# YOUTH CULTURE IN CHINA

The lives and aspirations of young Chinese (those between fourteen and twenty-five years old) have been transformed in the past five decades. By examining youth cultures around three historical points – 1968, 1988, and 2008 – this book argues that present-day youth culture in China has both international and local roots. Paul Clark describes how the Red Guards and sent-down youth of the Cultural Revolution era carved out a space for themselves, asserting their distinctive identities despite tight political controls. By the late 1980s, Chinese-style rock music, sports, and other recreations began to influence the identities of Chinese youth. In the twenty-first century, the Internet offered a new, broader space for expressing youthful fandom and frustrations. From the 1960s to the present, global youth culture has been reworked to serve the needs of young Chinese.

Paul Clark is a professor of Chinese at the University of Auckland, New Zealand. He is the author of *The Chinese Cultural Revolution: A History* (Cambridge 2008), *Reinventing China: A Generation and Its Films* (2005), and *Chinese Cinema: Culture and Politics since 1949* (Cambridge 1987).

# Youth Culture in China

## FROM RED GUARDS TO NETIZENS

### Paul Clark

University of Auckland, New Zealand

CAMBRIDGE UNIVERSITY PRESS
Cambridge, New York, Melbourne, Madrid, Cape Town,
Singapore, São Paulo, Delhi, Mexico City

Cambridge University Press
32 Avenue of the Americas, New York, NY 10013-2473, USA

www.cambridge.org
Information on this title: www.cambridge.org/9781107602502

© Paul Clark 2012

First published 2012

Printed in the United States of America

*A catalog record for this publication is available from the British Library.*

*Library of Congress Cataloging in Publication data*
Clark, Paul, 1949–
Youth culture in China : from Red Guards to netizens / Paul Clark.
p.  cm.
Includes bibliographical references and index.
ISBN 978-1-107-01651-4 (hardback) – ISBN 978-1-107-60250-2 (paperback)
1. Youth – China – History – 20th century.  2. Youth – China – History –
21st century.  3. Youth – China – Social conditions – 20th century.
4. Youth – China – Social conditions – 21st century.
5. Youth – China – Attitudes.  6. Popular culture – China.
7. Group identity – China.  8. Internet – Social aspects – China.
9. Technology and youth – Social aspects – China.  I. Title.
HQ799.C5C58  2012
305.235095109′04–dc23      2012002706

ISBN 978-1-107-01651-4 Hardback
ISBN 978-1-107-60250-2 Paperback

# Contents

# Illustrations

# Acknowledgments

A fascination with 1988, the most liberal moment in China since 1949, inspired this study, as did a frustration with breathless accounts of present-day social change in China. As an historian, I wanted to trace the roots of contemporary developments, building on an almost forty-year acquaintance with life in China. Many people and institutions have kindly enabled me to do this. A major grant from the Marsden Fund of the Royal Society of New Zealand provided much appreciated support for several visits to China. The Lee Hysan Foundation generously supported a two-month period working in the Universities Service Centre for China Studies at the Chinese University of Hong Kong. The Peking University Library was a productive home base for much of this research. Other institutions that helped include the Shanghai Library, the Library of the China Youth University for Political Sciences in Beijing, the National Library in Beijing, and the Shanghai Academy of Social Sciences. Research support also came from the University of Auckland, including its Faculty of Arts. Many colleagues and friends have helped along the way, including Philip Abela, Chris Berry, Tony and Susan Browne, Chen Xin, Brian Donovan, Hong-yu Gong, Anders Hansson, Wayne Lawrence, Haiqing Lin, Bonnie McDougall, Rumi Sakamoto, Robert Sanders, Rebecca Wu Xiaojing, and Zhou Xuelin. Bonnie McDougall and Stanley Rosen offered valuable advice at crucial points in the project. Linda Lew made good use of a University of Auckland Summer Scholarship to trawl the Internet on my behalf. Jeff Lau has helped keep me grounded. At Cambridge in New York, Eric Crahan and Abigail Zorbaugh provided vital encouragement and support. These people and institutions, along with numerous friends and colleagues in China whom I have not named, have made the research a pleasure and this book possible. I warmly thank them all, including those whom I have not identified. The book's shortcomings are mine alone.

# CHAPTER I

# Introduction

## *Finding Youth in China*

In the late 1960s, when American youth were longing for or enjoying summers of love, their Chinese counterparts were engaged in somewhat different activities. Some were still active as Red Guards, the shock troops who answered Chairman Mao's call for continuing revolution and for the overthrow of his rivals in the leadership. Millions of young Chinese had started the journey to rural exile, to learn from the peasants and deepen their Maoist faith. Youth culture, epitomised by Woodstock and the wider Western youth rebellion of the 1960s, seemed to have passed China by, though Red Guards represented their own kind of revolt against established norms. Twenty years later, China was more open to outside connections and young Chinese knew about Michael Jackson, the Beatles, and much more. Distinctive youth cultures had emerged in a nation undergoing rapid change. Forty years after Woodstock, young China formed the largest mass of Internet users in the world. Despite government efforts at control, Chinese youth took to the opportunities the 'Net offered with the kind of gusto with which American youthful rebels had embraced rock 'n roll and rebellion a generation or two earlier.

This book seeks to trace the emergence and elaboration of youth cultures in China over this forty-year period. It will show that China's youth, even in Mao's time, were as active in their own ways at asserting their ambitions and difference as their Western counterparts. Three historical junctures in the formation of Chinese youth identity – 1968, 1988, and 2008 – provide key moments on which to map the rise of Chinese youths' engagement with the world as China moved from the relative isolation of Maoist times to what appears to be invasive globalisation, symbolised by the Beijing Olympics. We will plot the emergence and elaboration of youth cultures from the time of the Red Guards in the 1960s through the 1980s to the current world of the Chinese Internet. The study will illustrate how the interplay between indigenous factors and foreign influences has continued, over more than forty years, to shape youth identities in the People's Republic. Chinese youngsters have seized on opportunities to turn hip-hop, the Internet, and other popular cultural elements to their own, particular, and varied purposes. In China globalisation of youth culture has a distinctive Chinese cast. This study raises the question of whether globalising influences might obliterate Chinese culture in a few generations. Or could Chinese youth culture enjoy the same currency around the world in this century that American popular culture achieved in the last century?

## THREE HISTORICAL MOMENTS

In 1968, China, seemingly cut off from the rest of the world, including parts that were in the throes of their own youth rebellion, was in the midst of the Cultural Revolution. The destruction of lives and the abuses of power in these years cannot be ignored. But, as Red Guards, some young people found a space to assert their difference from older genera-tions. The sending of millions of youths to the countryside starting in late 1968 gave these developments new impetus, by providing opportuni-ties for youthful exploration in new writing, performance, and collective artistic practice, as conditions eased and as this generation returned to the cities even before the end of the Cultural Revolution era in 1976.

By 1988 the innovations of the 'search for roots' and other post–Cultural Revolution intellectual and artistic movements had combined in popular youthful imaginations with greater knowledge and interest in the world outside China. Several of the developments that attracted young China in 1988 were related to film. Zhang Yimou's *Red Sorghum* struck a remarkable chord among young Chinese audiences with its por-trayal of a primitive, instinctual world without Confucianism, Marxism, or any 'ism' other than nationalism. The popularity of the film helped spawn a new kind of rock music that mixed folk with foreign elements to express youthful rebellion. The so-called hoodlum novelist Wang Shuo captured the mocking tone of the times in his stories, five of which were in preparation as films in 1988. The year marked a transition between the autochthonous youth experimentation of the late 1960s and the over-whelming global influences of the new century to come. The possibilities for further liberalisation seemed enormous in 1988, as even state-owned television broadcast (and soon after, rebroadcast) the documentary series *River Elegy*, which presented a new interpretation of Chinese history that largely ignored Marxism and most Communist achievements. In the fol-lowing year, however, state power brutally asserted itself against youthful rebellion on June 4 in Tiananmen Square.

The year of the Beijing Olympics saw a range of youth culture phe-nomena, including spontaneous volunteer service to help victims of disaster and to assist in presenting a successful international sporting festival. By 2008 young China had embraced the Internet with unexpected, complex consequences for themselves and for the rest of society. The global reach made possible by the Web brought increased international influences to the lives of young Chinese, adding to the range of choices the virtual world made available to the young. Japanese comics, Korean preppy fashion, Chinese-style hip-hop, and fandom for instantly created television stars were all part of the new, consumerist youth culture that many young Chinese were creating for themselves. A kind of nationalist undertow, in part encouraged by the state, worked behind this apparent popular globalisation.

By examining these three points in the development of youth cultures, this book hopes to avoid the kind of breathlessness about contemporary developments and rapid change that dominates journalistic accounts of present-day China. Tracing the origins of current phenomena and showing the ways in which these Chinese developments have drawn on roots springing from previous generations' experiences help explain how and why China has taken these paths to popular cultural modernity. The study hopes also to show that changes in Chinese elaborations in youth cultures, even in very different political and social circumstances, were often rather similar to the experience of Western societies. This book shares with Jon Savage's study of the emergence of the teenager the aim to tell 'the story of how youth struggled to make itself heard, if not totally on its own terms, then in terms it could recognise and accommodate itself to.'[1]

This study invokes the concept of subcultures, using for example Dick Hebdige's emphasis on self-styling as a means to promote a sense of belonging and distinguish oneself or a group from others. The idea of subcultures is relatively new in mainland Chinese contexts. The word for subculture (yawenhua) only began to be fitfully used by sociologists in the 1990s, a half century after its association with the Chicago school of urban research and more than twenty years after Hebdige's early studies as part of the Birmingham school of cultural studies.[2] In China the dominant political discourse in the second half of the twentieth century spoke of 'the people' and 'the broad masses,' an approach that seemed to deny space for subcultures. This book will trace the roots of subcultural practice among educated youth in the 1970s. When subcultures emerged publicly in the 1980s, they were not necessarily anticommercial, transgressive, oppositional, or spectacular, unlike their earlier Western counterparts. The following chapters, however, will show that elements of these characteristics were present and grew as youth cultures were further elaborated. Chinese young people tended to engage with gusto in the new mass culture and massification that came with economic growth and opening to the outside world. The attractions of the new commercialised mass culture were as all-encompassing or totalising as the earlier Maoist version of culture for the masses. The new, however, also offered space for subcultural distinctions.

## YOUTH AND THE CHINESE REVOLUTION

The concept of youth as a distinctive period in a person's life emerged in China at about the same time as in the Western world. An awareness of a period between childhood, with its dependence on adults, and the assumption of the full adult responsibilities associated with marriage slowly dawned in premodern China. Part of the perpetual appeal to Chinese readers of the vernacular novel of the eighteenth century, *A Dream of Red Mansions* (*Honglou meng*) lay in its indulgent depiction of a world of youthful dreams, ambitions, and disappointments. As a modern education system developed in the late nineteenth century, associated with efforts by Christian missionaries and separate from the traditional Confucian training that boys (and some girls) received, the concept of youth took hold. In the political disorder of the second decade of the new century, a New Culture movement called for a rejection of old values and habits. In the pages of *New Youth* (*Xin qingnian*), magazine writers called for the adoption of Mr. Science and Mr. Democracy, symbols of the Westernisation they saw as China's saviours. Student demonstrations in Beijing and other cities on 4 May 1919 gave the label May Fourth Movement to this effort to promote social and cultural modernisation. One feature of the movement was advocacy of free marriage choice for young people, in contrast to the usual custom of arranged marriages. Free choice tended to encourage later marriage, so that the period of youth, from puberty to setting up one's own household, was extended, providing an incentive for the elaboration of youth cultures. Frank Dikötter has noted the rise in the first half of the twentieth century of a focus on the young body as a site for the inscription of nationalist and modernist ambitions.[3] This present study will suggest the same has been true of the era since then.

In the midst of these changes the Chinese Communist Party was founded in 1921. A minor figure at the first meeting, Mao Zedong was himself a product of the ferment of ideas that had given rise to the May Fourth Movement. Throughout his life, Mao held tight to the idea that the future belonged to the young. The relative youth of many leaders of the Communist Party and its army during the War against Japan and in the civil war that ended with victory in 1949 was striking. In his new regime, Mao kept returning to the enthusiasm he associated with youth. Speaking to Chinese students and trainees in Moscow in 1957, on the second of the two trips he ever made abroad, Mao declared: 'The world is yours, as well as ours, but in the last analysis, it is yours. You young people, full of vigour and vitality, are in the bloom of life, like the sun at eight or nine in the morning. Our hope is placed on you.... The world belongs to you. China's future belongs to you.'[4] Youth may have been valorised in this way in the 1950s and early 1960s, but it was a dependent, politicised period in the lives of Chinese citizens, with limited opportunities for distinctive and independent expression. Youth in the Maoist era was often regarded as simply a junior version of adult commitments and responsibilities. Young Pioneers put red scarves around their necks as children and joined the Communist Youth League as teenagers in preparation for adulthood in the Party.

The Cultural Revolution changed this pattern and created spaces for the establishment of youth cultures expressing distinctive identities. As in the May Fourth era, political upheaval helped create the conditions for new ideas and patterns of behaviour to take root. Mao regarded young people as the vanguard force for his revolt against his own regime. For themselves, Red Guards seized the opportunities to indulge in rebellion against teachers, parents, and the establishment. Many groups took up creative activities to propagandise Mao's cause. The transfer of millions of youth to the countryside, the army, and to other occupations beginning in the late 1960s afforded many young people the freedom to elaborate further some of these creative activities. The purpose tended to shift to a different, even individual, urge to express themselves. In the absence of close supervision, underground creativity took hold as some rural sent-down youth became linked with urban salons discussing new ideas and new art.

The return to the cities after Mao's death in late 1976 and the end of the Cultural Revolution produced an explosion of youthful creativity, enthusiasm, and alienation. Soon 'reform and opening up' promulgated by Deng Xiaoping saw a widening of the resources available to China's youth in its continuing quest for self-expression. Foreign films, novels, television programs, music, fashions, and foods opened up new worlds for all Chinese, but the young took particular interest in the new possibilities. Concern about the impact of these new trends, combined with a determination that young Chinese had somehow 'lost their way' as a result of the Cultural Revolution, was behind an episode in 1980 in which a letter supposedly from a young woman named Pan Xiao sparked widespread media discussion on youth alienation and lack of ideals.[5] By 1983 elderly conservatives in the Communist Party were grumbling about 'spiritual pollution' among China's young, epitomised by permed hair, bell-bottomed trousers, and excessive fascination with Western popular culture. An official campaign against such alleged evils gained little traction and was abandoned. By the late 1980s the rhythms of Western,

Hong Kong, and Taiwan pop and rock music were competing with local versions for youthful attention. Breakdancing, bodybuilding, and sports provided exercise for young bodies, while some youth took an interest in the indigenous breathing exercises and seemingly magical powers of *qigong*. New spaces, such as the pool hall, bar, and video hall, emerged in which young people could gather to share a sense of solidarity and difference from older and younger citizens. China's youth keenly embraced a mix of international and local cultural practices.[6]

Continued economic growth opened up further possibilities for young Chinese. Income growth began to accelerate around 1995, so that, for those with money, life began to change dramatically. Private home ownership, private cars, and open choice in finding employment had become established by the turn of the millennium. A new space emerged for youthful expression, as the Internet became a fixture in young lives, first in Internet bars (cafés) and later in college dormitories and private homes. The virtual space of the Web brought new music, including from other parts of Asia, to youthful Chinese fans. A 'Korean wave' took hold and television talent quests made young Chinese dream of individual fame, while a foreign education became an ideal for others. Fans – of pop stars, film stars, talent show contestants, cartoon characters, or of more esoteric activities like cosplay (dressing up as fantasy characters) – found likeminded conversation partners through the Internet and in urban spaces devoted to idol worship. Globalisation took root in Chinese popular culture, with most young Chinese happy to live lives of global connectedness. But the indigenous and local could also find space in the new youth cultures, as indicated by the success of a televised talent show based on *A Dream of Red Mansions*, a novel enjoyed for centuries by Chinese readers. This hybrid mix of influences was characteristic of the new youth culture throughout the post-1978 reform era.

## DISCOVERING YOUTH IN CHINA

By the 1990s the rise and elaboration of youth cultures, and the new attitudes that these cultures reflected, were hard to miss. In the late 1970s and early 1980s the term *youth* (*qingnian*) had been stretched from its usual thirty-five years-old cut-off to include even people up to the age of forty-five who had lost ten years of their careers during the Cultural Revolution. By the 1990s youth was more narrowly defined, though some writers included those in their thirties. This present study applies the term to those aged from about fourteen to about twenty-five, from teenagehood to before marriage. We should acknowledge of course that a fourteen-year-old usually has different outlooks and tastes from someone who is in their mid-twenties.

Social commentators in the 1990s began to use a label that soon gained wide currency: the post-1980 cohort (*80 hou*, read as *baling hou*). It was coined to acknowledge the new kind of young Chinese who had been born in the first decade of economic reform. These young people had no direct experience of the economically straitened times or of political campaigns or movements (the events of the spring of 1989 and June 4 occurred in their childhood). The materialism and high expectations of China's new youth were nicely summed up and explained by this new label, 'post-1980.' As had happened in filmmaking in the mid-1980s when a critic identified a Fifth Generation of directors, a calculation of previous and subsequent generations was made. A post-1990 cohort (*jiuling hou*) was seen to succeed the slightly older group, with an allegedly even greater devotion to consumerism and their own pleasure. By 2011 a post-2000 label was being applied to some youth phenomena. Others counted backward and came up with a post-1970 generation (identified with events in the spring of 1989) and even a post-1960 group.[7] In the new century, printed collections of nostalgia for each of the decades beginning with the 1960s appeared frequently in Chinese bookstores. Profusely illustrated with pictures of everyday objects, television and movie stars, grain and cotton ration coupons, school uniforms, and favourite comic books, these works were a symptom of a sense of rapid change and growing prosperity. Chinese readers seem to have welcomed these collections as a kind of anchor for memories in a tidal wave of development and change.

This book prefers to map changing youth cultures across four decades in ways that avoid the restrictions that these group, cohort, or generational identifiers impose on what is a moving picture of differently paced streams of development. The twenty-year spacing between the main focal points of the study are less than the usual twenty-five-year gap granted generations. The fans of rock musician Cui Jian in 1988, therefore, were not the children of 1968's Red Guards. Only some of the netizens of 2008, hunched over computer screens in their bedrooms to escape the censure of parents who still listened to Cui Jian's ancient lyrics, were the offspring of 1988 rebels. The twenty-year space allows a freedom from generational labels that can offer more nuanced insight into the changes taking place over this period of forty-plus years.

A study like this is unable to cover the whole country and all of Chinese society. Given the differences between habits of life in village China and those in urban centres, there is a bias toward urban China in this study. Cities, especially large conurbations on the eastern seaboard were the nodes through which international and other new influences presented themselves to young Chinese. A kind of trickle-down effect, facilitated by the increasing movement of rural workers to urban workplaces, took new fashions and ways of behaving to the farthest reaches of the land. Pirated videotapes and DVDs, for example, could be found on sale or broadcast on ancient television sets in the remotest village, even if a petrol-powered generator drove the equipment. But the action, including innovations that created Chinese versions of new phenomena originating outside the nation, was in the big cities. Youth in Beijing, Shanghai, and Guangzhou were at the forefront of change, even if some indigenous responses, such as the Northwest Wind in rock music in the late 1980s, drew on remoter Chinese places.

This study also tends to examine young people with the resources to participate in the new cultural practices. These resources were not just financial, though the circumstances to buy new fashions, watch movies, attend rock concerts, subscribe to magazines, and use or own Web-connected computers were essential to access the real and virtual spaces of the new youth cultures. Resources also included the educational level to appreciate new writing and new ideas. Education was perhaps less important in terms of the body-related phenomena that helped constitute youth culture. Even if elaborate sports shoes might have been out of reach of poorer urban youth, in the 1980s at least, a cheap T-shirt and pair of jeans could be sufficient to make a statement of identity. The rhythms of the new youth cultures might at least be enjoyed from radio or television, even if attendance at rock concerts was beyond the resources of many urban youth.

In addition to these differences in social status, this study tries to acknowledge the importance of gender and regional differences in the youth cultures of these decades. As in most other societies, teenage boys and girls did not necessarily enjoy similar opportunities or appreciate the same pastimes or aspirations. Red Guards and sent-down youth in the 1960s and 1970s were imbued with a notion that boys and girls were equal and equally capable. Physical difference, especially different strength in farm labour, however, could not be overlooked. Much of youth culture in the 1980s took on a masculinist tinge. The popularity of the film *Red Sorghum* in 1988 was a distinctly male, and northern, phenomenon. The songs that took hold after the film, including Cui Jian's husky anthem 'Nothing to My Name,' appealed as much to young women as to their male peers, even if other rock groups tended to attract more young men. Cui and his rock cohort found their keenest fans in Beijing: Many Shanghai youth affected indifference. The rise of the Internet and its virtual connectedness had the potential to obliterate gender difference, but it also offered more opportunities (often anonymous) to elaborate these differences. Access to the 'Net and to mobile phones required a certain level of resources. The opportunities for niche cultures and narrow but widespread groupings of fans and mutual interests allowed for all kinds of differentiation, by region, gender, age, and inclination.

The research draws on almost forty years of personal observation in China, particularly in Beijing. Primary materials, including memoirs, films, magazines intended for youthful readers, and discussions and blogs on the Internet, have been augmented with sociological and other work by Chinese researchers. This latter material includes surveys, interviews, and a great deal of anecdotes and examples. Much of this kind of research in China is couched in terms of shaping policy for officials charged with what is called 'youth work.' But this purposefulness does not negate the usefulness of the content of these reports. We should acknowledge the pioneering work of Stanley Rosen in building on this Chinese research in his studies of the attitudes of youth during and especially since the Maoist era.[8] In his 2009 book, *Research on Contemporary Chinese Youth Culture*, Lu Yulin presents a useful and up-to-date overview of youth research in China, couched in a Marxist framework.[9] He includes coverage of popular culture among 14- to 25-year-olds, which is the focus of this present study.

In attempting to trace themes identified with bodies, rhythms, and spaces across five decades, this study has avoided a simple structure based around the three points in time that are our focus: 1968, 1988, and 2008. The first time-point is the subject of a separate chapter, but the natures of youth cultures at that time do not amount to a kind of baseline against which to measure subsequent developments. The other chapters range across the period since the Cultural Revolution, with a degree of concentration on the latter two dates. This matrix approach should not obscure the trajectories of nativist pride and global engagement that have driven changes in Chinese youth cultures in the reform period. Broadly speaking, the development from the late 1960s to the end of the 1980s was an elaboration of local cultural resources for youthful purposes in complex relationship with opening up to outside, particularly Western, cultural influences. In the two decades after 1988, these developments were intensified and complicated through processes that have not very usefully been called 'glocalisation.' This study suggests how complex these ostensibly local and international interactions and entanglements had become by the twenty-first century. The technologies of change had shifted from the radio to television, the video and DVD, and to the Internet and mobile phone. Bodies had been exhausted, built up, and displayed across these decades, to a changing soundtrack derived from a mix of the folk and the foreign, and in spaces that became at once more public and more intimate.

# CHAPTER 2

# Marking Out New Spaces

## *Red Guards, Educated Youth, and Opening Up*

The decade of the Cultural Revolution saw the creation of distinctive modes and spheres for the assertion of youth identity. The developments in these years laid the groundwork for the emergence of youth popular culture in the 1980s and later. The Cultural Revolution is conventionally dated from 1966 to 1976. The phenomena in the first three years associated with Red Guards account for the mapping out of a space in which young people could conduct their own activities, whether in support of the current political campaigns or from more personal motivations. When Red Guards became 'sent-down youth' (or 'educated youth'), starting in late 1968, the spaces for the development of youth popular culture extended to the countryside. Groups from the cities took their new sense of the possibilities for self-expression to the rural communes and even to the militarised settlements in harsher environments. Although authoritarian and bureaucratic control remained high in many areas of life, young people found an outlet by participating in performance troupes and other cultural activities. Some of these activities soon took the form of unofficial or underground cultural production. The hand-copied novels and poetry circulated among urban youth in rural settings allowed for considerable experimentation and creativity. Urban salons of returned youth and others provided a new context for discussion and debate on these new cultural phenomena. Mao's death in September 1976 allowed these youthful expressions of identity to emerge alongside mainstream discourse, setting off a further elaboration of youth popular culture as China opened up to more outside influences. But the Cultural Revolution origins of youth culture in China are unmistakable. This chapter will explore these origins better to assess the flourishing of youth cultures from the mid-1980s to the first decade of the twenty-first century.

The spaces for the expression of youth popular culture thus moved from cities (with Red Guards) to the countryside (with sent-down youth) and back to the cities (with literary salons and other groupings). Each of these spaces offered a wide variety of expression and tastes. The degrees to which official and orthodox culture attempted to confine or channel activities in these venues also differed widely. But once young Chinese experienced the opportunity to create distinctive spheres for their own cultural expression, they could not be expected to abandon such a heady sense of freedom and power. In a decade usually characterised by an emphasis on control and regimentation, these spaces for youth culture offered a new and long-lasting landscape in which to assert difference and even resistance.

Nineteen sixty-eight was a year of youth rebellion in North America and Europe.[1] In China the man at the pinnacle of the state had made his own call for youthful rebellion. In 1966 Mao Zedong had called upon China's young people to rise up against their teachers and other elders. A cultural revolution, in which old values, attitudes, and behaviours were smashed, would ensure that Mao's revolution would continue to transform Chinese lives, build a strong and proud nation, and spread this socialist transformation around the world. Despite the idealism, people were persecuted and killed in these years. Young people on high school and college campuses were organised, by themselves and school authorities, as Red Guards to answer Chairman Mao's call to arms. A heady atmosphere of disruption took hold as young people seized unprecedented opportunities to travel about the country, to boycott classes and denounce unpopular teachers, and to try to reverse roles in the running of schools, offices, and even neighbourhoods. Red Guards also created their own writings and performances to express their ideals and sense of solidarity, often in bitter rivalry with other Red Guard factions. The upheaval and destruction proved so powerful in many Chinese cities that the army had to be called in to restore order in the winter of 1968–1969.

By the end of 1968, as autumn prepared to give way to winter, the first groups of young urban Chinese left their homes in Beijing, Shanghai, and other centres for the remote countryside. There they would 'learn from the peasants,' as Mao exhorted them, and bring urban enlightenment to undeveloped parts of the nation. Soon a great wave of 'sent-down youth' made the journey out of the cities.[2] Most went to rural communes and militarised settlements in relatively distant parts of China. Some joined the army and others made their way to mines and other major development projects. Some young people, for a variety of family reasons, remained in the cities.

Many in these groups of sent-down high-school- and college-aged youth found their initial enthusiasm for Mao's cause was difficult to maintain in the face of the reality of poor, dull, even dangerous rural existences. On the Inner Mongolian steppes, in the fastness of the underdeveloped northeast, and in the subtropical climes of the far southwest among ethnic minorities on the borderlands with southeast Asia, doubts about the appropriateness and long-term viability of lives learning from the locals were hard to avoid. An emerging underground subculture of hand-copied fiction and poetry and an above-ground reworking of officially sanctioned cultural activities provided an outlet for youthful frustrations.

Within a couple of years, a steady stream of young people found reasons (legitimate or otherwise) to shift back to their urban homes. What they brought back from their official and underground cultural activities helped invigorate urban salons that had been formed by like-minded 'educated youth' in alliance with older writers and artists. This crucible of official Red Guard, sent-down youth and underground creativity forged the beginnings of distinctive youth popular culture in China. The emergence of distinctive youth cultures, a process that had been taking place over several generations in Western societies, got started only in the late 1960s in the People's Republic. It required broader changes in Chinese society in the 1980s to truly take hold, but youth culture had its roots in the Cultural Revolution.

The youngsters who formed the bulk of the Red Guards and sent-down youth can be considered the third generation in the People's Republic of China. Their grandparents' generation had fought the revolution that had established Communist rule in 1949; their parents had helped build New China; these high schoolers and college students were the children of this revolution. They had been taught to admire the heroic sacrifice of model soldiers such as Lei Feng and Dong Cunrui, full of the hope and confidence expressed in the songs they had learned as Young Pioneers and of the stories they had imbued in class struggle education exhibitions and through picture story books.[3] This chapter will argue that the awakening and assertion of identity by *laosanjie* (literally 'old three years': high school graduates from 1966 through 1968) and others in these years benefited paradoxically from the weakness of their formal education. Being denied completion of their schooling and being sent to the countryside or somewhere else in society produced in some an insight into their social position and potential that few young people growing up in the 1950s had ever achieved. This laid the groundwork for a flourishing of cultural innovation in the early 1980s.

## RED GUARDS

This book is not the place to present a complete history of the rise and failure of the Red Guards during the Cultural Revolution.[4] The usual view is that they were misguided because they were ultimately used by Mao and his allies at the highest levels of the Communist Party to serve factional purposes, becoming canon fodder in the waves of violence that swept through Chinese cities in 1966 through 1969.[5] Whatever their place in historical assessments, for three years starting in 1966, millions of Red Guards put their bodies on the line in the service of Mao's cause and in assertion of their confidence and enthusiasm in supporting him. Their activities included turning the music of the Maoist revolution into new tunes for their own uses. In these three intense years, Red Guards mapped out new spaces where youth identity was presented, questioned, and elaborated. This period saw the first steps in the emergence of distinctive youth culture in China.

The impact of the formation of Red Guard groups on their participants has often been overlooked in accounts that focus on factionalism and abuse. In a society in which personal and career paths seemed clearly laid out and highly determined, the spring and summer of 1966 offered an exciting sense of liberation to many young people. Chinese teenagers in this sense were no different from their counterparts elsewhere in the world. Adolescence demanded the assertion of rebellion against parents and other adults. Mao's call for a 'great proletarian cultural revolution' offered a wonderful excuse to take these assertions farther than any previous Chinese generation had ever dreamt of. On the surface, Red Guards rallying on campuses and shouting slogans against 'reactionary authorities' and 'revisionists in the party' or feverishly reciting quotations from Chairman Mao seemed caught up in a new regimentation of their lives. Mao was such a powerful figure that youthful rebels did not think to attack him but instead followed his directions. Nonetheless, for the participants, the opportunity to directly express their resentments at teachers, parents, and other authority figures presented an unexpected space for assertion of their sense of self. Some of this space was filled with violence, as students physically attacked their teachers and other groups. But these new spaces also opened up to such activities as publications, travelling around the nation, street theatre, plays and other artistic genres, and to more underground locations.

In responding to Mao's call for rebellion against his own establishment, young people naturally drew upon the resources that their education and upbringing had given them. As one pioneering scholar of the Red Guard movement noted, the efforts to exhort young people to learn from the story of model soldier Lei Feng and novels such as Luo Guangbin and Yang Yiyan's *Red Crag* (*Hongyan*, published in 1961) and Jin Jingmai's *Song of Ouyang Hai* (*Ouyang Hai zhi ge*, published in 1965) had a profound impact on readers in the seventeen years after 1949. These and other works had engendered in their young readers a sense of idealism, self-sacrifice, and hero worship. Yin Hongbiao, a pioneering researcher of the Cultural Revolution argues that school education had also become

more influential on young minds in the first half of the 1960s, after the
ideological uncertainties of the previous decade.[6] Given an opportunity to
act out the heroic imaginary in which their worldviews had been formed,
many young people were delighted to seize the moment. In addition to
the inspirations from Chinese authors, foreign novels and films also had
an influence in shaping this heroic self-image that many Red Guards
cherished. Nikolai Ostrovsky's *How the Steel Was Tempered* (translated
into Chinese in the early 1950s) and Irish writer Lillian Voynich's *The
Gadfly* (translated into Chinese in 1953) also presented highly appealing
images of rebellious heroes to young Chinese readers. Both were made
into films in the Soviet Union and released in China, in 1951 and 1956
respectively. Chinese youth saw in these often solitary heroic figures,
struggling in a society that refuses to recognise their superior aspirations,
models that reflected their own frustrations and idealism.

Heroes require enemies. Red Guards on college campuses in Beijing,
Shanghai, and other cities promptly responded to a 1 June 1966 *People's
Daily* editorial titled 'Sweep away all forces of evil [literally cow ghosts
and snake spirits]' (*Hengsao yiqie niugui sheshen*) by identifying dozens
of such alleged transgressors among their teachers. The attacks on school
authority figures continued through what should have been the summer
vacation.[7] By late August, the objects of youthful attack were the 'four
olds' (*sijiu*: old thinking, culture, customs, and habits), encouraged by
a directive from the Party's Central Committee. This shift partly dep-
ersonalised the Red Guard's vicious attacks on intellectuals and former
officials and made them into attacks on objects that represented China's
cultural heritage. Statues in temples, books, and antiques were obvious
targets of youthful iconoclasm. But it also could be applied to the dress
and habits of people whom the youthful zealots deemed bourgeois. In
Shanghai, coffee shops patrons were harassed: 'Chinese people do not
eat Western food.'[8] By late winter 1967, Red Guard groups in Shanghai
were beginning to fight each other for control of broadcasting stations
and other strategic assets. Fighting continued sporadically through 1967,
despite efforts by Party central authorities to restore order.[9]

Red Guard groups provided opportunities for young people to express
their frustrations with the quality of their teachers. At Fudan University,
Shanghai's top college, some students by late 1966 had formed a Sun
Wukong Fighting Group (*Sun Wukong zhandou zu*). They took their
*nom de guerre* from the monkey with supernatural powers that was the
hero of the much loved classical vernacular novel *Journey to the West*
(*Xiyou ji*). Sun Wukong featured in the lives of all Chinese children as
a mischievous companion to the more serious Buddhist devotees of the
story, immortalised in story books and cartoons. To name a Red Guard
faction after Sun was a touch of cheeky genius, and a far cry from the

more solemn (and highly repetitive) names chosen by most groups: East Is Red, Red Headquarters, and so forth. In January 1967, the Sun Wukong Fighting Group helped lead the gathering of materials to use against Zhang Chunqiao, future member of the Gang of Four and then leader of Party cultural and ideological activities in Shanghai.[10]

## Bodies on the Line

Youth is a time of physical growth, greater self-consciousness about appearance, and boldness in physical display, performance, and risk. Dress is an area in which youths express their difference from others. The Red Guard dress sense, however, was a shared effort to look like Communist Party army members and others in photographs from the Yan'an era during the Anti-Japanese War (1937–45). Some Red Guards were able to re-use genuine army uniforms from their fathers or older brothers. Most Red Guards took a more resourceful approach and modified worker's trousers and cotton Sun Yat-sen jackets (usually called Mao jackets in the West). Mothers and young women with good sewing skills could even produce a passable replica of a 1930s army uniform.[11] One major Red Guard concern was to ensure that the uniform did not look too new. Suitable wear and tear, especially on a right shoulder, suggesting the constant use of a carrying pole and highly visible to companions, was especially prized. This teenage and young adult urge toward sartorial uniformity seems to run counter to the expected declarations of sartorial individuality by such young people in other societies. But a desire to fit in with one's particular group can also be a youthful obsession. The ersatz army uniforms on Red Guards could anyway be customised with individual touches.[12]

One such touch was provided by the ubiquitous Mao badge, mostly featuring small bas-relief portraits of the leader on or surrounded by a red background. By 1967, Mao was on most young chests, sometimes in multiple versions. This was a new phenomenon and became for many young people an engrossing and politically infallible hobby. Produced locally or by army units, workplaces, universities, and other institutions, badges could identify membership in a particular group, unit, or faction. As Red Guards travelled to other centres, Mao badges were traded among friends, swapped with visitors from out of town, and prized for rarity.[13]

Another way in which Red Guard bodies expressed support for Mao's revolution and youthful vigour and enthusiasm was through performances. These were presented in a range of settings, including the street, workplaces, campuses, and theatres. The creativity of some performance groups was a precursor of the kind of innovation that would be further elaborated among educated youth in less visible settings. Performance for Red Guards offered another way of putting their bodies on the line, in less physically dangerous settings than fighting their rivals and enemies.

With the coming of the Cultural Revolution, the range of artistic activities, in the performing arts and elsewhere, narrowed and came under even tighter official supervision. By May 1967 the media had identified eight so-called model performances (yangbanxi) as the touchstones for a new cultural effort. These models consisted of five modern-subject Peking operas, two full-length ballet dramas, and a symphony based on the music of one of the operas.[14] Young people did not seem to have a part to play in this remodelling of cultural production and consumption. Peking opera, a centuries-old form, was not a strong drawing card for most Beijing teenagers or young people elsewhere, who largely ignored their own regional musical theatre forms.

On the other hand, the portrayal of the heroes of the new-style Peking operas and ballet-dramas had a direct appeal for young people, as they chimed with the self-image of many young Chinese. The heroism familiar from Soviet films and their Chinese counterparts was incorporated into the reinvention of the opera and ballet forms, with main heroes at the centre of a group of loyal and admiring colleagues smiting their enemies and emerging triumphant. The figures on stage and their stories were similar to morality tales that dominated children's literature in China.[15] Only a few youthful characters featured in the model performances, though they had prominent roles. Li Tiemei is the adopted daughter of a 1930s railway signalman who takes up the lamp of revolution upon her father's martyrdom at the end of The Red Lantern (Hongdeng ji). Another fictional 1930s young woman was the eponymous hero of The White-haired Girl (Baimao nü), in which there is a residual suggestion of young romance between her and an army officer, a hangover from an earlier nonballet version of the work. The young waterfront worker who is the principal recipient of fervent class education from the female Party secretary in On the Docks (Haigang), the only contemporary story in the model performances, was another youthful hero on stage.[16]

The professional resources, skills, and effort that had gone into the development of these works for up to a decade before their proclamation as models, would seem to exclude the possibility of youthful participation in their performance and further elaboration. The new-style model works included ballet, a form completely unfamiliar to most Chinese audiences. In parallel with the emphasis on the model works was a stress on the amateur.[17] Art and literature were to be wrenched from out of the hands of professional, and presumably politically unreliable, writers and artists. The broad masses, which included youthful enthusiasts, were encouraged to write and perform in the new, officially sanctioned modes. What Red

Figure 2.1. Sent-down youth in a typical Cultural Revolution performance combining art and labour.
*Source:* Xue Yanwen and Zhang Xueshan, *Zhiqing lao zhaopian* (Old photos of sent-down youth), Tianjin: Baihua wenyi chubanshe, 1998, p. 18.

Guards and other young people in the mid-1960s did, however, went beyond the strictures of the new cultural authorities. The creativity and innovation that some of these youth engaged in on the streets, in theatres, at schools, and in work places were striking. Their experiences in 1966 through 1969 can also be said to have laid groundwork for the mostly underground nurturing of cultural expression among sent-down youth in the subsequent decade. The mid-1960s youthful efforts also prefigured the new cultural turn in the 1980s, after the end of the Cultural Revolution.

In the first months of the Cultural Revolution, in the spring of 1966, Red Guards' first efforts at artistic creation were in street theatre. Troupes wrote, choreographed, rehearsed, and performed propaganda chants for passers-by in city streets. This kind of performance had roots in the Anti-Japanese War period and had been occasionally revived in the 1950s. Red Guards chanted slogans and quotations from Chairman Mao while moving in unison to form tableaux to emphasise the importance of their messages. Props, including portraits of Mao, were often used as the central focus of group alignments, red flags, banners carrying slogans, and oversised papier-mâché hammers, sickles, and even guns. In May 1967 such performances were still seen on city streets. Marking the twenty-fifth anniversary of Mao Zedong's *Talks at the Yanan Forum on Literature and Art*, which had set out cultural policy for the Party and its post-1949 regime, Red Guard performers took to the streets of Beijing and to Tiananmen Square. The anniversary was so important that the performers included more professional stage practitioners (described in standard practice as 'revolutionary workers in literature and art') alongside Red Guard amateurs. By this stage in the Cultural Revolution, such groups were identified as Mao Zedong Thought Propaganda Teams and incorporated into official cultural endeavours. Assuming frozen poses similar to those seen in revolutionary statuary – a phalanx of people all pointing toward the glorious future, for example, or indicating denunciation of enemies by pointing to the ground – these performers seem to have been welcome entertainment to many urban dwellers. The tableaux also drew upon folk performance traditions, such as clapper talk (*kuaibanr*), adding to their popular appeal.[18]

Some of these performances were further elaborated when they were staged in theatres, gymnasia, and other, often makeshift, venues. With this shift indoors, the scale of chant-and-mime performance usually expanded, with serried ranks of young people in ersatz military uniforms showing remarkable discipline and timing as they moved as one. The content of such group performances also expanded, to include, for example, the telling of village or factory histories through group singing (*cunshi lianchang*).[19] Beijing Red Guard leader Qu Zhe was a member of the Capital Red Guard Propaganda Team, which specialised in songs, particularly the relatively new style of 'revolutionary songs' (*geming gequ*), and dances.[20] In his memoirs of his Cultural Revolution experiences, Liu Jialing recalls how each propaganda team performance began with young male and female announcers declaring that 'the fight begins!' (*zhandou kaishi*). No matter what kind of performance, there were invariably two purposes: praise for the red sun (meaning Mao) and condemnation of feudal, capitalist, and revisionist elements (*gesong hong taiyang, pipan feng-zi-xiu*).[21] The former involved clenching fists and buttocks and raising arms and eyes skyward; the latter meant pointing to the ground and stamping. Liu later recalled his experiences as a member of a high school propaganda team in a small town in Manchuria as a mix of great solemnity of purpose and occasional high farce. Membership was a sought-after privilege among schoolmates. Youthful rebellion was not forgotten in the life of the team. A certain mispronunciation of lyrics or bung note in a massed song could reduce the team to suppressed giggles that had to be relieved by rushing outside, away from audience eyes, to have a mighty laugh together.[22] As a thirteen-and-a-half-year-old, Liu took on the responsibility of teaching songs to others, starting with the mother and daughter next door. As members of propaganda teams, the young found themselves in the unusual position of knowing how to perform loyalty and being able to offer their knowledge to ignorant, older persons.[23] School, street, and other public performances provided an arena for the young to assert an unexpected public importance. Most schools had closed by the late spring of 1966. The calls to rebel, made legitimate by Mao's statement that 'to rebel is justified' (*zaofan youli*), were seductive for teenagers and university students determined to have society recognise their talent. Street and theatre performance was a way to secure public recognition of their social and personal value.

Spoken drama (*huaju*) was an area of particular Red Guard creative achievement. The most foreign of performance forms, at least in terms of China's tradition of musical theatre, plays proved an easy arena in which to compose and present stories with contemporary relevance to the young activists and their audiences. From 1967 to 1969, Red Guard theatre troupes in Beijing, for example, created a range of dramas with both foreign and domestic settings. *In Lenin's Hometown* (*Zai Liening de guxiang*, 1967) told of the fictional, heroic efforts made in 1966 by progressive Moscow workers, sympathetic to Mao Zedong's attacks on Soviet revisionism, to print and distribute Mao's writings in the city.[24] Another Red Guard play, *Daring to Drag the Emperor from his Horse* (*Gan ba huangdi laxia ma*), was created by students of the Central Drama Academy in Beijing. The play was based on a contemporary reportage story headlined 'Madman of the New Age' (*Xin shidai de kuangren*).[25] Another Red Guard spoken-drama troupe adapted this particular report about a citizen who had written more than thirty letters since 1962 denouncing the now deposed head of state Liu Shaoqi. Confined in a 'Red Flag Insane Asylum,' he is assisted by Red Guards in getting word directly to Chairman Mao. Soon he is released and hailed as a perspicacious hero.[26] In 1918, a highly influential short story by China's most eminent modern writer, Lu Xun, 'A Madman's Diary,' had used the idea of a madman being more sane than others to mount an attack on Confucian values and society. In the summer of 1967 a madman was being used for similar critical purposes. By the spring of 1968 the Red Guard version of a madman's distopian but insightful vision was being denounced in the mainstream media. An article by a soldier in Heilongjiang, for example, applauded Tianjin colleagues who had exposed the play as a 'black' work produced by antirevolutionary forces to undermine the Cultural Revolution. Criticism of the play, which had been performed in Harbin, was itself a way to wage factional warfare.[27]

Red Guard performing groups also participated in officially organised events. *People's Daily* devoted a full page in May 1967 to a report on a large-scale amateur performance festival in Beijing. In addition to worker and peasant groups, prominent among the performers were Red Guard troupes. Their contributions ranged from a massed crosstalk (*duokousi*) called 'Down with China's Khrushchev,' an attack on Liu Shaoqi, to a short dance drama, 'Red Guards See Chairman Mao,' commemorating Mao's eight appearances in Tiananmen Square the previous summer. The prominence of Red Guards in this major concert and in the newspaper report (including in the single photograph illustrating it) gives some sense of how empowered many such young persons felt in these heady days of 1966 to 1967. In a stock phrase, the report refers frequently to 'Red Guard young generals' (*Hongweibing xiaojiang*).[28] In a society where social status had remained a key marker of success and prospects, despite almost two decades of Communist government, such standard terms undoubtedly boosted a sense of self-worth among these youthful rebels. When Mao Zedong was still presenting himself as rebel-in-chief, such slavish following of the chairman's wishes could still feel an act of defiance, at least towards parents and teachers criticised as being opponents of the revolution.

The Red Guard plays had started as a young person's amateur movement, with some performances involving up to six hundred participants in a massed choir. Other shows required audiences to join in the singing of well-known songs incorporated into the item. After about two years of vigorous activity, Red Guard plays began to shift in focus and style. By 1968 the school propaganda teams around the nation had taken on a somewhat professional tendency, specialising in performance as a full-time occupation while creating a narrower range of plays and other programmes.[29] Red Guard performances continued in some areas until well after the army stepped in to restore a firmer sense of order in China's cities in 1969. A report from Heilongjiang in March 1970, for example, describes the dedication of a high school Red Guard Literature and Art Propaganda Team in Mingyong county. The young women resolved to brave the falling snow and strong winds to take their show to the local old folks' home.[30] By then many of these young enthusiasts were showing their dedication to the revolution by heading out of the cities for the countryside.

### Rhythms Shared

Music was another natural arena for youthful creative expression during the Red Guard upsurge in 1966 and 1967. Although the scope for youth compositions and performance could not match the relative liberalisation of the 1980s, when Chinese popular music developed in ways that allowed for the emergence of rock 'n roll, in the mid-1960s many young people saw music as an outlet. Red Guard musical activities had origins earlier in that decade. Mao's 1962 call to 'never forget class struggle' formed the basis for an upsurge in popular artistic creativity, including

Figure 2.2. A militant performance drawing on Red Guard precedents.
*Source:* Xue Yanwen and Zhang Xueshan, *Zhiqing lao zhaopian* (Old photos of sent-down youth), Tianjin: Baihua wenyi chubanshe, 1998, p. 50.

massed singing and amateur composing activities. These phenomena built on over a century of mass singing in China pioneered by Western missionaries and strengthened in secular schools by their inclusion in Japan-inspired school curricula.[31] With the upsurge in youthful mass enthusiasm in 1966, singing was a natural part of expressing solidarity with Chairman Mao. It was easier, after all, to engage large numbers of classmates in a chorus than to organise and rehearse a theatrical show. Songs also allowed Red Guards to create their own lyrics, lauding the need to rebel, for example, and even their own music to accompany these highly political songs. Publication of words and music, in the simple numerical notation that had been used in China since earlier in the century and popularised after 1949, enabled these new works to reach a nationwide audience, even without broadcasting on the radio network. In June 1966, 'Take Up the Pen as a Weapon' (*Naqi bi zuo daoqiang*), a collective creation by junior Red Guards at the high school attached to the Beijing Aeronautical University, included the words:

Take up the pen as a weapon.
Focus fire power on the black gang.
Revolutionary teachers and students all rebel,
Cultural revolutionaries are daring generals.

The bluntness and forcefulness of the words foreshadowed Chinese rock music of a generation later. In the summer of 1966, *People's Daily* published songs from the high school attached to the Central Music Conservatory. The young writers had some advantage in their place of study, even though classes at the academy and high school had stopped. By August songs like these had more polish and finesse than 'Take Up the Pen as a Weapon.' Setting quotations from Mao Zedong, and even some of his classical poems, to music in the new decade was taken over by music professionals to ensure appropriate quality of production. In 1966, song writing and performance became part of the factional rivalry between Red Guard groups, each claiming to be more loyal to Mao and his cause than others. Lyrics denounced other groups and made claims to the superiority of one's own, as did whole suites of songs (*zuge*), performed by different groups, often in combination with other kinds of Red Guard performance forms, including group recitation and miming. By 1967, the venues for such presentations, including Tiananmen Square, were a mark of political success and superior connections. Professional standards were achieved by enlisting the input of musical professionals. The most successful songs were broadcast on China Central Radio.[32] We shall see how this Red Guard experience in musical expression and creativity became further elaborated among sent-down youth. Music could express solidarity, remorse, and longing in ways that could be shared with other young people.

## *Spaces of Difference*

The Red Guard years provided China's youth with unprecedented opportunities to explore new spaces, both real and imaginary, for the assertion of their distinctive attitudes and aspirations. Publications brought new writing and relatively unsanctioned statements to other young readers. More appealing to the young was the hitherto undreamt of opportunity to travel far and wide across the nation. New places and new experiences opened young eyes to a much wider world than they had ever known. The sense of liberation that such travel engendered meant that when Red Guards became sent-down youth they had stronger aspirations to assert youthful identity.

In an age before widespread access to telephones in homes, let alone the Internet, Red Guards spread their influence and shared views and experiences face to face and through publications. Accessing printing premises was a major ambition for rival Red Guard groups in many cities. The broadsheets and flyers that poured from mimeograph machines and presses ranged from crude calls to arms to sophisticated publications with regular features and columns. Much of the content of these newspapers was reprinted from well-connected Red Guard publications, but a lot was written by youthful reporters. In a nation in which regular newspapers told their readers little about actual developments, local or national, the Red Guard broadsheets filled a gap in ways greatly appreciated by readers of all ages and backgrounds. Readers formed long lines to buy copies as soon as they appeared. *Jinggangshan*, a paper from Red Guards at Tsinghua University in Beijing, at the centre of youthful activism, even set up printing locations in Shanghai, Guangzhou, Hangzhou, and Xi'an, supplied with copy flown in from the capital with government assistance.[33]

This proliferation of publications, called 'little papers' (*xiao bao*) to distinguish them from regular newspapers, provided an outlet for young writers. By the summer of 1967, cultural or literary sections became a regular feature in many small papers. Despite the campaign against the 'four olds,' poetry, the most distinguished literary form in Chinese cultural heritage, featured prominently. At first the poems amounted to little more than well-written chants to be performed as part of Red Guard street theatre. One popular poem chant was 'Set me free, mother!' (*Fangkai wo, mama!*): 'Set me free, mother! / Don't be anxious about your child / Everywhere are our comrades-in-arms / The thugs' spears are no big deal! … Wait for the report of our victory, mother! … To achieve a total victory in the great Cultural Revolution / Your sons have pledged a thousand years as an heroic kid (*qianqiu xionggui*) and to not come home!'[34] The words reflect the inflated and militant rhetoric of the times, but the underlying sentiment is strictly a teenager's declaration to parents.[35] Soon the Red Guard verse shifted from chant-friendly doggerel to the freer mode of modern-style poetry that had emerged in the twentieth century and had little audience beyond educated readers.

The Red Guard newspapers allowed a new cohort of youthful writers to see their words in print. Established writers, artists, and specialist editors were silenced or at least worked under close supervision. In the space vacated by these usually older men and women, youthful amateur writers took on a new prominence. Mao's China had always encouraged amateur creativity, particularly in such activities as mass poetry writing, during the Great Leap Forward in 1958. The Red Guard publications offered new opportunities for amateur writers. The 18 July 1967 issue of *Revolutionary Rebel Literature and Art* (*Geming zaofan wenyi*), for example, included pages of poems mostly written by People's Liberation Army soldiers stationed in Huhehot, the Inner Mongolian capital where the paper was published. One of the featured poems, by a 'Red Flag soldier' from the Forestry Institute, sang the praises of Ma Deshan, a local hero who had died trying to rescue a child from drowning.[36] Such heroic self-sacrifice had great resonance in teenage self-images in China and elsewhere. Two years later, in July 1969, the mass drowning of eleven sent-down Shanghai youth in Huangshan, who died while trying to save the production brigade's grain and fertiliser from raging waters, was commemorated in posters reproduced throughout China.[37]

Cinemas were a real space in which the young continued to congregate, as they made up a high proportion of film audiences in China's cities. Most Chinese-made films from before 1964 were banned by the spring of 1966, but some were chosen for controlled exhibition. These were frequently screened as 'negative teaching examples' (fanmian jiaocai) for organised groups of students, workers, and others. While the purpose was to highlight the sinister political shortcomings of the work, many viewers later reported other attractions in such shows. In an age before the VCR, opportunities to see films years after their initial run were rare even in normal times. In the years of demonstrations and closed schools, these special screenings offered real diversion and even delight in the forbidden features. In his 1994 film In the Heat of the Sun (Yangguang canlan de rizi, based on a Wang Shuo novella), actor Jiang Wen presents a nostalgic picture of the lives of a gang of army brats in Beijing. One of the group's diversions is to sneak into the screenings of banned films, both foreign and domestic.[38]

New spaces for the assertion of youth identity opened up through a kind of revolutionary tourism that captured the imagination of most Red Guards and of youngsters who aspired to be Red Guards. 'Establishing ties' (chuanlian, link-up) with like-minded youthful revolutionaries in other cities offered an excuse for young people to travel far and wide across the nation. This was unprecedented in a society in which mobility had been largely restricted to professional and work needs. Soon young people were boarding trains in centres and demanding that the guards allow them free travel as Red Guards or revolutionary successors. Many youngsters chose to journey to sites of Communist Party significance. Huang Jianzhong, in his mid-twenties already working at the Beijing Film Studio, walked eighty kilometres a day for ten days from Taiyuan, capital of Shanxi, to Yan'an, the anti-Japanese wartime Communist headquarters.[39] Future film director Tian Zhuangzhuang at age fourteen joined his older brother and his classmates on the train to Hunan (Mao's home province) and Shanghai. In the winter of 1966–1967 they staged their own version of the Communist Party's Long March of the 1930s by walking part of the way from Beijing to Yan'an.[40] Tian's future film school classmate Wu Ziniu took the train from Sichuan to Beijing, but was refused entry to the capital. Only true 'Red elements' could be allowed into Chairman Mao's precincts: A son of a 'black element' like Wu's professor father could not proceed past suburban Fengtai.[41]

In Beijing the influx of politically acceptable young travellers put huge strains on the city's infrastructure. Beginning in August 1966, city authorities converted cinemas into reception centres and mass billets for out-of-town Red Guards. Staff worked in three daily shifts, with the screening of documentaries during the daytime, when the visitors were visiting sites in the city. The total audience for the seven documentaries made of Mao's eight appearances on Tiananmen in front of a square packed with young followers numbered precisely 5,315,707 in Beijing.[42] The logistics of receiving travelling Red Guards and students in Shanghai also strained that city's resources. Almost four million Red Guards reportedly visited the city between August and December 1966. On one day in this period (22 November) 997,691 outside visitors were registered.[43] Some of the major Red Guard coordinating organisations in Beijing and Harbin, for example, had representative offices in Shanghai in parallel to official regional organisations in the city. These provincial 'embassies' helped sort out visiting Red Guard needs.[44]

For those arriving in the city, harried authorities tried to organise activities for the visitors: viewing the documentary of Chairman Mao inspecting Red Guards in Tiananmen Square, visiting class education museums in local factories and schools, and meeting to engage in political study, sing songs or chant slogans, including Mao quotations. With Beijing and Guangzhou declaring in mid-October 1966 that young people were allowed to travel out of those two cities but no more would be allowed to enter, Shanghai became a more attractive destination. Feeding and clothing these newcomers became a major challenge, with factories ramping up production of cotton-padded jackets and pants. As cool weather moved south, sickness among the often ill-prepared outsiders became a problem. Not all travellers were of sound mind: Some needed help with mental illness.[45] The Party leadership in Shanghai called on Beijing to halt all such travel after National Day (1 October), fearful of city services being overwhelmed by the influx of youth. But the young travellers continued to pour in. In the space of six months Shanghai saw visits by about four million students and others intent on 'establishing ties' and enjoying the unprecedented sense of freedom that such travel allowed.[46] From late November onward the numbers of visiting Red Guards dropped in Shanghai, a change not unconnected with the coming of winter.[47] On 7 March the newly established Shanghai Revolutionary Committee ordered fifteen hundred receiving stations in the city closed and one hundred and fifty thousand people involved in looking after outside visitors to return to their original workplaces.[48]

While Red Guards and other youth were pouring into Shanghai, a city associated historically with the founding of the Chinese Communist

Party and with fascinating bourgeois excess as a treaty port known as the 'Paris of the East,' Shanghai youngsters were leaving town. On 23–24 November, when over one hundred thousand outsider Red Guards arrived in the city, more than double that number of their counterparts from Shanghai headed in the opposite direction.[49] Hapless railway ticket clerks found it impossible to say no to hundreds of youths turning up together at stations and demanding passage north. Travelling to the nation's capital became a fashionable expectation among Shanghai university students in the autumn of 1966. They were not infrequently joined by their high-school-aged siblings, who also struck out on their own.[50] Through the winter of 1966–1967 young Shanghainese put a huge burden on food supplies in small, remote centres like Jinggangshan, where the first Chinese Communist base area had been established in the early 1930s. Local communities grew to resent these demanding outsiders, full of revolutionary righteousness, for the burdens they placed on limited resources. In early February 1967, a notice from Party central and the State Council (China's cabinet) instructed travelling youth to return to their schools and places of residence.[51] But central and local authorities could not completely control youngsters with a taste for adventure. While most travel to 'establish ties' ceased after the February notice, by late spring and early summer 1967, many young Shanghainese were again on the road.[52] In the summer of 1967, Liu Jialing, then in his early teens, used the excuse of 'establishing ties' to travel from his native Shenyang to Beijing. Returning to the Northeast in the deep autumn, he and his older siblings longed with a fever to return to the capital.[53]

One study of the 'establishing ties' tide puts the number of young participants at 10.1 million.[54] A proportion of these hit the road simply for adventure and to see the sights. In a nation where nonofficial travel was extremely limited, such opportunities for tourism seemed irresistible. Youngsters determined to show their independence from parents, teachers, and other adults were happy to seize the chances that arose.[55] As one youth who had set out travelling at age sixteen recalled in his middle age:

> You could say that those days of 'establishing ties' were the beginning of our entry into life and getting a real taste of life. You could say that 'establishing ties' was a richness for those of us of limited experience. Its value to us in later life has often been clear, and served us in all sorts of ways. You could say that the start of 'establishing ties' laid a kind of foundation stone for a generation's growth and establishing itself in society. It caused a generation from then on to approach maturity.[56]

'Establishing ties' helped establish Chinese youth culture.

Red Guards put their bodies in the service of Mao Zedong and his call for a cultural revolution. A pioneering analysis of Red Guards, published in 1991 by a Tianjin Communist Youth League teacher, argues that their adoration of Mao was not a Red Guard aim but a means by which they could achieve their ideals, the creation of a special status for youth.[57] Singing Mao's praises put a natural youthful activity, music and singing, to this same purpose. Broadsheets helped spread youthful viewpoints, while travel on an unprecedented scale broadened minds and reinforced youthful determination to change the world and their part in it. From the autumn of 1968, new arenas for the promulgation of youth cultures began to open up.

## SENT-DOWN YOUTH

By 1968, youthful rebellion was wearing thin in the eyes of central authorities. Order in the cities and the restoration of industrial production became more pressing priorities than indulging the young devotees of the chairman. Starting in the autumn, groups of tertiary and secondary students were dispatched from Beijing, Shanghai, Tianjin, and other major cities to life in the countryside. The Cultural Revolution phase of the movement to go 'up to the mountains and down to the villages' (*shangshanxiaxiang*) saw millions of young people sent in what amounted to internal exile. Rural transmigration for most youth meant assignment to a production brigade, a subsection of a rural commune. But in underdeveloped parts of China, a more militarised organisation was used, as the urban newcomers were grouped into educated youth corps to help break in new lands. Such groups worked in the Great Northern Wilderness (*Beidahuang*) in the far northeast and on the steppes of Inner Mongolia. A third kind of experience was on state farms, in places such as the far southwest. In Yunnan, for example, state farms were the locus for natural rubber production.[58] By 1973, 4.19 million youths were reported as having gone to the countryside.[59]

The manner in which young, educated Chinese made this apparently one-way journey was as important as the destination. City authorities organised them into groups, usually of classmates from the same school, college, or university. In many cases these groups had already been working together in Red Guard or similar, imitation organisations in the cities, as by 1968 schools began to restore more regular classes. The sent-down experience thus was generally not undertaken by individuals in the company of strangers. The educated youth remained with their peers from the cities, sharing the hardships and their responses to their new environments. Physical labour was of course the first duty of these transplanted, would-be peasants. For many urban youngsters this was a definite hardship. Others took up the spade or wheelbarrow with gusto, imbued in the early phase of this mass transfer with idealistic notions of learning

Figure 2.3. Sent-down youth bid farewell to city life in this propaganda shot.
*Source:* Liu Xiaomeng, Ding Yizhuang, Shi Weimin and He Lan, *Zhongguo zhiqing shidian* (Encyclopedia of China's educated youth), Chengdu: Sichuan renmin
chubanshe, 1998, p. 12.

from the peasants who had been the backbone of Mao's revolutionary
triumph in 1949. Among a diverse wave of eventually up to fourteen million urban youth there were inevitably those filled with less enthusiasm at
the prospect of a life on the farm or in the wilderness. Others found their
frail bodies could not match the demands of their idealistic heads. From
the first months of this mass movement from the city to the countryside,
there were those plotting to move back in the opposite direction.[60]

Our interest here is in the cultural lives of these educated youth. Bodies
continued to perform loyalty to Chairman Mao and his revolution, as
bodies also were sacrificed in accidents and sickness. The rhythms of
life in the countryside inspired in some cases a reworking of the musical
heritage, foreign and domestic, of these young people. Many sent-down
youth escaped to imaginative spaces, drawn from films, novels, and other
writings. These three domains saw further assertions of youth identity
and difference. In broad terms, cultural activities in the countryside and

other places of assignment can be divided into the official and unofficial. The word underground (*dixia*) is often used to describe the nature of the latter kind of activities. The officially sanctioned cultural production and consumption of sent-down youth should not be dismissed as empty performance without meaning to either makers or consumers. In these state-sanctioned activities many young people learned the skills and confidence to make their own cultural way in the world. Some waited for many years until they returned to the cities to assert their distinctive point of view, others did not.

## Bodies Performing Revolution

The kinds of performances that young people had produced in their urban homes were brought to rural audiences as well as to fellow educated youth by the newcomers. In early 1969, from across the nation at the first Spring Festival since the transfer of young people got underway, came standardised accounts of youthful enthusiasts finding fulfilment in putting down roots in the countryside, encouraged by welcoming peasants and other locals. On a Henan commune a range of artistic troupes organised by sent-down youth and by young and old locals took turns entertaining the assembled crowds. Some troupe members also trekked through rough country to take their performances to remoter parts of the commune. The combination of local stories of class oppression and the writing and performing skills of the urban newcomers reportedly made these performances most effective.[61]

The kind of Red Guard performances that included fixed postures and the recitation of quotations from Chairman Mao were taken to the great northern wilderness by young transferees from the cities. Yang Qizhang, himself from Heilongjiang, recalls his excitement at watching a tableau of young performers, all in a version of army uniforms, holding high banners with slogans and a portrait of Mao. As soon as they started reciting he realised they were almost all from Shanghai, their accents making that clear. They had been in the construction corps for almost two years already and had some claim to heroism in their exploits in quelling a fire, which has been widely reported. Yang noted the impact of the performance on its several hundred viewers, many of whom shed tears along with those on the stage. As his corps members trudged back to their quarters, an unusual silence prevailed, so moving had been the show.[62]

After a few weeks at their Sichuan commune in the spring of 1969, Chengdu youth Xie Qianhong joined between twenty and thirty other newcomers in the commune meeting room to help set up a propaganda team. The commune Party secretary saw it as a matter of local pride to be able to show off a group of youngsters performing the items they had

Figure 2.4. A model-opera aria sung in the fields.
Source: Liu Xiaomeng, Ding Yizhuang, Shi Weimin and He Lan, *Zhongguo zhiqing shidian* (Encyclopedia of China's educated youth), Chengdu: Sichuan renmin chubanshe, 1998, p. 44.

seen back in Chengdu. As an inducement the secretary announced compensatory work points, extra rations for the team members, and extra points on days that they performed. These bonuses and the escape from toil in the fields greatly encouraged Xie and his colleagues. They took Red Guard propaganda team items and adjusted them for their present circumstances, making sure that the model performances (*yangbanxi*), promulgated two years earlier, were given suitable prominence in a repertoire that included clapper recitations, comic dialogues (*xiangsheng*), flute duets, and a variety of items. Their venue was an old opera stage in the village, high above a flat area for the spectators with four stout columns holding the elaborate roof over the stage. Having started with 'The East is Red,' the first show moved to more lively fare, with a two-part song between performers playing local old men and educated youth, each group taking a line of lyrics. The content might have been about poor and lower-middle peasants, but the form had real roots among its audience. Even trouble with a fake old man's beard refusing to stay fixed to the young singer's face and falling off five times just added to the general delight in the first show. Two-part recitation (*duikouci*) by two young women followed, with the last lines: 'Chairman Mao's revolutionary line / If we don't defend it, who will? The proletarian literature and art stage / If we don't occupy it, who will? / We have arrived. / Having arrived, we will not leave. / We'll never leave!'[63]

Educated youth performance groups were expected to pay proper attention to the model performances at the heart of Cultural Revolution cultural practice. In the vast wilderness of the Northeast, even the exotic and highly specialised art form of ballet was part of the sent-down youth's performance repertoire. The Nineteenth Corps of the Construction Corps established a '*White-haired Girl* propaganda team' (*xuanchuandui*). As Mao Peiling recalled, after being sent down in 1968, the only cultural item available seemed to be a loudspeaker. 'Every day three times if it wasn't "Grandma, listen to my story" [from *The Red Lantern*] it was Yang Zirong on "hunting tigers up the mountain" [from *Taking Tiger Mountain by Strategy*]. Listening to it really bored us.'[64] Several propaganda teams in the battalion came together to create their own version of the model ballet. Mao Peiling alone in the newly estab- lished ballet group had any ballet experience, and that was just for three years when she was at primary school in Shanghai. They had no script, no musical instruments, and no costumes and rehearsed in a seedling shed. Performances were on any available flat area, including concrete pads, and the occasional hall. Given the Northeast's weather, performing in flimsy stage costumes could also be a challenge. The troupe became so well-known that it participated in a Shenyang military region festival in 1971 and at a 1973 Heilongjiang educated youth festival. Thus even the most orthodox of Cultural Revolution arts could offer diversion to sent-down youth.

In the same month that the first of the model performance films was released, the renewed effort to popularise these works as models for all cultural practice was evident in China's media. The push did not rely upon showing the new film, *Taking Tiger Mountain by Strategy*. Indeed, one source suggests that there were only thirteen copies of the new film in nationwide circulation.[65] Instead, disk sound recordings of the operas and reading and discussion of the printed scripts were the main means to encourage further interest in what by 1970 were highly familiar works. From photographs of these renewed propaganda efforts around the model performances it is clear that young people made up the main body of the activists.[66] In Anhui Shanghai, educated youth Zhang Ren was part of a mixed group of sent-down youth and local youngsters that presented the model opera *Shajiabang*. The novelty of the new-style opera became a local hit among the villagers in the district. They would invite Zhang's troupe to perform, preparing a much appreciated special meal for the vis- iting actors. In addition to the model operas, they also presented a range of songs, recitations, and skits.[67]

By the early 1970s, with the movement to the countryside well established, though no less unpopular with some participants, sent- down youth in many places were active in song and dance ensembles

Figure 2.5. Young sent-down women dance while the men play the music.
*Source:* Liang Yunping, *Shu shang de rizi* (Days in the trees), Guangzhou: Huacheng chubanshe, 2007, p. 193.

(*wengongtuan*). Such local performers did not simply perform arias from the model operas and songs popularised on national and provincial radio broadcasts. Performers also wrote their own material in a wide variety of genres, ranging from song and dance duets (*errenzhuan*) to short skits and longer dramas. These were all based on models sanctioned in the mainstream media, but they could also be tailored to local tastes and performance traditions such as these duets. A major mechanism for the testing of the acceptability of an expanding repertoire was participation in provincial and regional performance festivals. The Liaoning festival of amateur performers in 1975 proved a showcase for over three thousand performers and students from across the province. Forty-five days of preparation and three streams: spoken drama; song, dance, and variety performances; and operas attest to the scale of the exercise. Over half a million people watched the 357 performances. Culture in the Cultural Revolution offered more than just eight shows watched by eight hundred million people, as the old joke suggested.[68]

One sent-down youth's experience in the reinvigoration of official cultural work in the early 1970s is noteworthy. Future Fifth Generation film director Wu Ziniu had spent over two years completing physical labour hauling barges on the Dadu River in his native Sichuan. Adjudged to have the appropriate political attitude, despite the condemnation of his professor father several years earlier and the suicide of his older sister, Wu was relieved of his labouring job in late 1971. He was assigned to the Leshan District Mao Zedong Thought Literature and Art School, quietly assisted by some family connections. After eighteen months of study, Wu joined a travelling drama troupe in Leshan. Later he became a member of a spoken drama troupe in the prefecture. All the while he had been honing his skills with the *erhu* (two-stringed violin) and piano accordion and in writing poetry and skits.[69] This was a typical Cultural Revolution apprenticeship for many of the generation who would turn Chinese art and literature on its head in the next decade.

Sent-down youth creativity needed outlets other than underground sharing of private art. In early 1975, the network of agricultural reclamation sites in Yunnan, largely staffed by educated youth, held a festival of amateur youth performances. Young people from Xishuangbanna, Linlun, Dehong, and Honghe presented four programmes of song, dance, and other items. Two Shanghai youth wrote a so-called 'surge poem' (*langtongshi*) in praise of the value of sending young people like themselves to the countryside. Their composition, in short, exclamatory lines, was recited by a massed group with dramatic increases in numbers and volume accounting for the name of the style of work. This was precisely like the street tableaux of Red Guards seen in Shanghai and elsewhere nine years earlier. Items at the festival, such as 'New sprouts are sturdy' (*Xin miao zhuozhuang*), tried to present class struggle but reportedly needed more polish to be effective. Work on such officially sanctioned art was a means of strengthening the sent-down youth's own commitment to the whole rural transfer project.[70]

Participation in officially sanctioned cultural activities appealed to educated youth in places like the Yunnan construction corps for a number of reasons. Actual belief in the worldview presented in the model operas and other works of the Cultural Revolution should not be discounted. But the simple attraction of a diversion from what otherwise could seem a rather pointless existence, with little obvious chance of improvement or change in the near or medium term, was a major factor for many city youngsters. This was true of Yang Jianhua and his participation in an amateur ballet troupe in Yunnan.[71] The immediate motivation was the news in early July 1971 that the regiment headquarters would hold a concert on Army Day (1 August) and set up a regimental propaganda team. Yang Jianhua knew that a recently arrived young woman from Chengdu had danced the lead role in *The Red Detachment of Women* at her No. 5 Middle School. Yang happened to have bought the ballet script just before his move to

Yunnan. They decided to present the second half of the dance drama's first act. News of Yang's ballet plan caused considerable interest in the regiment headquarters. He and his star were invited to join the newly established propaganda team. As much as the opportunity to perform, the attraction of not having to do physical labour to earn work points was equally important. Of the twenty-nine members of the propaganda team, apart from three local Va minority colleagues, all were sent-down youth.

In anticipation of Spring Festival 1972, the propaganda team leadership decided that the complete *Red Detachment* should be presented. By making do with their own attempts at costumes, props, lighting, and sets, listening to records of the score, and watching a television version of the ballet to flesh out Yang's rather thin script book, eventually the Red Women's Detachment danced across a stage in a remote corner of Yunnan close to the Burma border. The regimental political headquarters deputy head took a special interest in the troupe's preparations. On one visit he urged the youngsters to practice on all occasions. One young man asked whether they should do so in the lavatory. Yes, came the firm reply. Yang does not record whether squatting *en pointe* became *de rigeur*. The original version of the dance–drama required over one hundred dancers. In Yunnan, Yang and his companions danced multiple parts. In order not to miss their cues, the dancers wore five or six layers of costumes, peeling the outer layer off as required. Some of the women accordingly appeared to start the ballet pregnant.[72]

Officially approved writing gave educated youth valuable experience that some applied to less official creation. Yang Yusheng in Jiangyou county, Sichuan, was encouraged by his commune to write a one-act play in preparation for a county performance to commemorate the renewed push in 1976 to study the agricultural model of Dazhai village. Within a fortnight Yang had produced a script for *Guardians in the Storm* (*Fengyun shaobing*), the story of an educated youth deceived by a class enemy in his plotting against the collective, but rescued by the production brigade Party secretary. Despite its orthodoxy, the commune leadership was divided on the script's political acceptability. But then came the 5 April Qingming demonstrations in Tiananmen Square and elsewhere. Once the Communist Party's central decision condemning the demonstrations, which were directed at the group later identified as the Gang of Four, was received in Sichuan, the commune Party committee gave the go-ahead for *Guardians in the Storm* to participate in the county performance.[73] As it turned out, the play was received well by the audience that mattered, local officials, including in the county literature and art apparatus. There was even a suggestion that the play be turned into a Sichuan opera (*Chuanju*) for the county Sichuan opera company to present. This local competitiveness was an area in which educated youth, with their writing and performance skills and experience often as Red Guard players, could contribute, bringing glory to their commune or village.

## Rhythms Expressing Solidarity

The start of the Cultural Revolution project to send young people to the countryside was full of a mix of excitement and dread. A student at the Chengdu No. 13 Middle School, Feng Zhicheng, on the night of 22 December 1969, heard a propaganda truck on the street. From the loud-speakers came the news of 'the latest announcement,' Then a song, using the theme tune of the 1964 film *Heroic Sons and Daughters* (*Yingxiong ernü*), but with new lyrics. 'The latest announcement has arrived, / We must leave our hometowns right now, right now. / Leaving their dear friends, educated youth must go to far away places, / Re-educated by poor and lower-middle peasants, / Shake up the world and temper our red hearts.'[74] The young people subjected to this enforced transfer to the countryside tended to present a less fervent picture of the departure from loved ones in some of the songs they themselves composed. 'Song of Wuhan Educated Youth' (*Wuhan zhiqing zhi ge*), for example, was a lament at saying farewell to a girlfriend. As Feng notes, there was a full range of feelings among the youth at the time they left their city homes.

Lamenting the failure of the countryside to match their idealised image of it, Sichuan youth gave new lyrics to a song from the 1930s. The new song became widely known in Chengdu and elsewhere as a plaintive expression of longing.[75] Love songs, often with reference to *zhige* (brother educated youth) and *zhimei* (sister educated youth), offered solace and an opportunity to raise issues generally denied in the somewhat desexualised public culture of the day. There were more practical considerations expressed in song. One lyric popular with sent-down young women read: 'Marry a soldier, guard an empty house, / Marry a cadre, be sent down, / Marry a worker, guard a kitchen, / Marry an educated youth is the most stable.'[76]

There were also the diversions of dancing the loyalty dances (*zhong ziwu*) that Red Guards had perfected, singing model opera arias, and at daily meetings singing songs such as 'Sailing the Sea Depends on the Helmsman' and 'The East is Red.' More special, because of the frisson of risk associated with the activity, was singing vulgar songs (*huangse gequ*, literally yellow songs). One of Wang Tianhui's Chengdu classmates had a copy of *Two Hundred Foreign Songs* (*Waiguo minge 200 shou*). One evening three girls were singing softly in the group kitchen when the militia platoon leader next door heard them and rushed over. On his order, the precious book was flung into the cooking fire, turning to ash before the devastated young women.[77]

The eight sent-down boys in the production team on a commune in An county to which Duan Detian belonged between them had two guitars, two violins, and a mouth organ. They used to call themselves 'Katyusha' (*Kaqiusha*, the name of a popular Russian song and of a Soviet rocket). When not making tunes, they used to entertain themselves by reciting in its entirety the dialogue from the 1934 Soviet film, *Lenin in 1918* (*Liening zai 1918 nian*), adding a silly or satirical tone to key lines. The film was widely shown in the late 1960s and early 1970s, when new Chinese feature films were either not being made or only slowly emerging from the reopened studios.[78] They earned such a reputation as performers that the task of playing the model performance operas (and earning political kudos) was given to the eight young men from Chengdu. They first presented scenes from *Taking Tiger Mountain by Strategy*, with its dashing hero Yang Zirong and his tigerskin waistcoat and goatskin lined cape, though they gave it a distinctly Sichuanese opera flavour. In addition, a few standards, such as the 'living report skit' (*huobaoju*) 'Don't forget class bitterness; always remember blood-and-tears hatred' (*Bu wang jieji ku, laoji xuelei chou*), rounded out the programme.[79]

The underground songs of the educated youth were a direct expression of their frustrations and aspirations.[80] Songs were a natural, collective activity, particularly as most rural youth were in regions where there was nothing to do in the evenings, and electricity was not available. Electric light might allow more concentrated activities, such as reading or study. Flickering lamps were more suitable for activities where concentration on reading materials was less important. It would be wrong to suggest that songs created and sung by sent-down youth in this kind of environment were all expressions of discontent with their lot. Many songs were their own versions of the kinds of songs promulgated by state radio and commune and other broadcast stations. These more orthodox songs were full of resolutions to serve the revolution and model their behaviour on past heroes. This kind of above-ground composition was typified by songs from the construction corps in Inner Mongolia, including 'Construction Corps Battle Song' (*Bingtuan zhange*) and 'The Hearts of the Construction Corps Soldiers Face the Sun' (*Bingtuan zhanshi xiong you chaoyang*). 'The blue sky our canopy the earth our bed, yellow sand in our food tastes fragrant, the wild wind sings a battle hymn for us, the vast sky and earth is put in battlefield order' was hardly a dissident cry.[81] Rather, its hyperbole had appeal in making sent-down youth's individual and small group efforts into something of earth-shaking import. Teenagers around the world evince similar grandiose attitudes.

The underground songs coined by educated youth had a different motivation: They featured homesickness, love, and frustration. At a time when such alleged bourgeois indulgence in nonclass-based expressions of feelings was politically incorrect, simply singing such a song represented an act of defiance or at least a release of pent-up frustrations. Many of these Chinese songs were as old as the 1930s. One Chinese song, 'The Blue Street Light' (*Lanse de jiedeng*), included the lines: 'I am crying, I am crying, no one knows me.... Whoever is singing, come softly over, it's the song I loved to sing when I was young.' Other songs, such as 'Moscow Nights' (*Mosike jiaowai de wanshang*), had enjoyed wide currency among all generations before 1966. Even the American 'Old Man River' (*Laorenhe*) was occasionally sung, its sombre tone appealing to unhappy youth.[82]

Sent-down youth also made their own songs, often by rewriting the lyrics of familiar tunes. Some were just sung as jokes. One such gem was 'Flying the Red Flag to Go Begging' (*Dazhe hongqi qu yaofan*). The rhythm of the title matched perfectly that of well-known, officially approved songs. Young people, working or resting together in the fields, were not reticent in bursting into such songs, as they sounded proper but made a sly, satirical point. Any peasant listeners could appreciate the joke. In Shaanxi, educated youth took local folk songs and wrote new words. The *xintianyou* style of folk song on the loess plateau lent itself well to expressions of youthful loneliness and love in the wilderness. This local song style was usually a male voice singing in high pitch, as if on the top of a mountain, and with a rough, uncultivated sound. The solitariness of these local songs had instant appeal to heartbroken urban youth who had grown up on a diet of polished, often syrupy tunes. In Shaanxi as elsewhere, during its circulation among the urban youth, the unofficially created songs had their lyrics changed as they were evolved and modified according to local circumstances. A similar process occurred in the passing around and recopying of hand-copied stories.

The creation and circulation of the songs depended on the different circumstances in which they emerged. Most of the youth sent to rural communes were billeted together as groups (separated by gender). This collective living arrangement provided conditions for the sharing of activities such as singing, studying, reading, and sports. With group monitors and other leaders close by, the songs that emerged from state farms and construction corps were more mainstream and less anguished. Unlike the sons and daughters of high-level cadres or with other good connections who regarded their rural transfer as temporary, the offspring of ordinary families provided the driving force for the musical creativity of urban youth in the countryside. These had little hope of arranging to return to the city, so instead focused on dealing with their new circumstances. Musical expression of their frustrations and feelings provided a welcome outlet and one that could be shared with others.[83]

The influence of local styles can be seen in many songs. Sichuan youth, sent to places in their own province, recycled the folk songs they encountered in order to express their own predicaments. Beijing and Shanghai youth, sent farther away from home, tended in contrast to not turn so much to local musical resources.[84] Some widely known songs shared a title and music, but the lyrics were different. 'Seeing Mother in My Dreams' (*Mengjian muqin*), for example, existed with differing words among youth in the Yunnan and Inner Mongolia construction corps at two ends of the nation. Titles could also co-exist or change, depending on where the song circulated. Yang Jian, in his study of underground literature, cites the case of 'Song of Nanjing' (*Nanjing zhi ge*). In 1971, the song was taken into army ranks by former sent-down youths who enlisted. It became popular among city-based soldiers, most of whom had spent time as educated youth. In Shijiazhuang, Hebei, the song was called 'My Hometown' (*Wode jiaxiang*), but at a Nanjing artillery school it was 'Lovely Nanjing' (*Ke'ai de Nanjing*).[85]

Songs circulated among the sent-down youth in a number of ways. There was a great deal of movement among youth in many places, as friends or groups from the same city visited other villages, brigades, and corps. Some moved out of the county and even to other provinces, in a shadow version of the 'establishing ties' of Red Guard travel in 1966 and 1967. Hand-copied versions of songs carried them far among other youth, just like the novels and stories passed among these groups. Returning to the cities at Chinese New Year, classmates and friends got together and naturally exchanged songs as well as experiences. Some former members of Red Guard performance troupes even organised 'underground concerts' on these occasions. Travelling singers and storytellers also emerged from among sent-down youth. These rare figures made a kind of living by moving around the countryside, using personal acquaintances and networks, and receiving payment in food and hospitality. Even those who specialised in telling stories also sang a song or two, helping popularise sent-down youth songs.[86]

The expression of youthful feelings and attitudes is the most notable feature of the sent-down youth songs. Free from an expectation to serve a political purpose, as was the case for officially promulgated songs of the period, these songs offer a direct entry into the aspirations and identities of the young people who wrote and sang them. Through these songs we can trace the changes in youthful fervour and hopes, from the initial period of enthusiasm on being sent to the countryside and longing for home through to more mature or measured desires. The early songs, from 1969 and 1970, show influence from Red Guard music, with reference in a farewell lament to parting company with comrades in arms (*zhanyou*) in a song like 'Beijing, Goodbye.' Chinese poetry has a long tradition of poems of saying good-bye to friends, often with metaphorical reference to time as river water flowing. 'Song of Guangzhou Educated Youth' (*Guangzhou zhiqing ge*) had similar imagery, using the Pearl River that flows through the city.[87] Starting from 1970, song themes shifted to reflecting life in the countryside and lost aspirations. As the song 'Madman' (*Jingshenbing huanzhe*, literally someone who has contracted mental illness) put it: 'People in the world jeer at me, a madman; my youth has been stifled (*maimo*: buried), who feels sorry for me?'[88]

Singing forbidden songs was a common memory of sent-down youth and could get youngsters into trouble. Yan Xiaoli from Chengdu remembered a day when she and four of her classmates found a quiet glade in the mountains. Usually these young women did not sing vulgar songs, unlike the young men in the production team. But the glade was so peaceful that Gao Rong, who had the best voice in the group, burst boldly into 'The Last Rose of Summer' (*Xiatian zuihou de meigui*), 'Oh, Susanna' (*Sushanna*), and 'Baby' (*Baobei*). The other four joined in with 'Katyusha' (*Kaqiusha*), and 'Moscow Nights,' among others. When they discovered the next day that some of the boys may have been listening, they refused to sing forbidden songs for a long time for fear of being reported on.[89] In the disciplined surroundings of the construction corps, it was more difficult for sent-down youth to enjoy these songs. Incidents abound of efforts by officials responsible for the urban youth to expose those who had sung such songs under the cover of darkness. A Heilongjiang construction corps platoon encountered trouble over the 'Song of Nanjing,' unaware of the fortunes of its creator. Ren Yi, a 1966 graduate of the Nanjing No. 6 Middle School, had been sent in late December 1968 to the Jiangsu countryside. One evening in late May 1969, he took a 1964 song about moving to Xinjiang as the foundation for a guitar version of 'My Hometown,' which others began to call 'Song of Nanjing.' In February 1970, Ren was arrested. Initially sentenced in April to death with a two-year reprieve, four months later he was given a ten-year term. These were extreme responses to the young people who chose to express themselves in the supposedly utopian climes of the Cultural Revolution.[90]

The music of sent-down youth's lives in the late 1960s and 1970s was varied, resourceful, and amenable to manipulation to express feelings and hopes that often could not be voiced in other ways. These youthful rhythms laid the groundwork for the emergence of an even more distinct youth music in the mid-1980s, when Chinese rock music has its origins. The success of this later phenomenon in providing a special soundtrack to the growth of youth cultures in a rapidly changing society indirectly owed much to the musical lives of an earlier generation.

## *Spaces: Imagined and Real*

The real and imagined spaces inhabited by sent-down youth during the Cultural Revolution provided arenas for the shaping of distinctive youth attitudes and aspirations. Three kinds of educated youth cultural practice can be associated with the three sorts of sent-down youth organisational or living modes. First were the construction corps (*jianshe bingtuan*), a semi-militarised existence in undeveloped areas, such as in Heilongjiang, Xinjiang, and Inner Mongolia in the north and Yunnan and Hainan Island in the far south. Living in the corps was a highly organised, disciplined experience. A second kind of sent-down youth experience was to end up in established but poor areas in less remote provinces, including Shanxi, Shaanxi, Jiangxi, and Liaoning. In such disadvantaged places, organisation among the city youngsters was weak, with most of them largely left to fend for themselves and to establish relations with the peasants among whom they settled. The third mode of educated youth existence was among those who had either remained in the cities or managed to find ways, sanctioned or otherwise, to return home. This third group sometimes came together in city salons, a new cultural phenomenon in these years, which grew from a constant interaction with youth in the countryside.[91]

Life in the construction corps was collective and shaped by military-style discipline. Accordingly, even the most basic of unofficial cultural activities, such as reading banned foreign and domestic books, were somewhat difficult, as supervision by officers circumscribed much creativity on the part of their younger charges. Cultural life in the corps consisted largely of writing officially sanctioned 'educated-youth literature' and performing propaganda shows of limited innovation. In poor villages, urban youth faced considerable isolation from the currents of cultural innovation. On the other hand, being remote from close supervision allowed a space for more interesting local developments or subcultures than official cultural production provided for. Enhanced by some contact with urban salons and other developments, cultural life in the deprived countryside incorporated such activities as the circulation and enjoyment of hand-copied novels. Indeed Yang Jian argues that the city salons and the unsupervised country youth enjoyed a mutual dependence. The latter provided background and material, the former new directions and support. Yang further identifies two distinct periods in these sent-down youth literary and artistic developments. Before 1972, the urban youngsters were still becoming used to their country circumstances. In the construction corps, poor villages, and the city salons, the new culture was putting out shoots and becoming extremely active. In the second period, until Mao's death in 1976, cultural production became more marked and increasingly distinctive.[92]

The growth of sent-down youth writing and its fostering of new imaginative spaces for youthful assertion of identity owed much to the official encouragement of publications in the construction corps. These broadsheets continued a Red Guard practice, though with tighter supervision. They were published for circulation among the construction corps in the Northeast and Inner Mongolia, among other regions. In the Sixth Regiment of the Heilongjiang Construction Corps, Yu Yinghua and several of her fellow platoon report writers (*lian baodaoyuan*) from Beijing produced *Red Sentry* (*Hong shaobing*) in 1970. Work in the wilderness was at a slow point and the youth were anxious to contribute more than just filling two blackboards outside their canteen. They also recalled the first published writings of Mao Zedong in the *Xiangjiang Review* (*Xiangjiang pinglun*) about sixty years earlier. Ink and paper were bought in town or from the regimental headquarters, which also lent a mimeograph machine. They printed the first issues in red ink, which had a satisfying impact on readers. Content was filled with the kind of rhetoric that made even the most ordinary activities, including reading unapproved writings, a matter of class struggle. A poor peasant woman's reheating of wheat buns in a steamer became a story about 'strategic buns' (*zhanlue mantou*). Soon readers were sending stories to the broadsheet. The corps leaders became concerned that corps money was being spent on *Red Sentry*, as the platoon only had two yuan a month to cover its expenses. They closed the broadsheet down, apparently because it offered unwelcome competition to the existing and more official *Corps Soldier* (*Bingtuan zhanshi bao*).[93] But this experience probably enhanced the sent-down youth's interest and confidence in creating their own underground writing.

In Inner Mongolia more than one hundred thousand youth came from Beijing, Tianjin, Shanghai, and Nanjing, making up about a third of the sent-down numbers in the autonomous region, the others being local young people.[94] They lived in three kinds of circumstances: herding, agriculture on state farms, and the wastelands being developed by construction corps. In the latter two places, the youth were subject to close organisation and discipline. Qu Zhe remembers a fellow corps member returning from a trip home to Beijing with a watch, a pen, even a radio, which offered a way of imaginative escape from the regimentation of farm life.[95] Youth in herding work, however, had space in which to create subcultures of their own. On the steppes, fiction, poetry, and creative prose (*sanwen*) began to flourish in the early 1970s. As some youth had opportunities to return to the cities on visits, and as others married urban newcomers or locals and set up home on the steppes, rich material for new writing and other cultural expression emerged. The hand-copied novel 'A Year' (*Yi nian*) from 1972 was written by Wang Koukou, the pseudonym of a young herder from Beijing. It told of the experiences of sent-down youth on the steppes and circulated among youths in the Abaga banner (district) where it was composed. In other banners in Inner Mongolia, similar hand-copied works, with their typical mix of melo-drama, emotion, and idealism, were widely read by sent-down youth. Poetry, as shorter form, was easier to compose and circulate. Five former classmates from the No. 2 High School in Beijing worked as a poetry col-lective, producing three 'volumes' of seventy-one poems in 1971 and 1972 in their banner. Other sent-down youth were inspired by their example, composing their own collections. The titles, such as 'Songs on Horseback' (*Mabei shang de ge*), sound like those of officially published paeans to the success of the 'up to the mountains, and down to the villages' project. But the collected poems were a more authentic expression of youthful hopes and identity than those on the shelves of the Xinhua Bookstores in the region. The start of the return to the cities around 1972 had a huge impact on sent-down youth on the plains of Inner Mongolia. The upsurge in unofficial compositions, in a range of styles and forms, from classical to experimental, and covering a broad variety of subject matter, from folk to deeply personal, was remarkable.[96]

In the Northeast, particularly in the northernmost province of Heilongjiang, the discipline of the construction corps would seem to have worked against artistic creativity among the educated youth from Beijing, Tianjin, Shanghai, and the provincial capital, Harbin. In 1968 and 1969, four hundred thousand such people were transferred to corps in the province. The closely organised corps included both official propa-ganda teams, attracting some of the most polished talents, and amateur performing and writing groups more geared to cater to the entertainment and relaxation needs of the young people. As elsewhere in the nation, some of the writings that came out of these activities were published with fanfare in collections intended to reflect the success of the urban–rural transfer project. But even in the most controlled circumstances, students from Beijing and other cities managed to produce original work. In some cases, the young writers wrote, edited, and performed in their platoons' newsletters, notice blackboards, and propaganda troupes, and in parallel wrote material of a more personal import. Each platoon (*liandui*) ide-ally included 'three members' (song teacher, blackboard newspaper edi-tor, and night school teacher), 'two teams' (art and literature propaganda team and a basketball team), and one room (a library). At higher levels in the construction corps in the Northeast, a degree of professionalism was apparent, with troupes performing the model operas and ballets and other creative personnel being largely released from productive work. From the ranks of these creative youth in the Northeast came the core of new writers in the post-1976 epoch. They had learned their craft in the officially sanctioned and underground arenas, including in the city salons.[97]

A major inspiration for young writers and their readers was copies of books they had brought from their home cities. Entertainment in the poor villages of Sichuan for educated youth included reading the novels some had been able to bring from home and reading Mao Zedong's collected classical-style poems. These volumes eventually were worn and battered, stained with lamp oil. Preparing to leave his native Shanghai for Fujian, Zheng Mengbiao dug out copies of the classic eighteenth-century novel *A Dream of Red Mansions* and a book of classical poetry that had been hidden under a lute table and stowed them in his luggage.[98] In Shanxi, Beijing sent-down youth Zhuang Weiliang read a hand-copied version of the same classic novel among other classical works in circulation.[99] When several of her sent-down classmates in 1973 were among those able to start university studies, Cai Yongxian turned to the pages of the three novels that educated youth in her regiment were by then allowed to read: *The Gadfly*, the Czech wartime *Notes from the Gallows*, and the Soviet favourite, *How the Steel Was Tempered*. She hoped that the trials of the heroes of these stories might provide guidance for her own life, apparently stuck in Yunnan.[100]

The simple act of writing letters to family and friends recording the initial wonderment at the novelty of life in the Southwest or wherever they were assigned and then the pains of a continued exile there became a major solace for many sent-down youths. Communicating with families and friends back home was made more vivid if youths could send visual records of their new lives. Zhou Que, a Heilongjiang youth, took an old camera with him when he was sent to the First Regiment of the Construction Corps. He managed to set up a makeshift developing apparatus. His fellow educated youth appreciated the opportunity to send negatives of themselves to their parents. Many handed over a roll of film to Zhou and asked him to fill it, not just for their families in the cities, but also for their own keeping. Demand in the district from urban youth and locals was such that Zhou set up a darkroom with an enlarger so that he could print photographs. From his account more than twenty years later, it is clear that the photos he took were not all reflective of the propaganda of the time. Exhausted and sorrowful subjects were also in his lens, providing a welcome record of reality for the educated youth to share among themselves and on occasion with their families.[101]

Some officials tried to supervise youthful writing like they did other areas of cultural activity among educated youth. In the Northeast, Han

Xiuqing was assigned to an 'Anti-Revolutionary Political Rumour' office, established at the Fifty-third Regimental Headquarters after the Qingming (5 April 1976) demonstration in Tiananmen Square by young Beijingers against what was later identified as the Gang of Four. A poem and cartoon with the slogan 'When will we be able to leave this place?' were submitted to the office for investigation. The writer of the poem and cartoon was a friend of Han, who she knew had a bad family background, her father having been condemned as a 'capitalist roader' with overseas connections. But the writer had already been assigned out of the regiment. Han Xiuqing decided to write a brief note to her friend warning her that her poem had fallen into the hands of the platoon leader and then to go through the motions of addressing the issue in a report to her superiors. As in a lot of cases, the arrest of the Gang of Four in October 1976 brought an end to her dilemma, as the rumour investigation work was abandoned.[102]

The imaginative space opened up by film viewing had been a major attraction for city youth in China before 1966. During their time as sent-down youth, young people from the cities continued to enjoy the worlds that a flickering screen offered to its enthusiastic audiences. A range of films made its way to rural youth, including titles from the seventeen years before 1966 that became extremely familiar after repeated screenings, as well as banned films and new works, including the model performances on celluloid and new-style feature films. The movies retained and even enhanced their power during the Cultural Revolution to offer imaginary spaces for youthful dreams and escape.

During these years, those in charge of the Chinese film enterprise made a major effort to facilitate popular access to the movies. To be assigned to a mobile projection unit, taking films to villages and other settlements across the commune or reclamation area, was a signal honour. The work could often be tough, battling the weather and terrain to bring entertainment and instruction to the countryside. But it also promised diversion and even a distant association with the still lingering glamour of the movie industry. These small groups used relatively portable 16 mm projectors, often powered by generators, to bring films to people who did not have easy access to cinemas. In the 1970s, even more portable Super-8 projectors were developed. During the Cultural Revolution, the number of projection teams nationwide increased substantially, just as the range of films available for showing shrank. Mobile projection teams, however, did not just show feature films: They also showed documentaries on national events and developments and educational films on new agricultural techniques, for example. According to one source, nationwide rural projection units, including mobile teams and fixed places where films were shown, increased four times over 1965 levels.[103] In Heilongjiang, where a large

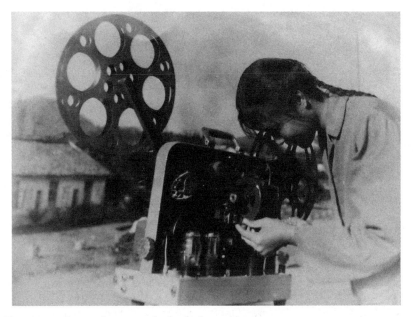

Figure 2.6. A sent-down youth checks her projector.
*Source:* Liang Yunping, *Shu shang de rizi* (Days in the trees), Guangzhou: Huacheng chubanshe, 2007, p. 167.

proportion of educated youth were sent, film projection units, including mobile teams, had almost doubled between before the Cultural Revolution and early 1973.[104]

The generally youthful members of the mobile projection teams often had broader skills than knowing how a projector and generator worked. Members saw themselves as part of a larger propaganda project. Arriving at new place, they would assist local propaganda team members with the preparation of blackboard posters, scripting recitals of poetry and other material, and rehearsing clapper rhyme recitals with a local twist or reference. A typical report from the Northeast describes how members of one team visited nineteen different workplaces in a small town to explain the historical background and parallels between *Lenin in 1918*, which they were to show in the evenings and the current political situation in China.[105] These propaganda tasks offered opportunities for sent-down youth, for they usually were more conversant with current ideology than less educated country folk. Such work included preparing educational slides to show before the main feature. One lauded all-female projection team in Heilongjiang made sure that the thirty-six hundred peasants in their mountain commune saw films twice monthly.[106] Apparently, however, some projection teams were less activist, happy to simply show a film without preliminary explanation and follow-up.[107]

A common generalisation about film in the ten years after 1966 is that all films made in the seventeen years before that date were banned. The implication is that Chinese audiences, among whom young people figured as prominently as in any other country, could not revive their fond memories of much-loved movies by actually watching them again. A perusal of newspaper advertising in the late 1960s and early 1970s indicates, however, that a number of pre-1966 films were available for young and old Chinese to enjoy. One kind of enjoyment was watching films condemned as antirevolutionary or decadent. Such films were occasionally shown for political education purposes. But going to watch a 'negative teaching example' did not mean that the audience was united in its voiced condemnation of the work. In the darkness of a cinema or work hall groups of young people could find pleasure in familiar songs, characters, and stories.[108]

More common were the 'old three fights' (*lao san zhan*) films, so named because of the word *zhan* (fight or war) in their titles: *Fighting North and South* (*Nanzheng beizhan*, 1952), *Mine Warfare* (*Dilei xhan*, 1962), and *Tunnel Warfare* (*Didao zhan*, 1965). These three stories of the War against Japan and the civil war of the 1940s in the case of the former, were shown continuously during the period from 1966 to the mid-1970s.[109] They became so well known that some young viewers liked to have fun by reciting the dialogue just ahead of the characters, to the amusement of most viewers. The same familiarity became true of a small number of foreign films. Works from the Soviet Union, such as *Lenin in 1918* and *Lenin in October* (made in the 1930s), were also subjected to joking recitals of the dialogue and other interruptions from mostly young watchers.[110] For Zeng Zhicheng from Chengdu the monthly film show was far from satisfying, especially as only four films were shown: the 'old three fights' and *Surprise Attack* (*Qixi*), a 1960 Korean War film. *Guerrillas on the Plain* (*Pingyuan youjidui*, 1955) was only shown once. The arduous journey to the battalion headquarters town was rewarded with the chance to buy candies and, for those so inclined, a book that would be devoured by all within a week.[111]

Films provided sent-down youth in the northern wilderness some access, though highly controlled, to the world beyond their assigned workplaces. Sun Chunming, from Beijing, remembers how he and his classmates in the depth of winter in 1972 resolved to walk the almost three miles through the snow to the regimental headquarters to watch a documentary, 'The Chinese Table Tennis Team Visits Four Countries, including the United States and Canada' (*Zhongguo pingpangqiu dui fang Mei, fang Jianada deng si guo*). A few had seen it before, but opportunities to watch films were welcome, besides this gave an insight into the wider world. Through the falling snow, a northwest wind, and snow drifts, the going was far from easy. Soon the young men and women were cursing everything in an effort at mutual encouragement. By the time they arrived at the clubhouse, the film was half over and there were no spare seats. Leaning against the walls, the youth watched the expressways, traffic, skyscrapers, and huge billboards on screen, marvelling at another world. What was that claim that 'two thirds of the world's people are oppressed ...'? In the environment in the film this didn't seem too bad a fate to the youngsters in Heilongjiang. On the way back, the snow had stopped falling and a weak moon shone across the path. Recalling what they had seen on screen, the youth heard one of their number start to sing from the back of the group. It was a popular song that had been banned. Its lovelorn lyrics were of separation between two worlds on each side of a river.[112]

Film diversions that city folk could enjoy in the early 1970s were generally unavailable to sent-down youth unless they were on a visit back to their home towns. In 1972 the North Korean melodrama *The Flower Seller* (*Mai hua guniang*) proved a huge success in Beijing, with ticket lines stretching around the block at the cinemas showing the film. In all, close to one-third of Beijing's population appears to have watched the film in 1972 and its rerelease in 1973.[113] But the effort in these years to make film prints in 16 mm and Super 8 formats meant that even youth from Beijing in the Thirty-seventh Regiment of the Heilongjiang Construction Corps could watch the Korean weepie. For Dong Qiangsheng and his Beijing classmates, walking more than three miles in the cold autumn air to see a movie was nothing. Nor was squeezing with two hundred other young people into the canteen, with no part of the floor empty of a little stool and no wall space not lent on. Beijing, Shanghai, Tianjin, and other accents all mingled until the lights went out and the film began. To general delight, it was *The Flower Seller*.[114]

In addition to film, there were other imaginative spaces to which sent-down youth could resort in seeking inspiration or solace. Playing cards could be used to tell fortunes. A sent-down youth at a commune in Fushun county warned readers of *Liaoning Youth* (*Liaoning qingnian*) against what he called this superstition. While most fellow educated youth were learning new outlooks and habits from the poor and lower-middle peasants, some urban youth were using playing cards to tell fortunes. The letter writer acknowledged that this use of cards was mostly a game, but it also ran the risk of spreading reactionary notions about people's fate being predetermined. The published letter, however, gave instructions to readers on what cards carried what meaning, including how to tell if someone was likely to return to their urban family. These could be used by readers to try the activity for themselves.[115]

The excitement of reading banned or vulgar books (*huangse shu*, literally yellow books) was welcome relief for those like Duan Zhishu

from Beijing, who had soon realised the difference between the propaganda image of sent-down youth and the reality in the construction
corps. Despite this he had been selected to attend a Communist Youth
League assembly. One day, at the clinic where he worked, his friend Wang
Chunsheng brought the news that a 'yellow book' was circulating in their
platoon. When she looked surprised at his interest, he protested that even
he needed to establish what such a book looked like. That afternoon
Wang handed over the book, in the manner Duan noted later, of clandestine Communists in the 1930s that they had seen in the movies. After
midnight, Duan locked the door of the clinic and, holding a torch under
his duvet, opened the dark green covered volume. It was *Autumn in Spring*
(*Chuntian li de qiutian*), published in 1932 by respected May Fourth
writer, Ba Jin (1904–2005), then under arrest. It was not a thick book,
so by dawn Duan had finished it. But where was the obscene part?[116]
Duan did not know that editions of works considered politically incorrect,
including translations of foreign novels and other writing, were published
in the Cultural Revolution with different coloured covers to indicate their
contents or origin.[117] One account from the far north of Heilongjiang suggested that underground or banned writings had wide circulation. A young
worker in Shangganling was in the habit of not going to his factory job
but staying in the workers' dorm reading what the report called pornographic novels. After attending a performance by the amateur propaganda
team in the district, he became eager to join the team.[118] Underground
fiction, hand-copied or copies of banned books, seems from this report to
have been available to readers other than sent-down youth.

In Yunnan, reading banned books had dire consequences. Two Shanghai
youths in one of the regiments of the Yunnan Construction Corps were
reading such works, when one of them, heading for the lavatory, knocked
over the oil lamp they were using. Fire broke out, but the two youths did
not raise the alarm, fearing being discovered with the risky books. The
fire caught hold and spread in the wooden building shared by the sent-
down youth. When it was put out, ten young women were discovered in
the ashes huddled together.[119]

In the great northern wilderness, private circulation of a battered copy
of the 1958 novel *Song of Youth* (*Qingchun zhi ge*) needed to be kept
away from the platoon leader, who would confiscate it. Whenever a com-
rade returned from a visit home to the city, the first question was 'Did
you bring any good cigarettes?' The second was 'Have you brought any
books back?'[120] A transistor radio might offer furtive opportunities to
hear Radio Moscow or even the Voice of America.[121] On a trip back
to Beijing, Wang Dawen was able to read two hand-copied stories in
the city: 'An Embroidered Slipper' (*Yi zhi xiuhua xie*) and 'The Second
Handshake' (*Di'er ci woshou*). Excited by them, but unable to bring

copies back north, Wang shared the stories with his sent-down companions. Soon others were making the trip to hear him tell the stories, which he elaborated further to please his listeners. He became quite fluent in retailing the stories, rewarded with bowls of boiled water and cigarettes, the best gifts available from his comrades. Wang's luck ran out, as his activities became known to the leadership. Summoned to explain his feudal–capitalist–revisionist stories, he discovered that the leaders had not heard of hand-copied novels. Wang was subjected to criticism meetings and obliged to write and revise a self-criticism. Initial efforts at satirical language were not appreciated, and rewriting went on. When sent to supervised labour, Wang found himself surrounded by tellers of stories: the pre-Cultural Revolution Chinese films *Youth on the Water* (*Shuishang chunqiu*), about two generations of swimmers; *Girl Basketball Player No. 5* (*Nülan wuhao*); and the spy thriller *The Mysterious Travelling Companion* (*Shenmi de lubang*). Soviet films from the fifties and Indian films all provided material for stories.

In the absence of many books or other entertainments, some sent-down youth found a niche among their peers in telling stories. Zhu Shenzhi worked in the Daxing'anling forests in Heilongjiang. She started her hobby by telling ghost stories in the dark to the dozen young women with whom she shared a room in part to stop them thinking too much of their homes in Shanghai. Soon this storytelling developed into a daily ritual for the men and women working in the forest. She would tell stories in the morning when they arrived at the place to be cleared, and they would all work in the afternoons. Zhu Shenzhi became adept at combining her memories of a range of disparate novels she had read, ghost stories, detective stories, and others. Some of her tales featured settings before 1949, when women wore tight, Chinese-style dresses and could hide evil intentions behind a beautiful face. Zhu started making notes, and, realising that her chances of being found out were not great, became bolder in writing down whole stories. One that achieved some fame was actually set in the Heilongjiang forests and was about a hunt for gold. A handsome young hero, riding a white horse and adept with a pistol, falls in love with a local aristocratic young woman. Zhu Shenzhi did not get to circulate a second story, as her platoon leader found out about her plans and threatened to record her transgressions in her personnel file. But she bought a good quality notebook and secretly wrote a fifty-thousand-word story titled 'The Boundless Wilderness' (*Manman de huangye*). Her older sister and mother in Shanghai were its first readers. Looking back, Zhu acknowledged the importance of this writing as an outlet for self-expression and for the romanticism of a young woman.[122]

Sent-down youth helped create the folk literature of the Cultural Revolution period and the spaces for the play of imagination that such stories allowed. Other types of folk literature included fables or tall stories, political jokes, and political songs. The stories were either tales of modern detectives cracking cases or tales of actual revolutionary heroes or famous people. These stories, with exciting titles like 'A Fading Piece of Paper,' 'The Plum Blossom Gang,' and 'Shi Yousan Enters the Forbidden City,' were in some places widely known and enjoyed. 'The Plum Blossom Gang,' for example, created a fictional world in which the wives of top leaders were American spies and brave Chinese rebels outwitted and exposed them. Other detective or spy stories circulating during the Cultural Revolution were retellings of earlier tales with settings and the names of characters simply changed.[123] Stories of contemporary figures, such as Zhou Enlai or former foreign minister Chen Yi, carried such titles as 'Outwitting Khrushchev.' These types of stories lent themselves to constant elaboration, with new details added to the basic story. Their style drew on traditional vernacular tales and was similar to that of the episodic stories that gained wide readerships in the early part of the century, before and during the May Fourth period, when more modern literary fiction also emerged.

The circulation of unofficial or underground writing in the 1970s could bring unexpected consequences in the works produced. The most famous hand-copied novel of the era, Zhang Yang's *The Second Handshake*, started out as a novella in 1963. By 1974, sent-down youth Zhang had produced his sixth draft of the story and was under investigation for producing an unsanctioned work. By then his creation, about a patriotic nuclear physicist in the 1940s and her desire to return to China to aid national construction, had taken on a variety of versions. All featured the heroine spending time living in the United States and her romantic entanglements. The titles of the different versions reflected the qualities that young readers looked for in such underground writing, particularly the romance and presentation of a noble, educated hero: *Red Flowers on the Fragrant Hills* (*Xiangshan honghua*), *A Dynasty of Lords* (*Yidai tianjiao*), *Mother of the Hydrogen Bomb* (*Qingdan zhi mu*), and *Return to the Homeland* (*Guiguo*), among others.[124] By the time the novel, given its title at some point in the early 1970s by a writer other than Zhang, was published officially in 1978 it achieved impressive sales, in part from a readership already familiar with it.[125] Another widely read story that first appeared in 1972 in Inner Mongolia captured the appeal of this kind of writing for its youth readers. *One Year* (*Yinian*), written by a Beijing sent-down youth surnamed Wang, recounted the experiences of such youth, describing them as 'wanderers over the earth' (*dadi de liulangzhe*). This self-image captured youthful alienation in the years of internal exile.[126]

Some of the unofficial writing that circulated among educated youth in the first half of the 1970s was of less obvious appeal to young readers.

Already in the summer of 1969, hand-copied poetry was circulating among sent-down youth. Some friends and other interested writers formed groups to share such poetry, including experimenting with new styles that deliberately rejected the positive and clear messages expected in official outlets. From these groups, with individual members moving between rural bases and urban homes, emerged the post–Cultural Revolution school of poetry labelled 'misty poetry' (menglongshi, literally obscure or hazy poetry).[127] Some of this innovative writing was encouraged in literary or cultural salons in Beijing and other major cities. These had in fact emerged as early as 1967. By the summer of 1972 there were even salons meeting in the housing quarters of the State Council and the Ministry of Railways. Membership changed constantly as writers and other intellectuals moved back and forth from the countryside or found work in the cities. These spaces adopted the name salon, in its transliterated Chinese translation shalong, because it had an elitist ring and was a term not used by officialdom. The independence of the groups was thus expressed in their name, even if most sent-down youth had nothing to do with them and did not take an interest in their literary or cultural outputs.[128]

A focus on sent-down youth in the countryside should not overlook the young people who did not go to learn from the poor and lower-middle peasants. A proportion of the age cohort remained in cities, working in factories and elsewhere. Others entered the armed forces. Many young people underwent both kinds of experiences during the 1970s. These young people assume less importance in accounts of the emergence of youth identity because they were often working and living in smaller groups of classmates and under closer supervision. The space for their own expressions in literature and performance was accordingly more confined. In Shanghai factories, for example, new young workers participated in literature and art propaganda teams in rehearsing the model opera Shajiabang. The opera was popular in the city, as it had started life as a Shanghai opera (Huju) and was set in Zhejiang, the province surrounding Shanghai.[129]

For those youth who remained in the cities, the kinds of spaces that allowed for expressions of youthful aspirations and identity in the countryside were unattainable. Zhang Jianya, a Shanghai high schooler whose doctor parents had been abroad on United Nations work, was allowed to stay in his home city. This was because his older brother had recently been sent to the countryside. The regulations allowed for a child to remain at home to care for parents. Zhang was assigned to the Jing'an district housing administration, where he worked as a carpenter. Having a talent for performing that earlier had been put to use in his high school propaganda team, Zhang successfully entered the Shanghai City Workers Cultural Palace drama troupe in 1973 as an amateur actor. From there he was recruited by the Shanghai Film Studio as it increased production in 1975.[130] But these were cultural activities organised and controlled by adults. The kinds of collective sometimes unsupervised living conditions that led to youthful creativity in the countryside were not available to such city-based youth.

MARKING OUT A SPACE

The youth culture that appeared in the circumstances provided by the Cultural Revolution was not accidental. It emerged from the social upheaval, disruptions, and experimentation of those ten years. Chairman Mao's call for the young to take the initiative in what passed for politics set many young people on a road to self-discovery and creativity that the elderly leader could not have foreseen. Officially sanctioned rebellion against parents and established authority figures made for exciting times for many Red Guards. The subsequent experience of rural exile also presented unexpected opportunities, especially where authority figures were also absent or at a distance. In these niches and cracks in the edifice of Mao's continual revolution, a real revolution occurred.

But we cannot argue that this youth culture created a road map for further developments. In part this was because it emerged before the unprecedented reforms and opening up of China that became official policy at the end of 1978. The national and social contexts in which youth cultures began to flourish were so different from the Cultural Revolution era as to produce new and unimagined changes. But in part the limitations of that era's youth culture lay within the culture itself. It was relevant and vibrant in the times that shaped it.

The key characteristics of Cultural Revolution youth culture were rooted in the times. First, it was a collective culture: The large group and shared experience took precedent over the individual or minority interest. Hand-copied novels were made to be circulated among hundreds, even thousands, of sent-down urban youth. Songs were meant to be sung by hundreds, should the circumstances allow. Jokes and satirical stories were a counterpoint to orthodox, mass cultural versions and were for everyone to enjoy. The official culture was so overwhelming that the youthful response also assumed totalising ambitions.

A second feature of youth culture in the Cultural Revolution era set it apart from the new cultures that followed. Young Chinese before the 1980s worked in a technological wilderness in youth culture terms. Widespread television access, tape players, even radios, let alone computers with all the possibilities that they opened up, were machines of the future. The founders of contemporary Chinese youth culture laboured in a world of the written word (printed or hand-copied), live performance, and film. Walter Benjamin's true age of mechanical reproduction had to wait to shape youth culture in China once economic growth allowed for the technologies to become more widely available. The comparatively long delay in the arrival of these mechanisms of cultural reproduction perhaps made their impact even more effective.

A third characteristic of youth culture by 1976 was the limited, though notable, international influences reflected in it. Youngsters who had grown up in the 1950s and 1960s had been exposed to a good deal of foreign films, songs, and visual culture. Many had embraced these exotic cultural products with enthusiasm. The scope of international cultural influence, however, was limited, controlled largely by official emphasis on socialist and Third World countries. To a degree, in the Cultural Revolution years, the foreign provided the possibility of a counter-discourse, or at least reminded young Chinese of alternatives to the national orthodoxy that filled official channels. Here, too, the much broader range of contacts with the world outside China in the 1980s made these small beginnings of limited value. But the openness to the world beyond China that Mao's regime had never stifled meant that the emergent youth culture of the 1960s and 1970s did not take a nativist path. On the contrary, it laid the foundations for the cosmopolitan thrust of the following decades.

### REFORM AND OPENING UP

From the end of the Cultural Revolution in late 1976 until the mid-1980s, the foundations for the flourishing of Chinese youth cultures were laid, building on the groundwork established by Red Guards and sent-down youth and seizing the opportunities presented by a new opening to outside influences. For the government, the period was one of restoring the credibility of the Communist Party, in part by withdrawing from ambitions to control the whole of the economy. Economic reform and opening up, promulgated in December 1978 by Deng Xiaoping, loosened the state's grip on agricultural production and marketing, on urban consumers and eventually on parts of larger state-owned enterprises. More significant for young Chinese, access to and knowledge about the world outside of China grew exponentially, including about the television programmes, films, and music enjoyed by their counterparts in Hong Kong, Taiwan, and beyond.

Young Chinese were not the passive recipients of popular culture from beyond China's borders. The creativity, innovation, and activism of the Cultural Revolution decade continued in the new era. The drawing back of Party intervention in the economy and (to a degree) in society opened new spaces for public assertions of youth concerns. The first of these, the Democracy Wall protests in 1978 and 1979 was directly facilitated by

Figure 2.7. Production still from the 1982 feature film about sent-down youth, *Our Fields* (*Women de tianye*), directed by Xie Fei, Beijing Youth Film Studio. *Source:* Author's collection.

Deng himself. He concluded that a fresh start required popular opportunities to vent frustrations and discontents that had been aired first during the heady days of demonstrations in late 1976 against the Cultural Revolution radicals epitomised by the Gang of Four. In late 1978, a wall around a basketball court beside a major shopping precinct in downtown Beijing was used for the posting of big-character posters calling for political liberalisation. Young intellectuals were the core of the critics who took advantage of this outlet. As university entrance examinations were restored and ambitious educated youth seized the chance to return to the cities and resume their educations, cities like Beijing were filled with articulate and radical young people with a sense of confidence engendered by their survival during the previous twelve years. One such critic was Wei Jingsheng (born 1950), a former Red Guard and soldier and then an electrician at Beijing Zoo, who wrote of the need for a Fifth Modernization (democracy) to go alongside the Four Modernizations (agriculture, industry, science, and defence) that Deng had revived as the central thrust of government policies.[131] The government kept a tight rein on the youthful unrest associated with Democracy Wall. In 1979 the wall was moved to a more obscure location in a park and then closed down. Wei and others were charged with antigovernment crimes, the wall having served its purposes as pressure relief for popular, particularly youth, protest.

The next major wave of popular unrest was also associated with the young. From 1985 to 1987, students at campuses across China protested at poor living and study conditions. The boycott of classes took on a more political tenor, as renewed cries for more political freedoms were heard. Although the movement's public figurehead was Fang Lizhi, a middle-aged astrophysicist teaching in Anhui, the bulk of the protests were made by students. Some were mature students, old enough to have been sent down to the countryside; most were newly minted products of the post-1976 educational system. High hopes about contributing to the nation's accelerating economic growth were dashed by the reality of crumbling, crowded dormitories, old-fashioned teaching, and cautious school leaders. When students at provincial centres began to link up with counterparts elsewhere, the central authorities stepped in. Throughout the winter of 1986–1987 a new campaign against 'bourgeois liberalisation' was mounted, with the usual 'spontaneous' response from the 'broad masses.' The media were filled with denunciations of student and others' selfishness, though the campaign had the air of going through the motions. It worked, however, to end the protests, at least for a couple of years.[132]

In addition to political activism, many former sent-down youth were instrumental in new cultural developments from the late 1970s into the new decade. The misty poets have been mentioned already. The experimentation and rejection of older models of nonclassical poetry emerged from underground to a mixed response of confusion and acclaim. Anger, resignation, and alienation all featured in these new-style poems, which were definitely an acquired taste for most readers. Another new development for readers also had roots in the Cultural Revolution experience of young Chinese. The search for roots (*xungen*) movement, seen in fiction and also to a lesser degree in film and fine arts, represented an effort to reconceive Chinese history in new, non-Marxist ways. One of the stalwarts of the root seekers was Han Shaogong, a Hunan writer and ex-sent-down youth, who in 1985 (at age thirty-two) produced an article titled 'The Roots of Literature' (*Wenxue zhi gen*). Han argued that, contrary to the standard, Yellow River-based account of the rise of culture, Chinese civilisation had multiple, local origins that should inform its literature. His own fiction was set in more recent times, mixing the fantastical with the real and expressing confusion over identity and in narrative uncertainty. This was a deliberate rejection of socialist realist certainties.[133] Another root searching writer was Ah Cheng (Zhong Acheng, born 1949), whose 'three kings' stories captured the educated youth experience with a mix of nostalgia and despair.[134]

More mainstream responses to Cultural Revolution trauma were shared by mass audiences including youth. 'Wound literature' (*shanghen wenxue*), named after a 1978 story by a former sent-down youth, and films in the same genre presented stories of loss and courage set in the previous decade. Even painters produced illustrations of humiliation and bravery during those years. The effect was a kind of national catharsis, at its most popular in several films by director Xie Jin (1923–2008). Even as late as 1986 the public response to his *Hibiscus Town* (*Furong zhen*) expressed a shared view of the excessive politics of the Cultural Revolution.

Most Chinese youth in the early 1980s were not reading the literary output of the root seekers or paying much attention to the films of Xie Jin. Instead, they tended to be sitting in front of a television set at home or listening to a cassette tape of imported music. Deng Xiaoping's opening up of the Chinese economy after 1978 included a massive widening of the popular cultural choices available to all Chinese. The young in particular grasped the opportunities, as we shall see in the following chapters. With the loosening of state control over economic activities, new kinds of publications appeared, usually on street stalls but also in privately run stores. The tabloid press catered to a wider readership than ever before in the People's Republic: Lurid tales of romance, villainy, and heroism found eager readers. Music cassettes and videotapes began to flow from abroad, particularly from Hong Kong, assisted by local pirate copiers. Hong Kong, Taiwan, and American pop and film stars began to find fans among China's youth. Perhaps most influential on both young and old was the rise of television ownership, from about ten million sets in 1978 to more than two hundred million by the end of the 1980s. Filling the screens in most urban households were local programmes, especially cheaply made dramas, variety shows, and imported shows.[135] Through the latter, Chinese audiences increased their familiarity with some of life outside of China, particularly in Western countries. The government strategy was deliberate, to show how relatively underdeveloped China was.

Television, cassettes, and videos also provided opportunities for young Chinese fans to mark out a space for themselves in ways impossible for Red Guards and educated youth. Fairly early in the process there was a backlash from conservative government leaders. In 1983 and 1984 a short-lived campaign was directed at the 'spiritual pollution' symbolised by the adoption of new, mostly Western, hairstyles, fashion, and musical tastes. Some in the older generations were clearly concerned at younger Chinese citizens' enthusiasm for new ways of expressing difference. We shall trace these activities in the following chapters.

# CHAPTER 3

# Bodies

## *Undressed, Fashioned, Admired, and Moving*

As a time of intensified biological development, youth is characterised by an obsession with bodies: self-image, the discovery of sex, and the bodies of others. In the 1980s, with youth establishing unprecedented (at least since 1949) importance in Chinese society and public culture, bodies became a central focus of young Chinese. This chapter will trace the rise of the body focus and youth through a discussion of several youth cultural phenomena related to the body from the late 1980s into the twentieth century. Bodies had of course been important to young Chinese during the Cultural Revolution period discussed in the previous chapter. Notions about all Chinese clad in unisex, shapeless clothing in these years and denied any suggestion of sexual difference in the cultural products at the heart of the Cultural Revolution culture are clearly misplaced. Bodies and sexual difference featured in the eight so-called model performances, particularly in the two dance dramas. Ballet was hardly a place to ignore bodies. As we have seen, sent-down youth responded somewhat like young people everywhere in the relative absence of parental and other adult supervision. Much of the unofficial circulated fiction in those years featured salacious tales of love and betrayal acted out by handsome men and beautiful, worldly women.

But in the 1980s and later, as space opened up further for youthful expressions of identity and distinction, the body became a much more central feature of youth cultures in China as it was in Western countries. With the widening range of choices in entertainment and recreation, the rise of the body and sex in public discourse was obvious. Young people led the way in public demonstrations of the importance of the body, of fashion and appearance, of relationships, and of fandom. This chapter will examine the rise of the body among young people through several phenomena in public discourse in 1988 in particular. It will start with a film that celebrated physicality and with the interest in the nude body in art in the late 1980s. An exhibition caused a sensation by including representations of the naked female body. The development of the body beautiful through exercise and weightlifting (*jianmei*) was another expression of the new importance of young bodies. Fans of movie and television stars expressed their adoration of ideal bodies, while sports fans shared the conviction that their team or chosen sport embodied their ideals. An awareness of AIDS as a threat to healthy bodies emerged in 1988, as did greater public acknowledgement of homosexuality in society. As an assertion of a uniquely Chinese way to healthy bodies, *qigong* (traditional breathing exercises) enjoyed a sudden revival in the late 1980s.

## THE *RED SORGHUM* PHENOMENON

Any discussion of the importance of bodies and sex in 1988 must acknowledge the cultural impact of a film that featured half-naked young men living life according to their physical instincts in a golden, sunny world without outside control or authority. The *Red Sorghum* (*Hong gaoliang*) phenomenon marked the emergence of a new space for youthful assertions of identity and difference. It was both an imaginative space and a real domain. The fictional space created in Zhang Yimou's film had powerful appeal to young audiences. The real-world activities associated with the film, including spin-off music and concerts, provided opportunities for many young people to form a sense of community among themselves which was in some form of opposition to older generations. Young people were not alone in admiring *Red Sorghum*, but the audiences who were most enthusiastic about the film and its offshoots were overwhelmingly youthful.

Two themes were powerful elements in the *Red Sorghum* case: one related to the body, the other to the nation. The former was particularly embedded in the imaginative world of the film itself, though it also meshed with other developments in the mid- and late 1980s around bodybuilding and the interest in the nude in art. The theme of the nation arose from the view of history that the film presented. The sense of myth and national threat in the film resonated with contemporary discussions of China's place in the international system and the place of traditional or folk culture in a modern nation. The reinvented folk songs that were such an appealing element in the film gave rise to a new kind of Chinese popular music, one with deep local roots that could take on the world. Here too the worlds associated with the film were enmeshed with other developments in 1988, including the reassessment of Chinese history seen in the controversial television documentary *River Elegy* (*Heshang*) and the valorising of the folk and traditional seen in the rise of the so-called *qigong* fever (*qigong re*). *Red Sorghum* thus serves as a particularly useful point of entry into youth culture in the late 1980s and after.

From the first moments of the film, it is clear that viewers are in a distinct, distant, and probably unreachable space. With the screen black, a voice announces: 'This is the story of my grandfather and grandmother.... Some people believe the story, others don't.' Like such narratives of longer standing, some choose to believe in the myth and others deny its truth. A shared suspension of disbelief in its veracity is indeed one of the appealing features of any myth. The first words of the unseen narrator thus establish this quality of legend. Viewers accordingly can expect a story and setting with legendary or larger than life characteristics. The connection with the present day is a mix of closeness and distance. The voice speaks of just a three-generation span, which would hardly qualify for normal legendary status. In contrast, the narrator's emphasis on people's uncertainty as to the reliability of the story we are about to see undermines any confidence viewers may have that what follows is real. Viewers, including the young men who formed the bulk of the most enthusiastic followers of *Red Sorghum*, were thus alerted to the seductive quality of the imaginative space that the world of the film created from the first seconds of the work.

The first images in *Red Sorghum* reinforce the sense of distance from the film's world and the importance of the human body in this world. The face of a beautiful young woman fills the screen. The narrator tells us this is My Grandmother. Once seated in a sedan chair, she defiantly pulls off a red cloth that had covered her face. Her reluctance to enter an arrangement with a much older and leprous distillery owner is indicated by her clutching a pair of scissors. For young viewers, an image mixing helplessness and resistance establishes the character of My Grandmother. Youthful rebellion is thus indicated from the beginning of the film.

At the same time, the young woman is presented on screen as an object for male viewers' desire. She is not a typical Chinese female beauty. Her skin is darker than conventional standards of female beauty, her lips are full and natural, held open to gasp in fear and discomfort as she bounces in the wedding sedan chair. A traditional Chinese beauty would never be presented with an open mouth like this. Here again, from the first moments of the narrative, viewers are alerted to the resistant or rebellious ambition of the film, while also enjoining in the usual, we might say traditional, relationship with female beauty on a film screen. Indeed the first sounds we hear from My Grandmother are of her sobbing from within the curtains of the sedan.

The emphasis on the physical attraction of the young My Grandmother is matched by the obvious physical strength of the palanquin carriers. The focus is on the leader of the group, the youthful My Grandfather, identified as such by the off-screen narrator. The spirit of rebellion is obvious. Most of the men have stripped to the waist, hardly traditional behaviour

Figure 3.1. The sedan carriers in *Red Sorghum* (Xi'an Film Studio, 1987).
*Source:* Author's collection.

at a regular wedding procession. As the group bounces the sedan chair up and down, they raucously sing a mocking song about an old pus- and lice-covered groom on whom any young bride would be wasted.

These youths clearly enjoy their camaraderie and collective power and ability to mock conventional behaviour. The attention of the young woman, however, is directed on one male body, that of the future My Grandfather. Her gaze, we see from a point of view shot, is fixed on the broad, sweaty, tanned, and vital back of this youth. The young woman's interest in the half-naked body in front of her is made clear, as she reinforces an impression that she does not behave with conventional demureness and restraint. When the procession is held up by an armed bandit, My Grandmother boldly grins at the hooded man when he pulls back the curtains. These two main ancestral characters are thus established in the first minutes of the film as unconventional, rebellious, and rejoicing in their physicality. This imaginary world had immediate appeal to youthful, mostly male, film audiences.

In the world of *Red Sorghum*, natural instincts and freedom prevail. My Grandfather expresses his desire for My Grandmother by seizing her while she travels through the wild sorghum gulch. He carries her roughly into the midst of the plants, then tramples down a circle of the tall sorghum. There he proceeds to have sex with the woman, who swoons rather than continuing to resist. The wild sound of several *suona* (Chinese bagpipes) and shots of the sorghum swaying in the wind enhances the moment of sexual pleasure. Later, after the unexplained sudden death of the leprous distillery owner, My Grandfather turns up drunk at the widow's home and distillery to claim his mate. He is tossed by workers into a huge vat, where he sleeps off his intoxication over three nights. Once sobered up, he follows his urges in urinating into the sorghum still. The red-coloured drink from this batch proves to be the best ever made, guaranteeing the fortune of the distillery enterprise.

The men of the distillery, including My Grandfather after he has become the partner of the widow and fathered a boy with her, live in a kind of primitive communism. The male staff share a large room in the distillery and regard themselves as an extended family. Much of their work, even more than for the sedan carriers earlier in the narration, is done while half-naked in a display of male bodies and bonding. The workers conduct a simple ritual to mark the first fruits of this season's liquor. They line up in two rows before what looks like an ancient, faded mural of the god of wine, each holding up a bowl of the new wine. Instead of a reverential ceremony of appreciation of the god, they burst into a rowdy song of praise for their own handiwork:

If you drink this liquor, you'll breathe well and you won't cough.
Your breath won't smell.
You won't bow down to any emperor.

Like the mural of the wine god, the ruined archway on the hill behind the distillery compound seems a marker of an earlier civilisation that no longer exists or no longer commands respect from these men and women living life in a natural state according to rules they seem to have invented for themselves.

The wild sorghum in Green Killers Crossing (*Qingshakou*) and the crumbling, broken archway mark off this free place from a world outside. Indeed, apart from the pistols, there is little to indicate the historical era of the setting. This enhances the mythic qualities of the story and its protagonists. Only the eruption of the outside world into this seemingly isolated realm indicates for viewers that we are in the mid-twentieth century. A Japanese army vehicle crashes through the wild sorghum into this playground. Soldiers round up the local population, whom we have not seen before, to act out a ritualistic, collective intimidation in which two local men are skinned alive. This action has the opposite effect, for not even the intrusion of the modern world can quash the natural instincts and sense of justice of the distillery family. Urged on by My Grandmother, the workers determine to take vengeance on the Japanese. They gain strength from another wine ritual seemingly of their own invention. Their ambush of a Japanese convoy goes horribly wrong, resulting in the death of My

Figure 3.2. My Grandmother addresses the distillery workers in *Red Sorghum*.
*Source:* Author's collection.

Grandmother and others. My Grandfather and the boy who becomes My Father are the only survivors.

The world presented in this story created an imaginative space into which Chinese young people in 1988 could inscribe their own aspirations and fantasies. The world of *Red Sorghum* was distinguished by one central absence, at least until the Japanese arrive about two-thirds of the way through the narrative. There is no external authority in the world of the sedan carriers and distillery workers. Generally the inhabitants of this world seem to ignore traditions, creating their own, somewhat egalitarian, big family with the benevolent factory owner and comradely workers.[1] When she sets out to run the distillery, My Grandmother tells the workers: 'What's mine is yours. We are all one family, aren't we?' Singing that they will not bow down to any emperor, these men and woman live in a world they seem to have created for themselves. It is a natural, uncultivated realm. The tall sorghum plants, growing wild at Green Killers Crossing, become a symbol in the narrative. Like the sorghum, these people have never bent to a cultivator's hand. Instead, the men and woman of the distillery live according to their instincts. In the case of My Grandfather, the instinct is the sex drive. My Grandmother responds to this primal urge by submitting to his lust. The attraction to young (and older) male viewers in cinemas across China is not hard to imagine.

Few of these young male viewers of *Red Sorghum* would have thought further to identify the broader absence in the world of the film. There are no 'isms' in the imaginative space of the film; no Communism, Marxism, Confucianism, Daoism, or Buddhism. It is a prelapsarian world where a primitive communitarianism prevails. As youthful Shanghai-based researcher Li Zhenzhi, writing in *Contemporary Youth Research* in the relatively open atmosphere of the spring of 1989, noted, the film addresses the layers of ideological clothing that Chinese had accrued over centuries and generations:

> People under a heavy burden (*runiufuzhong*) enter the cinemas. They strip naked and come out, feeling no sense of shame. On the contrary, with one voice they cry out: 'Terrific (*tongkuai*)! Terrific! Terrific!!! Living in an exceedingly uncouth, serious and slack way is the predestination of our compatriots, like a miniaturized version in a courtyard of the national quintessence. What should shame us is not a bare head or bare chest, not lice and stinky sweat, but those Confucian garments.'[2]

The response by young Chinese to *Red Sorghum* turned the film into a youth phenomenon, with spin-offs in popular music, fashion, and art. The imaginative space presented on the screen was matched by a physical space associated with the film, in which young people seized opportunities to express their enjoyment of the music associated with the film, their appreciation of the emphasis on the body in the film, and the assertion of a folk-based culture with roots in the yellow earth of northwest China. If there is an 'ism' in the film, it is nationalism.

What drew initial youthful attention to the film, however, was not its folk roots in China but its success internationally. In February 1988, at the thirty-eighth Berlin International Film Festival, *Red Sorghum* won the top prize, the Golden Bear. This was the highest international recognition ever received by a film from the People's Republic of China. In the 1980s, a few films had secured awards at festivals in Western countries. Indeed Zhang Yimou, the director of *Red Sorghum*, had been the cinematographer on *The Yellow Earth* (*Huang tudi*, 1984), which was successful in 1985 at festivals in France, the United States, and Britain. But to win the highest award at one of the top three film festivals in the world (the others being Cannes and Venice) in the then West Berlin, in the non-Communist world, was a signal development.

The response back in Beijing was unexpected. Any initial caution from the government's cultural apparatus, which had been typical of the reaction to the earlier film honours won in capitalist venues, gave way to a triumphant embrace of the success. The Berlin award made front-page news in both the more popular press, which young people read in greater numbers than the more official organs, and in *People's Daily* (*Renmin ribao*), the Communist Party's mouthpiece. Film Bureau and other officials rushed to the airport to greet Zhang, actress Gong Li who played My Grandmother, and their party when they touched down at Beijing Airport from Frankfurt on 25 February, two days after the prize presentation.[3] Television news gave proud coverage of the arrival and of Zhang's subsequent news conferences. It opened in Beijing on 3 March 1988.

Young people in China were already familiar with the successful director. Stripped to the waist, Zhang had made his film acting debut in *Old Well* (*Lao jing*, 1987). Directed by the head of the Xi'an Film Studio in Zhang's home town, the film was one of a series of Chinese 'Westerns' that the studio had begun to specialise in during the 1980s. Wu Tianming had become leader of the studio in 1984 in an experiment associated with the economic reforms of that decade. Granted unusual power to hire, fire, and decide which projects should get the go-ahead, Wu saw an opportunity to produce films with strong local roots in the northwest region around Xi'an.[4]

*Old Well* was one such regionalist work. Set in neighbouring Shanxi, the film told of the efforts by peasants to find water in their parched mountains. Generations had not succeeded until a group of young people, one with specialist training at a city technical college, manage to dig a well that produces water. Like *Red Sorghum*, this story was given a timeless quality on screen to emphasise how momentous present-day success was. Faced with finding competent actors to play peasants, Wu Tianming and Zhang Yimou, his cinematographer for the project, travelled to several cities and continued auditioning young actors back at the Xi'an studio.[5] Frustrated at the difficulties in casting the two youthful leads in the film, Wu turned to his cinematographer. After some persuading, Zhang Yimou was cast in the lead role as the peasant well digger. The crew went into the Taihang mountains in southern Shanxi in the early summer, shooting in remote, difficult locations until September 1986.

The results on screen, at least in terms of male bodies, gave a foretaste of *Red Sorghum*. As the local man who locates the successful well and has an affair with his childhood sweetheart even though he is already married, Zhang Yimou made an impressive debut. He looks the part, every inch a hardened, sun-burnt, taciturn but determined peasant. In creating the role, Zhang could draw upon his own experience working for three years as a sent-down youth in rural Shaanxi. When he appears climbing out of the earth carrying a huge slab of rock on his back, his broad chest streaked with sweat, his flat stomach taking the load of the stone, no one could doubt this was a local man. So convincing was the performance that, at the Tokyo Film Festival in September 1987, Wu Tianming won best director and Zhang Yimou took the best actor prize, despite competition from professional performers in other films. The box office success of *Old Well* in China and the Tokyo win meant that Zhang Yimou

Figure 3.3. Zhang Yimou (right) as a peasant youth in *Old Well* (directed by Wu Tianming, Xi'an Film Studio, 1986).
*Source:* Author's collection.

already had a following among young Chinese film goers even before his success in Berlin. The striking physical resemblance between his peasant character, shaven, stripped to the waist, and in voluminous, padded cotton, old-style trousers and My Grandfather in *Red Sorghum* only added to the impact of Zhang's film on youthful audiences in 1988.

Before going to Berlin, Zhang identified some of the aspects of his film that would appeal to its young audience. He spoke directly of the nationalistic pride the film embodied:

> Chinese should live more cheerfully. Our ancestors were once vivid and dramatic, living freely, dying without regret. But for the past several centuries we've been suffering. Today we should assert ourselves (*qiang qi lai*). Apart from economic strength, the important thing is psychological arousal (*xintai de zhenfen*). I wanted to express a human's intrinsic love of life, a hatred of those who threaten life. I set out to sing a eulogy for an ideal type of personality.[6]

Whether such youthful ambition would appeal to audiences was uncertain. At a Film Association discussion of the newly completed *Red Sorghum* in December 1987, somewhat conservative views were expressed about the film's celebration of roughness. But Chen Huai'ai, a veteran director, was convinced that the film would be a commercial success. Although in his sixties, Chen still knew how to appeal to audiences, having made his reputation with screen adaptations of well-loved Chinese operas.[7]

A year after Chen Huai'ai made his prediction, a set of statistics suggested that *Red Sorghum* had had only limited success at home, despite the triumph in Berlin. A list of the numbers of prints of feature films released in 1988 showed that Zhang's film was far from being the most widely distributed feature film that year. Topping the table was *Yellow River Knight-Errant* (*Huang He daxia*), a martial arts film, with 379 copies struck. Bernardo Bertolucci's *The Last Emperor* (a Sino-European co-production) reached 306 prints. *Red Sorghum* was a surprising number twenty-one on the list, with a relatively standard 206 copies.[8] These numbers, however, are a misleading guide to the impact of *Red Sorghum* on a segment of China's film audience.

Upon his return from West Germany, Zhang Yimou (along with his star and lover Gong Li) became a media celebrity, sought out for interviews on television and in print. The film was an instant hit. It was clear that young men, particularly in northern China, found the film an inspiration. The dry, wild landscapes of north China and the northwest (the film was shot in Shandong and Ningxia) for northern viewers represented a quintessential Chinese setting. Southern Chinese or the sophisticated residents of Shanghai were perhaps less inclined to identify with such uncultivated, parched representations of the nation. For them, the riverine mistiness of the Yangzi or the floating-in-cloud Karst mountains of Guilin were more 'national' in character. The popularity of *Red Sorghum* in the north can be seen as a rejection of these traditional Chinese landscapes. For its fans, the near desert and dust of the yellow earth was a more satisfying representation of Chineseness.[9]

Young men in the north instantly identified with the muscular roughness of My Grandfather and his mates. Adolescents, chaffing at restrictions and conservative parents, found the rebellious and instinctive lives of the film's protagonists instantly engaging. In the summer of 1988 in Beijing, young workers were apt to burst into a verse from the songs that were so much a part of *Red Sorghum*'s appeal. Jiang Wen, the actor who played My Grandfather with such obvious relish, was familiar to film goers as a noble and punished intellectual in *Hibiscus Town* and as the weak and cautious last emperor Puyi in *The Last Empress* (*Moudai huanghou*, directed by Chen Jialin and Sun Qingguo, 1986). He played against this type as My Grandfather, swaggering without a care in the world, like every young man's notion of a peasant rebel. In Beijing the film played simultaneously in an unprecedented twenty cinemas with eight screenings each day from early morning to past midnight.[10] The success in Berlin added to the film's attraction, as by the late 1980s Hollywood and other imported features, though strictly restricted in number, were

Figure 3.4. The sedan carriers in the wild sorghum in *Red Sorghum*.
*Source:* Author's collection.

proving more popular than Chinese-made films. Here was a Chinese feature film that could stand up to the foreign cultural invasion of China,
somewhat in the manner in which My Grandfather and My Grandmother
resist Japanese invasion on screen.

But others took strong exception to *Red Sorghum*. The debate over
the film and its appeal threw into greater relief the attractions of the
film as a space for youthful assertions of identity. Two articles on the
same page of a May issue of the *China Film Gazette* (*Zhongguo dianying
bao*) expressed diametrically opposed views. Cai Wanlin acknowledged
the shock of the new: 'We may not be used to it: a horror story, a mob
of unruly people, a blood-red tone. Unfamiliar, remote. Like a legend, a
nightmare.' But Cai went on to suggest:

> Getting over these limits of appreciation, we can savor an outstanding artis-
> tic realm and the mood of the makers' song celebrating life as ardent as fire.
> It is a 'declaration on freedom' for life (*shengming de 'ziyou pian'*). Here, life
> shines its light without any restrictions. Lust, hatred, fraternity...free and
> untrammeled, without dissembling (*bu jia yanshi*).

Cai concluded this paean to the delights of the film with an appeal to
patriotism: '*Red Sorghum* also gives...the Chinese people a galloping
inspiration: Chinese can do anything, all they need is self-belief.'[11]

Not all young people were enamoured of the film. On the same page as Cai Wanlin's article in one of the most widely read film periodicals was a piece headlined 'Red Sorghum is a film that uglifies Chinese.' The curiously anonymous 'D. W.' (initials like this are a rare usage in Chinese publications) outlined the usual conservative objections to the film: that it was vulgar and low-class, that it made heroes of hoodlums, and that it was unrealistic. 'How could a man drink for three days and nights but not eat anything and survive?' Public morality was apparently threatened.

> Now on screen there are embraces and hugs, the young people and students in the audience are in turn in the auditoria copying the kissing. One knows not how many young women have complained tearfully every day to the managers of cinemas about incidents where they have suffered hooligan humiliation (*liumang qiwu*) and fled the premises.[12]

*Red Sorghum* screenings were apparently no place for those of a refined disposition.

The impact of the film was so striking that *Popular Film* (*Dazhong dianying*), at the start of the decade China's most widely read periodical and still enjoying a circulation of millions, devoted a special column over the summer months to debate on the film. In the May issue, a reader from Beijing expressed surprise at the film winning an award. On the opposite page a Shanghai resident praised *Red Sorghum* for its skill in creating such a unique (and intoxicating) world on screen.[13] In June, a correspondent from Zhang Yimou's home province of Shaanxi wrote that 'sorghum people' (*gaoliangmen*) should feel proud of the film's international success. A local Suzhou government engineer noted the 'red extravagance' of the film, but approved of its national (*minzu*) qualities. A reader from Hebei University, identifying with the 'free sorghum,' hoped the director could present as impressive an account of life in present-day China.[14] The editors noted in the July issue the volume of readers' letters about *Red Sorghum* and promised a continuing column. Several correspondents regretted the way in which Chinese film goers seemed to require foreign approval of a Chinese film before they would take an interest in it.[15] Liu Zaifu, literary critic and social scientist, noted in an interview how the characters in the film 'dare to live, dare to die, dare to love, and dare to hate.... Those who say *Red Sorghum* is a display of the ugliness of the Chinese race and art enslaved by the West ... have no basis for saying so and ... are overcritical.'[16] The youthful fans of the film could not agree more. A doctoral student at Beijing Normal University noted the shock of *Red Sorghum* on many people: 'That totally satisfying (*tongkuailinli*) attitude to life displayed by [the film] to dare to laugh, dare to curse, dare to act, to do, to love, to hate, to die in our own lives seems so precious and so hard to find (*nanmi*)!' Guo Yuhua went on to explain some people's strong reactions against the film with reference to the conventional valorising of calmness, acceptance of one's station, and the Confucian ideal of the golden mean. In contrast *Red Sorghum* was a call for toughness and resistance.[17]

The view from the provinces revealed similar divisions about the film. In Huhehot, the capital of Inner Mongolia, an early review of *Red Sorghum* was headlined 'Causing puzzlement.' It started: 'Although the film *Red Sorghum* won a major international award, this writer is at a loss to say what the theme of it is.' The cinematography and artistic look of the film were no compensation for this lack of beauty (*mei*) in the theme.[18] Such conservative tut-tutting undoubtedly added to many young persons' determination to see and enjoy the film as a gesture of resistance to blue-stocking condemnation of *Red Sorghum*. A review in the *Tianjin Daily* in August seemed to take a similar line, laying out the objections to the film for its allegedly crude portrayal of Chinese who were far from heroic in traditional terms. But Li Houji concluded that people were being too simplistic in considering the film ugly.[19] This orthodox concern for beauty and ugliness, typical of conventional Chinese aesthetics, was precisely what Chinese youth, in an age elsewhere of the rise of punk, were rebelling against in 1988. One enthusiast of the film dismissed accusations that Zhang Yimou showed the ugliness of the Chinese. In a sarcastic reference to the 'high, wide, and handsome' (*gao, da, quan*: literally tall, big, and grand) heroes of Cultural Revolution operas, Xu Hongli in *Liaoning Youth* asked if the characters in *Red Sorghum* should be shorn of all imperfection.[20] In Fujian on the southeast coast, the provincial youth journal *Youth Power* (*Qingchun chao*) made no reference to *Red Sorghum* in its twelve issues in 1988.

Even *People's Daily* got into the act in September, writing on the front page about the '*Red Sorghum* phenomenon' in which divided opinions on the merits of the work were a lesson for leaders and others on the progress made in tolerating diverse views and their public expression.[21] Zhang Yimou's film could be seen as a barometer of the relative liberalism of the year in which it was released. To have a full-page reportage (*baogao wenxue*) story in *People's Daily* was a measure of the official attention Zhang's success in Berlin gained him.[22] Usually only national heroes (or on occasion officially condemned villains) had the privilege of such high-profile coverage.

To ordinary film fans, the director and his consort, Gong Li, had become big stars. Zhang took to the habit of moving about Beijing with a baseball cap pulled low over his face and a pair of large lensed dark glasses blocking much of his face. In an age when entertainment and tabloid magazines had not yet taken off nationally in China, he was usually spared the attention of paparazzi. Young fans who saw through the disguise greeted him with a mix of excitement and reticence, as how to behave as a fan was not well-established. But when in July 1988 he took to the stage at the Capital Gymnasium at a concert of rock music inspired by his film, the young crowd went wild. Many had paid a premium for tickets to the concert. At the packed entrances to the grounds of the gymnasium, ticket touts did good business on both nights of the show. Young men who did not have tickets or needed another for their girlfriend or companion stood in the crowd holding up a wad of notes, including coveted 'foreign exchange certificates.' These were the only Chinese currency supposedly available to foreign visitors. Their attraction was that they could be converted into foreign currency or to Chinese notes at a generous black market rate.[23] When the familiar opening bars of 'Little sister, go forward' from the film started up, the youthful crowd yelled with excitement. Zhang Yimou himself performed. His croaking rendition could have come from Pavarotti the way the fans reacted. The whole audience joined in the chorus. It was a great night.[24]

*Red Sorghum* was one of the highest grossing films of 1988. It spawned some spin-offs, including a dance drama *Sorghum Soul* (*Gaoliang hun*), choreographed by a young member of the Daqing Dance Troupe in the northeast.[25] In tourist performances in Xi'an and elsewhere, a sequence featuring a wedding palanquin carried by strapping peasant youths became a standard feature, joining the existing display of waist-drum dancing by young men inspired by the vigorous drum dancers in *The Yellow Earth*. Zhang Yimou's film added to the folkloric invention of the times. But it was the music of *Red Sorghum* that took the film and what it meant for young China to a new level. The invented folk songs gave rise to a 'Northwest Wind' (*Xibei feng*) that swept up young fans in a collective display of identity.[26]

### NAKED BODIES

The male bodies on display in *Red Sorghum* were not the only bodies that appealed to young Chinese in 1988. The film's emphasis on physicality and natural instincts, however, helped open up a public space for the presentation of other bodies, female as well as male, and for acknowledgment of the importance of the body to the young in particular. Nude art, body building, fashion, and even ancient Chinese conceptions of bodily well-being all emerged in the late 1980s as reflections of young China's body obsessions.

On 22 December 1988, the 'Exhibition of Nude Oil Paintings' (*youhua renti yishu da zhan*) opened at the China Art Museum in central Beijing. Organised by the official Chinese Artists Association and held in the most prestigious exhibition space in China, the display of paintings of nudes by Chinese artists from a range of ages was an instant success. Long lines of people, mostly young, queued up at the ticket booth, snaking along the street and into the nearby corner park. Tickets reportedly sold for ten times their face value and over fifteen thousand were sold in one day.[27] Having secured entrance tickets, the lines formed again to file through the packed galleries. The expensive hard- and soft-bound copies of the exhibition catalogue and the much cheaper guide and postcards sold out in record time. The usual opening times were extended to try to accommodate demand from art lovers. The exhibition broke attendance records for the gallery, with two hundred thousand people going through the galleries in eighteen days, a remarkable achievement given that in the past workers and students had mostly been organised in groups to see certain politically important displays there.[28]

In late 1988, the majority of those willing to stand for hours in the sub-zero cold of a Beijing winter were young and male. The paintings in the gallery represented for them a kind of liberation from conventional Chinese strictures on the public display of the body and of sex. Some of the most extensive coverage of the 1988 exhibition was in the pages of magazines directed at a youthful readership. The March 1989 issue of *Campus Life* (*Daxuesheng*), for example, featured two articles, one covering more than six pages with photos, headed 'China unprecedented: Snapshots from the Beijing model storm.'[29] This was followed by a shorter piece titled 'Walking out of the dizzying art gallery,' reporting on the excitement engendered by the display.[30]

The Beijing exhibition had a nationwide impact. In Nanjing, seven exhibitions of 'nude art' spontaneously appeared in the city in response to events in the north. In addition to work by students of the various colleges and universities in the city, the Nanjing displays included copies of well-known Western classical works of art, contemporary foreign paintings, photographs of women in bikinis, and even videotapes of nudes. The response of the city authorities was to require application and inspection of these and any proposed exhibitions and an official call for a more respectable level of appreciation of such works.[31]

The same issue of *Campus Life* that carried the reports on the December 1988 Beijing nudes exhibitions included photographic coverage, by a student of Renmin University, of the February 1989 'China modern art' exhibition in the same august venue. Police closed the exhibition the afternoon that it opened, after two young artists in a performance piece fired a rifle in the exhibition space. The photographic essay asked whether the laws should be allowed to restrict such 'breakthrough art.' After being closed for four days, during which students protested outside the gates and passed food and drink to the artists locked within, the exhibition reopened and the offending performers were released from custody.[32]

The emergence of a rebellious, even dissident art, like the relatively new move to display naked bodies in art exhibitions, was closely associated with educated young people in the 1980s. The February 1989 modern art exhibition even used a logo to identify itself. It looked like a gigantic traffic sign, featuring an arrow curved back on itself with a line diagonally across it indicating that a U-turn was not permissible. There was no going back to the old, restrictive days of conventional art created for the ready understanding of the broad masses, as in Mao's time. Celebration of nudity in art was just one part of this rebellious spirit.

The widening of the range of public possibilities regarding the body and sex had started over a decade earlier. The May 1979 issue of *Popular Film* caused a sensation when it included a still on its back cover of Richard Chamberlain embracing and kissing the eponymous heroine of the film *Cinderella*. Conservative readers wrote in, denouncing the image and accusing the editors of wanting to corrupt China's youth. In the winter of the same year, murals in a VIP lounge at the Capital Airport were also criticised for depicting naked Dai minority women in a tropical setting in Yunnan. Despite the relative inaccessibility of the murals, they were soon covered with floor to ceiling curtains.[33]

Nudes could be excused if the alleged purpose was artistic guidance. Publication of handbooks for artists had become a growth industry by the mid-1980s. The privately run bookstores that had sprung up across the road in front of the China Art Museum in the 1980s in mid-1986 displayed numerous guides for sketching or painting nudes. The dog-eared nature of the display copies attested to unusually high interest, although readers bold enough to invest in a copy for themselves seemed somewhat fewer than those sneaking a furtive glance. Students at the Central Arts and Crafts Academy, members of the graduating class of 1982, the first degree class since the end of the Cultural Revolution, were among the first to relearn life drawing with both male and female models.[34] As another report in *Campus Life* on the late 1989 Beijing nude exhibition noted:

> In the eyes of Chinese, so-called body art (*renti yishu*) is no more than a picture of a naked model. As a result, Chinese body art is skewed (*zoudiao le*, literally out of tune) and becomes model art. What this art displays is not the charm of the human body, but the body of the model. No wonder ordinary people are aflutter and artists are perplexed.[35]

A writer in *Youth and Society* (*Qingnian yu shehui*) magazine, published by the Communist Youth League in Yunnan, noted the surge in 1989 of publications of nude illustrations. Over sixty picture books had been brought out nationwide. 'Indeed, some people say: "1989, the Chinese body year"!' Li Hongbin, in his article titled 'China's "nude upsurge"' (*Zhongguo 'renti chao'*) listed some recent books: *Selection of Foreign*

*Nude Photographs* (published in Tianjin), *Nude Photographs* (Hunan), *Nude Oil Paintings from Chinese Colleges and Universities* (Sichuan), *Selection of Nude Oil Paintings* (Guangxi), *Foreign Nude Photography* (Hebei), *Artistic Nude Photography by Famous Foreign Photographers* (Guizhou), *Art of the Nude and Light* (Hainan), and *Bodies and Nude Art* (Beijing).[36] Like other commentators, Li concluded that this surge of interest was part of broader changes in China's openness to the rest of the world and to new views of life.

The idea of models had taken hold in the 1980s after French fashion designer Pierre Cardin pioneered fashion shows in China in the late 1970s. The young women Cardin recruited, tall and thin with impassive features, became objects of great public interest. In part the excitement arose from an assumption about the sexual morality of such models. Fashion models were lumped with life models in the public imagination as people with new and dangerous attitudes toward their bodies. Fashion models were also seen as representative of new, modern, and international lifestyles. In November 1988 China's first Fashion Model Competition was held in Guangzhou to find the top ten models in the nation.[37] Models were often included in the most unlikely events as a 'modern' element to lend glamour to an occasion. In Tian Zhuangzhuang's 1988 film *Rock 'n Roll Kids* (*Yaogun qingnian*), the protagonist, a male dancer, works as a director of fashion shows. To a contemporary Western eye, a fashion show in the film seems to disrupt the flow of the narrative, but to the young people who were Tian's target audience, this sequence had more significance. It was a display of youthful, modern bodies and, more important, of a new attitude toward personal adornment.

## BODYBUILDING

Another manifestation of the new emphasis on beautiful young bodies in the 1980s was the introduction of and public response to bodybuilding (*jianmei*). Physical fitness had been part of early twentieth-century efforts to strengthen the Chinese nation and culture in the modern world. Healthy bodies had always featured in Communist imagery of national construction. The emphasis on developing muscles and displaying them in competitions, however, was new in the decade after the Cultural Revolution. In November 1986 the Fourth National 'Warrior Cup' (*Lishi bei*) Body-Building Contest was held in Shenzhen, a booming new city and one of the newly identified Special Economic Zones where economic reform was particularly being promoted. The contest featured women in bikinis, including Sun Heng, the first Chinese woman to publicly appear clad in this garment. Sun won three runner-up awards: in the women's lightweight, mixed couple, and female duo competitions. The Shenzhen contest was covered by close to one hundred newspapers, seventy magazines, and thirty television stations.[38]

Bodybuilding had been introduced in China in the 1930s as part of a broader emphasis on physical activity and openness about physical beauty. Hollywood's valorising of female and male beauty, often revealed in stars wearing less than full coverage, was matched in Shanghai-made films and in the apparatus of fan magazines and other media. Male bodies, not conventionally part of Chinese attention in representations of the ideal scholar–official, became a feature of modern discourse on strengthening the nation in that decade. Physical activity for men and women continued to be promoted in the 1950s and 1960s. Two films from the period typify the public and private appeal of youthful bodies. *Girl Diving Team* (*Nü tiaoshui duiyuan*, 1964) and *Youth on the Water* (*Shuishang qingchun*, 1959) both featured young protagonists who spend much of each narrative clad in just brief swim suits. Bodies revealed were thus not absent in Mao's China.

What was new in the 1980s was a more widespread and more revealing emphasis on youthful bodies. *Fitness and Beauty* (*Jian yu mei*, published by *Sports News*), the major magazine promoting this activity, had appeared in Chinese bookstores in 1985. Most covers and inside covers (the only full-colour parts of the magazine) featured not local models, but Western muscle-bound men and women clad in tight Lycra or scanty bikinis, their huge bronzed arms and chests rippling under a layer of oil. For the men and women hair was big in these photographs, often set off by a multicoloured headband. Californian confidence and expensive dentistry beamed from the covers. The inside contents were a mix of articles on sports fitness in general. Judging from the many missing covers from the bound issues of the magazine in the Peking University library, the cover illustrations of a version of Western bodily beauty were the main attraction for some readers.[39]

Bodybuilding and the display of healthy bodies required new products for young participants to present themselves in the best possible light. Some were of questionable medical value, involving a mix of Western and Chinese traditional pharmacological traditions. Skin whitening potions, electrical devices that allegedly toned and smoothed muscles, hair removal creams, and other products were advertised. One page of *Youth Times* (*Qingnian shidai*) from early 1989 presented these kinds of products in a form that was more advertorial than direct advertisements. The items used cryptic headlines with decidedly Christian missionary overtones: 'Body-building good news [or Gospel, *fuyin*]' and 'Body-building heaven and earth, good news on becoming rich.' The radio station of Pingdingshan in Henan Province invited readers to send ten yuan to their Xinhua (literally new China) bodybuilding information service centre. In return readers would receive introductions to ten professionally minded friends.[40]

Twenty-six-year-old He Yushan, a railway worker from suburban Beijing, in 1989 spoke of his sacrifices since taking up bodybuilding six years earlier. He had travelled to training classes over 4,000 kilometres away in that time, taking four or five hours to make the round trip. He had put romance aside in order to pursue his sport. At the June 1985 Third National Warrior Cup Body-Building Competition, He won the eighty-kilo contest. Two months later he became a professional member of the Railway Bureau sports team. In Shenzhen in 1986, the national competition included 228 competitors in forty-eight teams. More effective coaching, along with higher and subsidised nutrition, enabled He to do better. In Kunming in 1989, at the seventh Warrior Cup contest, He Yushan won five titles.[41] The Huzhou (Zhejiang) Television Station's drama *Body-building Goddess* (*Jianmei nüshen*) told the story of a young bus conductor who faced opposition from her friends and family when they discover the contest she enters includes a bikini section. She wins them over through her dedication to her new hobby and succeeds in the East Asian contest.[42]

Attention on the body was evident in other youth publications. Teresa Teng, the Taiwan singer who had gained a huge following on the mainland during the 1980s, was reportedly a model for youth. In order to handle her concert schedule, her doctor devised a health regimen, including exercises (the term *jianmei* could refer to aerobic exercises as well as bodybuilding) and a healthy diet.[43] Cover and centrefold illustrations in periodicals intended for a youth readership, often published by provincial branches of the Communist Youth League, featured healthy young women. The November 1988 *Youth Times*, for example, featured a full-length photo of a model in a one-piece swimsuit, standing with her hands on her hips, looking away from the viewer as if to allow the latter to gaze carefully at her. The colour cover also included the name of the magazine and the colours of the rainbow (*chi, chen, huang, lü, qing, lan, zi*) and 'hope literature' (*xiwang wenxue*) in Hanyu Pinyin Romanisation. Beginning in the late 1970s, the use of Romanised words instead of Chinese characters was seen as a sign of the modern. *Popular Television* (*Dazhong dianshi*) had only one centrefold in the last two years of the 1980s, apart from a calendar for the following year in October 1988. The June 1989 issue, however, featured a centrefold with a tanned, string bikini-clad actress, Li Wanyu from Singapore, standing thigh-deep in sea water holding a palm branch over her head and smiling directly into the camera.[44] Despite Ms Li's healthy bronze skin, many young women had become obsessed with whitening their skin. A writer in *Youth and Society*, in an editorial piece titled 'Yellow skin

Figure 3.5. The November 1988 cover of *Youth Times* (*Qingnian shidai*), published by the Guizhou Communist Youth League.

cannot be washed white,' called on Chinese to be proud of their natural tones. 'Please remember the latest figure of speech: gold is also yellow coloured!' he concluded.[45]

The response of university students to this emphasis on the body is evident in a somewhat breathless report on campus sports from late 1988. The article talks up the manliness (*nanziqi*) on display on soccer fields in colleges, though the writer does cite an example of female students setting up a team with help from fourth-year physical education students. Tennis, thought of as a bourgeois game during the Cultural Revolution, had enjoyed a revival. A male student surnamed Chen displayed a male bodybuilder poster at the head of his dorm bunk. Unlike his classmates who pasted pictures of pretty women above their beds, this young man had put up his male poster to inspire him to work at building his own body: along with his muscles, 'his male consciousness is also swelling up.' Some students, interested in developing their English language skills as well as their bodies, lifted weights while listening to the Voice of America. At the unnamed S University, a notice seeking participants for a body-building class put up at noon had forty enrolments by four in the after-noon and sixty by the next day. Boxing was another means to strengthen male bodies. The campus report notes at length the impact of television sports on students' enthusiasm for being active. Ten years after the rein-troduction of university entrance examinations, this article seemed to reflect a growing concern at sedentary, unhealthy habits of young people who had spent years bent over books.[46] It was a concern that adults con-tinued to express in the new century.

## CLOTHES AND FASHION

One way for youthful bodies to display themselves was through clothing and personal adornment. When it was released in 1984, the film *Girl in the Red Dress* (*Hongyi shaonü*, directed by Lu Xiaoya at the Pearl River Film Studio in Guangzhou) caused a sensation by suggesting that young people could become obsessed with their appearance. Social commenta-tors solemnly declared that this was counter to dedication to the social good that was the proper concern of the young. By the late 1980s the scope for such personal expressions of taste had become much wider. Choices on how to dress and on hairstyles and makeup had expanded greatly and offered young people a world of opportunities to mark col-lective and individual difference. Fashion trends swept China's youth. Beijing, for example, in 1986 saw a craze for yellow dresses, in 1987 for military-style great coats, and in 1988 for black trousers. To be consid-ered fashionable, a young Beijinger needed to adopt the current style.[47]

Influenced in part by the Coca Cola advertisement's tag line about 'Can't stop the feeling' (*Dangbuzhu de ganjue*), young Shanghainese by the early 1990s were paying attention to feelings and making deci-sions based on them.[48] The case of Ms Wang, a college junior, showed the seduction of consumerism. From a poor family in northwest China, she found her city dormmates lived in a different world. When they were not around, she would hold their clothes in front of her body to see how she would look in them. Spending tiny amounts on food, she saved enough money to buy the latest fashions to keep up with the city girls. When asked why, she echoed the cola ads and spoke of 'going with the feelings of the city...the feeling of the city has embraced me, so I cannot lose.'[49] Master Sun, a Shanghai high schooler, proudly showed off his Western suit and American brand-name leather shoes. His outfit totalled 3,000 yuan (at a time when the average monthly wage in Shanghai was just a few hundred yuan). While Sun acknowledged he was not well-educated, he had a strong sense of social belonging (*guishugan*) through his obsession with brands, declaring: 'Wearing brand-names is a group thing (*you quanzi de*) ... [Besides] I trust the adverts [on TV].'

Another young Shanghainese, Ms Jiang, received about 700 yuan each month (a princely sum in 1992) from working at a foreign joint venture and overtime. Eighty percent of this she spent on clothes and appearance. 'Being fashionable gives me peace of mind (*xinqingshuchang*) every day. So many people around me staring, it's so stimulating, so much fun (*tongkuai*)!' When clothes were no longer in style, she sold them at a discount to her coworkers or to private traders. 'I don't worry about it being worthwhile or about cost. I only pay attention to feelings (*ganjue*) ... Look at you, wearing the same clothes for three or four years ... you must have no feelings at all in your life!' Ms Sun shot back at a researcher. A sense of self-worth based on how much you spent might seem to many Chinese from outside Shanghai a typical Shanghai attitude.[50]

Shanghai university students wore T-shirts not just because they were cheap and colourful: There were broader considerations at work. A female student noted that wearing T-shirts was a statement about the shared values among the wearers. It was also a conscious statement against obsession with more elaborate fashion, according to a male student. In the spring and summer of 1991, Shanghai youth joined their counterparts in Beijing and elsewhere in adopting 'slogan T-shirts' (literally cultural shirts, *wenhua shan*). These were plain white T-shirts with hand-drawn words, cartoons, poems, song lyrics, and other frequently jocular or satirical content. Slogan T-shirts had been worn by young people on occasion in the 1950s and 1960s. Then the slogans had been along the lines of 'Resist America, Support Korea; Protect home, support the country' (*Kang Mei, yuan Chao, baojiaweiguo*), 'Go to the mountains and villages, to where the nation has greatest need' (*Shangshanxiaxiang, dao zuguo zui xuyao de difang qu*), and '*Hao nan'er zhizaisifang*' (Fine men are eager to serve anywhere).[51]

But the early 1990s slogans reflected a different engagement with society or, more correctly, a disengagement. 'Downbeat slogan T-shirts' (*huise wenhua shan*, literally gray cultural T-shirts) were typical in Beijing and elsewhere in 1991. '*Fanzhine, bie li wo*' (I'm upset; leave me alone), '*meijin*' (I'm tired), and '*Wo hen chou, ke wo zuirou*' (I may be

ugly, but I'm really gentle). These assertions of rebellion were not without political implications, even if, two years after the June 4 crushing of
student demonstrations, politics needed to be carefully handled. A shirt
like '*Taiyang zhen du, wo re*' (The sun is cruel, I'm hot) might be just a
statement about the weather. But in a nation where the late Mao Zedong
was likened to the sun for ten intensively politicised years, the slogan
could carry more meaning. Giving hoary old slogans a new twist was
also a political act. '*Yi bupa ku, er bupa si, san bupa ni*' (First, not afraid
of hardship; second, not afraid of death; third, not afraid of you) added
a third phrase to the Maoist cliché in order to express the new individualism. Some shirts had a punch line on the back: on the front, '*Qianwan
bie ai wo*' (Please, please don't love me); on the back, '*Meiqian*' (No
money). Other shirts reproduced pictures or forms, such as household
registration forms, grain ration tickets, graduation diplomas, and marriage certificates. A portrait of Lei Feng on the front of a shirt would be
accompanied by a familiar quotation from the 1960s soldier hero on the
back.[52] Differences were evident between Beijing and Shanghai slogan
T-shirts: many in the latter city being less political and featuring photos
of girlfriends.

The three most popular T-shirt phrases were reportedly: 'I'm upset,
leave me alone,' 'I'm really tired' (*zhen lei*), and 'Carrying a heavy family
burden' (*lajiadaikou*). More than a third of the T-shirts sold in Beijing in
the summer of 1991 carried these slogans. As one of the inventors of the
product, Kong Yongqian, noted, the shirts could be understood against
the background of June 4.[53] One T-shirt was banned: It read '*zuohuai
buluan*' ('Chaste embrace' or 'Keeping it clean'), an ancient phrase describing platonic relations between men and women.[54] A social psychologist
saw the T-shirts as expressions of young people's disappointment with
the direction of economic reform and concern about corruption.[55] As one
Beijing researcher noted, this craze, like pop songs and youth slang, was
a marker of a distinctive youth culture, different from the mainstream
and beyond its control.[56] In an era before the Internet provided a space
for the expression of youthful rebellion and collectivity, cotton fabric on
young people's chests and backs was one space for the ironic airing of
difference.

Like T-shirts, jeans had become a symbol of youthful identity in the
reform era. Jeans had first attracted youths' attention in the first half
of the 1970s with the arrival of Western tourists. The denim garment's
origins in work clothes made them acceptable in Mao's China, though
few had access to them. They had become a marker of youthful Chinese
fashion by the late 1970s. Over a decade later, some students dribbled
different coloured paints or embroidered decorations on theirs, and some
deliberately made holes in their pants, treatments familiar in Western

countries. One art student cited practicality for his wearing of what he acknowledged were a kind of 'school uniform' on college campuses. Another long-haired youth told a Shanghai researcher:

> Jeans have an anti-traditional, anti-conventional, anti-fashion, and anti-snob [literally anti-aristocratic *fan guizuhua*] significance. They express a kind of pure and natural appearance, so they can stay cool (*jingjiu bu shuai*) for forty years. People today respect nature and a return to purity and simplicity. Jeans really fit those aspirations.

One of his classmates added her voice:

> Jeans are a kind of language, one that just about all we young people can understand. That's why they are favoured by young people, it all depends on expressing connotations. They can express a kind of frame of mind with anger and resistance. They can express a kind of holding yourself aloof from the world (*yushiwuzheng*), a state where ignorance is bliss (*nade hutu de jingjie*). They can also express an attitude towards life that is unconventional and uninhibited (*luotubuji*) where I'll stick to my own way of doing things (*woxingwosu*). Jeans are a language for young people to express themselves.

Their own bodies provided a space for young people on which to present a sense of difference.[57]

Fifteen years on, in a new century, the notion of clothing as a reflection of youthful difference and aspiration had been firmly established in the public eye. By 2008 bodily awareness among young Chinese matched that of their counterparts in Western countries. Fashion magazines, television and film stars, and television talent contests bombarded the young with idealised bodies – slim, confident, and pale. Whitening creams became a major segment of the personal care market for men and women. In the 1970s women and men had used moisturising lotion, at least in the dryness of Beijing's winter. By the end of the first decade of the new century, L'Oréal, Olay, and other global companies were pushing whitening creams. Television and magazine advertisements emphasised the success enjoyed by young women and young male executives when their skin was pale and they smelled good. Young women in particular were subjected to impossible ideals of slim, wide-eyed beauty. This pressure was probably worse than for their counterparts in Western countries, as evidence of a counter-discourse in the media was hard to find.

By 2008 fashion magazines, for men as well as women, were an established part of the middle-class urban landscape.[58] Beautiful images on covers at newsstands and on advertising billboards were impossible to avoid. These visual exhortations to health, beauty, and spending had replaced the equivalent ubiquitous advertisements of the mid-1970s, large red billboards at strategic intersections emblazoned with the truth and beauty of a short saying by Chairman Mao. By the 2000s fashion trends among the young were as changing and as guided by commercial, media, and other influences as was true for Chinese youth's counterparts in North America, Japan, or Europe. To be considered out of fashion for many young Chinese had become a social blunder, though it would not result in the kind of persecution brought on by political mistakes in an earlier generation of young people in Mao's time. Television, magazines, and the Internet brought waves of fashion trends into the lives of young Chinese with disposable incomes. Korean youth styles, fashions from Tokyo, and fashion seen on the bodies of comic book characters and by cosplay (short for costume play) participants were successively adopted by fashionable young China.[59]

Those young people who found all this consumerism overwhelming could turn to guidance from experts. Bookstores offered advice books on grooming, fashion, and consuming in general. Some books were themselves fashion statements, capturing the e-world of their readers on the printed page. One good example is *Pure Teenager* (*Chuncui shaonian*) from 2001, which offered advice to youth on how to behave, how to interact with friends and with young women, and how to dress. Also included are horoscope profiles, lists of things like what women most dislike in a man, and hints on diet and fitness. All these are illustrated with cartoons and English words (beauty boy, something healthy, hair stuff, must have, attention please, and so on).[60] In a different vein, *Fashion Guilty* (*Shishang youzui*) served as both a guidebook to current fashion and fads and a critique of much of this new bodily consumerism. It covered a full range of wealthy, youthful obsessions typical of 2005: bars, cigars, perfume, underwear, antilabel consumers, cohabitation, skateboarding, and the different local characteristics of men and women in major Chinese cities. But the cartoon illustrations and the historical notes (including a list of annual major fads from 1978 to 2002) showed a more sceptical approach to fashion.[61]

One related adornment of the body deserves brief mention. Tattooing has a long history in China, at least as a punishment or identification for criminals. In the 1990s young Chinese, like their counterparts in Western countries, began to adorn their bodies with permanent marks. By the mid-2000s the fashion for tattoos was more widespread, with a definite focus on the young. Several men and women in their twenties who had a tattoo told a sociologist of the attractions of the mark: a wife thought it looked good, vaguely Buddhist beliefs could be expressed and protection from evil achieved, English soccer player David Beckham and other foreign celebrities looked good with them. Sometimes the interest in tattoos came in waves or clusters. A 2001 report identified Harbin high schoolers as youngsters who wanted the permanent bodily adornment that ink in skin provided.[62]

SEX AND RELATIONSHIPS

New choices and the new emphasis on appearance and the body by 1988 were part of changes in public discourse about sexual relationships. In her article on nude art models Jian Mei went so far as to write 'We can say 1988 is the year of sex culture' (*Keyi shuo, 1988 nian shi "xingwen-hua nian"*).[63] A curious sidelight on sexual relations was provided by an unusual drama from the television production arm of the Harbin Spoken Drama Theatre. *Wild Feelings* (*Ren yexing*) told the story of a university student who is kidnapped by some mythical, primitive inhabitants of the Shennongjia region of Hubei province, renowned as a centre of speculation about wild men living in the mountains. Ke Zhen (her given name refers to loyalty or chastity) realises her captors mean well and decides to defend them against the depredations of local hunters and her erstwhile boyfriend, an anthropologist. Production stills, reproduced in *Popular Television*, show actors in wigs, furs, and blackface playing the primitives, armed with spears. This fascination with so-called primitive or even Stone Age life in China's ancient past had been reflected on cinema screens in the mid-1980s. It was a less sophisticated allusion to life before the "isms" of civilisation took hold than that reflected in the world of *Red Sorghum*. This television drama, like many of the films, had a distinct frisson of sexual excitement at the suggestion of intimate relations between hairy primitives and innocent Han Chinese young woman. This was not very far, in ideological terms, from the world of the original *King Kong*.[64]

In the relatively open climate in the spring of 1989, the widely read *Popular Film* featured an ongoing discussion of sex and nudity in the cinema. The April issue asked 'How should films present sexual love?' and 'Should nudity be shown?' in a two-page spread at the front of the magazine liberally illustrated with recent Chinese film stills of mostly women in states of relative undress, in bath tubs and on beds, among other settings. Ten points of contention around these questions were summarised by the magazine's editors, outlining their readers' responses to the raising of these questions in the March issue. The editors presented a pro and con argument under each of the ten questions, which asked if sex and nudity were now excessive, whether these scenes were an integral part of the drama, and whether they were ahead of public attitudes (the writers used the expression *guoqing*: condition of the nation), among other issues.[65]

Sexually explicit reading materials were another indication of the rise of the body in youthful public discourse. Titles such as *Lifestyles of Hollywood Stars* (*Haolaiwu mingxing shenghuo*), *True Romance* (*Qinglian*, also called *Cohabitation*, *Pinju*), and *Gate of Youth* (*Qingchun zhi men*) made up the sixty-five percent of bookstall bestsellers that were considered pornographic (*seqing*). In late 1988, there were 700 book-stalls in Beijing alone. The bulk of the books were reportedly translations from Japanese, English, and other foreign languages. A local work like *A Prostitute's Regret* (*Qinglou hen*) had a 1940s setting rather than one in post-1949 China.[66] This was similar to a lot of the hand-copied stories that circulated among sent-down youth in the early 1970s. Although in the 1980s most of the customers for such material were between thirty and forty years old, there was concern about the unhealthy interest that some young people showed in it.

One new section in youth magazines was the personal column, featuring listings of readers seeking life partners or friends. *Youth Era* (*Qingchun suiyue*), for example, included a page or more with such ads in each monthly issue in 1988. Most were from men in their mid-twenties and older, suggesting a concern that their marriageable age was passing. The listings gave their height, information on their educational levels, family status (noting parents and dependents), and even in many cases monthly or annual income. Interested readers were invited to write directly to the person described, preferably including a photograph of themselves. Advertisements by women were greatly outnumbered in these pages. In the past finding a spouse had usually been resolved through efforts by parents or other family members. These 'marriage partner' (they were all labeled *zhenghun*) ads suggest a weakening of the attraction of those efforts. Like the emphasis on beautiful bodies, expectations for the qual-ity of a future partner were rising. Finding a wider pool of potential mates could raise the possibility of finding someone closer to the new more demanding ideals. *Youth and Society* added an element of romance, not expected in such efforts in the past, with a subtitle on one of its columns, 'Cupid's arrow' (*Qiubite zhi jian*) and a photo of an Italianate Cupid statue.[67]

A similar example of self-advertisement appeared in the pages of *Popular Television*, though the purpose was to attract casting directors as well as reader interest. Each month's issue from June 1988 until December 1989 included a page of usually eight 'young stars' in their teens and twenties with a head shot, height, and a note on their personalities, hob-bies, and sometimes on their roles to date. In total, 142 actors appeared in these eighteen months, too many to be considered true stars with any substantial fan base. Their appearance, however, suggested how fanship had become a recognised pastime for readers of a similar age to the fea-tured players. The page in each issue was usually marked with a logo of 'telescreen matchmaker' (*yingpin hongniang*), suggesting the kind of ide-alised relationship with readers sought by these young actors. Under the logo appeared the four-line slogan: 'welcome recommendation, welcome self-recommendation, welcome selection for a position, welcome to employ them' (*huanying tuijian, huanying zijian, huanying linxuan, huanying luyong*). It seems these photos were directed at both general readers and television casting directors. Their photos and short bios were the equivalent of the marriage personals in youth magazines at the time, though the latter never included photos of the individuals featured. Unlike marriage ads, these television pages did not include addresses to contact the young person pictured.[68]

## BREAKDANCING

One way to meet potential marriage partners was through dancing. Several dance crazes swept 1980s China, with one in particular attracting youthful enthusiasts and a cultish following. Social or ballroom dancing was too sedate for most youngsters, who left it for older urban siblings, their parents, and even grandparents to discover (or rediscover) in the 1980s.[69] Disco dancing was one of the relatively few words in contemporary Chinese that was transliterated from English. *Disike* became a label in the 1980s for any freeform dancing to pop or rock music with a powerful beat. The excitement of a hotel dining room or college gymnasium transformed with the addition of a mirror-covered ball in the centre of the ceiling and a tape recorder plugged into loudspeakers attracted youthful attention. This was in part because of the association of loud music with youthful rebellion. Dances were also a new form of social interaction, revived after falling into abeyance during the decade of the Cultural Revolution, which appealed to adolescents looking for ways to interact with the opposite sex.[70] There were also other benefits from the 1980s dance craze. One small-time Shaoxing opera actress in her twenties noted the appeal of working as a taxi dancer in a dance hall. She had not much hope of becoming an opera star, but on the dance floor she could feel free to satisfy her urge to make an impact on viewers. 'This is also a kind of stage, I act, but the audience is different. My status also changes. When I'm here [in the dance hall] my income is much higher than when I'm playing bit parts.' Disco dancing in high-class hotels in Shanghai could even be a means of going abroad through finding a foreign husband.[71] When the term *disike* was extended to early morning exercises favoured by older citizens in public parks, disco began to lose its youthful cachet.[72]

The urban youth dance phenomenon of 1988 was breakdancing (*piliwu*). At a time when the number of Hollywood movies officially released in China was limited to about ten a year, any of these titles was expected to attract a lot of movie goers. *Breakdance: The Movie*, the story of a multicultural group of Los Angeles youths who do well in their shared interest in a new dance style, was released in China in 1987.

That summer in public parks in Beijing, it was not unusual to find a group of young men and women standing in a circle watching a few young men twirl and spin on the ground, usually on a shiny board, to the beat of rock music from a portable tapeplayer. A 1988 article in *Popular Film* indicated a somewhat broad definition of the dance phenomenon. There were three kinds of breakdancing: robotic dancing or moonwalking (though Michael Jackson and his *Thriller* album [1983] go unmentioned), the kind of spinning on heads and backs seen in the movie *Breakdance*, and similar dancing by couples who avoided contact between each other. The female lead in *Breakdance* states: 'I dance with my heart, not for other people to watch.'[73] A national breakdancing contest took place in September 1988. Twelve thousand spectators watched the competition in the Workers' Gymnasium, a venerable Beijing venue constructed in 1959. Reportedly only one of the contestants in the individual and group categories was a university student.[74] As with the young protagonists in the American film, the attraction of this dance form among Chinese youth was that is provided a way to assert identity and to increase social standing.

Contestants in the Beijing contest confirmed in a radio report these attractions of breakdancing.[75] Although some said that the American inventors of the moves had been influenced by Chinese martial arts movement, the phenomenon was a distinctly foreign one. Like for 'seniors' disco,' there were those who wanted to censure the import: It's "neither fish nor fowl" (*sibuxiang*).... Save those empty souled children.' Winner of the first prize in the group competition was the Shock Troupe (*Zhendong dui*) from Beijing. One of its members, nineteen-year-old Zhang Dawei, from the China Musical and Dance Theatre, told the radio interviewer:

> For me, I'm a professional dancer. My basic job is to dance ethnic dances (*minzuwu*). The rules for doing ethnic dances and break-dancing are opposites, completely different. It's pretty terrific and looks good.... Break-dancing requires some real effort, especially in the movement rules. You can't just pick it up, you have to work on it. I want to dance it well, because then lots of people will want to watch it.... Some of the skills in break-dancing can enhance my abilities and can help me with my ethnic dance skills. Now I like this kind of dance. For me, since I dance this, I can win prizes.

Chen Qiushi, an amateur breakdancer from Xinjiang in the far northwest, explained his interest:

> Whatever your pastime, none can be considered low grade. So long as you put your heart and soul into something, it shows you're a genuine person. What's the point if you only listen to what other people say: they tell you to do this, you do this; do that, you do that. In the past, loyalty dances [to Chairman Mao] were not a pastime; they were controlled. Ballet relies on skill, the traditional skills of standard dancing have a kind of beauty. These

also have a kind of accepted artistic value. But dances as a pastime depend on a person's feelings and the free development of emotions. So things that are pastimes will always reflect your values in life. You can't do without them. Losing them means you lose your own self-worth. The key is this era is the 'me era' (*ziwo shidai*). People like break-dancing, and like these pastimes. That's the way it is. No-one resists this wave.

In the Workers' Gymnasium the breakdancers performed while roaring the songs 'Go Forward Boldly, Little Sister' from *Red Sorghum* and Cui Jian's anthem, 'Nothing to My Name' (*Yiwusuoyou*). Outside the venue the radio reporter asked a Peking opera singing *erhu* player what he thought of breakdancing. 'It's something for youngsters. Each to his own.'[76]

A reporter from *Dance* magazine interviewed the six young men in the team from Tianjin, who had paid their own way to be in the Workers' Gymnasium competition. Why did they like breakdancing? Because it made them feel good (*tongkuai*). Huang Xianguo also noted the parallels between the youthful interest in breakdancing and the Northwest Wind in songs that swept China at the same time. The inside front cover of *Dance* showed young men from the Beijing contest in lurex jumpsuits, or tank tops and parachute pants, on stage or at rest.[77]

This was not just a Beijing phenomenon. In Guiyang in the southwest, the local branch of the National Youth Federation and other organisations in early May sponsored the Dongwei Disco and Break-dance Television Contest. A brief note with photos of dancers at the event observed earnestly:

> Break-dancing is a kind of do-as-one-pleases (*suixinsuoyu*) dance. It uses natural and unrestrained dance moves, and freely releases people's inherent passion. Owing to the fast rhythms and beat, movements strange and rapid, and including the impact of lightning and thunderclaps, it gives people powerful stimulation in vision and feelings.[78]

No wonder China's youth had taken to the fad with gusto in 1987 and 1988. A fan in Shanghai described how he and his classmates at the Shanghai No. 2 Middle School in mid-1986 saw a classmate from Hong Kong perform some moves. For the upcoming school concert, he and a group of friends asked the Hong Kong boy to teach them this 'incredible' (*bukesiyi*) dancing. Having won a special award at the concert, the group became more serious. That winter, even in the coldest weather, they practiced in a nearby park at 6:00 A.M. every morning before school. Their skills got better and after six months they started creating their own moves. At that time the American film *Breakdance* had not yet been released in China, so very few Chinese knew about the dance style. A skit in a Shanghai television contest incorporated the robotic moves of the dance and won them a prize. Soon the group was invited to perform for payment at shopping centres and similar places. One of their number, Lu Xianbiao, by 1988 studying at Shanghai Medical University, did not like this development: He took up the dancing because it gave him good feelings and friendships, not for the money. In early 1988's national university student song and dance television contest he won a prize, which was enough.[79]

In the summer of 1988, noted young director (and former classmate of *Red Sorghum*'s Zhang Yimou) Tian Zhuangzhuang was filming *Rock 'n Roll Kids* (*Yaogun qingnian*) at the Beijing Film Studio. The director's motives for this, for him, startling change of subject matter were obvious, though when asked why, he responded facetiously, 'Why not?'[80] Tian was under pressure to produce a commercial success at a time when the whole film industry was in the midst of earnest discussion about how to make commercial or entertainment movies instead of standard propaganda fare or the kinds of art-house works typical of Tian's Fifth-Generation film school classmates.[81] Having started his directing career with two unusual (and for many viewers, incomprehensible) ethnic minority films and an adaptation of a 1940s novel that had not set the box office on fire, Tian had become almost a figure of fun. In a widely publicised interview in 1986, he had responded to accusations that audiences did not understand his films with a typically throwaway line about making films for twenty-first century viewers. Deng Xiaoping, then China's highest leader, reportedly snorted in response: 'Let him wait till next century to collect his salary then.'[82] By mid-1988 Tian had something to prove. The breakdance craze offered a way forward.

*Rock 'n Roll Kids* tells the tale of a professional dancer in a state-run company who leaves his secure employment to set up a modelling and fashion business. This entrepreneurial move, and his relations with his girlfriend who lives alone and allows him to stay overnight, captured the social and economic changes accelerating in the late 1980s. Such living arrangements were virtually unprecedented on China's screens. For youthful viewers the appeal of the kissing and new sexual morality in the film was considerable. Such scenes were still unusual in Chinese feature films. Tian shows how older neighbours express their disapproval of the hero and his partner, underscoring the identification of his intended audience with the youthful protagonists. But a lot of the immediate appeal of the film lay in the numerous dance sequences. The film starts with a group of breakdancers. As pop music swells, the young men (the dance phenomenon was distinctly gendered in all its guises in China) twirl and jerk. Then the lights are raised: They are performing these late twentieth-century moves in front of the Meridian Gate, the southern entrance to the Forbidden City palace complex in central Beijing. New and old could not be more clear, though more thoughtful viewers may have also realised that the gate was just behind Tiananmen, marking the northern edge of China's most sacred political space. These wisps of youthful rebellion are all the more ironic when we note that most of the young dancers were professionals from the People's Liberation Army air force song and dance ensemble, among others.[83] *Rock 'n Roll Kids* captured several strands in youthful assertions of identity and invention in the late 1980s. Thirty-six-year-old director Tian himself explained that his purpose in making the film was to encourage young people to lighten up and enjoy their youth. He contrasted his own experience when in his twenties, when politics was of paramount importance. Worship of Mao had been replaced in the 1980s by worship of money, but both were unwelcome pressures for the young. Liu Yiran, the scriptwriter, noted the various aims of the film: to react against several thousand years of feudal mentality (as in breakdancing in front of the Meridian Gate), and to show how young people are breaking free with their own personalities and expressing themselves (by dancing their own dances and singing their own songs). But most important was to set free their creativity: '[T]o dare do something you've not dared do before; to take the road that people had earlier not been able to take.'[84] The filmmakers clearly knew precisely what would appeal to their young audience in late 1988 and early 1989.

### THE *QIGONG* CRAZE

Another bodily phenomenon attracting youthful attention in 1988 was not new. Instead it had roots deep in the Chinese past. The attraction of *qigong* (breathing exercises) to young adherents lay precisely in this national cultural association. Following *qigong* for many was an antidote to the headlong rush to copy foreign models in 1988. With its origins in Daoist explanations of the body and in Buddhist refinement of these notions, *qigong* held a powerful sway over many youngsters who in other respects were adopting very modern lifestyles. With its alternative 'scientific' account of the workings of the body and mind, *qigong* and its associated martial arts offered a China-derived science for the modern world.[85] *Qigong* appealed to middle-aged and older citizens in large part because of its potential physical and mental health benefits. For most youth, however, *qigong* was more a source of entertainment than a body of belief and health practice.

The English translation of *qigong* does not do it justice. A major attraction of the regimen of breathing exercises, diet, discipline, and contemplation associated with the term was the way highly expert practitioners of the art could develop extraordinary abilities or powers. In 1987 and 1988 a wave of interest in the subject swept China. Much of this was fuelled by *qigong* 'masters' (some of whom were women) demonstrating to enthusiastic audiences. Eight thousand tickets, for example, were sold for five nights of demonstrations in a Guangzhou hall in December 1987.[86] Typically such performances would include the master's ability to make inanimate objects move purely through his or her thoughts. Other displays were of 'mind reading,' feats of exceptional strength, or the ability to withstand pain or temperature extremes. In Qingcheng, Inner Mongolia, a September 1988 demonstration in a local gymnasium by two masters (aged forty-six and fifty-five) from Shanghai filled the sell-out crowd with enthusiasm. The display included feats of strength, bending metal, and making people standing several meters away move without touching them. According to the reporter from the *Huhehot Evening News*, the masters also used their powers to treat sick members of the audience, including having a young woman who had not stood up for eight years walk.[87] A Jiangsu high school teacher urged more high schoolers to become involved in the movement to popularise *qigong*.[88]

A sceptical writer in Huhehot claimed 'the golden age of *qigong* is not in the past, it's right now.' Ke Jun cited what for him were ludicrous stories about *qigong* forcing satellites out of their orbits and curing people thousands of kilometres away. The many advertisements for *qigong* classes and the packed stadiums for demonstrations by masters showed how the '*qigong* fever' (*qigong re*) suited 'national characteristics' (*guominxing*) that included a propensity to fall for 'fevers': Western clothing fever, climbing sacred Mt. Taishan fever, disco fever, and mahjong fever, among others.[89]

But Ke Jun's was a minority voice of scepticism in a chorus of approval. At Peking University, the 'PKU *qigong* fever' had been listed as one of the top ten campus developments in 1987. At China's most renowned university, investigation of the special powers of *qigong* was hailed as promising a new scientific revolution. There in October 1987 two thousand students and teachers had attended a demonstration in which a young master had 220 volts of electricity passed through his body for three, then ten seconds, while he continued talking to the audience. Other students attested to the benefits of practicing *qigong*. One reported that after three days of the exercises, he felt no need to eat, realising this was probably the ancient practice of 'avoiding eating cereals in order to achieve immortality' (*pigu*). Another felt no tiredness at one in the morning, a useful attribute for students working on due assignments. One student agreed with the ancient notion that *qigong* users emitted a distinctive, sweet body door, an attractive trait in the heat of the summer in a crowded dorm room. In a group of fifty, moving slowly through exercises in unison with eyes closed, students reported a glowing sense of beauty. This student account of *qigong* at Peking University suggested that feelings of contentment and autonomy, free of disturbance from others came with the skills. *Qigong* and science were certainly not incompatible; indeed this was at the root of campus interest in this ancient Chinese art.[90]

Yan Xin, the most publicised of the *qigong* masters, was relatively young (born in 1950) to be accorded the accolade.[91] In November 1987 Yan gave a lecture and demonstration to two thousand people in the assembly hall at the Central Party School in Beijing. A former student of traditional Chinese medicine in his native Sichuan, he made his Beijing appearance in a Western suit and tie. Yan showed how he could withstand 220 volts passing through his body and light a 100-watt light bulb. He was even able to lower the voltage to 200 volts, then 180, then 150, all the way to forty volts and then back up to 200 volts. He did this three times in succession. Powers like this were apparently impressive. Yan held his audience in his thrall in a lecture that started at 8:00 P.M. and ended over seven hours later at 3:20 A.M. The *Youth Times* reporter himself felt a strange power over his body five hours and twenty minutes into this lengthy presentation. He ended his report with three words: 'mysterious, magical, enrapturing' (*shenmi, shenqi, shenwang*).[92] After a demonstration by Yan Xin in Kunming, enthusiasm for *qigong* swept the city. In a typical nationalistic reference to the modern relevance of this ancient Chinese practice, a *Youth and Society* reporter noted: '*Qigong* is a quintessence of our national culture [*guocui*, which the report misspelled]. It is a rich and marvellous cultural heritage which we successors of the yellow race are obliged to perpetuate.'[93] Yan toured the country in 1988 giving demonstrations in gymnasiums and colleges. More than five thousand people flocked to see him in three performances in early January in Sichuan. Part of his message was about the health benefits for young and old of practicing *qigong*. A photo of one occasion shows a huge crowd in a gymnasium, with patrons in wheelchairs in the front row. Young people make up a large proportion of the crowd.[94]

Nationalism, and even political orthodoxy, could be associated with this enthusiasm for mysterious magic from China's past. An analysis of science and *qigong* took a similar view, pointing out that the first '*qigong* fever' had been at the turn of the century when the so-called Boxers (*Yihetuan*) had used its powers in an attempt to resist Western imperialism. The second such fever had begun in 1979, coinciding with the start of economic reforms. Science could secure *qigong*'s place in the modern world.[95]

A Ph.D. student at Beijing Normal University took a different view, noting that the 1980s were struck by three great waves of enthusiasms: 'everybody after diplomas' (*quanmin zheng wenping*), 'everybody getting into business' (*quanmin gao jingshang*), and 'everybody practicing *qigong*' (*quanmin lian qigong*). The latter could be seen everywhere on the roadside, in parks and on college campuses. Guo Yuhua mocked the excessive interest in the ancient exercise regime:

> [T]oday we face our race's last opportunity to stand up in the global forest and confront the possibility of failure in this undertaking. Under the huge pressure of maintaining our membership in the community of nations, can we afford to close our eyes and enter a vast fantasy world? Can we use this divine achievement [*qigong*] to overcome this heavy sense of impending racial crisis?...The way of thinking of Chinese traditional culture and its rhythm of life are too far out of step with this world and these times.[96]

Guo's was a minority voice. Writers in other youth periodicals were enthusiasts both of the seemingly magical powers of *qigong* and of the alleged potential of *qigong* to add a new dimension to modern scientific knowledge. Wang Hongguang in Shanghai's *Youth Era* (*Qingnian yidai*) in January 1988 uncritically cited cases of astonishing medical cures through *qigong*. In an ancient imperial building in the Western Hills outside Beijing during the summer of 1985, Wang Jiping, the eighteenth generation in the Longmen school of Daoism, had used his powers to cause all the animals in the hills – rats, foxes, frogs, rabbits, snakes – to gather around the four sides of the pavilion. In another display, a *qigong* master moved pills out of a sealed bottle without touching it. Wang ended his breathless account by calling on twenty-first century science to learn from this ancient art.[97] In an age of rapid globalisation, *qigong* offered young China a source of pride in the national heritage. But by the late 1990s, popular *qigong* in the hands of older citizens took on a political dimension when Falungong adherents protested in Beijing, leading to the banning of the movement. Meanwhile, youthful enthusiasm had moved on to other bodily matters.

### SPORTS FANS

Sports is an area in which the twin focuses on the body and fandom came together in the 1980s. There were precedents for sports fandom in the 1950s and 1960s, with keen support in those decades of China's table tennis representatives in international competitions, for example. In the 1980s, however, participation or spectatorship in some sports provided a useful marker of youthful difference. In the late spring and early summer of 1988 an enthusiasm for pool or billiards swept Beijing, major cities, and many smaller centres. Like the karaoke singing room craze, which had taken hold in 1987 and 1988, the pool fever particularly involved youth. Much of the evidence was literally on the streets, in an era before the widespread adoption of summer air conditioning in restaurants and places of entertainment. Pool tables dotted the fringes of the eastern Third Ring Road, for example, in Beijing in 1988, with groups of young men and women standing around them. Enterprising business people seized this opportunity to set up tables, often rather small and rickety affairs, and charge players for a match or by the hour. Hucksters with advanced skills ignored the official ban on gambling and persuaded gullible punters to try their luck. In the long summer evenings these tables became social centres, with curious onlookers outnumbering players.[98]

Even *People's Daily* noted the phenomenon of tables set up in front of apartment complexes, shopping centres, and cinemas or video parlours.[99] An informal survey counted more than 200 tables in a ten-kilometre stretch eastward from Beijing's inner city Chaoyang Gate. According to the paper, this was the 'third big fever' currently hitting Beijing, along with seniors' disco and *qigong*. The deputy secretary of the China Billiards Association expressed delight at increased public interest but concern about the need to 'strengthen leadership,' meaning controlling gambling and other unsavoury elements in the craze. Ma Hua, a thirty-three-year-old manager at the pool room of the Chaoyang District Palace of Culture (*wenhuagong*), acknowledged the overwhelming predominance of young people in his hall. Their interest had been piqued by two television broadcasts of billiard competitions in the late spring. The other reason for youthful interest was the absence of much to do in their spare time. Dance halls were too formal and expensive, whereas a game of pool was relatively cheap and easy to learn. Mr Ma ended his reported remarks with an earnest plea for newspapers to make clear that 'billiards is a genteel (*gaoya*) activity, and so those who want to play in their clothing, manner and language should also be genteel. Be a little civilised (*wenming*), and you shouldn't damage the pool-hall equipment.'

Leaving the thirty-year-old players who had moved up the value chain from street-side tables to pool rooms, the intrepid *People's Daily* man approached some young people around a table on Jintai West Road, outside the Third Ring Road in Chaoyang district. The owner of the table, a thirty-something private businessman (*getihu*) in a faded army uniform, had paid 270 yuan for the table. The young players were all his neighbours. The manager of the sporting goods shop that had sold this table told the reporter that interest had soared since April, especially for tables costing less than one thousand yuan. The best sellers were priced between 220 to 270 yuan, close to an average month's wage in 1988. The shop had sold forty tables in the first month and could sell between 150 and 200 if stock was available. His customers calculated that they could recoup their investment in just a month or two. But this shop manager was concerned that people were setting up tables as a business without securing the necessary permits or registration. Should the Commerce Ministry be running this or the Ministry of Culture, which looked after sports? Neither seemed to want to take responsibility. This manager was also quoted as emphasising the refined origins of the sport in Western countries, where it was grouped with golf and tennis as the 'three great gentleman's ball games' (*san da shenshi qiu*).

The attraction of pool playing as a marker of rebellion was implied by this shop manager's concern that the official attitude to the phenomenon was not clear: Did the government want to allow it or ban it? The police district commander in Chaoyang district recognised that his beat was the focus of the fever in Beijing. There were problems with the craze, especially with the outdoor tables occupying space and blocking foot and vehicle traffic. Twenty tables sat outside the Qingsong Cinema, for example, making leaving after a show difficult. Gambling was an issue, as was noise from morning to late at night around tables in neighbourhoods. Some youths also got into fights around the tables. The policeman acknowledged that an outright ban would not work, but would merely drive the activity underground. The best response was 'a "Dayu controls the water" method, adjusting methods to circumstances, and guide it to an eventually healthy direction.'[100] The pool table craze of the summer continued in Beijing at a lower pitch into the autumn. As the days grew cooler, the attractions of youthful gatherings on the street to pass the time and enjoy a shared interest began to fade. By the following spring in 1989 other distractions emerged involving university students that provided a welcome spectacle for young Beijingers in general.

Soccer engages legions of youthful and not so young fans around the world. China in the 1980s was no different. As Liu Hongsen, a Shanghai sociologist, observed in an analysis of Chinese ball game fans, young people made up the overwhelming majority: 'Young ball fans are a social grouping with special interests and demands (*teshu liyi xuqiu*). What kinds of demands are actually satisfied with balls and ball game competitions?' Liu identified three key elements for ball game fandom: the process of games, playing area rules, and stars (*qiuxing*). Fans enjoyed the unpredictability of competition, with a similar degree of involvement to those watching a film or play. But unlike the latter, a ball game lacked a script and could take unexpected turns. Ball fans were also more prone to display their feelings: yelling, cursing, and leaping to spur on their teams or to express disgust with their performance. These feelings and their display were generally not seen in everyday life. Youth were more demonstrative and demanding. Previous generations had given them a basic script for life (when to eat, when to sleep, work, marry, become a parent). While acknowledging this inheritance, young ball game fans naturally wanted to find their own path.

> Youthful ball-game fans are addicted to competition, and this stems from their feelings of being fed up with and resisting (boring!) the play-acting of real life. The addiction stems from the thirst for endless possibilities and expectations (live life to the fullest!) which are displayed everywhere.[101]

Liu Hongsen went on to discuss sports star icons and psychological compensation for youth. Sport stars earned respect from their skills and ability to turn a game and were more respected around the world than most political leaders or beauty queens. But what, asked Liu, was the psychological basis of young sports fans' adoration of their favourite stars?

> As members of a race that has experienced many vicissitudes in life and which in politics, economics and culture has fallen behind the rest of the world, Chinese youthful ball-game fans are extremely sensitive to their own limitations when faced with the world. Because they have no experience of comparisons, they often don't enquire about the cause of the status quo. All they do is take an exaggerated view of present differences, hence their sorrow and low self-esteem. Consequently young sports fans frequently in their subconscious hope that through watching sport, through watching a contest in which the Chinese team utterly routs the 'foreign devils' they can gain compensation for their low self-esteem and satisfaction of their self-respect.[102]

Fans identified themselves with the sports stars in a kind of 'inner modelling' (nei mofang), so that the stars' success was their own success and failure was a shared responsibility. This could lead to emotions boiling over: 'Youthful arrogance is fuel to the flames.' Especially when Chinese teams played Western and other foreign teams, victory made them national heroes. Defeat for these Chinese stars, who were stand-ins for the fans, led to sometimes wild recrimination by disappointed fans. For Liu Hongsen, young sports fans were undergoing a kind of psychological training for life's challenges. He saw parallels with the determination of breakdancers to practice their art.

The May 1985 riots outside the Workers' Stadium in Beijing were an illustration of Liu's points about the emotional instability and dependence of youthful sports fans. But in May 1988 a similar protest in Sichuan also offered evidence of the kind of psychological transference that he identified. The earlier Beijing incident followed the Chinese team's draw with the Hong Kong team in an Asian regional qualification match in the buildup to the 1986 Football World Cup. The result meant that China was again excluded from the competition. As the two teams left the field, young spectators pelted them with bread and soda bottles, shouting 'Disband the Chinese team,' and 'Zeng Xuelin [the Chinese coach] is a bastard,' among other, reportedly less salubrious, chants.[103] Abuse was also hurled at the police in the stadium. Having left the grounds, more than one thousand people in a mob gathered and intercepted buses, taxis, and cars, including those of foreigners. This continued for over an hour until a show of force by newly arrived police squads put a stop to the riot. Two members of the Communist Youth League Central Research Office surveyed 116 young men detained by police that night. Forty-eight of those interviewed had been bystanders caught up in the riot outside the stadium; the other sixty-eight had thrown bottles in the stadium, and a small minority had smashed car windows and done other damage on the streets. Eighty-five percent of those detained were under twenty-five, with twenty-one under eighteen and seventy-eight aged between nineteen and twenty-five. Only three men were over thirty. The explanation of why they had rioted revealed that the roots lay in youth fandom.

The riot had been spontaneous, but reflected a longstanding grievance among young fans since the Chinese team's failure four years earlier in the previous World Cup preliminaries. The shock of failing to demolish the Hong Kong team and go on to meet Mexico was too great. 'When I saw the girl beside me crying bitterly,' noted a twenty-one-year-old Youth League member, 'I too felt really upset, and without thinking hurled a bun.' The researchers observed that these young people were respectable citizens who lost self-control as strangers around them began to express their anger and frustration as the end of the game approached. A young worker from Luoyang, awarded a trip to Beijing for his excellent work performance, had spent a lot of money on a ticket to the match. At the end, he was seething with anger and rushed to join in the rioting: 'I was really like a madman. I changed into this totally different person.'[104] Some of the young fans sang two Communist anthems, the *Internationale* and 'We Workers Have Strength' (*Zanmen gongren you liliang*), in a derisive way when they saw the police massed outside the stadium.

Frustration extended beyond the soccer match. A twenty-year-old worker, when asked why he had smashed the windows of a taxi, responded that he worked hard every month for just a few dozen yuan, whereas a taxi driver got several hundred yuan in his hands each month. Two-thirds of the men surveyed were employed in enterprises and service industries and about one-fifth were in high school. The group included four university students and five cadres. Even more remarkable to the researchers was the discovery that thirty-three of the 113 men under thirty years old were Communist Youth League members: twenty-nine percent in a population cohort in which membership averaged twenty-one percent. This published report makes no mention of the fact that the offending visiting team was from Hong Kong. In Beijing and North China then (and today) people from Hong Kong tend to be looked down upon as lacking a suitable cultural level and only interested in making money. That a team of Cantonese from a British colony could thwart China's team added to the particular sense of humiliation behind the riot. The researchers did note, however, the unwelcome influence of news about soccer riots in Western countries that had undoubtedly provided a model for the Beijing youths' bad behaviour.[105]

In 1988 the Sichuan soccer riot was on a much larger scale than the 1985 Beijing event and again drew attention to youthful attitudes of alienation and frustration. The trouble had begun at a soccer match between the visiting Tianjin team and the Sichuan side in Nanchong, a major regional centre in the east of the province. Unhappy at what they saw as the early end to the game when it was drawn one all, the crowd spontaneously erupted in anger. A young man who ran across the pitch to the officials' seats was first handcuffed, then released, which seemed to only make the crowd angrier. Outside the grounds they waited for the Tianjin team to emerge. The troubles extended to a nearby hotel, which had its windows broken and was set alight. Reportedly many people observing the riot likened it to what they had seen during the Cultural Revolution. Indeed one young cook, Tang Xiaogang (later sentenced to ten years in prison) told a reporter he thought this must be the kind of excitement and liberation Red Guard protesters had felt during that decade.[106] Yang Min, a well-built young man who enjoyed martial arts, had been struck by a stone outside the stadium and gone to hospital to have his wound tended. Headstrong and impetuous at the best of times, he returned to the stadium to yell slogans, chanting like a Cultural Revolution troublemaker, according to a reporter.[107] Song Xiaolong (later sentenced to five years imprisonment) had not even been at the soccer match, but when a couple of buddies told him that the streets around the nearby Unity Hotel were bustling with excitement, he rushed over. A fan of Sylvester Stallone, whom he had seen in *Rambo: First Blood*, Song later recalled that when he started throwing bricks and stones, he felt so excited it was as if an electric current had passed through him. Wang Guofu had left school after only four years of primary school and worked with his father in a neighbourhood metal workshop. Though self-conscious about his short height, he took up dancing in Beihu Park, played pool on the street, and sang in his spare time. He liked in particular belting out Northeast Wind songs like those from *Red Sorghum*. Swept up in the excitement of the day's events that May, he thought it was even better than the feeling he got when singing 'The Flame' (*Yi ba huo*). A three-wheel cart rider who had moved to Nanchong from the countryside and had registered the year before as a private business, Lin Weihe was overwhelmed by the risks of that evening, helping to rock a car:

> Lin Weihe suddenly felt as if he had become an amazing soccer star taking a beautiful shot from a teammate and breaking into the penalty area. He felt that an even greater sensation and becoming famous overnight awaited him. In his mind it seemed there was a voice: 'Look at me!' Then, he kicked a burning flip-flop sandal to beside the gasoline tank. All he heard was a 'woosh' and the car was on fire.

Lin ended up also serving a five-year term.[108] The excitement and group solidarity that these five rioters temporarily felt that afternoon and evening are clear. They had copied the overturning and setting fire of vehicles, the reporter suggested, from foreign films and television reports. They also modelled their behaviour on Cultural Revolution protests. Overweening pride of locality, in this case Sichuan province and Nanchong city, was also a factor behind the May 1988 riots.[109] For the young participants, it was clearly an opportunity and a space for displaying their feelings that could not be resisted.

Even in the relatively sombre, post-June 4 days of the summer of 1989, young sports fans could still show their enthusiasms and contempt for authority. A China–Iran soccer match (again part of a World Cup buildup) in mid-July that year caused a near riot in Shenyang over availability of tickets. Four days ahead of the game, those who could not get tickets through other means started lining up at the stadium ticket booths. Two days later thousands were there waiting, most of them young men. Someone reportedly paid a massive 370 yuan for three tickets. But there were no riots in Shenyang that year, just complaints about the inefficiencies of ticket distribution.[110]

Sports stars became objects of fan attention in the 1980s. One of the first objects of youthful fandom in sports from the late 1970s was the highly successful national women's volleyball team. Their matches against Japan in particular attracted huge television audiences, becoming accustomed to the new experience of watching sports broadcast live in their own homes. The exploits of the women volleyballers formed the basis for a thoughtful and artistically innovative film about a volleyball player. *Sha'ou* (named after the lead character, but also known in English as *The Drive to Win*) was directed at the Youth Film Studio by Zhang Nuanxin in 1981.[111] The film's message was about winning being less important than the effort put into taking part. A scene in the Yuanmingyuan (Old Summer Palace) among the iconic remains of Western armies' looting in 1860 underscored the nationalist commitment of the film that had appealed to young viewers. The latter also identified with the novelty of the youthful central character lamenting at the unfairness of life.

Nineteen eighty-eight was an Olympic year. China's performances at the Seoul games were the subject of post-mortems by Beijing and Wuhan university students. One communications student at Renmin University in the capital noted that the media talked up Chinese teams' chances before a contest and then switched after a team fell short of these expectations to prattling on about the importance of simply participating. The pressure of public expectations on athletes was the concern of a Beijing Normal University graduate student.[112] A junior communications student at Wuhan University argued that the educational level of the Chinese team members was less than ideal, which meant many could not handle the challenges of international competition. A law student noted the pressure on athletes, carrying on their shoulders the national hopes of more than a billion people. According to one of his classmates, sportsmen and women such as gymnast Li Ning, a gold medalist four years earlier in Los Angeles, had lost their pleasure in sport and focused on fame and money. Other participants in Wuhan noted the need to keep raising skill levels, as Western athletes seemed to manage. In the relatively liberal atmosphere of late 1988, the students called for less government control of sports and more popular management.[113]

Li Ning was one of the first youth celebrities in 1980s China and the first in the realm of sports. Born in 1963 in Guangdong, Li's triumph at the 1984 Los Angeles Olympics received wide media coverage. The official sports and propaganda apparatus regarded him as a suitable model for the young in the new, more international era. A healthy young man able to out-compete the best in the world offered distinct attractions as a representative of his generation and those younger. But international and national distinction in the new age also offered other potential. When he retired from gymnastics after the Seoul games, Li joined forces with Jianlibao, a Guangdong beverage company, to turn his fame into commercial success. The proprietors of Jianlibao wanted to create a Chinese soft drink brand that could compete with Coca Cola and Pepsi. The former had entered China in the late 1970s and in the following decade became the standard drink with restaurant meals, apart from tea or beer. Jianlibao helped Li Ning establish his eponymous brand of sports clothing and shoes. The opportunity had arisen when, after the June 4 incident in 1989, Li lost his previous contractual arrangements with Western sports equipment manufacturers. By the 1990 Asian Games in Beijing, Li Ning had opened his first store in Wangfujing, the city's top shopping street, and begun to equip some of China's teams. The Li Ning brand equivalent of Nike's swoosh was a familiar sight on young Chinese chests beginning in the 1990s. The close resemblance with Nike's symbol showed the copycat nature of the business but also its ambition to take on international companies like adidas and Puma.[114]

Another sports person to excite China's youthful attention was a giant of the basketball court. Like Li Ning, Yao Ming came to public notice through the Olympics. But he achieved real fame through recruitment into the United States NBA, joining the Houston Rockets in 2002. Yao's career was symbolic of the increasing globalisation and commercialisation of China. He was a key figure in the NBA's marketing in China, where millions of fans, a high proportion of them young, followed the fortunes of American basketball franchises through direct and delayed broadcasts. As injury took its toll in 2009, Yao made a move back to China with his investment in the Shanghai Sharks team in the Chinese league.[115]

A third sports celebrity needs mention here, though his following among China's youth could be said to be more purely a sporting matter. Liu Xiang, a Shanghai runner born in 1983, won gold in the 110-meter hurdles at the Athens Olympics in 2004. Late that year Liu published his autobiography, *I Am Liu Xiang*. While conceding in a postscript that he was a little young to publish his life's story, Liu argued he was just an ordinary person.[116] Of humble origins (his father was a driver for the Shanghai water company), Liu's account of his life is punctuated by quotes from his parents, classmates, and others declaring what a fine young man and indeed model youth he is.[117] The kind of national pride that had given Li Ning a following among the young in the 1980s can be seen among Liu's fans twenty years later. On a far more obvious scale than for Li Ning, Liu Xiang became the front man for a range of products, including an international credit card and Amway.[118] In the 2008 Olympics advertising campaign for the latter, Liu appeared alongside American hurdler Allen Johnson on billboards and television ads. Expectations built hugely as the Beijing Olympics approached and China's world champion prepared for the contest.[119] On the day that August that Liu did not run a step, withdrawing because of injury just before his heat in the hurdles, the public response was a mix of condemnation and sympathy. Young netizens vented their frustrations in discussion groups, a space for fandom that did not exist when Li Ning was leaping the vault.[120]

## COSPLAY: NEW BODIES AND VIRTUAL WORLDS

A body phenomenon from the later 1990s and 2000s shows how far youth cultures in China had become elaborated, embedded in cyberspace and in globalised circuits of exchange. Cosplay is a contraction of 'costume play' and involves its participants dressing up as fantastic, fictitious, or historical characters. This pastime first emerged among Tokyo youth and developed from the kind of costumed activities carried out on weekends in Harajuku Park that became famous in the 1980s. The kinds of personas embodied by cosplayers drew heavily on Japanese manga, with blond-haired, androgynous young men in makeup to accentuate eyes and lips. By the 2000s cosplayers were using the Internet to find fellow players and share images of characters. Digital manipulation allowed characters to be placed in suitably complex settings to create fantastic virtual worlds. The Internet also provided a means of sharing the techniques and skills used in creating these characters and worlds. Cosplay became a transnational phenomenon, with activities in Japan, North America, South Korea, and elsewhere shared on the Internet and in publications.

Although much of this activity was conducted and shared on the Internet, glossy books appeared in 2006 and 2007 in China offering a mix

Figure 3.6. Cosplay as Western fantasy: 'Dream in Venice'.
*Source:* Manyou wenhua, *Manyou COSPLAY 100 xilie: pianyi huanxi-ang* (Cartoon Friend Cosplay 100 series: on the wings of fantasy), Harbin: Heilongjiang meishu chabanshe, 2006, p. 79.

of images of cosplay participants and advice on how to achieve some of the costume, prop, and makeup effects. These volumes showed the range of cosplay imagery and ambition. Blond-haired young women played manga-inspired pre-French Revolution lovers from Versailles, vampire fantasies, or Venice in the pages of one book, alongside more East Asian fantasy figures from vaguely premodern or legendary times. The book also contained pages of news and photos from the United States, Japan, Hong Kong, and various cities in China. Also included were brief 'how-to' pages on achieving certain makeup and prop effects, including a Lolita look and ancient metal finishes on newly created buttons, swords, and other accessories.[121] But the realm of cosplayers could accommodate a range of interests. Another glossy volume featured mostly young men in fantastical outfits, clearly inspired by Internet-based games and manga characters. A single cosplay character is presented in a series of photographs, offering insight into the hair, makeup, and costume effects. In addition practical advice on how to achieve the looks is offered. Several of the young men are portrayed in more regular clothing, with their Chinese names, cosplay names (often Japanese style or modelled on Japanese names), with details of birthdates (most are young teenagers), height and weight, hair and skin colour, personality, and a statement about the boy.[122]

These cosplay details seemed a long way from the plain personal ads in youth magazines in the late 1980s. In twenty years the worlds of bodily beauty and adornment had expanded hugely as realms in which young China could parade and celebrate difference and control over their own bodily identities, real or imagined. By the twenty-first century the body focus of Chinese youth had shifted from the androgyny of the Cultural Revolution, through celebration of manly vigour and refusal to bow to authority, to a more complex, in many ways highly sexualised, concept. As with the rhythms and spaces of youth culture, new technologies and media were instrumental in shaping these changes.

# CHAPTER 4

# Rhythms

## *The Soundtracks of Connection and Assertion*

It is impossible to reimagine the emergence of youth cultures in the United States and Western Europe in silence. Music made by and for young people was an integral part of the generational shifts of the 1950s and 1960s that established youth as a powerful and assertive group that reshaped consumer tastes and popular culture in general.[1] In China, the noise of a youthful soundtrack to accompany the emergence of new groups in society blasted out in a much shorter time frame than in the Anglo world (the North Atlantic and Australasia), essentially in the single decade of the 1980s. The interconnectedness with the musical developments in the Chinese advanced or outlier societies of Hong Kong and Taiwan, Japan, and with the Anglo world drove this Chinese process in unexpected and hybrid ways unique to the conditions in the People's Republic. By the 1990s, youth music had been further elaborated by local artists working from international and domestic inspirations. K-pop (from South Korea) joined the chorus, which received new impetus in the new century from the commercialised world of television talent contests.

Discussions of the rise of youth and rock music in China tend to begin with Cui Jian, the former trumpeter in the Central Philharmonic Orchestra and Korean–Chinese. Cui's most famous song, 'Nothing to My Name' (*Yiwusuoyou*), became the theme song of the late 1980s, sung by the protestors in Tiananmen Square in the spring of 1989 alongside the more ancient and orthodox Communist anthem *Internationale*. Cui Jian's career from his emergence in 1986 as the inventor of Chinese rock music (*yaogun yinyue*, literally shake and roll music) to his reemergence in the 1990s and his continued performance in the new century offers us a way of mapping the continued relevance of youth-oriented music to successive generations over three decades.

The more syrupy tones of Taiwan singer Deng Lijun (known internationally as Teresa Teng, 1953–1995) and the sentimental, polished warbles of Li Guyi helped establish a space for songs full of sentiment and private feelings that represented a shift from the more politically engaged songs that had provided the soundtrack for the Red Guard and sent-down youth generation. As we have seen, private feelings through song for these youth tended to be the domain of foreign songs, heard in the covert singing of 'Moscow Nights' by groups of classmates in the safety of darkness in the constructions corps billets in Inner Mongolia, Heilongjiang, or Yunnan. This is not to argue that the songs popularised by the Chinese state after 1949 were all resolute hymns to the glory of the Communist Party and the importance of loyalty to it, even if titles such as 'My Country' (*Wo de zuguo*) and 'Aunty Wang Wants Peace' (*Wang Dama yao heping*) might suggest otherwise. By the early 1960s, less blatantly militant songs were part of the Chinese repertoire. Songs like 'The Fish and Rice of Dongting Lake are Fragrant' (*Dongting yu mi xiang*) and 'Horsey, Slow Down a Little' (*Ma'er a, ni man xie zou*) allowed for more domestic and affectionate affects, even if the former could still be considered a praise song for the bounties of socialism.[2] Many of these songs were popularised through their inclusion on feature film soundtracks. The standard two-song sequences by the late 1970s, as in previous decades, proved a highly effective means of taking the messages of a film to audiences beyond the cinemas and other film viewing venues.

Li Guyi achieved fame in the 1980s as the singer of such film songs. One of her early successes was the film *Little Flower* (*Xiaohua*, directed by Zhang Zheng, 1979), the story of a brother and sister separated during the civil war of the 1930s and reunited years later. The emphasis on individual feelings and the focus on the personal story at the expense of much coverage of war and resistance made *Little Flower* a major hit on its release, for it fit the new era's relative spurning of directly political stories.[3] Sentiment and feeling triumphed over a singular focus on duty in the film and its songs. Li had a similarly influential hit in the 1981 movie *Longing for Home* (*Xiangqing*, directed by Hu Bingliu and Wang Jin), which told of a young man torn between making a new life in the city and his affection for the girl he left behind. Theme songs for the ubiquitous television series that filled China's screens added to the popularity of Li Guyi and her southern equivalent, Zhu Fengpu.[4] These two singers were trained in the bel canto (*meisheng*) singing style, different from the popular (*tongsu*) or folk (*minzu*) styles. Their successors in the 1980s proudly adopted the latter two modes, as we shall see.

In the early 1980s young Chinese seeking a new soundtrack for their lives had more choices than ever both in the origins of the music and the means by which they listened to it. The rise of the cassette recorder, at first as large, box-like stereo sets or as medium-sized, portable players, allowed the growth of a market in cassette tapes and the copying of tapes by individuals and organised businesses. By the mid-1980s the Sony

Walkman was (expensively) available in China's major cities. By then the availability of taped songs from Hong Kong and Taiwan, regarded by Beijing as integral parts of China, brought new song styles and languages to Chinese fans. Canto-pop (songs sung in Cantonese, the language of Hong Kong and Guangdong) had an appeal, with catchy tunes sung in the (for most Chinese) exotic language being a way of showing to friends and others within earshot one's modernity.[5] Privately run hair dressing salons, for example, took to playing Canto-pop in the mid-1980s as an assertion of their novelty and style.[6] A kind of generation gap emerged, according to some young fans: 'The Hong Kong and Taiwan songs are about stuff close to us; the mainland songs seem so distant.'[7] Despite having origins on the margins of China's cultural sphere, these songs were attacked in the adult moral panic that arose in the early 1980s about 'spiritual pollution' (*jingshen wuran*), a short-lived campaign against new Western influences such as bell-bottomed trousers, permed hair, and excessive makeup. This campaign, reflected in *People's Music* (*Renmin yinyue*) asking in June 1982 'How can we differentiate against decadent (*huangse*) songs?,' gained little traction and spluttered out in 1983 and 1984, as the force of new tastes and expanding choices swept aside all such publicly mobilised, conservative responses to rapid social change.[8]

Nonetheless, during the 1980s the place of popular music (*tongsu yinyue*) had to be secured in the official pantheon of music genres. Personal sentiments tended to be the domain of the folk song, often performed by an ethnic minority singer, though even these songs were usually given a more stiffened political point than was customary in the traditional versions.[9] Even as late as 1988 a writer in *Youth and Society* magazine, intended for youthful readers, remarked that he no longer was disturbed at hearing a popular song sung on television or by a family member returning from work. The change in his attitude to such music had been relatively recent. Some people became addicted to such music; others opposed it, shaking their heads and sighing at its unseemly influence on young fans who could become almost drunk with excitement at certain song performances.[10] In early 1988 a speaker at a national conference on this music noted its role in bringing pleasure and liveliness to a broad listenership. Cheng Yun admitted that he had been among those in the early 1980s prone to too readily compare the new popular songs with the 'decadent songs' (*huangse gequ*) of the 1930s that had been regularly condemned after 1949. Cheng noted the stages in the rise of the popular song since 1978, associating them with the growth in ownership of tape recorders and television sets.[11] TV serials from Hong Kong in 1981 and 1984 played a key role in introducing these songs to mainland audiences.[12] By the end of 1989, quasi-official attitudes to popular songs had become much less generous, judging by articles in *People's Music*. The titles indicated the shift: 'How did popular music fall to such a low ebb?' and 'Musical culture must pay attention to "ecological balance."'[13] Youth music had become a target in the post-Tiananmen reaction after the events of June 4, for the young people in the square had flaunted their delight in popular songs from the mainland and from other Chinese places.

Throughout the 1980s it was hard to avoid Hong Kong and Taiwan singers in the pages of the increasing number of magazines aimed at a youth readership, competing with other titles through illustrations and articles on these stars. This pitch coincided with the ubiquity of television series from Hong Kong, with their theme songs played nightly and the rise of tapes, legal and otherwise, containing this music. In 1984 Hong Kong singer Zhang Mingmin sang his song, 'My Chinese Heart' (*Wo de Zhongguo xin*) on the most watched television programme, the Spring Festival Television Gala on CCTV.[14] By the end of the decade, however, the prime position occupied by singers from these two outliers of the mainland had faded with the rise of local performers and singing styles, such as the Northwest wind.[15]

Taiwan singer Teresa Teng became a major star on the mainland in the 1980s. Her songs of unrequited love, longing, and strength, were in modern, standard Chinese and drew upon instrumentation and tune styles familiar to mainlanders. Deng's personal rise from child star to wholesome pop diva added to her appeal, which was distinctly cross-generational. Deng's songs were a staple of TV variety shows in which popular songs played alongside funny skits, comic dialogues, and more orthodox praise songs for the wisdom of the Party and government. While Deng Lijun helped create a space for the popular song, her wide appeal also prepared the ground for a more assertive, youthful, and mainland-rooted response.[16]

Beginning in the early 1980s, young Chinese singers, performers of romantic or socially responsible ballads, emerged on television and on tape. Their rise and promotion was an official response to the influence of Taiwan and Hong Kong singers on mainland audiences. They were packaged in much the same way as Teresa Teng and her Hong Kong counterparts.[17] One such star was Fei Xiang, tall with a distinctly Western look and almost blue eyes under carefully coiffed hair. His song 'A Fire in the Winter' (*Dongtian li de yi ba huo*) took off, as, despite its somewhat syrupy delivery, it captured youthful tastes and yearning for a love connection.[18] In the absence of a well-developed recording industry – the China Record Corporation (*Zhongguo changpian gongsi*) monopolised manufacture and distribution – television played a major role in popularising songs and singers. Liu Huan (born in 1963), for example, first made his name by singing the theme songs from several popular television series.[19] Given the Chinese television habit of showing a multipart series nightly until its end, such theme songs rapidly became very familiar to Chinese viewers. By the late 1980s televised youth singing contests attracted excited and partisan audiences across the nation anxious to see local stars make good on the national stage.[20] This area of cultural life was undergoing the kind of commercial transformation occurring throughout the economy. Despite a strict 1983 Ministry of Culture prohibition on performers moonlighting and making money from concerts outside of those endorsed by their own work units, many performers took advantage of more liberal times to organise their own musical events. One such singer was Mao Amin, a young ethnic singer, who in the two years prior to mid-1988 was alleged to have made herself over a quarter million yuan in this manner.[21] Some of the more fringe or youth-oriented rockers often belonged to a mainstream performing organisation, be it the Oriental Song and Dance Troupe, reconstituted after the Cultural Revolution and open to commercial opportunities of all sorts, or military performance troupes. Even the venerable China Record Corporation signed up young musicians, released albums, and tried to monopolise the distribution of tapes and disks from Hong Kong, Taiwan, and the rest of the world.[22]

Western popular music had also taken hold among young Chinese in the 1980s, aided by the tape recorder and the television set. The first noted rock concert by Western performers was by British duo Wham in Beijing's Workers' Stadium in 1985, although the first Western group, Spyz from New Zealand, had performed in China three years earlier.[23] By early 1988 a writer for *Youth and Society* wondered how music from the outside world – American country music, pop songs, disco beats, classical music reworked with a fast tempo and strong beat, Hong Kong and Taiwan songs – could now fill China's sound waves with no one really noticing the shift. Jing Yufeng thought that the appeal to Chinese youngsters of Karen Carpenter and other singers was because this music for Chinese 'clearly expresses themselves.' This music had a seductive hold in capturing feelings and attitudes about life.[24] Michael Jackson's 'Thriller' reached Chinese fans not long after its release in 1983, mostly through pirated tapes. The urban beats in the film *Breakdance* of the same year took hold of many youthful imaginations.

## CUI JIAN AND A ROCK ALTERNATIVE

Cui Jian (born 1961) and his band entered the consciousness of China's youth in May 1986 at a televised concert titled 'Fill the World with Love' (*Rang shijie chongman ai*), presented in Beijing's Workers' Gymnasium to mark the International Year of Peace. Ironically, this activity, so reminiscent of Moscow-centred socialist unity efforts of the 1950s, gave the impetus for a brand-new kind of music and musician to capture young

China's imaginations.[25] Cui's style was resolutely that of a countercultural rock singer. He often wore a Mao jacket on stage, sometimes with a 'Mao cap,' complete with red star. In an age of forward thrusting economic growth and modernisation, this was a deliberate harking back to roots and a collectivist ethos that was being lost. Many of Cui's songs also had a backward connection. His March 1989 album was titled 'Rock 'n Roll on the Road of the New Long March' (*Xin Changzheng lu shang de yaogun*). The original Long March (1934–5) was part of the founding myth of the Chinese Communist Party regime; economic reform after 1978 was sometimes likened to a new Long March. Most promoters of this notion probably did not include rock music as part of the present effort.

Cui Jian's was not China's first rock group. In 1980 at the Second Foreign Languages Institute in Beijing four classmates set up a group named after their surnames: Wanlimawang. They performed on campuses at a time when such music and bands had huge novelty value.[26] By 1982 other groups emerged. Ding Wu and Wang Di, with others, set up the 'Fuchongji Band.' its name sounding Japanese. These two and others (including Sun Guoqing) established Daruma or Weeble Wobble (*Budaoweng*, the Chinese name of the roly-poly, round-bottomed Japanese doll). They mostly sang Chinese covers of Japanese songs and reportedly were the first mainland group to use electric instruments.[27] Cui Jian's own prehistory included his first disk release in November 1985, a single titled 'The Prodigal Returns' (*Langzi gui*), emblematic of the outsider status cultivated by rock musicians.[28]

The 1986 Workers' Gymnasium peace concert put Cui Jian and Chinese rock music on the map. He distinguished himself among a hundred musicians involved in the event with two songs, 'Nothing to My Name' (*Yiwusuoyou*, literally I own nothing) and 'It's Not that I Don't Understand' (*Bu shi wo bu mingbai*). Sung in his rasping voice, accompanied by himself and others on guitar and drums, including two foreigners (a Hungarian bass player and a guitarist from Madagascar), the former song became an immediate hit among concertgoers. It was included on the album of the peace concert and then appeared in March 1989 on Cui's 'Long March' first album. Cui sang 'Nothing to My Name' at a CCTV concert on the eve of the Seoul Olympics in September 1988, reaching a huge audience. 'Nothing to My Name' became the anthem of the generation that in the spring of 1989 occupied Tiananmen Square in protest at official corruption and in favour of political reform. March 1989's concert in Beijing by ADO, Cui Jian's band, marked the height of the so-called Cui Jian current (*chao*). Eighteen-yuan tickets, considered expensive for the time, were changing hands for fifty yuan. At the concert banners were held up in the audience: 'Cui Jian, we love you' and

Figure 4.1. Cui Jian, the godfather of Chinese rock music.
*Source:* Cui Jian and Zhou Guoping, *Ziyou fengge* (Freestyle), Guilin: Guangxi shifan daxue chubanshe, 2001, p. ii.

'Peking University Cui Jian backup team' (*Beida Cui Jian houyuan dui*). The crowd insisted that Cui perform for half an hour, even though he was only one of the acts that made up the concert. Crowds sang along with Cui, waiting at his likely exit point from the venue, continuing to sing his songs.[29] Unlike the polished voices of Li Guyi or Fei Xiang, Cui's husky croak was easy for any ordinary fan to imitate or join in.

Cui had reached such a position that the *People's Daily*, the nation's newspaper of record and official mouthpiece of the Communist Party, included the words and the musical score of 'Nothing to My Name' along with an article explaining Cui's popularity in July 1988. Having noted the enormous appeal of the singer to students, teachers, workers, and private businesspeople, the writer argued that the attraction lay in the words and style of the song itself. Its gut-wrenching sound and its honest presentation of loss of love were the song's secret. 'What the work reveals are a generation's feelings: loss, confusion; what it voices are emotions from the bottom of people's hearts, so that it meshes with tens of millions of people's tastes and life experience.'[30] In part the song went:

> I've been asking you for ages:
> When will you come away with me?
>
> But you just keep laughing at me,
> 'cause I've nothing to my name.
>
> I want to give you my hopes,
> I want to give you my freedom.
> But you still keep laughing at me,
> 'cause I've nothing to my name.

As the writer in the *People's Daily* observed, the lyrics and their delivery were not downbeat, but represented instead pride and self-belief. These qualities made the song the unofficial anthem of the young protesters a year after this laudatory comment. At the end of 1988 Cui Jian received a top level of support in a 'Ten Years of the New Era Golden Songs, 1988 Golden Star' poll, despite the considerable caution about him and his band that some officials had evinced a few years earlier.[31] By early spring 1989 Cui was performing another song, 'A Piece of Red Cloth' (*Yi kuai hong bu*), often with a red strip of cloth over his eyes like a blindfold. Ostensibly another love song, the lyrics about not being able to see the real world and being led around blind ('You asked what I could see / I said I could see happiness') had obvious political undertones. *People's Daily* reported on Cui's Beijing solo concert with ADO at which he performed this song, noting the enthusiastic response to the music from the young crowd, many of whom joined in the singing.[32]

Cui Jian's appeal to China's youth from 1986 to 1989 cannot be explained by reference simply to his alleged political engagement. Cui himself consistently adopted an ambivalent attitude to politics that was not just a self-protective strategy. His songs were much more than politics, for the singer and his fans. They can be read as a deliberate attempt to put politics in its place, by making music out of wider, more personal issues of confusion and alienation. Politics is just one part of this youthful domain of searching for attachment and loyalty.[33] Writing in the relatively august pages of *People's Music* in the excitement of the spring of 1989, young critic Jin Zhaojun cited the lyrics of several of Cui's songs as evidence of his ability to capture the anxieties and aspirations of the young.[34] As another writer had noted in the summer of 1988, '"Nothing to My Name" has become this generation's shared name, and the birthmark of their own cultural emergence.' Liu Qing went on to observe:

> These people, all turning up in the world around 1970, have not gone through any kind of large-scale difficulty. Their understanding of the 'Cultural Revolution' comes only from textbooks. They're regarded by their

parents' generation as lucky children, because they have had a stable and regular education, they have had the opportunity to enter university, have had their every financial need and anxiety taken care of by doting parents and they are able to find work and make their fortunes. They've had the kinds of richness and freedom to make spiritual and material choices denied to our people until now. And yet amazingly they say to their parents: we have nothing to our name.[35]

Liu argued that this new cohort of young people were more realistic in their thinking than the Cultural Revolution sent-down youths that the poet Bei Dao spoke for in his 1976 poem, 'The Answer' (Huida), which included the lines: 'Let me tell you world / I – do –not – believe!'(wo bu xiangxin). The younger folk saw through the philosophical and political focus of the older group and were just not interested in it. Such older obsessions were futile and lies. Liu Qing noted: 'As I see it "Nothing to My Name" on the one hand is a bold declaration of the fervor of their rejection of tradition. On the other hand, it is an unavoidable lament full of loss and perplexity.'[36] The generation growing up in the era of reform and opening up could simultaneously feel an unexpected jealousy for the earlier certainty of their youthful predecessors, while sensibly carving out a new space for themselves. But the popularity of 'Nothing to My Name' did not mean that contemporary youngsters lived in a 'spiritual vacuum' (jiazhi zhenkong). 'Their thorough suspicions, thorough rejection and thorough tiredness ultimately amount to their own particular set of values, which I would call a roving spirit (liulang jingshen) ... understandings of conventionally significant socialisation and self identity are just hard to apply mechanically to this generation. Because "roving" has no sense of belonging, so individualism is another of their most important characteristics.'[37] Liu Qing went on to note that action was a watchword of the new youth: 'I feel good, so I do it.' In the summer of 1988, when for many Chinese the possibilities for change seemed at their greatest since 1949, Liu's analysis of the appeal of Cui Jian's most popular song hit the mark. Liu Qing labeled the youth of the 1980s the 'Newborn Generation' (Xinsheng dai). When coupled with an awareness of contemporary Japanese discussions of young people as 'New Humans' (Xin renlei, in Japanese Shin-jinrui), the label began to stick. It was to be succeeded in the first decade of the new century by '1970s generation' (70 hou), '1980s generation' (80 hou), and its successors.

Despite his close association with the student protestors in Tiananmen Square in the spring of 1989, Cui Jian proved remarkably resilient, seemingly undamaged by the more restrictive politics of the post-June 4 period. Liaoning Youth even featured his song 'Fake Travelling Monk' (Jia xingseng), with lyrics and score, on the inside front over of their National Day 1989 issue, embellished with a portrait of Cui and labeled

'Song Request.' Its lyrics read in part: 'I want to go from white to black....
If you love me, don't fear regrets.'[38] In January 1990 he was back on the
concert stage in the Beijing Workers' Gymnasium, in a fundraiser for the
Asian Games to be held in Beijing that year. A Peking University graduate
student (possibly remembering when the song first became a hit) remarked
at the time on the enduring power of 'Nothing to My Name':

> The force of this song causes people to feel overwhelmed, and unable to dis-
> cuss together with other people. As soon as you hear it you are completely
> honest and not bad tempered. When I hear [the song] I feel shaken up. One
> song embodies a generation's frustrations. Hearing this song, I know who I
> am. My basic nature should be that of the guy in the song. Songs I listened
> to before it were all purely entertainment. But [this song] definitely isn't. I
> found myself in it. Good songs are like that: such a song comes to you and
> makes you want to come to it. Really, Cui Jian is so great! He allowed a
> generation to find its standpoint in his song.[39]

As this fan suggests, the appeal of Cui Jian lay in his declarations that
the task of rock music was to take off masks and be honest and direct.
Confronted with the music, all people, no matter high or low, were
equal.[40] In a society undergoing rapid change and growing expectations,
these sentiments had an obvious impact on the young.

Cui Jian continued to negotiate the collective memory of his own and
other generations. His 1994 album, *Balls under the Red Flag* (*Hongqi xia
de dan*), with its use of the red flag metaphor for the unchanged government and its emphasis on the lack of ideals and loss of direction, served as
a powerful and appealing indictment of China's situation. The title balls,
worn smooth under the red flag, represented the personalities of the singer
and his audience. Chinese unwillingness to cause trouble and an urge to
comply outwardly with society's expectations were the target of the title
song. Young people, prone to rebellion in any society, and all those who
had seen the liberal promise of 1988 smashed in June the following year,
could read the song as a lament for a lost but still vivid past.[41]

## OTHER ROCKERS

Cui Jian was not alone in carving out a new space for rock music and
the youth culture that it fostered. Among other rock groups that emerged
alongside Cui were Tang Dynasty (*Tangchao*) and Black Panther (*Heibao
yuedui*). The two band names reflect two streams in youth consciousness
in the mid-1980s: the native and the global. The Tang dynasty (C.E. 618–
907) was an era of exceptional cosmopolitan relations between China
and the rest of Asia and the world. The Tang capital in Chang'an (today's
Xi'an) included quarters for Arab, Jewish, and other traders. This period
is also regarded by Chinese as a highpoint in the development of their

cultural heritage. Naming a rock band after the Tang was both an ironic comment on the new music's foreignness and an expression of native pride. The black panther was a sleek and powerful symbol: The name had no connection with the African American political group. Usually, however, there was a more direct linkage made between the rock group and another American phenomenon, Bon Jovi.[42] Black Panther pioneered tours by Beijing-based rock bands to the economically advanced south of the country, playing in Shenzhen in May 1989.[43] Cui Jian and others in the 1990s followed their example, often when large-scale gigs in the capital proved politically unwelcome. These kinds of concerts – Cui Jian attracted thirty-five thousand fans to a 1995 concert in Zhengzhou in Henan[44] – were occasions during which the enthusiasm of hordes of young fans was clear: weeping, screams, waving of clothes, cigarette lighters, and flags, and generally grooving to the music. These were all behaviours familiar at a Western rock concert and underscored the similar rebellious appeal of rock to China's youth.[45]

Tang Dynasty had been formed in 1988 and initially included two American Chinese musicians, an international connection that influenced the new music they played. The band specialised in heavy metal (translated into Chinese as literally as the English: *zhongjinshu*). All relatively tall, the band members grew their hair extra long, adding to the dramatic effect when they performed. In 1992 their album 'Dream Return to the Tang Dynasty' (*Menghui Tangchao*) was distributed in Hong Kong, Taiwan, Japan, South Korea, and Southeast Asia.[46] Another group that had started in the late 1980s singing standard Western pop songs and then in August 1989 began to take an independent path was the band '1989.' Even the name, a provocative choice, reflected rebellion.[47] Also worth noting was the all-female band with the assertive name Cobra (*Yanjingshe*), two of whose songs were titled '1966' and 'Our Own Heaven' (*Ziji de tiantang*).[48]

Sun Guoqing (born in 1959), originally a cello graduate of the Central Conservatory, started his rock career as a member of Daruma, China's first home-grown rock band. Sun was among the first mainland artists to record an album for a Hong Kong record company. He was among a number of singers who made their names in the mid-1980s by turning venerable and well-written songs of praise for Chairman Mao and the Communist Party into rock songs by altering the tempo and adding a heavy beat and guitar instrumentation. These singers included Li Xiaowen, noted for his reworking of 'Chairman Mao's Words Are Remembered Deep in Our Hearts' (*Mao zhuxi de huar ji zai women de xinkan li*), and Zhao Li, whose 'On Beijing's Golden Hill' (*Beijing de Jinshan shang*) was a rock version of a much-loved song. At a concert in the Capital Gymnasium, the home for the emergence of Beijing

Figure 4.2. Tang Dynasty, a rock band formed in 1988.
*Source:* Lu Lingtao and Li Yang, eds, *Nahan: weile Zhongguo cengjing de yaogun* (Scream: For China's former rock), Guilin: Guangxi shifan daxue chubanshe, 2008, p. 154.

rock music, in July 1988 Sun Guoqing belted out 'Great Oaks from Little Acorns Grow' (*Gaolou wanzhang pingdi qi*) in his inimitable style. The packed young crowd, mostly there for the Northwest Wind songs promised in the programme, clearly enjoyed the rock song and also the considerable frisson that came with turning this raspy rock treatment on a classic of the Cultural Revolution.[49]

The contexts, international, technical, and industrial, in which youth rock emerged and grew in China were integral to the paths it took in the 1980s and the following two decades. In parallel with the increasing globalisation of the Chinese economy, youth cultures took on global dimensions. We have already noted the participation of foreign musicians in the rise of rock music in Beijing in the early 1980s, when youths associated with embassies in the city formed groups with local friends. Part of the appeal of Cui Jian's ADO band was its international mien. The influx of foreign songs, not just rock music, formed the background to these developments. Television was an important vehicle for the promotion of foreign and new local music. Theme songs from foreign and domestic serials, concert shows televised on festive and other occasions, and special programmes all brought new music to viewers, including the young. While Cui Jian and his buddies (the revival of the Chinese equivalent expression *gemenr* in the second half of the 1980s is notable) were doing their thing with foreign band members and performing in bars in Beijing where foreigners hung out, there was another route to forming your own band. In late December 1987 China's first 'private enterprise art troupe' (*getihu biaoyan yishu tuanti*) was established in Tianjin, 120 kilometres from the capital. Formed by fifteen unemployed youngsters and farming music hobbyists who pooled over one thousand yuan, the group took the name 'song Nirvana' (*Ge tihu*: a homonym of the Chinese for 'private entrepreneur').[50] A month later a writer for *People's Daily* noted the importance of the cultural marketplace where equal competition allowed new music from anywhere to compete for consumers' attention. Control of rogue elements in the new culture was impossible without acknowledging the role of the market in promoting it.[51]

Another new mechanism for music distribution was the karaoke laser disc player. Beginning in the mid-1980s, Chinese cities and towns sported signs for *kala OK*, the Chinese transliteration (including the two Roman letters) of the Japanese word for 'empty orchestra.' Beijing's first karaoke venue opened in June 1989, hardly an auspicious start. But the activity soon proved as popular in the city as it had become in other parts of East Asia.[52] Corresponding with the rise of private enterprise, karaoke bars offered a means for entrepreneurs to make money from a new means of entertainment. Most of the songs available in these places, however, were foreign, which was bad for Chinese rockers and others, but did attract young and old crooners to the facilities.[53] Home karaoke players enjoyed brisk sales in the early 1990s, with hundreds of thousands sold in Beijing and Shanghai. As one young Beijing factory worker noted, 'I can practice at home to get better, then go to the karaoke lounge. In my workshop section more than thirty young colleagues have bought machines.'[54] As an army researcher on youth issues noted, karaoke was an ideal, healthy, and collective outlet for youth to express themselves. Vigilance, however, was needed to root out harmful songs and to ensure Chinese songs received enough attention. Some youths even wore the currently fashionable slogan T-shirts to karaoke lounges, displaying their negative expressions to young patrons.[55]

Foreign recording companies played an important part in facilitating the reach of the new music. One device important in the 1990s in particular was the *dakou* CD. These were imported music CDs with a small bite taken out of the edge (spoiling the last song), to allow their discounted disposal on the Chinese market. The CDs brought a wider range than might be expected to young Chinese listeners. Their distribution was mostly through stall holders and small shops that also acted as conduits for pirated videotapes, tapes, VCDs, and CDs.[56] Canny recording companies in Hong Kong and Taiwan took an early interest in the rise of mainland rockers. Soon after the release of their first albums in China, stars like Cui Jian and Tang Dynasty were signing contracts with music companies in the British colony and beyond. A glimpse of the music tape market in 1989 reveals an increasingly complex picture. Where once the China Record Corporation had a monopoly there were now over 200 producers of tapes which in 1988 made over one hundred million tapes, mostly of popular music. This built on rapidly expanding ownership of tape players, particularly after 1984. Young persons made up the bulk of consumers of these tapes, but the commercial interests of the producers were the main driver of the direction of developments.[57] The second half of 1988 was described as the most chaotic in the marketplace, despite the regulatory efforts of the Ministry of Radio, Film, and Television. The buying and selling of 'permit papers' (*zhaozhi*) with the required tape registration number (similar to book and magazine standardised numbers) had grown out of control in the rush to make money.[58] Indeed popular music was one of the first areas of Chinese life where commercial realities were encountered by local consumers and entrepreneurs within the first ten years of economic reform. The nature of the encounter helps explain the rampant nature of piracy in music and motion pictures that has characterised the Chinese market since.[59]

## THE NORTHWEST WIND

One of the most notable new trends in Chinese writing, avidly devoured by young readers, in the early 1980s had been the 'search for roots' (*xungen*) movement. Writers of fiction in particular set their stories in the Chinese countryside, often in primitive conditions, or borrowed from the newly imported magical realist writings of Latin America to create fantastical versions of Chinese folk customs. This writing trend can be interpreted as a response to the Soviet-inspired straitjacket of Cultural Revolution orthodoxy. The new writing offered new, China-based mythologies and alternative, non-Marxist or pre-Marxist versions of social relations. Many of the writers had been sent-down youth in the 1970s, so drew upon their own experiences rooted in Chinese soil. Out of this root seeking also emerged a remarkable television documentary series, broadcast twice in the summer of 1988 by China Central Television. *River Elegy* (*Heshang*, literally a river that does not reach the sea) was the work of relatively young filmmakers and writers intent on presenting an overview of Chinese history different from standard Marxist accounts. They emphasised the nation's need to leave the native, yellow earth and plunge into the global, blue sea. In early June 1989 a student flag flying in Tiananmen Square carried the words 'national elegy' (*guoshang*, suggesting a nation unfulfilled).

It took time for Chinese popular music to establish its own roots. We have seen how the influx of Hong Kong and Taiwan pop songs inspired local emulation, with and without official encouragement. Cui Jian and the film *Red Sorghhum* were key players in youth music going native. Although they did not initiate the new song style, both contributed to the rise of the Northwest Wind, a new kind of pop music with folk roots in the loess plateau of northern Shaanxi in northwest China. Peasants there had been singing songs in the *xintianyou* style for generations: The melodies tended to be lonesome songs of loss or rugged pride. Listening to these folk melodies, it was easy to imagine lone figures on mountain tops roaring their anger, sorrow, or love to the skies.[60] In 1986 Wang Sidao, a singer attached to the Pacific Music and Film Corporation, launched her song titled '*Xintianyou.*' She sang in a forceful, throaty way in the manner of Shaanxi singers. But the label for the new kind of pop music came from Tian Zhen's singing of 'Hills of Yellow Earth' (*Huangtu gaopo*). Her lyrics included the lines: 'My home is in the yellow earth hills. / The wind blows from the slope. / No matter if it's a southwest wind, or a northwest wind, they are all my songs.' Cui Jian strictly speaking was not a Northwest Wind singer, but his style, seen in 'Nothing to My Name,' was so similar that he became associated with the success of the new style and made his own contributions to it.

The appeal of these songs, seen on television in particular, represented a reaction against the predominance of Hong Kong, Taiwan, and soft music from southern China.[61] The Northwest Wind was a temporary phenomenon driven by the particular circumstances of the late 1980s when Chinese rock was in its infancy and the very concept of popular music, as we have seen, was novel.

> [Y]oung people suddenly felt that those Hong Kong and Taiwan songs had become floating on air and insubstantial. They would go no further with all that chattering about self, lovey-dovey (*chanchanmianmian*), indecisive, feeble chants. They used the plain 'Northwest Wind' to replace the sweet, smooth, charming and gentle; they took up the in-your-face and intense force to displace the subtle, and the far reaching, remote and vigorous instead; they used anything-goes and vigorous feelings to remove those old ways in songs. They took up the brutal and the bleak to attack the pain caused by the excessively soft and the too gentle [in those other songs].[62]

A nativist stand, rooted firmly in the dust of the yellow earth, is redolent in this 1993 assessment of the new song style's impact on young China. Similar admiration for its Chinese qualities was expressed in the pages of *Huhehot Evening News* in Inner Mongolia in the summer of 1988. One reprinted article was subheaded: 'Seeking a genuinely Chinese proud style.' It reported how fifty-four thousand tickets for the Capital Gymnasium Northwest Wind concert in early July had sold out in a few hours. At Peking University the campus broadcasting station frequently played this music. When the students returned to their dorms in the evening, the buildings were filled with the sound of these songs.[63] The directness of the new song style – nothing to my name means nothing to my name, my hometown is not beautiful means just that – was a major part of its attraction, mirrored in other aesthetic fields by the late 1980s.[64] One writer in *People's Music* in early 1989 resorted to quoting American psychologist Erik Erikson on youth development to answer his question as to why university students felt a strong connection with the Northwest Wind. Tu Keshan explained, however, after formative years being looked after by parents and teachers, students entered university to find, not the rose-tinted campus of their imaginings, but a cold, friendless space in which they had to rely on their own psychological resources. Naturally the proud, lone cry against the world of the singer in Northwest Wind songs had immediate appeal. So too the directness and lack of adornment of these songs engaged students, even when they sang of love, a major student obsession.[65]

The new-style rock music with local roots really took off among China's youth after the release of the film *Red Sorghum* in February 1988.[66] The raucous, proud songs of the sedan bearers and distillery workers in the free, natural world in the film greatly enhanced its impact, particularly on young men in North China, who were perhaps more inclined to connect with the men in the film than were their counterparts in the smoother, reputedly more sophisticated southern centres like Shanghai.[67] The work of composer Zhao Jiping (born 1945), himself from the Northwest, with lyrics in part by director Zhang Yimou, the film's songs extended the reach of the movie far beyond the cinema. Soon tourists in the Northwest were being entertained by rollicking sedan chair carriers performing to the songs, which had become a kind of reinvented folk song.[68]

By late 1988 a writer in *People's Music* was wondering how long the Northwest Wind would blow. Young fans, Han Yinghong suggested, could be fickle and abandon these songs should a well-written song in another style come by. Blazing new trails was, after all, the attraction of popular music.[69] A few months later, some critics were lamenting the sameness of current popular music, with bluntness in excess and not enough sweet polish.[70] Even in mid-1988 an anonymous music expert was quoted as describing the music as 'neither local nor foreign' (*tu bu tu, yang bu yang*), but 'claptrap to cajole the public' (*huazhongquchong*).[71] In April 1989 in Guangzhou the audience at the National Popular Song Singer Contest reportedly cried out, after three hours of items, 'sing something we like!' in reaction to the stream of Northwest Wind songs.[72] By late May, at a time when students were occupying Tiananmen Square, critic Jin Zhaojun was back in the *People's Daily* somewhat ruefully commenting on the decline of popularity of the Northwest Wind, even in its Beijing stronghold. For Jin, the commercialisation of the song style, with every singer adding this kind of song to his or her repertoire (and turning female voices to sound like men) had led to its declining fortunes, starting in the south and moving north.[73] Even the anthem of the Northwest Wind craze, 'The Hills of Yellow Earth,' came under direct attack. In an article dripping with sarcasm, Duan Ruizhong wondered why, in an age of rapid modernisation and looking to the future, these songs dwelt on backward, rustic notions of home. He also took strong exception to the ubiquity of the Northwest Wind songs, which were a reminder of the totalitarian ambitions of the Cultural Revolution regime.[74] A vigorous defence of the song appeared in August 1989, two months after the young people who were its biggest fans had been cleared from the centre of Beijing. Xiong Xiaoming and Li Shiding argued that it was perfectly natural for people in the midst of rapid modernisation to look forward to the future and look back with regret at what was being lost.[75] This was certainly the attitude of the new generation in the late 1980s, who felt a degree of nostalgia for what they thought of as the simplicity (and honesty) of earlier decades.[76]

In the new century a curious remnant of the Northwest Wind was seen on China's television screens, heard in bars, and occasionally on stage. Abao (original name Zhang Shaoting) performed dressed as a Northwestern peasant, with a wooly sheepskin jerkin over old-fashioned black pants, cloth shoes, and a white towel knotted on his head. Born in 1969 near Datong in Shanxi, at age twelve Abao succeeded in the fierce competition to enter the Datong Arts School. After graduating at senior high level in 1986, just as the Northwest Wind was beginning to blow, he began a career as a wandering singer. The CCTV talent contest 'Star Road' (*Xingguang dadao*) in 2005 brought Abao to national attention.[77] In contrast to the 1980s Northwest Wind, Abao sang in a more genuinely folk style, but with the rasping directness that had endeared those older songs to young China. In a new world of gleaming modernity, Abao's rustic air, combined with obvious marketing skills, was a remarkable reminder of one of contemporary youth culture's roots.

## INTO THE 1990S

At the turn of the new decade, the Northwest Wind was blowing out of puff; its performers and anthems had become perhaps too familiar, especially as Chinese entrepreneurs tried to cash in on the craze. This is not the place to present a comprehensive survey of pop music in the 1990s, but several trends became apparent. There was a weakness in talent available, as the first wave of stars who had real (often classically trained) skills gave way to younger talent. What new talent that did appear was often somewhat manufactured by record promoters eager to make a quick

killing in an undeveloped or distorted market. Investment in the industry was fragmented and inadequate, hardly surprising given the rise of
pirated tapes and CDs and the beginnings of the large-scale importing of
*dakou* CDs.[78] But new developments should not be overlooked. In 1990
a group of high school students formed Matchbox (*Huochaihe*), inspired
by Taiwan boy band Little Tigers (*Xiaohu dui*). The following year, twenty-two high school soloists or groups competed in a national contest for
high school pop musicians in Beijing.[79] The contestants' ages indicate that
pop music was no longer the domain of performers in their twenties. In
February 1993 a mock 'farewell party' was held at Maxim's, the French
restaurant in Beijing that had seen many Cui Jian and other concerts, for
the shift of rock music from underground to aboveground.[80]

There were more independent, underground developments in the music
scene in Beijing and elsewhere. New kinds of performing venues, such as
bars and clubs frequented by Chinese and foreign patrons, became available in the nineties, providing spaces in which more experimental and
less commercial sounds could be trialed. Beijing's Modern Sky record
company, for example, emerged mid-decade as a vehicle for these new
rock groups. One way to attract bands and to spread knowledge of them
was through music festivals. The Modern Sky and Midi outdoor summer rock concerts had small beginnings in the mid-1990s. By the middle
of the following decade, now held in places like Haidian Park, near the
college quarter of Beijing, they were attracting a mix of older fans from
early days and newer, younger followers. In the new century, performers
included local acts and foreign bands.[81] From the start Chinese punk
bands such as New Pants (*Xin kuzi*) offered youthful fans a rebellious
alternative to mainstream rock and the sedate presentation of popular
music to a wider audience through television.[82] In a study focused on the
mid-1990s, Jeroen de Kloet observes that, like their counterparts elsewhere, young musicians and their audiences in China relished the resistant qualities of their music. He examines the various music 'scenes' in
Beijing, using a term that Ryan Moore offers as a useful alternative to
the term *subcultures*.[83] De Kloet traces rock's articulation of space, mapping a geography of Chinese rock that locates Hong Kong and Taiwan
in the 'commercial south,' and emphasises the central role of the 'cultural
north,' explaining why Beijing became China's rock music capital.[84]

The view from Xi'an offers a way to modify our understanding of
the development of youth music in China. Pop music, geared to a youth
audience, emerged in the city on the back of a so-called moonlighting
(*zouxue*) craze encouraged by the arrival of Taiwan and Hong Kong
popular songs. Bands and performers, often with professional musical
backgrounds, played at freelance gigs around town. The first such group
formed in 1982. Named New Bud Band (*Xin lei yuetuan*), they created

their own songs and also wrote lyrics to sing to U.S. and European pop music. They made several tours to Beijing, where they performed with the highly professional Oriental Song and Dance Troupe. In 1988 Xi'an's first rock group, In a Twinkling (*Shunjian yuedui*), brought a number of accomplished soloists together, including Li Xin (then thirteen) and former members of New Bud. Several members had links to the Xi'an Conservatory, a pattern of rock band formation seen decades earlier in Britain and other countries. The newly established TV unit in the Xi'an Film Studio, which had produced *Red Sorghum*, made a two-part television programme in 1989 on rock music featuring works by In a Twinkling, but the show never aired. The band remained a largely underground phenomenon. Again following apparently global rock band patterns, In a Twinkling broke up the following year. Xi'an youth had to wait until December 1993 for the first original rock music concert in the city. Organised by the band Flying (*Fei yuedui*) at the Xi'an Foreign Languages Institute, this student origin followed the pattern set a decade earlier in Beijing. This was the first time Xi'an audiences had heard and seen their own, home-grown rock bands. The close ties between professionals and rock was reflected in the person of Cheng Gang, a 1992 graduate of the composing department of the Xi'an Conservatory who hosted a radio programme on rock music. Cheng formed his own band, Dinosaur Egg (*Konglongdan*) in the spring of 1995. His radio role gave Cheng a platform to promote rock music to Xi'an listeners, primarily the young. That same year several bands combined to issue a rock album, *Northwest Big Rock, Volume 1* (*Xibei da yaogun, di yi ji*).[85]

A report on these Xi'an developments sheds light on the actual conditions which aspiring rockers, both players and fans, faced in the provincial city. Given the usual loudness of the music, it was hard to practice in the neighbourhoods. Finding space at a school or similar institution meant facing threats from people who disliked the music and what it represented to the young. Basement bars and nightclubs could be used during the day. Nonprofit 'parties' (the English word was used) in these venues provided ways to find listeners and fans, and to hone musical and performance skills. The other mode was concerts at tertiary educational institutions around the city. These events made it easy for rock's biggest fans, college students, to enjoy the music. They paid about five yuan for a ticket, a sum within reach of many students but which barely covered costs of hiring lighting and sound equipment. Occasionally bands had opportunities to perform on real stages, but they usually could not play real rock music as these events were designed to make the kind of money that student audiences could not provide and featured a range of music.[86] Rock music retained its marginal status in Xi'an, with much of the action underground and in the hands of youthful enthusiasts. Many of Xi'an's best rockers went on to Beijing seeking the big time, for that city was China's rock music capital, the focus of youth fans' attention.[87]

As had been the case decades earlier in Western countries, the response of social commentators and sociologists to the youth music phenomenon ran the usual gamut from condemnation and alarm to welcoming diversity and expression. One Shanghai radio producer complained in late 1990 of the official attitude that underrated popular music and privileged more conventional bel canto-style songs. Having encouraged pop music celebrations and karaoke competitions on television to raise public support for the 1990 Asian Games in Beijing, the organisers used only old-style songs at the opening ceremony. As an expression of youthful enthusiasm and attitudes, rock music had a legitimate place in Chinese popular culture.[88] At a discussion in Shanghai on rock music's popularity in late 1990, one speaker observed that Beijing rock (in the hands of Cui Jian and Wang Di, among others), had a political tinge, unlike its Shanghai counterpart.[89] A rock musician attending the roundtable noted that there were seven rock bands currently in Shanghai. Zheng Yaohua argued:

> For Chinese, rock music doesn't provide a kind of big sound, but a new kind of attitude: You can do anything; whatever you want to do, just do it...one part of rock declares 'I've got these worries' and another part says, 'This is how I'm forgetting my worries.'... For us here, novels won't cut it, jeans won't cut it, break-dancing won't cut it. It seems we can't find a form to express youth's real (literally serious *yansu*) culture: maybe ROCK is an opportunity.[90]

A survey of 300 high-school and university students in Anhui in 1993 came to similar conclusions. Almost half the students agreed with the statement that 'a singer's performance takes me to a place I like, far from the worries of complex society.' Forty-five percent felt the singers 'enlivened busy lives,' while half that number felt a collective sympathy with the similar fans around them. Only about one-quarter admitted to liking rock music, compared to almost two-thirds who liked Hong Kong and Taiwan songs. Students could choose more than one type of music in the survey, so one-third also selected 'foreign stars singing in English' and one-third selected 'mainland folk music.' Three in ten chose the safe, mainstream, 'mainland popular songs.' Perhaps a clearer indication of the resistant or rebellious attractions of pop music was the fifty-four percent of respondents who liked 'lively song and dance performances, but not affected ones,' a dig at the carefully crafted emotions of Chinese bel canto and other singers. Five point six nine percent boldly confessed to liking 'irritating, provoking performances' (*cijixing you tiaodouxing deyanchang*), though not one female high schooler indicated this.[91] The excitement of collective enjoyment of music that annoyed adults was evident at the 'New Masses' concerts presented in Shenzhen in 1994 and 1995. These shows included an American saxophonist, a Japanese musician, and groups from the newly developed cities Hong Kong and Guangzhou. The use of the hoary Communist word 'masses' was a distinct provocation.[92]

Interviews in 2002 with university and high school students and young employees revealed the extent to which popular music infused young Chinese lives.[93] Wu Hao, a nineteen-year-old freshman at Harbin Engineering University, often listened to American rap music, R & B, soul, pop rock, rock, and soft rock. To him 'the feeling of Korean pop songs is "cool," lively, and has the power of youth to it. You can feel your heart set free (*shifang*), an identification of feelings and a sudden enlightenment towards life (*ganqing de rentong he dui rensheng de dunwu*).'[94] In an interesting note of generational succession in pop music tastes, Wu Ze, a twenty-four-year-old salesman from Heilongjiang, nominated Liu Huan's 'Starting Over' (*Congtou zailai*) as the song that had most influenced him, as it expressed what his mother had been through in her youth.[95] Guangdong high schoolers in 2002 not surprisingly asserted their preference for Hong Kong singers, who mostly sang in Cantonese.[96] Interviews with Beijing high school and university students and with employed youth showed half-generational change: A fourteen-year-old high schooler spoke of first being aware of pop music through South Korean groups H.O.T. and NRG, while a twenty-five-year-old journalist and a university student cited songs by Liu Huan as their first experience of popular music. One high school student said she liked to listen to Hong Kong and Taiwan music, though occasionally she put on a foreign album, such as one by the Backstreet Boys. Sheng Ying, a seventeen-year-old, did not like Korean groups, as she thought the dyed hair made them look too weird and alternative (*linglei*). Li Jie, a teacher at a university, confessed that in senior high his taste shifted from boy bands like Little Tigers from Taiwan to rock bands, especially Cui Jian and then Black Panther. Rock could really express inner feelings. Now twenty-five, he rarely listened to music. Westlife had their fans among Beijing senior high students. One complained that a lot of her male classmates liked foreign rock music and rappers, which she felt led to a negative outlook on life. Wang Hong, twenty-five, noted that her parents liked Li Guyi and similar singers on New Year's television concerts. They regarded songs as having a worldview (*you sixiang*), not like today when it was all about expressing love and feelings. Li Jie observed wisely that the Peking opera his parents liked to listen to was the 'popular music' of their generation, a reference to the model operas of the Cultural Revolution decade.[97] Cui Jian found favour with some younger fans, those born in the 1980s and 1990s, being regarded as the godfather (*jiaofu*) of Chinese rock.[98] All these comments reflected the diversity of popular music influences and origins by the new century.

## THE KOREAN WAVE

A new cultural influence in the 1990s expanded the arsenal of tools for self-expression available to Chinese youth. This was the influx of cultural productions from South Korea from the late 1990s onward. The impact of the Korean Wave (*Hanliu*, or Korean current: in Korean *Hallyu*) was felt across Chinese society, not just by teenagers and young adults. Television, a major factor in the rise of popular music and rock, played a similar part in this cultural development. Television drama serials, presenting stories of family tribulation and romantic misunderstandings in contemporary South Korean society, transferred well to the small screen in China (and indeed in Japan, Hong Kong, and elsewhere). One suggested reason for Chinese interest in Korean television soap operas was the shared Confucian ideals of family hierarchy and loyalty that the serials tended to promulgate.[99] Certainly some of the biggest fans of the TV soaps from Korea, dubbed skilfully into Chinese, were women in their thirties or older. The tribulations of mothers, daughters-in-law, and other inhabitants of the world of Korean serial drama seem to have had a resonance with the lives, or at least attitudes, of such Chinese viewers. Some Korean serials were aimed at a younger audience, or included storylines about teenagers and sons and daughters reaching marriageable age. We should not overlook the broader context of interest in South Korea as a kind of model for modernisation for China. It was essentially a highly conservative model that suggested that traditional values could coexist with modern development.[100] Koreans' trajectory toward prosperity and modernity could show ordinary Chinese viewers what the future might entail for Chinese more persuasively than similar images of Western societies. Universal television ownership, a highly developed pirate DVD and publishing market, and increased access to and use of the Internet helped create the essential conditions for the rush of the Korean Wave.[101]

The Korean world of rhythms had the greatest impact on young China, particularly in the new millennium. Music stars from South Korea became stars in the People's Republic, followed by their big and small screen acting counterparts. Young Chinese began to copy the music, clothing, and hairstyles of their Korean idols. Among the first young Koreans to gain a strong following in China was the five-person boy band H.O.T., who topped pop charts in the mainland and Taiwan in 1998.[102] A similar impact was enjoyed by CLON, a singing and dancing boy band who also performed in Beijing in 1998. Their Chinese name, *Kulong*, combined the local slang for *cool* (*ku*, literally cruel or excessive) with dragon, an apparently irresistible and somewhat pan-East Asian nationalistic combination.[103] As one young Chinese remarked: 'The people in Korean TV dramas all pay attention to clothes and make-up, making them pleasing to look at. Those are much better to watch than our so-called idol dramas. We are all Asian, and look pretty much the same, so it's easy to accept those fashions that have gone through a fusion of East and West.'[104] It was in South Korea, rather than Japan, that the fad for dying one's hair blonde or some other colour first took hold and spread to Japan, China, and elsewhere in East Asia. By early 2002, a Korean commentator noted:

> The brand new species (*xinxin renlei*) in China is using what amounts to the monthly salary of a university teacher to buy expensive, oversized Korean-made T-shirts, low-rise pants, and wearing wobbly, over-sized fashionable sports shoes, with a Samsung MP3 player, from top to toes thus uniformed for battle. From Beijing, Shanghai, and Guangzhou to eastern region Special Economic Zones, all places have such figures.[105]

By 2008 the China–Korean cultural nexus was strong. Parts of the Chinese film industry, for example, were closely tied with South Korean counterparts, providing investment money and post-production skills to many Chinese, Hong Kong, and Taiwan productions. Joint productions and location shooting in China became almost commonplace in the first decade of the twenty-first century. These ties cemented the influence of Korean youth culture in the People's Republic.

For many youth in China, the more unruly and most modern elements in South Korean culture held the most appeal. There was crossover, however, as some singing stars first made their names in domestic dramas. This was the case of Jung Ji-hoon, one of the young actors in *Full House* (*Langman manwu*, 2004), who became better known as Rain, pop star and East Asian mega-celebrity.[106] After the boy band H.O.T. performed in front of thirteen thousand fans in Beijing in February 2000, Chinese magazine *Contemporary Singers* (*Dangdai getan*) for five continuous months sold record numbers of monthly issues by featuring the band and their cohorts. Issues with H.O.T. sold four hundred thousand copies, and those with the band NRG sold half that number. Korean pop culture had a particular appeal to Chinese aged from fifteen to their twenties.[107] When H.O.T. failed to take first place among foreign bands in a contest on Shanghai's Oriental Radio in 2001, forty upset fans marched to People's Square in downtown Shanghai with banners demanding that the station admit that the competition had been rigged.[108] Young fans sounded like teenagers everywhere:

> In fact, the people who should listen to H.O.T. are some super-serious teachers ... [the songs] aren't hard to appreciate, you just need to want to

hear them.... Only we know what our needs are. We only want to live our lives in our own way. We don't want adults deciding for us, because we are the future![109]

An English researcher reports some of the fan statements she garnered in 2003 from Internet chatroom responses to her questions on the attractions of Korean pop stars:

The first time I saw [H.O.T.'s] second video – My God! They were so cute. Their cuteness was unrivalled. I'd never seen such cute guys. I instantly liked them. Completely the opposite image from 'front line warriors' [the alleged Chinese male ideal].

Many of their songs have expressed out heart's feelings ... the pressure at our schools is so high, the H.O.T. brothers' songs give us lots of encouragement. They are our companions in study.[110]

Doing fieldwork on the Chinese Internet and elsewhere in mid-2003, Rowan Pease reported an impression that the interest in Korean pop music had waned, occupying a mere two percent of the imported music market (which counted Hong Kong and Taiwan music as imports).[111] Given the importance of the hard-to-measure pirate music market in China, this figure may be a misleading indicator of youth enthusiasm. Certainly in the years after 2005, Chinese bookstores displayed well-thumbed copies of fan books on a range of Korean pop stars and film actors, both men and women.[112] A typical fan book is *New Century Edition Korean Wave Summit Archive* (*Xin shiji ban Hanliu dianfeng dang'an*), edited by a Hong Kong-based writer but published in Hainan in south China in 2003. It offered fans a comprehensive directory of Korean pop stars, actors, TV serials, and films, all richly illustrated. The birthdates, height, weight, family makeup, blood type, and other details for each of the featured performers are provided to readers.[113]

Korean television serials were the major vehicle for the transmission of cultural influence on China's youth. In 2002 sixty-seven Korean titles were shown on Chinese television. Two years later CCTV broadcast three such titles, one of which had 200 parts. Hunan Satellite TV, an innovator in Chinese media, increased its nationwide viewership figures by a multiple of three through showing Korean serials in 2005.[114] The Chinese convention of showing local and imported serials at the same hour, often in primetime (the 'golden hour' or primetime in China), daily, weekends included, until the series was finished probably compounded the impact of these dramas. A weekly screening or a twice a week show could not have achieved such high profiles for the most popular series. The contents of many contemporary serials, including young people rebelling against strict, old-fashioned parents, achieved a resonance with China's young. There were also more superficial influences. The kind of short hairstyle or a fashionable scarf seen on television on actors in the contemporary family drama *Winter Sonata* (*Dongji lian'ge*) soon appeared on the streets of Chinese cities.[115] An Internet survey in the mid-2000s indicated that 83.12 percent of respondents liked Korean television dramas (and that 67.81 percent of Internet users were young people).[116] Television dramas, starting in 1993 and given impetus in 1997 when CCTV broadcast *What Is Love?* (*Aiqing shi shenme*), opened the way for youth interest in Korean films, pop music performers, and other products of South Korean popular culture. In 2003, for example, a Wuhan music and video store close to a high school sold on average daily at least fifteen CDs containing music from Korean serials and ten VCDs of such song performances. A Beijing publishing company kept selling out of titles in its pop star series 'super Korean Wave' (*Chaoji Hanliu*).[117] Korean novels for youth readers, particularly young women, proved a good earner for Chinese publishers. These romantic stories were bound in attractive covers featuring floppy-haired, androgynous young men and baby-faced, doe-eyed young women. By 2005 one publisher had issued eight titles starting in July 2002, selling about one hundred thousand copies per title, a major success in the Chinese book market.[118] The pop music radio programme 'Seoul Concert Hall' (*Hancheng yinyueting*), broadcast in ten major cities, was heard by four to five hundred million listeners in 2002, with a regular audience of thirty to forty million, according to the host.[119] In 2003 three-quarters of the Chinese computer game market was held by Korean imports.[120]

As we have seen, clothing was an arena for youthful expressions of group belonging and difference from other social groupings. The South Korean 'look,' evident among the handsome male stars of Korean films and TV dramas, served as a powerful model for many young Chinese. Pastel polo shirts with the collar worn up and Paul Smith spectacles were part of one look. Other chose low-rise baggy jeans and thick-soled skate shoes or basketball boots or the exaggerated stylings of hip-hop. Both looks were American in origin, but reached China's youth through the mediation of Korean media products.[121] Korean movies had special appeal: 'Compared to Western-made films, they are relatively Eastern. Compared to Third World movies, Korean films are relatively modern. Compared with arty directors' films, they're relatively populist. They use art to show the emotions and lives of everybody. Whatever you say, Korean films at least have found their own, suitable place.'[122]

For the young, the hip-hop music and other fashions presented by Korean youth offered more important models for Chinese youth culture. These models were East Asian rather than directly from North America or Western Europe.[123] One transnational phenomenon in the Korean Wave was the incorporation of Chinese singers in Korean bands and the duplication of Korean-style groups with Chinese performers. One such singer was Han Geng, born in 1981, who became the only Chinese member of thirteen-member boy band Super Junior. SM Entertainment, a South Korean company, ran auditions for Chinese singers. Han was a dance student at the Minorities University in Beijing. After four years of training in Korea, he debuted with the rest of the Super Junior group. Han's popularity in China soared in 2008, when a subgroup of Super Junior, Super Junior M, was introduced. This group was aimed at the Chinese market, with Han Geng as the leader and two other Chinese performers in the new lineup. In the same year Han was voted on the Internet as one of the torchbearers in the lengthy Olympic torch relay in its progress around China. The Beijing Olympic organising committee concurred with the popular vote and gave Han Geng this honour.[124]

There is a possible parallel between the Northwest Wind and the Korean Wave twenty years later. The former can be understood in nationalist terms, emerging from the same impetus that encouraged the search for roots by Chinese writers in the post–Cultural Revolution period. The 1980s were a time when many Chinese felt that their traditional culture had been destroyed in the ten-year period from 1966 to 1976, while the new writers set out to find new sources for regional and national pride in their heritage. The popular consensus on the Cultural Revolution, encouraged by the official verdict on the era, was that the last vestiges of Confucian decency had been destroyed by the vicious political culture created at the encouragement of the Gang of Four. These four leaders, headed by Mao Zedong's wife, provided a convenient way for the post-1976 Chinese leadership to quarantine the era as a period of madness now over. But the popular view by the end of the century was that communal relations, characterised by respect for elders, a sense of hierarchy based on age and social position, and a community spirit that considered other members of society beyond one's immediate family or work group, had been obliterated by the excesses of the Red Guards acting at the behest of evil conspirators in the Communist Party.

In this context at the end of the century, the arrival of television dramas replete with respectful (or rebellious) children, strong hierarchies of social control in families, work places and more widely, and a respect for age and traditional ritual sparked a natural curiosity. These Korean serials showed a society that might have been China without the upheavals of the Cultural Revolution and other impacts of Communist Party rule. Korean culture was not just an alternative way to modernity, but a standing criticism of the cultural nihilism alleged to characterise China in the twentieth century. Though Korean, these were originally Chinese or pan-Asian virtues on display on small and large screens.

Even for young Chinese, claiming credit for Korean progress by emphasising a shared cultural heritage had some salience. Korean youth culture offered a reworking of Western, essentially American, youth cultures, but through an East Asian filter.[125] This made Korean youth culture easier to adopt and modify in China. This response to the influx of Korean music, drama, clothing, and food has parallels with the rise of youthful excitement at the Northwest Wind in the mid-1980s. The appeal of the reinvented folk songs of Cui Jian, Tian Zhen, Sun Guoqing, and others was that they were a local, China-rooted version of contemporary youth music. Young Chinese embraced the nativistic implications of these Chinese-style songs, for they showed that Chinese youth could create and enjoy their own emblematic cultural products that could stand direct comparison with imported models. Twenty years on, the Korean Wave could be seen as a great returning of Chinese cultural values through the vehicle of Korean modernisation. This view could apply even to the most modern of Korean youth culture. This reclaiming of shared values back from the Korean peninsula could be made even by the hippest young Chinese fan. The Northwest Wind and the Korean Wave can paradoxically be seen as two routes to local pride.

## SUPERGIRL AND CHINESE IDOLS

On a warm evening in late August 2005 tens of millions of young Chinese television viewers watched the grand final competition of the Chinese equivalent of *American Idol*. In the climax of the *Supergirl* (*Chaoji nüsheng*) song contest from Hunan Satellite Television, five contestants (soon to be reduced to three) belted out their songs to an excited live audience, while millions watched at home to see what would happen to their favourite singer. Viewers had become engaged in the contest through a novel device, at least for China, voting using their mobile phones. The contest had proven a phenomenon in other media as well. Newspapers, local and national, responded to the public interest in the innovative contest by including coverage of the contestants and the rituals surrounding the competition on a regular basis.

On the final night, three contestants stood out. The winner, Li Yuchun, a twenty-one-year-old from Chengdu, received over 3.52 million text votes of the nine million cast. Runner-up Zhou Bichang, twenty years old from Guangzhou, took 3.27 million votes. In third place, with a much lower 1.35 million votes, was twenty-year-old Zhang Jingying from Chengdu.[126] Young people formed the vast majority of the fans. *Supergirl* created a space for youthful fandom and young aspirations to be acted out in public view. The excited groups of supporters, holding up posters of their idols and clapping and crying out their encouragement when their favourites took to the stage, were concrete expressions of the more scattered supporters. Some had organised fan clubs for their favourites at a local level. More of the latter took to the virtual spaces of the Internet to express their fandom in blogs, websites, fan groups, and other conglomerations of atomised supporters brought together in cyberspace.

The theme song of the contest, sung by the group of winning and unsuccessful contestants each week, captured the appeal of the show to young viewers:

> I'll sing when I want to, I'll sing loud and clear.
> Even if there's nobody to applaud me,
> At least I can still boldly appreciate myself.
> I'll sing when I want, I'll sing loud and clear.
> Even if this stage is really huge
> There'll always come the day that will see the torch of glory.[127]

This theme of self-reliance, of 'me against a hostile world' resonates among adolescents in all cultures. It echoed a strong element of the Northwest Wind songs of 1988. As we shall see, the ways in which the contest developed, its content and imagery, and its impact on the young all reflected this new sense of individual struggle.

*Supergirl* was much more than a television event. It became in 2005 a youth cultural phenomenon, combining the glamour and broken dreams of show business with the potential to bring people together provided by the Internet. The opportunity to influence the outcome of the contest by freely and (if preferred) privately casting a vote for your favourite was an added attraction, with implications far beyond the singing contest. Li Yuchun and her fellow contestants served as models for youthful aspirations and behaviour as powerful, in the new circumstances of the start of the twenty-first century, as Lei Feng had been for young people forty years earlier.

The 2005 season of *Supergirl* was the second; it began in 2004 with the contest confined to Changsha. In its second year, *Supergirl* took on national ambitions, with regional contests in Guangzhou, Zhengzhou, Changsha, Chengdu, and Hangzhou. Text message voting by viewers and analysis by jurors chose which singers would go on. Fifty contestants in each location were whittled down to thirty-one local champions. Fifteen finalists went on to the grand final in Changsha, where, over eight drawn-out weekends, they went from fifteen to identifying the supreme winner and two runners-up. The scale of the second series in 2005 was much greater than that in 2004, with nationwide audience numbers surpassing even the hugely popular CCTV Spring Festival broadcasts, which had become a national institution by the 1980s.[128] While learned commentators ruminated on national television about the vulgarisation of popular culture, young China took *Supergirl* to its heart. Others spoke of 'grassroots democracy' (*caogen minzhu*), struck by the popular excitement over cell phone text voting.

Nationwide, one hundred and fifty thousand aspiring singers had registered to compete. Twenty million viewers tuned in each week, ten percent of the television audience. This was a major achievement in a highly fragmented television market, with most urban households having access to several dozen channels from around the nation. Both singers and viewers seemed to agree with the head of the Hunan Provincial Radio and Television Bureau's declaration: 'Supergirl represents the coming of age of the people's own amusement (ziyuzile de shidai).' The normally sombre Sanlian Life Weekly (Sanlian shenghuo zhoukan) magazine, seeing lines of would-be contestants lining up for three and four kilometres over several days, observed: 'This is an era of general carnival' (zhuzong wanghuan de shidai). On Google, 1.64 million pages were devoted to Supergirl, while the Baidu Internet portal had more than ten million pages. Internet users considered Zhang Jingying's rendition of 'Don't Cry for Me, Argentina' one of the ten best performances in the contest.[129]

In a lengthy account of the rise of Supergirl, published just weeks after the 2005 final, Lü Hui identified several factors in the audience appeal of such talent shows. First, the 'zero threshold' (ling menkan) for entry allowed ordinary young persons of whatever background to dream of participating. In a system in which many stars (in entertainment or in politics) rose through the effective use of the kinds of personal relationships that had always oiled the workings of the Chinese system, audiences appreciated seeing the 'little guy' having a shot at the big time. As a university student observed: 'I was really attracted [to try in the competition] by the "equality" (pingdeng) in it. These days in society or at school, opportunities to compete on terms of real 'equality' are too few.' Even the period of the local contest in Chengdu saw daily reports on progress in the local newspapers and much public interest. A local drycleaner provided contestants and their supporters with water. Noodle and other snack shops did a roaring trade and offered discounts to participants. The level playing field quality of entry into the contest clearly struck a public chord.[130]

The Supergirl contest in 2005 also appealed to young viewers because of the opportunity it provided for individuals to achieve success. As a successful Sichuan aspirant, Zhang Li, noted: 'I hadn't thought I'd get to whatever round. I just thought those fifteen minutes on the stage belong to me. That's enough.' On the first day of the Chengdu regional contest, a Saturday in mid-May, ten thousand women lined up to register to enter. Some contestants waited more than nine hours to register in the local contests. In Zhengzhou, thirty-one thousand women initially registered for the contest. Lü Hui observed that the aspiring singers, all born in the 1980s, were mostly from one-child families and had grown up in relatively nurturing surroundings despite the pressure to do well at

Figure 4.3. The finalists in the 2005 *Supergirl* contest, with Li Yuchun (fifth from left).
*Source:* San Bao, *Chaoji nüsheng baodian* (*Supergirl* treasured book), Beijing: Xinhua hubanshe, 2005, p. 104.

school. What they lacked was 'a real space to express themselves' (*ziwo zhanshi de zhenzheng kongjian*).[131] Eighty percent of those registering in Chengdu were senior high schoolers.[132]

*Supergirl* chimed with what reporter Lü Hui identified as audience members' psychological desire to seek novelty and sort out the good from the bad. This was a natural desire in all people; the contest proved the ideal vehicle for it. The parallels with the success of Fox Television's *American Idol*, which began in 2002 and regularly outrated all other programmes except *CSI*, are obvious. Both the American and Chinese programmes offered viewers a sense of belonging and identification: 'How would I perform if I were the person up on that stage?' Likewise, reactions to the comments of the judges provided another avenue of engagement with the programme. Fans followed the fate of their favourite singer, disagreeing or concurring with the judges' comments, and either delighting in their favourite's success or lamenting elimination. The judges' rather blunt responses to some of the contestants in the early local rounds were unprecedented on Chinese television, where bland and generally supportive comments were the norm, with the dirty work done by the scores accompanying the judges' words. Asking a singer whether she was trying to reproduce one of the steps in the Maoist radio mass calisthenics or telling another singer that she should stick to her day job (hairdressing) or that she had no sense of rhythm gave viewers a vicarious thrill at such bold, direct public statements.[133]

A similar attraction for viewers was the use of instant elimination, called 'PK' (short for 'player killing' and rendered in the Roman alphabet), a concept borrowed from the computer games popular among young Chinese. This applied the idea from the virtual world to real life, broadcast live with real consequences for the winners. After the text votes the thirty-one-member mass jury then voiced its views and indicated its votes. The fortunes of the contestants could swing wildly: Excitement and fear of (PK) elimination predominated.[134] The emotions on display were another part of the appeal to the predominantly young followers of the contest. Tears could be relied upon when two contestants stood on the PK dais waiting to see the vote tallies. The brief visual summary of the eliminated contestant's road to that point, backed with tear-jerking music, would also reliably induce sobs. The unlucky singer was also required to read out a previously written letter of departure, often with words of encouragement for fellow contestants. Another device for tear inducement was taped messages of love and support and recollections of family suffering from the contestant's parents, played after she had performed. As one *Supergirl* fan noted, the television channels were awash with false tear shedding in melodramas and serials. This contest had real tears, showing real emotions.[135]

Text messages (*duanxin*) were a major element in the success of *Supergirl* in capturing the attention of its mostly youthful audience. In the regional contests there was no limit on how many votes one cell phone could cast. Groups of particularly ardent fans reportedly cast tens of thousands of votes. For the national final contests, each cell phone was limited to fifteen votes. Fans urged people on the street to vote for their favourite, bought phone cards, and opened bank accounts to support their preferred singer. One factory owner reimbursed his staff for the cost of the text messages they had sent for each weekend's contest.[136] Ignoring the revenue that Hunan Satellite Television was making from these votes, young fans were captured by the opportunity to vote: 'We have the power to spend our own money on something meaningful.'[137] Commentators even began to speculate on whether this 'entertainment democracy' represented by text voting provided a model for political democracy.[138]

The winner of *Supergirl* in 2005 was an androgynous singer from Sichuan, a student of the Sichuan Conservatory, which gave training in popular singing. Li Yuchun was unusually tall and had short hair and square shoulders. Whether in the trousers provided by the producers or in her own choice of mannish jacket and unknotted tie, Li presented herself as far from the standard ideals of Chinese female beauty. She looked like a boy. By the time she won, her website was receiving several thousand postings a day, many more times those received by major Chinese pop stars at the time. Chinese reports characterised Li's look as 'asexual' (*zhongxing*, literally middle sex). The runner-up on 26 August, Zhou Bichang (also a music conservatory student), had this quality too, though she was shorter than Li and wore dark-rimmed glasses that enhanced her boyish appearance. In striking contrast, third place winner Zhang Jingying had shoulder-length hair and conformed more to conventional Chinese notions of womanhood. When Zhang, from the Guangzhou regional contest, and Li, from the Chengdu finals, were put together in the national face-off, fans were reportedly torn between the two. 'Guys liked her as she could be a "buddy" (*gemenr*) and friend, girls for their part were enamoured of her and worshiped her.'[139] There were even calls for a new kind of hero to be identified, replacing the Cultural Revolution era 'high, wide and handsome' ideal with a new hero image, reflecting the triumph of *Supergirl*.[140]

For our purposes the most significant element in *Supergirl* 2005 was the fans themselves, called *fensi* (literally vermicelli made of bean starch) as a transliteration of the English word.[141] In his long reportage piece, Lü Hui described them as 'a group of people who were the most infatuated and frenzied' (*zui chiqing he fengkuang de yi qun ren*). On the weekends these real 'fans' took the whole programme very seriously. Their support for a particular contestant tended to become the centre of their lives, almost like a job, receiving their whole attention, feelings, and money. Loyalties were fierce: Supporters of Li Yuchun (as we have noted, called Yumi) were strongest among female university students and white-collar workers. Followers of Zhang Jingying, the third place winner and most conventionally feminine of the trio, were relatively older and evenly split between men and women. Zhou Bichang, with her short hair and glasses making her look like an awkward teenager, enjoyed most support from fans under the age of eighteen. Fans of the other contestants in the national finals all created clever labels for themselves, sharing a linguistic invention as a group identifier in chat rooms and among friends.[142]

These ardent young fans were active even at the regional contest level, creating dedicated sites (*ba*, literally an exclamation at the end of a sentence) for their favourites on the Baidu portal. These sites proved a major force in promoting interest in the contestants at the later stages and building connections among the fans. A Mr Yang in Beijing reported being approached by a group of young women on the street who offered him twenty yuan to borrow his cellphone to send fifteen text votes. In return they gave him a photo of a sweet young woman, whom he later identified from watching *Supergirl* as one of the contestants. Other 'hardliners'

(*qiangyingpai*) were less polite. A Mr Zhang in Changsha found himself
mobbed by a group of what he described as 'girls' and forced to hand over
his cell phone so that they could send in the fifteen vote maximum.[143] In
August a dozen teenagers at a Shijiazhuang shopping mall, along with an
office worker of about thirty, urged passers by to vote for Zhou Bichang,
explaining to those unfamiliar with texting how to send in their vote.[144]

Fans published posters, postcards, flyers, and name cards urging people to vote for particular contestants. Groups pasted up flyers, in defiance of local ordinances, and created chants to express their support for
their favourite singer. Some printed photos of their choice onto candy
wrappers and T-shirts, handing them out to encourage strangers to vote
accordingly.[145] Come the final contest, the most ardent fans made the effort
to travel to Changsha to see their idols in the flesh. This caused problems
for the security of the contestants, who had to move their accommodation
in the city to avoid being mobbed by fans from all over the country. Some
of these loyal fans were anxious to hand over their choices' favourite foods
or medicine to protect their throats. Fans were mostly well-behaved, realising perhaps that riotous behaviour could damage their singer's chances
in the contest. Unlike Chinese soccer fans on other occasions, *Supergirl*
fans accepted the elimination of their idols with reasonable calmness.

On the Internet, blogging fans gushed, in this case well-known blogger
Lü Yao (literally Green Goblin):

> You are an idol. You are the most dangerous (*xianjun*) of that school of idols.
> The day after tomorrow [Monday?] professional training will only help you
> polish your tricks some more. But your primary strength still comes from
> your inborn cultivation (*xiantian xiulian*). You were lucky to be born into a
> family filled with real love. Although not rich or distinguished, you possess
> the goodness, honesty and forgiveness of human nature. Each time *Supergirl*
> gets to the elimination (PK) stage, when the camera lights on you, your eyes
> are always filled with smiles and encouragement. On the competition stage,
> this kind of friendliness is revealed as just like pure gold.

> Maybe this fever can continue for a long time, no matter what, I cannot feel
> any regret this summer. I have seen a woman called Li Yuchun. She stood
> quietly in the midst of a wild *party* [the word was in English], in the heart of
> a tempest launching a tempest, yourself as serene as a dew drop.

> Although we all know this is just a game, although we know that the rel-
> evant businessmen are laughing to their hearts' content at our silly enthu-
> siasm, but as adults we respect this game and quietly send our not worth
> mentioning vote. As if protecting one self of many years earlier, that incor-
> ruptible and stubborn youth.[146]

Some ardent fans stayed in Changsha for a month in order to support
their idol. One leader of a fan club spent twenty thousand yuan for her
sojourn. A doll that Zhang Jingying's fans gave her after her third place
win reportedly cost three thousand yuan, about twice an average urban

worker's monthly wages. Fans could even use cyberspace to undermine the campaigns of rival singers. Li Yuchun was subjected to alleged 'gay pictures,' created by using a computer to put her head on another person's body and posted on the Internet.[147] Rival fans even fought on the street in Shanghai when they were soliciting votes for their favourite finalist. Jurors in the regional and final contests came under attack on the Internet and in person. Ke Yimin, herself a singer, announced her withdrawal from the Changsha jury after a fellow juror's car had been shot at in Guangzhou and after a sustained attack on her by fans of Zhang Jingying. Ke had been prone to bursting into tears while fulfilling her duties, adding to the emotionalism of the contest that appealed to many young fans.[148] Frustration with the jurors was such that a petition circulated on the Internet calling for the abolition of jurors and reliance entirely on texting fans.[149]

The response to *Supergirl* and to the eventual emergence of Li Yuchun as the grand prize winner involved a sense of national pride. As one entertainment journalist noted: 'Usually we have to tag behind Hong Kong and Taiwan reporters to interview stars from those places. Now at last the mainland has a star and Hong Kong and Taiwan reporters have to tag along behind us!'[150] This sentiment was shared widely in the media and the general public. Here was a star who had truly emerged from within China: *Bentu* (native land) was the phrase commonly used in these accounts. Even when Li Yuchun started selling CDs abroad under her androgynous English name, Chris Lee, her fans remained loyal.[151] When the winners went on a publicity tour to Beijing after the contest, even the reporter from *Elle* had to wait her turn for an interview. The level of public attention was indicated by the way in which pop and movie stars were asked for their views of *Supergirl*, rather than being questioned about the CD, concert, or film they were supposed to be promoting. In Inner Mongolia, Cui Jian, the inventor of 1980s pop music, found himself after an interview faced with the headline: 'Cui Jian doesn't know anything about *Supergirl*.'[152]

To China's youth the special quality of the popular appeal of *Supergirl* was clear. It was a programme about youthful hope and confidence. Li Yuchun's triumph in late August embodied this element perfectly. 'The mainland had at last given birth to an idol: not one, but a whole group!'[153] It was also a new kind of entertainment in which the audience had unprecedented influence. For reporter Lü Hui, the contest possibly heralded a major shift in approaches to entertainment and audiences in China. Instead of the standard, officially sanctioned, saccharine national-minority song with a pretty girl in ethnic costume and jewellery backed by hordes of similarly clad dancers, *Supergirl* reflected the new times, with young women alone on stage singing songs of love and pain. Ordinary people could express their own preference among the contestants and directly influence the outcome through their text votes. *Supergirl* told the masses: 'You want entertainment, you'll get it. Great entertainment, unrestrained entertainment, entertainment as *you* want it (*suixinsuoyu de yule*)!... I'll sing what I want to: an open society (*kaifang shehui*) inevitably has boundless prospects.'[154]

The reception afforded Li Yuchun after her victory confirmed the historical significance of *Supergirl*. In a parallel to the return of Zhang Yimou in early 1988 after the triumph of *Red Sorghum* in Berlin, five or six hundred of Li's fans waited in excitement at the Capital Airport when she flew from Changsha on a postcontest publicity tour. But they were deeply disappointed when she was taken via a VIP exit directly to her waiting car. Enterprising shopkeepers in the city of Xidan produced a series of products on the same day after the final that included cell phone covers, key chains, and others costing from three to sixty yuan and featuring photos of Li and the other finalists.[155] In September the release of the first CD from the show, *Supergirl: The Ultimate Elimination* (*Chaoji nüsheng zhongji PK*) showed its popularity was being sustained. Six hundred and fifty copies of the disc sold out in one store in one day, and a follow-up print run of one million more also sold fast. This level of interest was unprecedented in China. Meanwhile finalists in the show, bound by eight-year contracts that they had been obliged to sign with the Shanghai Tianyu Company, presented their own concerts around the country. Bookstores sold a range of richly illustrated books about the contest and the key finalists. Wei Wenbin, the head of the Hunan Provincial Radio and Television Bureau, announced that the 2006 *Supergirl* contest would be bigger and better and more deliberately geared toward a youth audience. He also suggested that there would be a 'Superboy' (*Chaoji nansheng*) contest out of Hunan.[156]

Debate on the significance of the contest continued after the triumphant conclusion of the 2005 version. Much attention was paid to the particular appeal to viewers of the androgyny of Li Yuchun. Her appearance – she had always worn trousers rather than skirts growing up – her voice – hard to tell as female on a blind listening – and her Ricky Martin-style Latin dance moves were in striking contrast to expectations. In a loosely hanging black singlet, with a shock of short hair falling over her face, Li Yuchun embodied a new sexuality, reminiscent of some characters in the Korean television dramas and cartoon novels now popular in China. But she also echoed the kind of male–female gender crossing seen in the characters in the classical Chinese vernacular novels and opera that high schoolers were obliged to read as part of their studies. With such diverse associations, the particular character of Li Yuchun touched a rich chord in young Chinese viewers' minds. The chatrooms showed the high level of interest in this aspect of Li's character, with 'open letters' declaring love apparently from teenage girls and darker allegations of homosexuality. Gays and feminists allegedly text voted enthusiastically for this idol.[157]

One obsessive young fan of Li Yuchun in Changchun was so eager to support her idol that she broke the law. Twenty-year-old Liu Miaomiao had joined the 'Yuchun fan base' (*Yumi jidi*) group established in Changchun, making new friends in the process of fulfilling her infatuation with Li Yuchun. Liu resolved to send Li Yuchun a new pair of sneakers (a contestant had remarked on Li's shabby footwear). To pay for the Nike shoes, Liu Miaomiao resorted to stealing from her fellow fans by tricking them on the Internet to buy tickets for an alleged plan by Liu's employer to bring Li Yuchun to Changchun. In all, Liu conned almost four thousand *yuan* from fellow fans to spend on sneakers and a T-shirt for her idol.[158]

A year after the completion of the 2005 *Supergirl* contest, talent quests had become a television staple in China. A partial listing in September 2006 included thirteen singing competitions (six of them from CCTV), six nonsinging talent quests (three from CCTV), along with two martial arts, two dance, two acting, and seven model competitions.[159] These relatively cheaply produced programmes offered television stations and their advertisers a means to reach youthful audiences increasingly diverted to Internet-based entertainment. Liu Hong, a middle-aged professor at the Communication University of China, noted how young people no longer read books and enjoyed the programmes of previous generations. Today they wanted books and entertainment written by and featuring young people like themselves. Idol culture (*ouxiang wenhua*) reflected greater commercialisation than earlier model or exemplar cultures (*bangyang wenhua, mofan wenhua*), and was possible in the context of the relaxation of official cultural controls. *Supergirl* produced the fans' popular choice of winner, unlike those successful on CCTV shows, who all seemed to enjoy an official imprimatur.[160]

The slump in 2006 in the appeal of the multitude of talent shows, in contrast to the real achievement of the three winners of the 2005 *Supergirl* contest, was widely noted. The earlier show had emerged at the right time, with little competition and novel and wide engagement with its youth audience.[161] Young people in Beijing and Changsha seemed to share this view, while recalling the appeal of *Supergirl* one year earlier. Zhao Zhidong, a student in Beijing, observed: 'I think that kind of style [with popular voting] is good. I feel the lives of many Chinese are too restrained (*lei*). They should have an opportunity to present and express themselves.... Whether for performer or viewer, there's a feeling of empathy.' He went on to warn against the commercialisation of these talent shows. Nineteen-year-old Lin Fan in Beijing was concerned that very young people might lose a sense of perspective from these shows with their promise of instant fame and fortune.[162]

Two years after Li Yuchun's *Supergirl* triumph, her male equivalent had emerged from Hunan Satellite Television's *Happy Boy* (*Kuaile nansheng*) contest. Winner Chen Chusheng, a twenty-six-year-old resident of Shenzhen though he entered the Xi'an regional contest, was supported by his fans, who called themselves 'Peanuts' (*huasheng*, incorporating the second of his given names). Whereas *Supergirl* attracted about fourteen million text votes, *Happy Boy* involved 3.32 million votes in the final. About three-quarters of the fans for the other two finalists in the 2007 male contest were young women: For the acoustic guitar playing Chen, four out of ten of his keen fans were young men. Young female fans of Chen Chusheng called him 'Prince Chu' (*Chu gongzi*) and spent time on the Internet discussing his clothes and hairstyle in each round. His male fans used the standard 'Old Chen' (*lao Chen*) and reportedly focused on the music.[163] *Happy Girls* (*Kuaile nüsheng*) had a run on Hunan Satellite TV, the inventors of *Supergirl*, in 2009. It attracted attention, but, in now crowded marketplace, lacked the impact of the original.[164] The careful, marketing-driven planning behind the organising and presentation of such shows, and their associated advertising and spin-offs, was revealed in a book-length report on the *My Hero* (*Jiayou! Hao nan'er*) televised talent contest of 2006.[165]

Talent quest shows had become a staple of provincial television stations, available to viewers across the nation. On Beijing TV, *Dream of China* (*Mengxiang Zhongguo*) attracted about two dozen young men and the same number of young women competing in contests based on the eighteenth-century vernacular novel *A Dream of Red Mansions*. The aspiring actors took on the main roles from the novel in a series of skits and then answered questions about the novel, much read over centuries and sprawling with details. A well-known professor of *Red Mansions* studies (*Hongxue*) was tasked with judging the answers to his questions. Other judges were acting and performance specialists. Unlike *Supergirl* and the other talent contests, which had been derived from the British *Pop Idol* and the *American Idol* originals, *Dream of China* could boast strong Chinese roots.[166] Chongqing TV's *First Heartbeat* (*Di yi ci xindong*) also featured groups of young men and women singing and acting, though in a contemporary context inspired in part by the androgynous models of Japanese *anime* or manga. Each episode featured individual interviews with a panel of judges, led by actress Liu Xiaoqing, herself from Sichuan. Each Saturday night viewers tuned in to see what transformation had been achieved by Liu, whose changing hairstyles and costumes (often more suitable for a woman decades younger) were an object of considerable fascination. Ke Yimin, the lounge singer who had helped judge

*Supergirl* in 2005, was also on the panel, along with a male singer. The relative vulgarity of the show was confirmed in a slanging match between a male contestant and Ke, who was reduced to tears and subsequently left the show, as she had done in the 2005 contest, citing the emotional toll of judging. In August 2007 the show was suddenly pulled from broadcast several weeks before the finals.[167] The State Administration of Radio, Film, and Television announced at the same time that talent contests involving popular text voting were now banned. By that time, despite the commentary from youth administration researchers about youthful idol worship, these talent contests seem to have lost their appeal to youth and had almost become parodies of themselves.[168] In mid-2010 a weekend dating show, *If You Are the One* (*Fei cheng wu rao*), on Jiangsu Satellite TV came under government fire for vulgarity. There were echoes here of the 1983 through 1984 campaign against 'spiritual pollution.' Many viewers felt that the twenty-four single young women who acted as a jury selecting male dates were out to make money from their hapless new partners, judging the young men on the size of their wallets more than anything else. One of these women, model Ma Nuo, became an instant celebrity with her outspoken comments about preferring to sit in a BMW crying than on a bicycle smiling.[169] By then the 2005 *Supergirl* contest seemed like a time of innocent fun.

## NEW RHYTHMS

By the new millennium Chinese rockers had become an established part of global youth music circuits. Xie Tianxiao, for example, and his band Cold Blooded Animals (*Lengxue dongwu*) were hailed as China's equivalent to Nirvana. Xie was featured at the South by Southwest festival in Texas and toured other centres in the United States.[170] The band's name expressed expected youth rebellion, even if the bars in Beijing in which it played appealed to a relatively prosperous clientele. More marginal were the young men (and some women) who came from all over China at the turn of the century to study rock 'n roll at the privately run Midi Music School in the rapidly growing northern suburbs of Beijing just north of Peking University. At its height the small suburb of Shucun (literally tree village) had 230 rockers leading hand-to-mouth existences while practicing and performing their music in an underground mode.[171] In September 2007 the Beijing Pop Festival, organised by Rock for China Entertainment (staffed by a mix of Chinese and foreigners), was held in Chaoyang Park in eastern Beijing city. The headliners included Nine Inch Nails, American punk group New York Dolls, Russian group Mumiy Troll, Chinese punks Joyside (formed in 2001), Xie Tianxiao and his Cold Blooded Animals, Brain Failure, and the Honeys. The Japanese garage rock band Doc Holliday & Apache Train was also in the lineup for this third edition of the festival. Muma and Third Party, a Chinese group, had emerged from art school in 1998. Also featured was Cui Jian in his first outdoor concert in Beijing.[172] The range of international and local musicians, attracting an audience of Chinese and resident foreigners, reflected the global ambitions of Beijing one year out from the Olympics. It also illustrated how global Chinese youth tastes had become since the days of Teresa Teng and Canto-pop.[173]

In 2006 *Liaoning Youth* marked the twentieth anniversary of Chinese rock with a single page in an August issue. Four musicians were covered, with a 'classical phrase' (*jingdian yulu*: classical saying, a phrase used in Buddhism, Neo-Confucianism, and by Mao Zedong forty years earlier) provided for each. Cui Jian's was: 'If our music doesn't value progress, then it's a disgrace.' Second named was Zheng Jun, who had emerged in the 1990s with gentler songs: 'We live only to keep each other warm.' Third up was the band Catcher in the Rye (*Maitian shouwangzhe*), whose new, somewhat rustic style had been a breath of fresh rock air in 1998. Their slogan was not so fresh: 'Live in our world.' New Pants, whose 1998 debut album had been ranked number two in a Hong Kong music magazine's list of top ten Chinese-language records from the decade, rounded off the brief overview of twenty years of rock progress with the quote: 'Fashionable music is all the rage.'[174] Five years earlier, a Chinese music magazine had devoted one page to farewelling rock music and its appeal to China's young, arguing that drugs and general excess had destroyed its claims to rebellion.[175]

Toward the end of the first decade of the new century, the musical tastes of China's young were an unsurprising mix of the old, new, foreign, and domestic. Cui Jian was still performing, mostly for the parents of today's teenagers, though with some fans among the young. Korean boy groups and copycat home-grown versions still attracted young fans. Korean male singers had their Chinese counterparts, with their carefully shaped casual hairstyles and (for female fans) nonthreatening, even vaguely feminised appearance.[176] Hip-hop (*xiha*), often filtered through South Korean or other reworkings, was incorporated into local performances, for China already had a centuries-old 'speak-sing' (*shuo-chang*) performing tradition that mixed spoken words and singing.[177] A typical mid-2000s rap, 'Life is Struggle' (its title was in English only), from the Taiwan-based Song Yueting (Shawn Sung), expressed typical youthful alienation and bravado:

> Each time I get home from school and put down that heavy backpack
> There's nobody at home:
> Only the smell of your perfume remains.
> Then I know

You have to work overtime again that night.
I open the fridge and take out the cold, microwave dinner.
Grandpa comes home at two in the morning, drunk.
From the midst of my dream I hear you arguing,
There's no way I can focus on tomorrow's exam.
Teacher – he doesn't like me; I don't like him either.
I'm fed up with wearing the uniform, I'm fed up with school
I'm fed up with the looks of the dean of students, fed up so I'm tied up.
*That's true*
Lots of people disdain my attitude
They say I'm too *cool.*
The cops they think I'll be arrested
*I don't give a fuck about* what people say.
They say whatever they want to,
But who the hell are they.
Nobody can use his criteria to judge me;
The guy in charge is me.
Whatever other people think,
I'm still me.[178]

Increasingly such rap performances and even syrupy love songs included some words in English, as if a marker of musical globalisation.[179] A Beijing researcher noted a typical hip-hop scenario: 'Youngsters buy a pair of Andl sports shoes and go play basketball [on the streets]. In so doing they send a coded message to other people: I'm not wearing Nike or adidas, because I'm a street ball player. I don't like regular basketball, I like the *free* spirit of street basketball.'[180]

Youth music had come a long way from the dulcet warblings of Li Guyi on a film soundtrack and the lone wail of the Northwest Wind. The MP3 player and cellphone put music into the control and ready access of young fans, replacing the tape players of twenty years earlier. Global musical circuits were equally accessible to young China. Moreover the music of twenty-first-century youth was just one part of a bigger picture of self-expression, consumerism, and shared values. Youthful bodies grooved to their own soundtracks, just as they had done twenty years earlier, but the rhythms were a more eclectic mix of the local and the global. They echoed in a space made seemingly infinite by the virtual world of the Internet.

CHAPTER 5

# Spaces

## *Real, Imagined, and Virtual Arenas*

In the five decades that are the focus of this study, the spaces in which Chinese youth expressed their evolving and distinctive identities changed and expanded considerably. From furtive group singing or reading of banned materials in the safety of a private space in a village or barracks, spaces for youth-driven activities extended to urban dance halls, parks, and gymnasiums in the 1980s. At the same time whole new imaginary spaces were constructed. We have seen how the film *Red Sorghum* created a fictional landscape on which teenaged men inscribed something of their own fantasies and ambitions. In the same decade a new style of fiction, labelled 'hoodlum writing' (*liumang wenxue*), reached readers, who saw in the hip, alienated, and amoral stories parallels with their own lives in a rapidly changing social context. The work of Wang Shuo in particular appealed to young readers and television watchers. By the mid-1990s a virtual space was beginning to open up, populated overwhelmingly by people under twenty-five years old. The Internet produced a vast expansion in the spaces available for the expression of youthful distinctiveness and shared values.

This chapter will discuss physical spaces before moving on to the imaginative spaces associated with the pen of Wang Shuo, then examine how television and film also opened up for youth unreachable spaces, real and imagined, historical and contemporary. The rise of youth Internet activity and the uses to which Chinese netizens put these virtual spaces will form the bulk of this chapter's analysis. Several themes will reoccur that can be broadly grouped around the labels commodification, manipulation, and deterritorialisation. Youth idols emerged who were in part the creations of companies and organisations intent on selling the products and the ways of living and attitudes that youth perceived them to engender. The groups backing the new heroes may have had benign, even noncommercial intentions, but the ways in which these 'products' interacted with the youth 'market' represented a further commodification and manipulation of Chinese cultural production and consumption. I have suggested elsewhere that this strong linkage between culture and commodity was strengthened greatly in the perhaps unlikely circumstances of the Cultural Revolution. The cult of Mao Zedong can be read as a giant advertising campaign, and the presentation of the central cultural products of this era, the new-style operas and ballets that made up the 'model works' (*yangbanxi*), presaged the reassertion and rise of commodity culture in the 1980s.[1] By the first decade of the twenty-first century this tendency infused all contemporary Chinese cultural practice. Youth consumers were inextricably bound in this nexus between culture, commerce, and manipulation.

On the other hand, developments from the mid-1990s that reached a zenith in 2008 gave Chinese youth new freedom to manipulate their worlds for themselves. This was facilitated by the deterritorial nature of the worlds of the Internet, in which a netizen could 'visit' places unreachable in other media or in daily life. These new virtual spaces included both the domestic and international, despite the efforts of the army of Internet patrollers that made up the staff of the so-called Great Firewall of China. Young users of the Internet found ingenious ways to work around official manipulation of these virtual spaces and form a range of connections with others. These links could be to share enthusiasm (or otherwise) for a *Supergirl* contestant, a particular movie, or a pastime such as cosplay. The links could extend far beyond China's territorial borders, to the Chinese diaspora and to sites across the globe. By the end of the new decade, commodity, control, and contacts were watchwords in Chinese youth cultures.

## YOUTH SPACES IN 1988

As in all societies, no matter what level of economic development, home, school, and work were domains in which young people spent most of their time and made most effort, under instruction or not. Slowly, however, other spaces for youth began to open up in China's cities. The dance hall, the video parlour, and the pool hall had all become youth spaces by 1988.

Economic opening up to the rest of the world brought expansion to cities like Beijing, Shanghai, and Guangzhou of hotel accommodation to cater to rising numbers of international tourists. These travellers included overseas Chinese, as well as numbers of Taiwan-based visitors after 1986, when travel to the mainland became possible after the lifting of almost forty years of martial law on the island. Three-star hotels, built by state-run and collective enterprises, sprang up in major cities. Each of course included at least one dining room. With the rise of social dancing for all ages, and of the disco for younger groups, enterprising hotel managers saw an opportunity to use space and increase revenues. Tables and chairs were moved from dining rooms, a mirrored ball or coloured lights were installed, loudspeakers were set out, and the hotel disco was born. Generally a weekend phenomenon, these dance halls provided a place for older teenagers and those in their twenties to date and share exploration of new music and dance styles. For most such youths, these were new activities that they had not enjoyed while at school or college. In a society in which marriage was an unquestioned expectation for all, the dance hall was a vital venue for youngsters to try to find potential mates, even if parents still aspired to having a big say in final commitments.

The video parlour was another space for youth exploration in the 1980s. When videocassette players first appeared in the Chinese market, they were prohibitively expensive. It took about ten years for VCRs to become a normal item in big-city homes. In the interim, both the pirated or officially sanctioned videotape offered new, imaginary spaces for youthful viewers. The places in which they could be watched were also a new space for youthful learning and indiscretion. Even the smallest towns by the late 1980s had a few places where videotapes were watched by a range of punters. Frequently these parlours were a room or a portioned area of the lobby of the local cinema. These usually well-located institutions, owned by provincial or urban film distribution companies, suffered a major slump in attendances for films in the 1980s. Video screenings offered a way to increase revenue streams. Private entrepreneurs, newly encouraged to establish business enterprises, also took up the video screening opportunity. Both kinds of establishments often showed few scruples in screening pirated, foreign, and even pornographic tapes to appreciative audiences of all ages.[2] Hong Kong martial arts films became a particular favourite of young Chinese by means of these widespread, relatively cheap parlours. Soon officials began to express alarm at moral and physical safety issues associated with this form of video viewing. These concerns were encouraged by several dreadful fires and by police raids on all-night screening establishments, which were often associated with local bathhouses, a conventional means of finding cheap accommodation overnight. Bar owners, too, saw advantage in installing a television and VCR system.

Bars, nightclubs, and similar establishments also offered spaces for young Chinese to enjoy music and conviviality, but the major development of these spaces took place in the 1990s. Some of these changes were associated with foreign residents of major Chinese cities. In Beijing, for example, the first bar on South Sanlitun opened in 1989, modelled after European and United States bars.[3] Sanlitun had been designated in 1960 as a new area for foreign embassies and organisations, which had

sprung up in the subsequent two decades. The bars in the district had primarily a foreign clientele: Before 1996, ninety-five percent of customers
were foreign. By 2003, after a massive expansion in the number and variety of establishments in the area, the 1996 Atlanta Olympics and 1998
Football World Cup in France, and the interest of beer company marketing departments, this proportion had dropped to less than one-third.[4]
These statistics obscure the importance of locations like Sanlitun in large
Chinese cities from the late 1980s as a place where young Chinese with
money or access to others with money could hear musicians like Cui Jian
and Tang Dynasty when they performed in such venues. Foreign-owned
or frequented bars, coffee shops, and nightclubs offered a degree of cover
for local musicians and other performers who might be vulnerable to official interference in purely Chinese venues.

Two other locations for youth to congregate and share interests in 1988
were the karaoke lounge and the pool table. The sudden rise of interest
in playing pool was noted in the discussion of sports in Chapter 3. This
was essentially a young male fad that manifested itself in the summer of
1988 on the streets of cities and in pool halls. The latter sometimes were
part of a mix of entertainment options, including video shows and, in the
subsequent few years, karaoke lounges. As in the bars and nightclubs,
these youth spaces were highly commercialised and tried to cater to a
wider customer base than just young people. The rise of the pool hall and
karaoke lounge by the start of the 1990s matched the decline of the hotel-
based dance hall, as habits of entertainment shifted to compete with the
near saturation penetration of television ownership in China's cities. The
rise and decline of the Internet café (or *bar* in Chinese, though *room* is a
better English equivalent) was linked with the rise of personal computer
ownership and broadband access, as will be discussed later.

## WANG SHUO'S HOODLUM APPEAL

In 1988 there were five feature film projects under development at Chinese
studios based on novels by so-called hoodlum writer Wang Shuo. Thirty
years old in that year, Wang had emerged as a new, alternative voice in the
cultural ferment of the 1980s. Turning away from many young writers'
obsession with the historical and cultural roots of contemporary Chinese
culture, Wang adopted a rebellious, yet indifferent pose. His stories were
set in contemporary times and expressed a contemporary morality. His
anti-heroes created a new kind of protagonist in Chinese fiction, in which
moral or political lessons seemed of no importance. What mattered were
survival and results. Wang's work was a distinct rejection of the focus on
moral centralism shared by both Maoist writing and much post–Cultural
Revolution fiction. These stories offered youth readers an imaginative

space in which to explore the issues of rebellion that were a natural part of taking on adult responsibilities. Wang Shuo's career serves as a barometer of the changing cultural climate and the rise of youth culture.

Wang was a new kind of Chinese writer in a decade when other new-style writers had achieved some notoriety. The 'misty poets,' for example, had emerged from underground poetry salons that had operated in the second half of the Cultural Revolution decade. They deliberately made their creations obscure and difficult to follow in a direct rejection of Maoist clarity and political devotion. The 'search for roots' writers, active during the same period, occupied an important segment of orthodox literature. While their exploration of older or marginal Chinese traditions and legends to forge an innovative, non-Marxist literature was new, they shared with more orthodox writers a serious, even pompous conviction about the importance of writing and writers as the conscience of society. The novelty of Wang Shuo, from his first appearance, was his loud refusal to be taken seriously or to take literature seriously. His attitude, and that of his novels, gave rise to the label 'hoodlum writer' (*liumang zuojia*). It was a badge that Wang wore with pride and that youthful readers embraced with even more enthusiasm. Rebellion on the page, and then on screen, had a strong appeal to the young.

Wang Shuo's early novel, *The Troubleshooters* (*Wanzhu*, a.k.a. *Masters of Mischief* or *The Operators*) told of a group of young men who set up their own company to provide services to a range of people from contemporary society. For an aspiring writer who has no hope of being taken seriously, let alone receiving awards, they organise a literary prize giving celebration. For a busy young man, they offer to stand in on dates with his girlfriend. For other clients, the young men provide the kind of companionship and support that had supposedly once been part of Chinese society but which was now, in the age of economic reform, conspicuously absent. The comedy and satire reinforced the novel's commentary on alienation and the commercialisation of a society cut loose from Maoist austerity and strictures. The characters in Wang's stories were a major part of their appeal to youth. They were also young, rejected adult authority whenever they could, and often were marginal figures in society. In *The Troubleshooters*, one of the young entrepreneurs lives with his girlfriend, sharing a bedroom in his father's apartment. Such a lifestyle was shocking in 1980s China, in part because unmarried cohabitation was difficult in the tight housing market.

Other features of *The Troubleshooters* (and the film made in the year after the novel's publication) that appealed strongly to youthful readers (and viewers) were the sardonic tone of the story, the language used both by the story and by the characters in it, and the attitudes and lifestyles of the protagonists. Wang's self-conscious use of the language of everyday, including a great deal of slang and swear words, set him apart from mainstream writers. This so-called hoodlum stance chimed well with the attitudes and aspirations of his young readers. The characters in these early stories did not subscribe to high-minded ideals and tended to be of rather ordinary social status and wealth. As regular urbanites, their lives reflected the changes in their readers' lives. In post-Mao society, these characters belonged not to what the Communist Party called 'the masses' (*qunzhong*) or even 'the people' (*renmin*). Starting in the 1980s, and endorsed by writers like Wang Shuo, a new label for such ordinary people began to gain currency. *Laobaixing* (ordinary people; literally 'old hundred surnames') had a long pedigree from at least the time of Confucius (fifth century B.C.E.). *Laobaixing* was a term that Wang's readers could embrace as their own. In a society that was determinedly breaking away from a strictly Marxist classification of social status, use of the word was itself a political statement of rejection of earlier class-based terms. Presented in an amusing, satirical tale of self-delusion and free-market action, *laobaixing* was typical of Wang Shuo's ability to make points full of political implications and yet keep his readers highly entertained.

In 1988 Wang Shuo became a celebrity writer. This phenomenon was itself new in the increasingly commercialised world of Chinese cultural production. Finding equivalent figures in the period before the 1980s is difficult. Yang Mo, the writer of the hugely popular novel *The Song of Youth* (*Qingchun zhi ge*, 1956), had enjoyed the attentions of legions of young fans in the late 1950s, as her novel and the 1959 colour film made from it proved to be huge hits. Hao Ran, a writer of lengthy novels set in the collectivising countryside, enjoyed considerable fame in the 1960s and 1970s. But both these writers were utterly mainstream and orthodox. Yang's story of youthful idealism in the 1930s cleaved entirely to the founding mythology of the Communist revolution. Hao Ran's more ordinary heroes also reflected the 'high, wide, and handsome' ethos of Cultural Revolution art and literature. In complete contrast to these predecessor celebrity authors, Wang Shuo was his own (and his youthful readers') man.

Born in 1958, Wang Shuo grew up in an army compound in Beijing. His 1991 novel, *Wild Beasts* (*Dongwu xiongmeng*), told the story of a gang of young teenagers spending their days during the 1970s getting into trouble and chasing girls in an army compound. The story was adapted by *Red Sorghum* actor Jiang Wen as his directorial debut, *In the Heat of the Sun* (*Yangguang canlan de rizi*, 1995). Youthful readers of the novel and watchers of the film were attracted by the extraordinary freedom the young men and women enjoy in the story despite the heightened political tensions of the Cultural Revolution that form a mostly unseen background to the story. By the mid-1970s Wang was a teenager himself. Graduating

Figure 5.1. The buddies enjoy the freedom of the bathhouse in the 1970s in *In the Heat of the Sun* (directed by Jiang Wen, 1995).
*Source:* Author's collection.

from high school in 1976, just a few months before the death of Mao, Wang was enlisted in the navy by his army officer father. His first published story (in 1978), about a young woman anxious to leave the stifling direction of her parents, was typical of an outpouring of melodramatic (and nonpolitical) writing in the late 1970s.[5] Wang quit the navy in 1980 and spent the next three years as a clerk in a Beijing medicine wholesaler. During this time he also dabbled in the kind of dealing with the new household appliances (televisions, VCRs, and washing machines) that had become de rigeur for urban Chinese families. This experience gave him the background for the anti-hero Shi Ba in his *Emerging from the Surface of the Sea* (*Fuchu haimian*), made into the 1988 film *Samsara* (*Lunhui*).[6]

In 1983 Wang Shuo became a full-time writer. His debut novella, *Air Stewardess* (*Kongzhong xiaojie*), appeared in the prestigious literary journal *Dangdai* (*Contemporary*) early in the following year. Wang's young readers saw in the story of premarital cohabitation and splitting up another welcome reflection of contemporary life, though with a degree of gloss associated with airline staff and access to apartment space. *The Troubleshooters* followed in 1987 and *Playing for Thrills* (*Wanrde jiu shi xintiao*) in 1989. These were present-day stories written with an obviously present-day attitude. Political slogans only appeared to be made fun of: A prostitute recycles Mao's exhortation in claiming to 'serve the people' (*wei renmin fuwu*); a rebel makes sardonic comments on his predicament with 'self-reliance and working diligently despite difficulties' (*zili geng sheng, jianku fendou*). The Beijing slang in the stories chimed perfectly with the fashion of students in the city to adopt the local, informal language as a marker of their distinction. It also served as a shared element for young people from across the nation. In the days before the Internet made youth language easy to share and elaborate as an identity marker, the stories of Wang Shuo served the purpose of helping popularise a youth patois.

The urban shift in the 1980s, part of the general move away from Maoist orthodoxies, had its most engaging spokesman in Wang Shuo. Even the pages of the official media featured items about the popular author. In the fall of 1988 the literature and art page of the *People's Daily* included a discussion of the rise of 'popular literature' (*tongsu wenxue*), a term that carried overtones of low-brow taste and vulgarity, similar to the equivalent term in music. The more high-minded literature of political example and exhortation had clearly lost ground since the end of the Maoist era. The burgeoning of popular publication, both books and periodicals, was a feature of the early period of economic reform. Registered publishers found ways to widen the range of their offerings to readers, even selling their publication licenses to privately owned publishers so that the latter could appear to be within the law by including an official publication number on their products. Beyond this official and semi-official publishing enterprise was a host of even more entrepreneurial publishers, cashing in on the tastes for scandal, shock, and celebrity displayed by the Chinese public.[7]

A subset of this newly popular reading material came from abroad, enlarging the imaginative space available to youth readers. Beginning in the late 1970s, the translation of a wide range of Western fiction, including the kinds of bestsellers and airport novels which more fastidious foreign and Chinese critics might despise, brought unprecedented choice to Chinese book buyers. Before the 1980s appropriately serious novels from the Soviet Union and other socialist nations had taken pride of place in Chinese publishing, and access to more unusual fare (translations of American novels from Salinger or Kerouac) had been controlled through more restricted circulation. Now Chinese readers could get hold of translated fiction from all over the world and across a broad spectrum of literary worth. By one reckoning, 172 works of foreign literature were published in translation each year in China in the thirty years before 1980. By 1989 that annual number had tripled to 657 works, with a surge after 1985. As significant was the shift in content. In the first thirty years of the People's Republic, almost two-thirds of the translated works came from the Soviet Union and eighteen percent from Britain, France, and the United States. Between 1980 and 1987, Soviet literature accounted for a mere six percent, whereas the latter provided almost six out of ten titles. By 1988 almost half of Western translations could be considered popular writing.[8]

For several Chinese filmmakers of the new Fifth Generation that had emerged after the Cultural Revolution, adapting Wang Shuo's writing to the screen offered a route out of an apparent entrapment in the late 1980s in rural and historical allegories of the nation. The urban and contemporary settings of Wang's stories and his determinedly modern and apolitical sensibility could provide young Chinese film with a way forward that was more substantial than simply trying to copy Hollywood's or Hong Kong's success with purely entertainment films.[9] Huang Jianxin filmed *Samsara* in the summer of 1988. The story of a petty dealer in stolen goods, though from an established military family, the film included a so-called last supper shared by the protagonists, including a young Chinese woman who has returned from abroad (as had the actress who played her). The hero's words are quoted: 'Buddies and gals (*gemenr jiemenr*) have come from all corners of the world have come together from a shared revolutionary purpose – to drink!'[10] The satirical reference to revolution was typical of Wang Shuo and what made his attitude so appealing to young readers. In a year in which 'main melody' (*zhuxuanlü*) propaganda films, new-style entertainment films, and art-house features were all having difficulty attracting viewers, Wang Shuo adaptations created their own opportunities for success and offered the film industry access to the youthful audiences it craved.

Zhang Yimou was under considerable pressure to match the success of *Red Sorghum* with his second film as director. Expectations were high, but cynics wondered if the young director could even remotely match the first film's impact. Zhang saw the popularity of Wang Shuo's writing with the kind of audience that had taken so enthusiastically to *Red Sorghum* – especially young men who related to the untamed and hard-living Grandfather figure in that film. Adapting a Wang Shuo story to the screen offered some hope in matching the enthusiasm aroused by *Red Sorghum*. An urban, contemporary story could also help shift the ground in audience judgment of his second feature. The hero of the piece, a young delivery man who rides a three-wheeled cart around the streets of Beijing, adopts an exercise and nutritional regimen in order to enter a bodybuilding contest. The low social status of the protagonist and the highly topical subject of bodybuilding were typical features of Wang Shuo's writing, as was the Beijing setting in the *hutongs* and clogged streets of the capital. The delivery man finds himself turning into a woman, hence the female–male elements in the title, *Yinyang Man* (*Yinyang ren*). Zhang spent many months working with Wang on writing a screenplay from the original story, *A Man and a Woman* (*Nanren he nüren*).[11] Even an unusual story of an ordinary young man's gender

Figure 5.2. The anti-hero of Wang Shuo's novella *Samsara* (in director Huang Jianxin's 1988 adaptation, Xi'an Film Studio).
*Source:* Author's collection.

change as part of getting ahead in today's more competitive society could not be made convincing on screen. Zhang turned to another project likely to appeal to young male audience members, an international hijacking thriller involving handsome antiterrorism officers and a beautiful airline stewardess, played by *Red Sorghum* star Gong Li. The political dimension, portraying unprecedented but secret cooperation between Taiwan and mainland authorities, added to the promise of the project, both for the Beijing authorities and for youthful fans of spy stories. The Wang Shuo film idea was abandoned and Zhang's *Code-name Puma (Daihao 'Meizhoubao')* was born.

By early 1989, when the *People's Daily* published a story on him, Wang Shuo had joined with several fellow writers and artists in establishing the Seahorse Film and Television Creative Centre. For such a commercially successful writer, whose work was being adapted for large and small screens, this was a logical next step. Two of his partners in the venture were the authors of *Rock 'n Roll Kids* and *Red Sorghum*, Liu Yiran and Mo Yan respectively. Wang took on the chairmanship of the board.[12] At a time when much of the Chinese film world was earnestly discussing how to make Chinese films more entertaining and lamenting the weakness of the local industry in this regard when compared to Hollywood, the new company aimed to strengthen Chinese efforts to compete for the entertainment yuan.

In late May 1989, hundreds of students from Beijing and around the nation had been camped out in Tiananmen Square for several weeks. Their protests against official corruption and rising inflation and for vaguely democratic ideals had attracted strong support from the people of Beijing. An almost carnival atmosphere pervaded the central square, despite the increasing tension as the authorities considered their options for bringing an end to the unprecedented upheaval.[13] In this charged atmosphere, Wang Shuo's latest novel, *Playing for Thrills*, appeared in China's bookstores. A review in *People's Daily*, itself a signal distinction, headlined the 'Beijing flavor' (*Jingweir*) of the work. This strong Beijing connection in the book, with the latest language and expressions popular among the young in the city, was reminiscent of the Beijing atmosphere in the novels of Lao She (1899–1966), like Wang Shuo a member of the Manchu ethnic minority that had formed the last ruling dynasty of China. But Wang's story was set in the thriving new cities of the southern seaboard of China.[14] Despite this geographical distance, the somewhat sleazy narrator and the humour of the story had a distinctive Beijing flavour, as the youthful protagonists sought thrills and play acted at life in typical Wang Shuo fashion. The story was neither tragedy nor comedy: Readers would in turn laugh or cry at the black humour, according to the reviewer.

Events in early June 1989 might have threatened Wang Shuo's position as a kind of spokesman for contemporary youth through his writing and public persona. Youthful rebellion in the pages of his novels and in the films based on them had become political in the spring of that year with a disastrous outcome. But, in a case similar to that of singer Cui Jian, Wang's public profile appears to have not suffered much. Ironically the mid-year issues of one of China's most widely read magazines, *Popular Film*, featured a two-part article on Wang titled 'A "philistine" who dares to despise convention.' This was perhaps not the ideal way to appear in the mass media in the tense months after the June 4 events.[15] The somewhat breathless account of Wang's life emphasised the social upheaval and youthful rebellion of the Red Guards in the first years of the Cultural Revolution and the young Wang's run-ins with the law. His part-time activities while still in the navy as a broker of household appliances and other scarce goods are described with admiration for his energy in flying around the country making deals. In his exit interview before leaving the military, Wang reportedly asked for support in being nominated to join the Communist Party, but was refused. All these escapades were recounted in the pages of the magazine in a manner similar to the exploits of the hoodlums in his novels, even including parenthetical references to similar events or characters from some of his better-known works and quotes from Lu Xun, Herzen, Montesquieu, Goethe, and others. He lived for a time off the wages of a flight attendant, an experience he turned into his first widely acclaimed story. He later met his wife, dancer Shen Xu, and lived with her for two years before they were married. From the *Popular Film* account, Wang Shuo came across as a version of the kinds of characters who populated his novels: disrespectful of convention, out to seize any opportunity to make money or a name for himself, and overall an almost admirable anti-hero. Unlike the literary writers of the 1950s to the 1970s, Wang was not afraid to say directly what he meant. Nor did he feel a need to coat his observations of society with a gloss of lazy morality. The timing of this account seemed to be breathtakingly bad, as the optimism of 1988 and 1989 among many educated youthful Chinese gave way to a numbed silence.[16]

Wang Shuo's fortunes in the media provide a barometer of the warmth or coldness of the cultural climate. By 1992 his contributions to the scripts for two highly popular television serials, *Yearnings* (*Kewang*) and *Stories from the Editorial Office* (*Bianjibu de gushi*), had secured his place in the entertainment world of Chinese viewers, both young and middle-aged. The former was a relatively mainstream telling of a tale of young love, separation, and yearning set in contemporary Beijing. *Stories from the Editorial Office* was a better reflection of the cheeky, sharp observation of urban life with which Wang had established his reputation in the 1980s. In an officially endorsed public culture with little room for satire, the serial's poking of fun at the bureaucratic caution and subservient rebellion in a magazine office was a welcome relief from po-faced praise for the wisdom of leaders. A third television serial, *I Love You Absolutely* (*Ai ni mei shangliang*), followed. All three serials played at primetime on CCTV.[17]

In the new decade, while his star rose strongly through the vehicle of the television serials, Wang Shuo remained the object of what can only be called moral panic on the part of some commentators.[18] Three new books ensured interest in Wang Shuo received a new impetus. *Wang Shuo: Great Master or Rogue?*, published in 1993, collected a large number of critical comments and outright attacks on the writer. It was one of several books that tried to cash in on his popularity, including Wang's own *I Am Wang Shuo* (1992) and *Critique of Wang Shuo* (1993).[19] The size of the print runs for these volumes, thirty thousand for the latter book and a reprint to forty thousand copies in the case of Wang's own autobiographical contribution, indicated the publishers' expectations of public interest. The (for China) immodestly titled *I Am Wang Shuo* comprised a transcript of a lengthy interview with Wang about his life and then about his writing, with his own assessments of his major works and comments about his style and attitudes toward fiction. A third area covered in the interview transcript was literature in general, including foreign writers such as Milan Kundera. The interview made occasional reference to Shen Xu, a performer with the Oriental Song and Dance Troupe. Celebrity writers apparently needed a glamourous partner.[20]

The two authors of *Critique of Wang Shuo*, published by the respected Chinese Academy of Social Sciences Press, noted in their introduction that Wang Shuo even in 1992 remained hot (*re*), indeed hotter than film or soccer stars.[21] *Wang Shuo: Great Master or Rogue?* expressed the most mixed views of the celebrity author's success. In 246 pages were reprinted a selection of the hundreds of short and long responses to Wang's work that had been sent to the newspaper *China Youth* (*Zhongguo qingnian bao*) after it published in a supplement on 30 January 1993 a pseudonymous article titled 'A brilliant and colourful poisonous spider' (*Yi zhi secaibanlan de du zhizhu*). Also included in the March 1993 book was a selection of articles published in response to the debate on the value and impact of Wang Shuo's writing. The book was graced by a provocative introduction by 'Old Stupid' (*Lao Yu*), author of the original piece in January, who repeated the notion of Wang's work being a poisonous influence on society.[22] Such so-called debates helped sell books. Wang Shuo himself had long operated under the principle that all publicity was good publicity, a rebellious notion that seems to have endeared him to his youthful fans.[23]

The appeal of Wang Shuo's cynical attitude toward the conventional regard in which writers were held in China was nicely indicated in a 1993 interview with the celebrity author in the pages of *Beijing Youth* magazine. What he said in the interview was perhaps less important than the way the interviewer described going with Wang Shuo from a bookstore book signing to lunch in McDonald's in Wangfujing, Beijing's premiere shopping street. Wang had a Big Mac and a chocolate shake, his interviewer a chicken burger and an ice cream. This was obviously not the way a more orthodox writer would conduct an interview about his work.[24] The subsequent interview, conducted in his home, was vintage Wang. He freely acknowledged he cared about money and having a good income, something he learned in his journeys to wealthier Guangdong as a wheeler-dealer over ten years earlier. Literary people engaging in business was a natural development, an attitude many young readers in the 1990s would have found refreshingly candid. Pompous or righteous talk about literary value and the social function of literature belonged in an earlier age: 'I want to become a cultural broker, and help some closeted writers, unable to publicise themselves, to manage things according to commercial rules.'[25]

Wang continued to adapt to the times, the trajectory of his fiction mapping the evolving commercialism in Chinese art and literature. Wang became one of the new-style, cultural–commercial icons of the new century's culture. No longer dominant in youth culture, he sustained his prominence in the new digital age. By 1994 he had established a company, Current Affairs Cultural Work Consulting Company (*Shishi wenhua shiwu zixun gongsi*), in which he was president.[26] After fourteen years of writing, freshness of subject matter and language had become harder to maintain. Turning to business was an opportunity to take a break from writing, remould himself, and help some friends. Besides, his considerable experience with television serials gave him special insight into which scripts could work on the small screen.[27] Reportedly there were already 700 television stations in China by 1995, only a handful of which made drama serials. This huge demand for product to fill the screens on over three hundred million television sets offered considerable scope to the entrepreneurial Wang, so well-tuned as he was to the tastes of youth audiences. The new company targeted the thirty-seven provincial and major city stations, which reportedly made a profit of twenty-six percent on advertising, though in some cases this rose to as high as fifty percent.[28] In an interview quote, Wang stated that one lesson from his earlier Seahorse company was that the most reliable and cleanest relationships in business were contractual relations. East Asian people relied too much on mutual obligation: If someone does you a favour for free, you remain subordinated by that obligation. Relationships based on money were a lot clearer, more efficient, and less complicated. This somewhat steely attitude captured the restlessness of his younger fans with the kinds of abuse and complications that conventional relationships entailed. A rapidly changing society required new norms. Youth wanted to escape the familial and other obligations that restricted the freedom of many of them to take advantage of new opportunities. As Wang Shuo jokingly noted: 'Before [as a writer] I was a 'secret prostitute' (*anchang*), now [as a businessman] I've started to 'put a required price on my wares' (*mingma biaojia*).'[29]

In addition to films and television dramas, Wang Shuo's new company aimed to publish books. The latter included series pitched at a youth readership, including young women. Some of China's most renowned post–Cultural Revolution women writers appeared in Wang's series, an indication of the clout Wang could bring to enhance their readership pool. Another series included writers who had emerged in the 1990s, but had not achieved first-rank status in the officially endorsed literary pecking order because their works may have lacked literary pretensions, being more concerned with the nitty-gritty of everyday life.[30] A third series was pitched also at youth readers. Titled 'A Dog's Eye View of the World' (*Gouyan kan shijie*), it was a comic book series. The series' name came from a comic scripted by Wang Shuo himself, working in collaboration with cartoonist Chen Xilin. The two dog characters in the comic were called Little Dog Wang and Little Dog Chen (*Wang xiaogou, Chen xiaogou*). The first two volumes in the new comic series were *Dream of Giving Up Football* (*Mengduan zuqiu*) and *City Rock 'n Roll* (*Chengshi yaogun*), both contents and format of obvious appeal to youth.[31]

To assess the tastes of his youthful audience and to generate publicity, Wang Shuo's new cultural services company conducted a large-scale survey in early 1995. Nine thousand respondents in Beijing and almost twelve thousand in Shanghai indicated their most and least favourite films and actors from 1994, and their all-time favourites.[32] Actress Gong Li had the distinction of being named the best actress of 1994 in Beijingers' eyes, but the worst in the opinion of Shanghai respondents, who chose the somewhat more elegant Pan Hong as their favourite. Beijing and Shanghai respondents agreed, however, that Gong Li was the best actress when all years were included.[33] Chen Kaige won best director in 1994 recognition in both cities, probably because of his then banned film *Farewell, My Concubine* (*Bawang bieji*, 1993). Indeed Shanghai voters named it as their favourite film of all time, selected by thirteen percent of those surveyed. Beijingers chose the highly orthodox revolutionary history epic, *Great Decisive Battle* (Da juezhan, 1993), selected by 9.4 percent. Veteran director Xie Jin, famous for his melodramas on recent shared historical experience, was named favourite director of all time.

The selections for favourite television programmes and actors confirmed Wang Shuo's skills in pleasing audiences. His *Guobayin* (*Getting One's Kicks*), a forty-part series about an on-again, off-again romance, was a clear favourite in the two cities, with close to one-half of respondents selecting it as the best 1994 television programme. Close to twenty percent of participants named the serial as their all-time favourite. Jiang Shan, star of the series, was nominated by half of those surveyed in Beijing and Shanghai for 1994 television shows and by a smaller margin as favourite television actress ever. Wang Zhiwen, lead actor, received best television actor for all-time accolades, with half of the Shanghai respondents naming him for 1994 appearances. Feng Xiaogang, director of *Chicken Feathers* (*Yi di jimao*), a satirical look at negotiating with petty power holders, took the top spot for best television director in 1994 and ever. As the youth magazine reporter noted, the survey results showed that audiences preferred works and actors that reflected the reality of contemporary life. These were precisely the content and style that distinguished Wang Shuo's works and attracted their legions of youthful readers and viewers.

By the end of 1995 Wang Shuo had put down his writer's rice bowl and picked up the sandalwood chopsticks of a film director, as the headline in *Beijing Youth* described it.[34] Wang confessed to not wanting to continue writing on subjects drawn from his youth and finding it difficult to write about strictly contemporary society. The opportunity to direct *I Am Your*

*Dad* (*Wo shi ni baba*), based on one of his own stories, arose when his friend Feng Xiaogang decided to act in the film and give up directing it. Feng Xiaogang would shortly afterward become a major celebrity by inventing the New Year event film and directing a string of such works, mostly in a comic–satirical vein. These hit movies were targeted particularly at urban youth with money to spend on tickets (and on the products strategically placed on screen) and with the ability to spot the contemporary, hip allusions and jokes.[35]

By the turn of the century Wang Shuo's preeminence as an influencer of youth cultures and hip articulator of resistance to mainstream culture had faded. In the multiple possibilities offered by a youth space increasingly dominated by the Internet, perhaps no one could succeed to the kind of position that the now forty-one-year-old Wang Shuo had achieved in 1988. If we must name a single personality who could be said to have come close to this sort of impact on China's youth, it would be hard to ignore Wang's erstwhile collaborator Feng Xiaogang. His Chinese New Year blockbusters proved sure-fire hits for several years in a row. Hollywood actor Donald Sutherland even starred in one of these, *Big Shot's Funeral* (*Da wanr*, 2001), a satire on Chinese commercialism, worship of the foreign, and obsession with celebrity. Ironically the film helped secure its director's celebrity status. Through film Feng Xiaogang captured the kind of contemporary currents and ethos in the 2000s that Wang Shuo had strikingly put on paper in the 1980s.[36]

Wang Shuo meanwhile did not sit still. Debate continued among literary types on the merits of his fiction, though the consensus appeared to be that it would endure. A cover story in a mass-market magazine in 2007 typified Wang's enduring twin status as bad-boy rebel and cultural wheeler-dealer. The title 'Wang Shuo wild' (*Wang Shuo xiongmeng*) was a play on the title of his 1994 novella *Wild Beasts* (*Dongwu xiongmeng*), from which the Cultural Revolution nostalgia film *In the Heat of the Sun* had been adapted.[37] The twelve-page feature, subtitled 'Middle-aged Wang Shuo's enlightenment and redemption,' started with a quote over a full-page photograph of the middle-aged author: 'Why after 1991 did I adopt self-effacing [self-extermination] behaviour. For example, I want to separate myself from the mainstream of society. From *Yearning* onwards I have been channeled into the social mainstream. I'm really uncomfortable with that. I'm against society. What is society? Middle-class, hypocritical.'[38] As he approached fifty, Wang represented the brashness of the 1980s and the general fragmentation of social cohesion that had accompanied the accelerated economic growth from the mid-1990s onward. This admiring overview of his career noted his ability to remain at the forefront of popular taste and attitudes. A pioneer in recognising the power of the media in the new reform era, Wang continued to somewhat self-consciously lead opinion in his reassessments of China's literary and cultural heritage. Admiration for the classic novel, *A Dream of Red Mansions*, and dabbling in cosmology, Buddhism, and his own versions of Confucian morality primers and other classics represented the kind of diversity of interest and pastime that the Internet allowed for youth. Young people by now simply regarded Wang as something of a grand old relic of the possibilities of resistance. Judging from this article, youth attitudes to Wang by 2008 appeared to be a mix of admiration for his studied cynicism and acknowledgment of his role in opening up a public space for direct expression of personal views. By then, however, a technology and social phenomenon (the Internet) had taken over that role.[39]

There was still a market for a book analysing Wang Shuo's views of fiction and life, though it provided a good measure of changes in the nature of popular culture between the late 1980s and the late 2000s. The commercial bent of the new work was more obvious than that of the early 1990s publications. *The Wang Shuo Code: Solving the Riddle of the Wang Shuo 'Success'* (2007) tried to cash in on Chinese interest in the international bestseller Dan Brown's *The Da Vinci Code*.[40] The book covered a range of topics about Wang's taste in art, his judgments about earlier generations of Chinese writers (including the late and much-loved Beijing writer Lao She), and his views on recent Chinese movies. The inside back cover flap helpfully listed thirteen films adapted from stories by Wang. Reportedly in 2008 his publishers paid three yuan per character for his latest novel, totalling 3.5 million yuan, an unprecedented high in Chinese publishing history.

Not to be left behind, in late March 2007 Wang established a website called Fresh Flower Village (*Xianhua cun*) to coincide with the release of a new book. This project, like the feature article outlined earlier, marked the most active public appearances of the writer in more than seven years. Indeed some reported it as a 'return from retirement' (*fuchu*).[41] The website was to include on its plain first page links to blogs, a shopping centre, discussion forum, and registration. Further in were news pages, a literary page, new writings, and selected classical writing. Even before its official launch the site had attracted more than one hundred thousand visits. A money making enterprise, the site charged ten fen (cents) for a visit to the blog Wang put on the site. With a new blog and one hundred thousand visitors every day, he stood to receive ten thousand yuan (dollars) daily. Wang would be the first Chinese blogger to charge for access to his blogs. By early 2007 there were 17.5 million blogs on the Chinese Internet, with 7.7 million of them active.[42] Although having not published any substantial works since 1991, Wang argued that he had been writing continuously in the intervening years, so there was plenty of new material to offer to website customers. He claimed visitors would discover that he had been experimenting with new language and ideas. Moreover, his habit of shooting from the hip in commenting on fellow writers and celebrities promised an entertaining time to his internet fans.[43]

There were other attractions in a website. Offering access to a writer's works through a website was a means for any author to undercut pirate publishers (*daoban*) who brought out unauthorised editions of popular novels. Another advantage of a website was the selling of memberships in an author's or publisher's fan club. Membership could offer an opportunity to chat online with Wang himself. As he acknowledged, he had never had any difficulty talking. Taking full advantage of the possibilities opened up by the 'Net, website members might in the future order a personalised version of a book by Wang. The cover could feature, for example, a photo of the author and fan together, signed by the former, on special paper with fancy binding. Advertising and sales of music and film downloads would also provide revenue streams for the entrepreneurial author–celebrity.[44] With this venture, Wang Shuo ended the first decade of the new century in an equivalent position to that which he had established for himself in the 1980s. On both occasions Wang was at the cutting edge of trends. His hoodlum stance that had held so much appeal for China's youth in the late 1980s had merged into a cynical posture in the new century, one just as aware of trends in the youth cultural space and not shy in acknowledging the importance of money and consumerism to all those in that space, including his fellow artists and his readers.

In a way, handsome writer Han Han (born in 1982) was the Wang Shuo equivalent for the new century. With film-star good looks, unlike the somewhat flabby Wang, and a lifestyle of race car driving as well as writing, Han's career was even more characterised by commercialism and commodification than that of his 1980s predecessor. He had come to public attention as a teenager with a novel on the examination pressure on high schoolers. A high school dropout, Han earned enough money with the bestseller to buy five cars, which impressed many young Chinese more than his literary accomplishment.[45] Such was his instant celebrity that his father produced an account of his son, published in 2000 by one of the most established Shanghai publishing houses.[46] Taking advantage like Wang of the new technologies, Han was one of the most popular bloggers on sina.com. Such was his celebrity by 2008 he was able to make sarcastic comments on official discourse and relatively sensitive political matters on his blog while escaping much censure from the authorities. Fame and fandom put Han Han above the law to a degree that only the Internet could allow. His role was perhaps as a kind of safety valve to

Figure 5.3. Racing car driver and author Han Han adorns the cover of a collection of his stories.
*Source: Han Han zuopinji* (Han Han: Collected works), Beijing: Shijie zhishi chubanshe, 2006.

allow a limited degree of political commentary, read mostly by the young and unnoticed by older Party leaders. Han also set up his own online bookstore on taobao.com, making recommendations for readers, and he began publishing a magazine in 2010, after the manner of Oprah Winfrey on the other side of the Pacific. His books featured photos of the author on their covers, reinforcing his attraction to both male and female youthful readers.[47] Even in his heyday Wang could not measure up to the glamour of this new novelist and media celebrity. Han Han was very much a product of the age of idol worship (*ouxiang chongbai*) that the triumph of *Supergirl* and its successor programmes had secured in the minds of young China.[48]

## THE RISE OF THE CHINESE INTERNET

By the first decade of the new century, the Internet provided a multifo-cal, multilocal virtual space for the construction, elaboration, and shar-ing of youth identities in China. From about nine million in 1999, the number of netizens, those who used the Internet, had increased to over three hundred and fifty million ten years later. The vast majority of users were under the age of thirty, with those under twenty-four years old pre-dominating.[49] Virtual worlds enhanced the space available for youthful expressions of difference, resistance, and solidarity to an extent impossi-ble before the new century. While parents, teachers, and authorities fret-ted about the effects of Internet use on the young, Chinese youths with the resources to respond adopted the new technology and its potential with gusto.

This rapidly growing youth phenomenon attracted sociologists and youth policy workers keen to understand the changes and bend them to their purposes. Surveys were conducted, often producing results that respondents thought the researchers wanted: a characteristic of survey results in a society in which frank expressions of opinions to strang-ers were always circumscribed by political caution. Rather than depend on what netizens claimed that they did on the Internet, a more produc-tive approach examined actual usage. In a 2005 survey conducted in Guangzhou, researchers compared the importance in these respects of tele-vision, print media, radio, and cellphones. For entertainment, the Internet was the first choice of 71.6 percent of Guangzhou youth surveyed. For self-expression, the figure was 74.9 percent.[50] Given the relative control exercised over broadcast and print media in China, these figures should come as no surprise. The 'Net was a virtual world of comparative free-dom for young people. One researcher argued that on the 'Net children from single-child families could express themselves more easily to peers rather than being confined to discussion with their parents.[51]

A 2002 survey of almost eleven hundred Beijing university and high school students with an average age of 16.25 years provides a useful snapshot of usage and purpose. About one in eight had started using the 'Net before 1998. By the year 2000 'Have you been on the 'Net yet?' (*Ni shang wang le ma?*) had become a fashionable greeting, in place of the usual 'Have you eaten?'[52] Gender differences were clear in reasons for using the 'Net. About half of female students said they searched for mate-rials related to their studies, while only 35.1 percent of male students claimed to do the same. Playing Internet games likewise attracted 46.9 percent of males, but only fifteen percent of females. Whereas half the male Beijing students most often looked for news of Internet games, only 17.8 percent of their female classmates did. On the other hand, forty-one percent of the women used the 'Net to find news of film and television stars, while only 23.8 percent of the boys did. For news on sporting stars, in contrast, twice the proportion of boys used the 'Net than girls (30.9 to 15.8 percent). Like their counterparts worldwide, boys far outnumbered female students in seeking information on computing and hardware (29.5 to 11.2 percent respectively).[53]

An early positive view of youth and the Internet came in mid-2002 from two researchers in two of the most progressive cities in China, Guangzhou and Shenzhen. Liu Lanping and Hua Tongxu listed the characteristics of the 'Net and its use: It was technical, virtual, interactive, open (*kaifangxing*), global, empowering (*zizhuxing*), and creative. These qualities and the potential of the 'Net to contribute to cultural development among youth could outweigh the negative features of the 'Net, including the prevalence of junk or harmful content, the opportunities for addiction and isolation, and its particular impact upon youthful values.[54] A pioneering comparative study of high schoolers and university-level Internet users in late 2004 in Zhejiang, Hunan, and Gansu provinces showed that the virtual, anonymous, and equal digital world offered a space for new kinds of youth conduct and characteristics.[55] In finding information, seeking friends, playing games, or downloading films and music, young men regarded the Internet in an instrumental way, as a useful tool, whereas young women saw it more as a means of satisfying feelings.[56]

The new language of the 'Net was one attraction for young people, as well as a marker of distinctive youth culture and identities. New language conventions, mixing alliterations of English words, child-like repetitions, and other informal changes to standard usage, emerged in the chatrooms and BBS ['bulletin board system'] networks. This new language, as a kind of resistance to the numbing orthodoxy of approved public discourse, was a major attraction of the Internet for many young people. It was the equivalent of the satirical, underground playing with language that had entertained some sent-down youth in the 1970s and emerged aboveground in popular jokes in the 1980s. By the start of the new century, the Internet had become an important feature of youth social life and friendships. Fan groups, formed around shared interest in a particular kind of music or celebrity, or interest groups could set up websites and interact with each other and with newcomers. The possibility of anonymity on the Internet seems to have been a major element in its rapid rise as a tool for youthful interaction and expression. As in the case of the contrast between official and Internet language use, so in this respect, the contrast with the real world was considerable. In the latter a Chinese citizen could feel helpless and never quite alone. In front of a computer screen, a netizen could do things impossible or more risky in real life. One of the most revealing questions in a 2005 survey of high school students in Ningbo asked if respondents felt happier or more in control of their lives on the 'Net than in real life. The students split down the middle: Forty-six point three eight percent agreed; the rest did not. One in five was always thinking about going online. One quarter of the Ningbo students thought that their parents and teachers did not really approve of their attitude toward the 'Net.[57]

Authority figures saw the dangers in youthful autonomy on the 'Net. A researcher at the Chinese People's Public Security University expressed concern at the baleful influence of the Internet. Wei Hongxin offered one illustration of her points, a nineteen-year-old in Dongguan in Guangdong. This young man discovered a pornographic website and in the space of two months had browsed the 'Net more than seventeen thousand times.[58] A counterpart at a Hunan police college concurred. Ouyang Yanwen discounted the Web as simply creating virtual 'subcultures' (ya wenhua). These might provide a channel for youth socialisation, but offered more dangerous temptations also. The Internet furthermore offered a means for further onslaught from foreign culture and a weakening of Chinese identity.[59] As a teacher at Fujian Normal University thundered, in real life there were winners and losers and many people found it hard to find respect from others. But on the Internet 'your status is virtual, just like taking part in a costume party. There are no ugly ducklings; everyone is a prince or princess. But it's all virtual.'[60]

The rise of the Internet bar [wangba] in China revealed the impact on patterns of youth consumerism and the official concern at regulating their use by young people. The first such bar had been established in Shanghai in 1995.[61] It was modelled on Internet cafés in Taiwan and an hour at a screen cost between twenty and thirty yuan, which was expensive for the time.[62] Soon the first Internet bars were competing with games halls for young customers by installing computer- and Internet-based games. By 2007 there were an estimated one hundred and twenty thousand such registered sites. Unlike Internet cafés in Europe and the Americas, which catered to a broad cross-section of society, had few gamers, and offered coffee and food, Chinese Internet bars were more the domain of young people.[63] Even at a time when ownership of personal computers at home was increasing rapidly, the use of Internet bars was growing at an even faster rate.[64] Most young Internet bar customers were unmarried, with few responsibilities at home or work, allowing time for other pursuits. As one bar user noted: 'If the Internet bar disappeared, I really don't know how I would spend the evening. Hanging round at home watching TV with the parents would be so boring!' The Internet bars had become a cheap way to pass the time, especially compared with regular bars, the movies, or other entertainment choices.

Debate about the negative effects of Internet bars on youth morality and social stability appeared almost as soon as the first such bar. Official interventions increased, often prompted by appalling incidents such as deadly fires in poorly regulated bars like the one that occurred in Beijing in 2002. As in other areas of Chinese life, real conditions often fell short of government ambitions.[65] From December 2005, for example, the authorities introduced requirements for users of Internet bars to show identification to prove they were at least eighteen years old. At such a bar in western Beijing, high school boys in uniform rode up on their bicycles and rushed to resume playing a new, highly appealing 'Net game. At twenty past five on a Friday afternoon, sixteen of eighty computer stations were occupied by minors in school uniform. Others, about fifteen years old, had changed out of their school clothes. In Jinan, a reporter discovered a student in a Shandong Normal University Attached Middle School uniform at a glowing gaming screen in the 'Strange Space' (*Yidu kongjian*) Internet bar adjacent to the university. Acknowledging their dependence on youthful customers, some Internet bar owners turned to a device with precedents in Communist Party practice. A 'private room' (*neishi*), along the lines of such restricted areas for Party members in bookstores before the 1980s, could be set up to cater to underaged netizens, either within a bar or adjacent to one. In one such fifty-square-metre space in a Beijing bar, eighty screens had been set up, probably breaking fire regulations as well as Internet use rules. Bar managers dismissed a lot of official efforts at control as simply money making, with fees charged for inspections of equipment and the establishment of associations of Internet bar managers. In the countryside, where supervision was usually weaker, 'black Internet bars' (*hei wangba*) did good business with minors.[66]

The young were particularly vulnerable to the allure of Internet games. One Tianjin thirteen-year-old was so attracted by the world of the games that, thinking he too could fly, he extended his arms and stepped off the roof of a twenty-four-story building. In case of failure, he had left a note stating that he was going to look for his heroic friends from the Internet. Other teenagers were reported to have physically attacked their parents when refused access to the Internet. In order to keep playing Internet games some young men went without food, sleep, bathing, or interacting with parents. One-third of juvenile delinquents at a Beijing detention facility in early 2006 habitually visited Internet bars to play games and seek pornography.[67] As a researcher at the Tianjin Social Sciences Academy observed: 'In the virtual world of Internet games you can casually kill people, set fires, you can marry or fall in love. All these things have no real consequences or require responsibility. The still unformed and immature view of life, values and ethics of minors can be easily distorted in this world.' A Beijing psychologist agreed: 'Students who in real life have poor results and cannot feel successful through Internet games can go higher and higher in [the game] levels and feel more and more encouraged and triumphant, rapidly gaining the pleasure of success. But the result is the wastage of time and damage to their studies.'[68] One response was to push for the creation of games that drew more upon the glorious traditions of Chinese civilisation. Thus game playing could reinforce feelings of national identity among the young. At the Tianjin Game Academy (*youxi xueyuan*), the first lessons were on national pride, patriotism, and ethics. In April 2006 a nationwide effort promoting the 'civilised Internet' (*wenming wangluo*) got underway, with ninety days beginning in early May marked in Beijing for the inspection of Internet bars.[69] On 23 January 2007, president Hu Jintao spoke of 'establishing an Internet culture with Chinese characteristics.'

Fifteen Beijing university students who identified themselves as 'Internet addicts' revealed the attractions of the 'Net in interviews in 2007. One declared: 'Classmates tell you a whole lot of ins and outs on an issue. If you get on Baidu [the most popular Chinese portal] for yourself, you can grasp things immediately.'[70] The relative ease and lack of pressure in communicating with friends and others on the Internet was a distinct advantage to these college students. 'No one knows anybody on the 'Net, everyone is pretty polite and you don't have to be too hesitant. It's unrestricted and open (*changkai xinfei*, literally fling open the doors to your heart) communication. That's really hard to achieve in real life, where you can't say much about anything. This includes dorm mates, where heart to heart communication is rare.'[71] Regarding relaxation and the 'Net, one student said watching films or listening to music on the Web was as good a break as going out with classmates, but often classmates did not have the time. Others noted the escape from assignments and other pressures that playing a Web game provided busy students. Success in playing a game might even compensate for lack of classroom achievement. Mastery of a game earned respect from others both on the Web and in the dorms.[72] On the negative side, the Beijing university students acknowledged that a lot of time could be wasted on the 'Net. Some dorm mates chatted on QQ (the dominant instant messaging service) until one or two in the morning.[73]

The new 'Net-based technologies produced youthful entrepreneurs, often lauded in more traditional publications. Li Mingming had only sixty yuan to his name when he arrived in Beijing after graduating from high school in 2000 and slept on the streets initially. A job transporting computers in Zhongguancun, the science and technology district in northwest Beijing, gave Li the opportunity to begin to learn about Web pages. Five years later, sporting the 'Net name 'Pop-top' (*yilaguan*, a pull-tab can), he was enjoying financial success and renown with 'flash' (*shan*) animation on the 'Net and on cell phones. He had pioneered for Chinese users a way to create 'flash' animation and established an identity as Pop-top which could mean users would pay more than usual for his products.[74]

### NETWORKS, NATIONALISM, AND MOBILE PHONES

The BBS intranets, mostly on university campuses, offered researchers an opportunity to examine the virtual communities that their use constructed. A Tsinghua University sociologist in 2007 analysed the society created by the Shuimu (literally water and wood) BBS used by students at that top Beijing university.[75] The research revealed three different kinds of interaction and socially constructed virtual spaces: 'communal society' (*gongshe shehui*), 'stratified society' (*keceng shehui*), and 'public square society' (*guangchang shehui*). In the first space, mostly classmates interacted using their real identities in friendly and sharing ways. The second kind of society was more formalised, in which interactions between teachers and students resembled their relations in the real world. The third kind of community Zhang Yu observed in BBS usage at Tsinghua, unlike the former two, was not stable or fixed, but shaped by the participants in this 'square.' It was a freer and equal space for interaction, with shifting alliances and a lack of strong bonds tying the society together. This virtual society was like the usually temporary 'societies' associated in the real world with such gatherings as temple fairs, coffee bar salons, or spontaneous demonstrations. On the Internet, such gatherings were more anonymous and even more fleeting.[76]

Zhang Yu applied these three kinds of Internet interactions to exactly how users used the BBS site in February and March 2006. The communal users prioritised the entertainment potential of the site, with Chinese chess (*weiqi*), TV games, pop music, dancing, swimming, and WoW [*World of Warcraft*, a popular game programme] among the top key words from this group. The 'public square' nodes (points of interaction) far outnumbered those of the 'communal' group. The smallest community, when measured by nodes, was clearly the stratified community.[77] The number of contributors or participants in particular pages (*banmian*), for example, those grouped under 'Friends together' (*hao pengyou zai yiqi*) or 'Memories' (*si shui liu nian*), was just a few dozen in these two months. Swimming, ice skating, and other sport pages, on the other hand, attracted one to two hundred people who left comment. The 'public square' pages attracted users in the thousands: The Newsexpress page saw over forty-five hundred visitors who made comments, while FamilyLife and Career-Plaza attracted just over and under thirty-five hundred participants respectively. Passive visitors to these pages, who did not leave notes, were of course much more numerous: The news or FamilyLife pages on the Shuimu BBS each week attracted over twenty thousand visitors.[78] Zhang Yu measured the relative intimacy or closeness associated with the users of the different kinds of pages in her three broad communities by analysing the connections and shared pages between users. She discovered that the most intimate connections were with the communal users, of 'Friends together,' and those pages associated with particular provinces: 'Central plateau beauty: Henan' and 'Jilu world: Shandong.' The least degree of intimate connections could be seen in the news and other more informational pages.[79]

Informal or unofficial groups among university students had increased in importance to participants between the 1990s and the 2000s. About one-third of such groups involved just two or three students, and another third consisted of from four to ten people.[80] At Wenzhou University, in the boom town of Zhejiang, about forty-six percent of such informal groups comprised male students only, and thirty percent were for women, with the remainder mixed. These groups even adopted names for themselves: Corn (*Yumi*) consisted of four female classmates who always sat together in class and, in the absence of any member, took notes for the missing classmate. The Three Guys (*Sanrenxing*) were all students in art class, but from different years. They got together and worked on designs for advertisements, which they made money from. A third example was a group of female schoolmates from several departments. They were known by others as Women with Power (*dajieda*).[81] Such groups were self-forming and fluid, with members leaving or joining a not uncommon occurrence. The BBS-based group was the largest, with a core of about ten members and a total of up to thirty participants. All groups had a strong element of democracy: Two-thirds of surveyed students said that in their alliances members spoke out freely (*changsuoyuyan*). Over three-quarters reported group discussion and decision making on issues.[82] A member of Corn noted: 'There are parents at home and teachers at school, so we don't have leeway to develop ourselves and have no freedom or equal trust, and no real democracy. The reason we got together and our aim was to free ourselves (*jiefang ziji*) and to happily live our lives. Only together with our close classmates can we feel we can keep no secrets from each other. We feel worry free and relaxed. Why? Because things are really democratic among us, our interactions are completely equal dialogues, genuine discussion. Our dialogues reflect equal shared influence and a process of shared inspiration.'[83] In contrast, participation in school-organised groups was clearly from utilitarian motives, for the benefits to be derived from being seen as active in these official groups.

The informal groups were concentrated, intense groups. When one member of Corn was embarrassed by an English teacher asking her to speak in class, the group of four drew a cartoon of the teacher after class to the amusement of other classmates. None of the group came to the next day's English class in what they called 'collective resistance' (*jiti kangyi*).[84] The larger such groups had core members who helped keep the collective going through the respect they commanded. The final feature of these informal student groupings was their ability to pass information in an unobstructed and timely way. This gave members a sense of empowerment, and of course mutual dependence, thus enhancing attachment to the alliance.[85] At this relatively new university, it was clear in 2006 that informal groupings were more important to students and their assertions of identity than any officially endorsed school organisations, even if the Wenzhou University researcher chose not to take his conclusions quite that far.

Youthful nationalism had been a driving force in the political and cultural development of modern China. The Internet provided a new space in which to share and build nationalist sentiment among the idealistic young. The summer of 2003 saw a period of rising anti-Japanese sentiment among Chinese youth. The tensions started with another upsurge of popular anger at Japan over the disputed Diaoyutai (in Japan, Senkaku) islands in the East China Sea northeast of Taiwan. The islands (along with any resources in the surrounding seas) are claimed by both China and Japan. This claim is indeed a point of agreement between the authorities and general public in Taipei and Beijing. A popular movement, apparently unsanctioned by officials, emerged in June with the aim of planting the Chinese flag once again on those rocky outcrops. By August more than ten thousand people had signed a petition opposing the use of Japanese technology on the Beijing–Shanghai high-speed train link then under development. In the same month more than one hundred thousand netizens had put their name to a petition calling on the Japanese government to clean up and pay compensation for the poisonous gas bombs they had left behind in China upon surrender in 1945. As summer drew to a close, in September came anger at Japanese tourists visiting prostitutes in Zhuhai in Guangdong. Such activities by Japanese men abroad in Asia were hardly new, but the popular response, assisted by the Internet, was unprecedented. Finally on 29 October, Northwestern University students in Xi'an took to the streets in demonstration against Japan. Student street protests had been virtually unheard of since mid-1989.[86]

In the summer of 2003 these activities gave rise to the concept of 'Internet nationalism' (*wangluo minzuzhuyi*). The day after the annual commemoration of the 18 September 1931 start of the Japanese seizure of Manchuria, a Chinese magazine headlined an article 'Internet nationalism is not the same as the Boxer Rebellion.'[87] The latter, in 1900, was a nativist, quasi-religious movement suppressed in part by foreign armed intervention in Qing Dynasty China. In popular minds, the Boxers were a patriotic group but also a symptom and hastener of China's international humiliation at the time. Discussion of this new nationalism continued until 2005, when China–Japan relations again took a turn downward, associated with resentment at Japanese ministers' visit to the Yasukuni shrine war memorial in Tokyo. Internet discussion remained at the heart of this attention to national issues among China's youth throughout the decade. This new means of communication played a vital role in perpetuating popular attitudes toward Japan that had been forged more than seventy years earlier.[88] There were of course also positive reasons for youthful nationalism, including officially encouraged pride at the return of Hong Kong and Macau to Chinese sovereignty in 1997 and 1999 respectively and in the preparations for the Beijing Olympics in 2008. This 'e-nationalism' represented a new stage in popular political participation, but one not susceptible to control or limitation. Netizen independence was manifested by the lack of ideological coherence and practicality of much of the expressions of nationalist outrage expressed on websites. Some Chinese commentators characterised this unmediated manifestation of nationalism as a twenty-first century equivalent of the activities of the Red Guards during the Cultural Revolution. The latter historical parallel was thought to capture the emotion and potential destruction inherent in the Web discussions.[89]

The Internet and mobile phone opened up realms of opportunity for China's youth in areas apparently far from interference by parents, teachers, or the state. From his study of young Chinese use of mobile phone SMSs (short message services), Kevin Latham argues the need to reconsider standard assumptions about the relationship between Chinese media and society. Models of propaganda versus free speech and of control versus democracy seem inadequate to comprehend the complexity and possibilities that something as simple as text messaging by mobile phone opened up for their users.[90]

SMS greetings at festivals, particularly Spring Festival, represent a high point in telecommunications usage each year. SMS also offers easy access to information services: news, sports results, weather forecasts, and so on. It greatly enhances interactivity between audiences and the media, as seen in the response among the young to the *Supergirl* singing contest in 2005. A year earlier China's first text message novel was published. *Out of the Fortress (Chengwai)* was 4,200 characters long and sent out twice daily in instalments of about seventy characters (enough for a paragraph). Written by a business man, Qian Fuzhang, rather than a professional writer, the episodic nature of the SMS novel recalled the style of storytelling characteristic of the classical vernacular novels much loved by young Chinese readers for centuries.[91] Latham makes the distinction between what he calls 'orderly' and 'disorderly' media, a paradigm based on government attitudes and behaviours toward the media. Orderly media are those readily controllable by the state, the disorderly are media which are 'more individualised or small-group focused.'[92] Latham suggests that SMS fell between the two media kinds and helped bridge them. Individual use is disorderly, but accessing information puts users in touch with a controlled sphere.[93] In April 2005 text messages on mobile phones were the means to rally demonstrations against Japan (in another round in the history textbook dispute between the two countries) in several major Chinese cities. Anonymous messages called on citizens to be patriotic, condemn Japanese war crimes, and boycott Japanese goods and services. Forwarding such messages provided rapid and widespread awareness, and in many cases mobilisation. As one Beijing recipient noted, 'Now the revolution comes from the mobile phone' (*Xianzai geming shi cong shouji laide*).[94]

The mobile phone gave young Chinese a sense of liberation from the confinement imposed by parents and school. A survey on cell phone use in 2005 confirmed this contribution of the technology to the development of youth identity.[95] The mobile phone matched the computer as means of youthful escape and had the advantage of portability. The little device opened up a new virtual space for interaction with other young people. High schoolers surveyed claimed they could speak to their parents and friends more confidently by phone than face to face. Texting allowed classmates or friends who had quarrelled to make up less awkwardly than in the past. Cell phones also became an arena for competition as a status symbol: Showing off an expensive, imported, or the latest model was appealing to many students.[96] The researchers concluded that the cell phone gave students greater freedom: The instrument expanded the space students felt part of, allowing them unsupervised access to friends, news, and events. As one student noted: 'I especially thank my cell phone, thank it for letting me know many people. I also thank it for making my life less empty. Every day...I wait for my phone to bringing some more new things.... It's not so easy for me these days to see television, so I [rely on] text messages. I'm a soccer fan, so [my phone] every day can bring me some soccer news. I started in second year of high school: there's no way I could change this habit now.'[97] In an educational system that put particular pressure on high school students through the national university entrance examinations, the liberation from pressure that the mobile phone offered teenagers meant a great deal. The small instrument constructed a 'personal space' (*siren kongjian*) for each user. In 2002 more than two hundred million text messages were sent daily. In 2003, seven billion such New Year texts sped over China. Ninety-five percent of young people sent such greetings. By that year a mobile phone had become the number one requirement of eight in ten university students.[98] Cell phones allowed young people to let off steam. One example was mockery of the national soccer team, a perennial favourite in unofficial public discourse in China since at least the 1980s.[99] Ironically, while making communication easier, the mobile phone also helped create a strong sense among students of insiders and outsiders (*quanzhong ren* and *quanwai ren*), defined by those with whom you exchanged text messages. The mobile phone, however, could also become a weapon to harm others, *Liaoning Youth* (*Liaoning qingnian*) magazine warned its readers in late 2005. As a character in *Cellphone* (*Shouji*, directed by Feng Xiaogang), the top box office Chinese film that year, had noted: 'The hand phone (*shouji*), if not used properly, could turn into a hand grenade (*shoulei*).'[100]

Several Internet 'incidents' from 2006 revealed the extent of the influence of the 'Net on young users.[101] The 'cat cruelty video' (*nüemao shipin shijian*) appeared on the 'Net in March 2006. A woman in high heels killed a cat in a particularly cruel way and the video was put on the 'Net to entertain. The thousands who responded to the posting felt no such amusement. Within a week, the names of the woman, the videographer, and the planner of the incident were known. A second incident was known as the 'hugging incident' (*baobaotuan shijian*). In November 2006 a Changsha blogger proposed that Chinese youth start a 'free hugs' movement, like that in Western nations seen on the 'Net. These two rather different phenomena shared some features. The responses to both revealed people's human feelings, as over one million netizens visited the pages and most reacted against the animal cruelty and endorsed the lighthearted hugs proposal. For both phenomena, the act of looking at the Web posting was an expression of involvement. The Internet was also the means to share feelings.[102]

The hugging craze attracted mostly netizens in their twenties who connected in informal small groups, motivated by an urge to show that ordinary people could be nice to others, even strangers. Just as in Western countries, the growth in population numbers and geographical spread of cities in China had strengthened feelings of isolation and indifference among urban dwellers. Like their flash mob counterparts in the West, the 'hugging groups' of young people wanted to resist this tendency. The Internet provided the means to team up with likeminded peers. In twenty days from their first appearance on the streets of Changsha on 21 October 2006, more than twenty other cities had joined in. Chatroom groups in different cities – such as Panda (*Xiongmao*) and Mars (*Huoxing*) in Beijing, Lefthand (*Zuoshou*) in Shenyang, and EBI in Shanghai – had joined in QQ discussions of the 'hugging groups' idea. This occurred in virtual space before the enthusiasts hit the streets of their cities to demonstrate their social engagement physically. This kind of organisation was only possible on the 'Net and could not be accomplished on this scale with a chain (*chuanlian*: the Cultural Revolution term for travelling about the nation to learn from other Red Guards) of text messaging. Some saw the hugging phenomenon as a youthful rejection of 'indigenous culture' (*bentu wenhua*) and acceptance of Western ways. The seduction of the young by Western culture allowed this Chinese version of 'free hugs' to appear in late 2006. The phenomenon was also a reflection of youthful rebellion, a rejection of traditional notions of proper, cautious social behaviour. The novelty of it all was a big attraction for youth.[103]

Two other mass phenomena on the Internet in 2006 were the 'steamed bun murder case' incident and the 'selling oneself to save one's mother' incident. The former was a parody of the historical fantasy film *The Promise* (*Wuji*). Director Chen Kaige appears to have regarded his new film as an answer to the immensely popular and officially welcomed historical drama *Hero* (*Yingxiong*), directed by his former film academy schoolmate Zhang Yimou. Chen's film readily lent itself to parody with its fantastical mix of supernatural characters and a revenge and redemption story. A young Shanghai advertising man, Hu Ge, reduced the story of *The Promise* to its simplest and illegally used clips from the film to tell this story. The legendary pomposity of the film appeared now as a ridiculous tale of death and destruction caused by a childish prank involving a purloined steamed bun. Hu's title, *A Murder Case Caused by a Steamed Bun* (*Yige mantou yinfa de xue'an*), captured the banality many viewers saw in the original epic film. Starting in February 2006, millions made visits to Hu's video clip, with tens of thousands leaving comments. Responses swung back and forth in support of Hu or criticising his reworking of someone else's material. In general, however, ordinary netizens were delighted to see the supercilious Chen Kaige taken down a peg or two.[104]

The 'selling oneself to save one's mother' incident occurred in September 2006. A high school girl offered to sell herself for one hundred thousand yuan to raise money for her seriously ill parent. Chen Yi's appeal prompted much debate. Some admired the Confucian filial loyalty the posting seemed to suggest. Some who knew her questioned her honesty and suggested she was a fraudster. In late October, when Chen's mother died after a failed operation, 'Net opinion shifted to censure those who had questioned the girl's motives.[105] These two incidents on the 'Net showed both the enormous enthusiasm with which mostly young netizens approached the two matters and the pattern of swings in attitudes to the phenomena. The 'mantou' parody was an example of the grassroots attitude of Hu Ge and the egalitarianism common among netizens challenging the refined position of Chen Kaige.

Such parodies, both on the Internet and in other media (including television) became known by 2008 by a new label, *shanzhai*, literally 'mountain fortress.' Derived from the label given copycat cellphones made in back-country workshops, the term was applied to a whole range of copycat phenomena, including fake designer bags and clothes and impersonators of famous stars on the television talent shows that took off in popularity around this time.[106] *Shanzhai* (copycat) captured the spirit of egalitarianism with its suggestion of rural lack of sophistication. The buffoon could puncture the pretensions of the sophisticate or appear just as elegant in fake finery. In a survey of 400 university students in Hangzhou, seventy percent expressed their support of a *shanzhai* attitude.[107] This delight in the grassroots quality of 'copycat' culture extended to a similar, new phenomenon promoted on the Internet, parody or spoofing (*egao*). Hu Ge's 'mantou' Internet sensation was just the most prominent in the slew of such mocking entertainments from individuals or groups like the self-styled 'Back Dorm Boys' (*Houshe nansheng*).[108] The attitudes reflected in these spoofs and copying had distinct similarities to the kind of studied cynicism and wit seen in the slogan T-shirts worn by young people in the early 1990s.

## BLOGS AND Q CULTURE

Blogs by 2008 had become a major feature of youth Internet use. Three years earlier, 92.61 percent of China's bloggers were under thirty years old. Blogging became a new channel for youthful participation in society, as it created a public space for communication, discussion, and debate. In contrast to the print media, radio, or television, blogging was a place of empowerment (*zizhuhua*), and was individual and fashionable, among other desirable qualities. Other media offered the voices of other people, blogging offered youth an unmediated, democratic space for the expression of views across differences in location, wealth, occupation, and education.[109]

The QQ instant messaging service (and China's equivalent of a social networking site) by February 2005 had over ten million users, almost all of them young people. The phenomenal success of the service lent its name to a whole range of youth subcultural phenomena that came to be called 'Q culture' (Q *ban wenhua*, literally Q-page or Q-print block culture). Enterprising entrepreneurs were soon attaching the letter Q to products, including mobile phones (the Q28 model was particularly popular among young women). Q literature became fashionable on the 'Net, with its deliberate playing with language and the expectations of mainstream writing. There were four main sources of the Q subculture, according to a Guangzhou sociologist.[110] First was Q cartoons, originating in the 1980s in Japanese *manga*. The characters had a distinctive look, with head, body, and legs in equal proportion. Second was the rise of 'cute' culture, another Japanese phenomenon associated with young women and the concept of *kawai* (Chinese *ke'ai*: loveable, cute). This movement, represented by international behemoth Hello Kitty, arrived in China in 2001. The third stream in Q culture's origins was the QQ social networking site, which itself had roots in ICQ ('I seek you'), at a time when university students had no access to the global Internet and so were drawn to QQ as a chat site. A fourth, somewhat unexpected, source came from eight decades earlier. Lu Xun, the most important figure in the invention of modern Chinese literature, in 1921 and 1922 published his serialised 'True Story of Ah Q' (*A Q zhenzhuan*). His self-delusional, anti-hero protagonist represented Lu Xun's dissection of the faults in the Chinese personality. The well-known satirical figure of Ah Q in the new century took on a new guise as a self-reflexive parody of pleasure-seeking and escapism.[111] One of the most visible examples of Q culture was cosplay, discussed in an earlier chapter. A degree of infantilism, in clothing, demeanor, and behaviour was characteristic of some young Q culture followers, derived from the Japanese 'cute' obsession. Another marker of Q culture was the distinctive use of Q language (*Q yan Q yu*), a mockery of conventional expression in which mainstream and traditional cultural tropes were given a new twist. A Q version of *The Romance of the Three Kingdoms*, for example, acted out in cosplay images, used plays on words and new coinages for characters and their situations in this reconceptualisation of the classic vernacular historical novel much loved by generations of Chinese readers over centuries.

Chatting on the Internet by the middle of the decade had become so commonplace that new variations emerged to add interest to the habit. One new fashion was 'naked chatting' (*luoliao*, short for *luoti liaotian*), using computer-mounted web cameras.[112] The practice was not widespread: According to research in Jiangsu and Henan, 3.9 percent of respondents had on occasion agreed to participate in such revealing 'Net intercourse and 8.2 percent had tried it (apparently visiting a site, though perhaps not removing any clothes). Participants were mostly male, in rooms alone or after midnight when their dormmates were asleep. It was an apparently headless or at least faceless exchange, with no real names or identity revealed and entry to the chat controlled with passwords.[113] This new take on youth interest in the body could be addictive: 'Before I used words to have conversations on the 'Net. But from the moment I first came across naked chatting, I discovered that it was completely different from what I had imagined. A new thing, a new person, a new way of chatting, a new experience … it all took me in deeply so that I could not rid myself of it.'[114]

There were less dramatic ways to find friends on the Web. The kind of personal adverts that had appeared in youth-oriented magazines in the late 1980s were succeeded by electronic equivalents in the 2000s. Both were expressions of the desirable qualities sought in friends or a life partner by the respective generations of advertisers in the two decades.[115] Almost two-thirds of the adverts on a Nankai University website, for example, were men seeking partners and about sixty percent were posted on behalf of others. The latter may have been outsiders to Nankai in Tianjin, making use of the campus BBS to find a better class of potential partner. Almost half of the roughly sixty percent of advertisers who were students were graduate students doing or having completed masters degrees, an indication of the pressure young Chinese felt by their mid- to late twenties to find a life partner.[116] By September 2009 the main social networking websites, kaixin001.com and xiaonei.com (literally on campus) had millions of users and might one day challenge the predominance of the QQ instant messaging software of the Tencent company.[117]

The Internet provided a vehicle for fans to form interest groups, linking likeminded young people in their enthusiasm for a star, show, or activity either at great distance or just around the corner. For the latter kinds of groups, chatrooms and discussion groups replaced or enhanced face-to-face gatherings. For fans scattered at greater distance, the 'Net was a boon for the sharing of individual or local devotion to the chosen fan object in informal fan club groups (*fensi julebu qunti*). An example of such fan groups, and an indication of their scope, was for young Chinese-speaking followers of South Korean pop group JunJin. In mid-October 2007, JunJinChina had over forty-three thousand registered users. The DoubleJ Chinese-language site had almost forty thousand users, and Baidu's JunJin forum (*tieba*) had 8,186 members.[118] Bound by adoration of their chosen idol, the members of the 'Net groups enjoyed the company of peers who spoke their own language and displayed their own tastes. Unity or solidarity within the group were watchwords. Each separate group had their own symbols and slogans and was in competition with other subgroups of the idol's fans. Groups received attention also from the record companies and promoters of idols, who saw advantage in encouraging such devotion.

Internet fan groups required organisation. Many groups had management and ordinary members, the former including task forces for website management, design, publicity, and translation (in the case of foreign stars). The group websites allowed the fan managers to organise fans to attend public activities (an airport arrival, for example) by their idols. Those attending would in turn report to the wider membership. Fan groups on the 'Net generally were rather open organisations, where the educational level, age, occupation, and other details of members were not required, simply an email address and declaration of gender. Having joined up, members could send in postings for the website, although some members were more active than others and gained prestige among their fellow fans by their postings.[119] Fans could use the Internet to push for other media to pay attention to their idol. In late 2006, organised postings on the Phoenix Satellite Television (Hong Kong) station website urged the station to make a programme on their Korean idol. After such insistent pressure, Phoenix relented. The fans had triumphed.[120] Of course, educationists and other workers with youth felt that there were negative aspects to Internet fan groups, which allowed young people to waste a great deal of time and attention to fandom at the expense of other activities, including study and work. Some members spent inappropriate amounts of money to express their fan loyalty: Chinese JunJin fans gave gold and the latest high-tech gadgetry to their idol (and even his father) to mark the Korean singer's twenty-eighth birthday.[121]

The role of the Internet in maintaining a fan base for Korean pop music in China into the first decade of the twenty-first century is clear. Rowan Pease describes how a small, fan-run site for fans of Kangta (singer An Ch'ilhyôn, a former member of the band H.O.T.) was the work mostly of a twenty-one-year-old unemployed woman in Sichuan, along with two other young women in other provinces. They had never met and managed the site closely, sifting through potential material, updating news, and blocking troublemakers. Pease notes how the unique language of the Internet, with its mix of Chinese characters, *Hanyu Pinyin* Romanisation, and slang helped enhance the sense of community felt by users of the Kangta site. 'The group identity was of a family of Kangta's protectors: they expressed their indignation at anyone who threatened Kangta – or their image of him – such as his record company, the press, rival singers, or any woman photographed with him.' Members adopted nicknames and created personas for themselves on the site. Based on their postings members were given a status by the site. 'These rankings, along with the whole structure of the site, were a fantastic mix of the fans' real-life Chinese communities and the play-world of their Kangta: the party-state and the pastel escapist girls' world. Puns abounded as members rose up through the ranks from 'floating population' to 'women's alliance [federation] secretary' to 'minister of finance.' They earned cow dollars [Kangta was symbolised by a cow] and eventually gained access to the secret meeting room of the street management committee.'[122] The Kangta website's anonymity allowed members a great deal of creativity in expressing their fandom and a freedom in showing their own feelings in ways that would not be possible in the real world.

A glance at bookstores in Beijing in 2008 suggests that Pease may have overstated the decline of the Korean pop star. Among glossy picture books of pop stars, the faces (and bodies) of Korean stars such as Rain and his more androgynous compatriots seemed to compete with similar fan books on male Chinese singers. Indeed it was often hard to tell, for an outsider, whether the white-faced, pouting boy on the cover and in the pages was a Korean or Chinese star. Pease notes the tendency on the Kangta fan site to feminise their idol.[123] This was certainly reflected in the bookstores.

The Internet provided a virtual space for the formation of a wide variety of youthful interest groups. One new such phenomenon in 2008 was 'gay-groupie girls' (*tongren nü*), young women who shared their fascination with reading stories about homosexual men.[124] Something like this tendency has long been identified in analysis of Japanese (and subsequent East Asian) *manga*, in which androgynous young men are the love interest in highly romanticised stories. In some such tales, the beautiful young heroes seem to have a more than manly interest in other young men. In the *manga* fan world these became known as BL ('boys' love') works. The magazine selling booths of China by 2008 also included publications with illustrated covers featuring beautiful young men in 'dubious acts' (*aimei*), in a genre labelled 'aesthetic' (*danmei*) that attracted devoted readers. On the Internet, such texts and their suggested subtexts could be written about, shared, discussed, and enjoyed by likeminded female readers (and men pretending to be female).

The 'gay-groupie girls' were not necessarily products of an excited indulgence in Japanese visual culture, including manga. Many such young women found inspiration in Chinese cultural traditions, especially that of the 'knight errant' (*wuxia*) from which a Chinese 'aesthete' obsession could be found or invented.[125] They ranged in age from fourteen to twenty-five. As one follower, named Li Luohe, wrote: 'I feel in fact that love between men is much more simple, and more real! I like pure loving (*chuncui lian'ai*), that relatively simple sort, relatively difficult, only together can they allow us to think of wishing them happiness.' In a similar, gushy vein, Liu REI (as she styled herself on the 'Net) wrote: 'I like how in BL [boy love] the two people seek love: "Love has no boundaries." I'm not here opposing BG [boy-girl love], just expressing my own feelings. I remember the first time my friend showed me a BL publication. Although I did not understand homosexuality, I was really deeply moved by them [the characters]. I suddenly associated it with my own experience, at least no need to be at a loss anymore. As long as you understand your own behaviour and have examined your own real feelings, I'll give my whole soul to "love." Why care about other people's gaze? This is what I have "seen" [realised] in BL.'[126] Such young women reportedly formed a part of the fan base for South Korean pop stars, boy bands, and their Chinese copycat equivalents. The 'gay-groupie girls' were growing in number in 2008 and their average age was falling.[127]

## INTERNET LITERATURE AND LANGUAGE

The issue of what was 'Internet literature' (*wangluo wenxue*) and what was its value came under discussion by the start of the new century. In some sense the discussion had parallels with the vernacular literature movement that Lu Xun had helped pioneer almost 100 years earlier. Like the debates in the 1910s, the discourse about Internet literature was also concerned with a new kind of writing that to some seemed too close to everyday language to be properly considered literature. The new writing's novelty could be found in two aspects: the content and the form. The stories in Internet fiction were closely related to the everyday lives or the aspirations of young netizens. The style of the new writing was different from the carefully 'dotted and crossed' (*quandian huagou*) emphases and discretion of traditionally crafted, mainstream writing. Instead, elegance on the page, unique effects, and inclusion of illustrations were central concerns. Well-known novelist Wang Anyi (b. 1954) saw parallels between Internet literature and mainstream writing and the differences between audiophiles and music lovers. The former are concerned with techniques and equipment. Likewise writers on the Internet try to display techniques through using new-style language and subject matter: 'The peculiarities of Internet literature are time and again emphasised, but that may be a superficial understanding of literature.'[128] Wang had made a name for herself in the 1980s as an innovative expresser of a new individualism and female subjectivity. In the new century, new-style writing in a new medium threatened the paramountcy of the fictional space she had helped create for youthful readers twenty years earlier.[129]

Four kinds of Internet literature could be identified: the refined (*ya*), the popular or vulgar (*su*), the hooligan (*pi*), and the sinister (*hei*, literally black). The popular included knight errant and other fantasies as well as love stories. Hooligan writing, to Xue Yali, was a continuation on the 'Net of the kind of fiction with which Wang Shuo had made his name in the 1980s, using humour, exaggerated techniques, and splashiness (*dasixuanran*). All these kinds of writing shared several characteristics. First and foremost was autonomy or the expression of the individual writer. Other features included creativity in content and style, manipulation (*caozuo*) of its appearance on the screen, and fast food style (*sushihua*) in its writing, editing, and production. To its youthful readers and its critical supporters, Internet literature was the ideal expression of the spirit of the times: fast, innovative, and a diverting virtual space for its readers.[130]

One major feature of the new virtual space that the Internet opened up for Chinese youth was the language it made popular. The use of new or special expressions, often a mix of Chinese and other elements, a play on words, or a clever pun, were one means of defining the boundaries of this new youth space. The border lay between those who used and revelled in the new language and those for whom the expressions seemed foreign and alienating. A 2002 survey offered an early glimpse into these usages among 134 Beijing university undergraduates. The list of the ten most popular expressions did not include any Internet invented words, except perhaps for *ku* (literally cruel or extremely) used as a Chinese version of 'cool,' which had spread from Hong Kong and Taiwan and been popularised by the Web. But the list of the next most popular expressions was awash with Internet usage, including QQ (the instant message service), TMD (initialised form of *ta made*, damn or shit), MM (*mei mei*, literally beautiful eyebrow, but a homophone for little sister), and 886 (the pronunciation of which, *ba ba liu*, echoed *baibai le*, the Chinese version of bye-bye).[131] The usefulness of these new expressions in asserting and strengthening youthful identity was indicated by only 3.5 percent of the students saying they would use the words at home with their parents.[132] These were words for the exclusive use of the young speaking or otherwise communicating with their peers. Gender differences were generally small, except for tolerance of swear words, which was (perhaps unsurprisingly) much greater among male students.[133] The Internet had spawned a strange ersatz language, combining Chinese and English in mostly playful expressions. '*I fule you*' (I fooled you, or I was kidding) combined two English pronouns with two Chinese characters, *fu* (to serve) and *le*, indicating changed or completed action.[134] Chen Si, a Renmin University Chinese Department staff member, noted how the young had remained at the forefront of cultural innovation over the past several decades: 'The books young people loved went from *How the Steel Was Tempered* [a Soviet favorite] to *Song of Youth* [published in 1956] to "Internet novels" (*wangluo xiaoshuo*); entertainment went from "massed singing" (*dahechang*) to watching movies and reading novels to "spending time in Internet bars" (*pao wangba*).'[135]

The language of the young on the Internet was a means to separate youthful users from parents, teachers, and other older adults in their lives. Using this language also of course strengthened bonds between 'Net users, for they were capable of understanding what others outside their group (however defined) could not necessarily comprehend. Even numbers became a kind of code: 5843344521 sounded almost like *wo fashi shengshengshishi wo ai ni*: 'I pledge generation after generation that I love you.' Similarly 7456 stood for *qisi wo le*: 'I'm really fed up.' Numbers could also play on foreign languages. For example, 121 (in English, one two one) was a way of saying 'I want to speak to you person to person [one to one].' Using '007' meant 'I have a special secret I want to share with you,' based on the reference to the James Bond films.

Initials were also used: MM for *meimei* (younger sister) and BB for *bao-bei* (or 'baby'). The numbers 3166 (*san yao liu liu*) stood in for *sa you na la* (literally scatter, leisurely, that, pull) which was a transliteration of the Japanese *sayonara* (good-bye). As one Shanghai researcher noted, using this language gave young netizens a sense of equality, power in communicating so easily, achievement, and pride. These were feelings not easily satisfied in other aspects of their daily lives.[136] The use of nicknames on the Internet enhanced anonymity, expressed a sense of self-identity through the selection of a name, and connected with likeminded netizens. Unlike a real name, selecting a Web identity did not involve registration at a police station.[137]

The language of the Internet was a major element in defining youth subcultures. The incomprehension of parents and others was one of the major attractions of this language to its users. Employing this language was a marker of difference and a symbol of connection with those of similar attitudes and tastes. The 'bricolage' (*bintie*) and creativity in youthful language invention were striking.[138] Two examples of youthful extension of language were the label 'dinosaur' (*konglong*) for an unattractive female netizen and the ungrammatical addition of *hen* (very) to a word to express the particular quality of a person or object, for example *hennanren* (a manly person).[139]

One language subculture on the Internet was 'Martian language' (*huoxing wen*), an expression of youthful freedom and individuality even as it aroused grave concern from some sections of society. 'Martian' generally involved using Chinese characters with the same sounds and the same elements as the normal words in a sentence, but choosing wherever possible characters with different, additional elements (particularly radicals). The effect was a visually more complex version of a sentence, with more complicated characters, although the meaning could fairly easily be discerned by mentally paring away the additional elements of each character.[140] It was as if a fog had been laid over the normal language, a visual equivalent of the thematic and expressive obscurity of the 'misty poetry' that emerged in the late Cultural Revolution (when it was underground) and immediately afterward. Both phenomena, separated by a quarter century, were a means of expressing youthful distinctiveness and dissatisfaction with the orthodox or mainstream.

The origin of this invented language appears to have been inspired by a line of dialogue in the hugely successful Hong Kong comedy, *Shaolin Soccer* (*Shaolin zuqiu*, 2001). The frustrated coach of the hapless soccer team, played by actor–director Stephen Chow (Zhou Xingchi), says to his goalie: 'The earth is a dangerous place. Why don't you go back to Mars!' Similarly, in popular conversation, a person whose speech is not understood can be invited to return to Mars. The usage on the 'Net started in Taiwan among young people attracted by the eye-catching 'otherness' of the so-called language. By 2007 mainland primary and high school players of Internet games like *Paopao tuan* [*Pawpaw Group*] were exposed to this 'language,' which they used to create their noms-de-guerre for their presence on QQ, MSN, when playing Internet games, and on BBS systems. Eighty percent of the users of 'Martian' were aged between fifteen and twenty years old and found it fun to write in this way as well as expressing their generation's difference from others. The secrecy that such pseudonyms offered and the obscurity of the characters used meant that 'Martian' became for those born in the 1990s their own kind of 'secret password' (*jianghu mima*).[141]

Obscurity of language seems to have been one of the attractions of the Internet and text messaging for young Chinese in the twenty-first century. A Liaoning youth magazine in 2005 offered readers a two-page key to some new and particularly indecipherable terms. The writer likened these expressions to the use of local dialect or the specialist language of particular occupations, also hard for outsiders to comprehend. The first example was inspired from a line of dialogue of the Monkey character played by Hong Kong's Stephen Chow in the two-part slapstick film *A Chinese Odyssey* (*Dahua Xiyou*, 1994). Only moderately successful in Hong Kong, the two films became mainland cult favourites, particularly on the campus of Peking University. The Mandarin dubbing actor for Chow spoke Mandarin but used the word order of Cantonese grammar, producing a strange, back-to-front request to 'give me for making this statement your reason' (*gei wo ge bu zhidao zhei juhua de liyou xian*). The linguistic invention appealed to netizens, who used the phrase and versions of it in chatrooms as a way of suggesting that their conversation partners were writing nonsense.[142] The Internet not only created new expressions and ways of using the language, it also was the means by which these youthful linguistic innovations were collated and preserved. Online dictionaries and guides to the new language were a source of amusement and enlightenment. One useful compilation was a twenty-five-page listing of expressions on the 24xuexi.com website.[143] This was not a simple listing, but a guide to the new-speak, along the lines of 'don't say xx, say [in the new language] yy.'

Political commentary was not absent from the new language of the Internet, despite the apparent indifference of the new generations to the kind of political engagement that had seen their older peers occupying Tiananmen Square in the spring of 1989. Almost two decades later, the kind of popular social concerns that had animated the public response to the student demonstrations of the late 1980s were reflected in the younger generation's new expressions. To invite friends to eat and drink, for example, was referred to as *fan fubai* (oppose corruption), as in 'Let's

go and oppose corruption.' This was a sly commentary on the continuing abuse of power by Communist Party leaders at all levels of society, including indulgence in high living on the public purse. Mixtures of
English and Chinese had become commonplace by the 2000s, including adding the suffix -ing to a Chinese character to express continuous
action, for example *shang wang-ing* (using the Internet). Some youthful
Internet expressions were transliterations of Japanese words: for example, *da zhangfu* (literally big husband or big brave man) sounded like the
Japanese *daijōbu,* 'no problem.' Such incorporation of foreign-sounding
words presumably gave a cosmopolitan gloss to the users of such language.
Chinese usages associated with Taiwan, Singapore, or Cantonese speech
had a similar attraction. Many expressions exploited the visual potential
of the computer screen: for example, +U stood for the Chinese *jia you* (literally add oil), the usual cry of encouragement to athletes. Some Internet
expressions favoured by the young had somewhat sinister associations.
*Luoli,* for example, referred to a sexually attractive (the online listing
used the words *ke'ai,* lovable in quotation marks) young woman under
sixteen years old. It was a transliteration of the title of the Nabokov novel
*Lolita.* Her male equivalent was *Zhengtai* (in Japanese Shota), from the
Japanese manga *Iron Man 28* (*Tieren 28 hao*), whose protagonist was
named Kaneda Shotaro.[144]

The Internet in early 2009 provided the means for a large-scale, sly
poke at government censorship. The rise of the so-called grass-mud
horse (*caonima*) became a measure of the extent to which the authorities were helpless in the face of youthful protest on the 'Net. The name of
this mythical animal, pictured in drawings and stuffed toys as a creature
resembling an alpaca, sounded very much like an obscene expression in
Chinese. A fake children's song about the horse on YouTube attracted
1.4 million viewers, a nature documentary on the habits of this nonex-
istent creature drew one hundred and eighty thousand viewers. Stores
began to sell grass-mud horse dolls. The story of the battle between
the horse and an evil river crab became a public talking point.[145] The
Chinese for river crab (*hexie*) is a close homonym of the word for har-
mony (*hexie*), an important part of the Communist Party's lexicon under
president Hu Jintao. Indeed, by 2008 'being harmonised' had become
a new way of saying a website or other expression of resistance had
been shut down by the Chinese authorities. The irony of an innocent
children's song, undetected by sophisticated software aimed at rooting
out disharmonious thoughts on the Chinese Web, being full of foul language made a strong point about the continuing tendency of the Chinese
state to infantilise its citizens. Cui Weiping, a professor at the Beijing
Film Academy, compared the government's antismut campaign that had
started on the Web in early 2009 with 1983's campaign against 'spiritual

pollution.' In both eras, the changing morality and lifestyles of young Chinese were the targets of official concern.[146] In both cases officials could not stop the new trends.

### YOUTHFUL VOLUNTEERS: JOINING SOCIAL SPACE

In 2008 a relatively new phenomenon emerged among China's youth, the rise of the volunteer, which created a new concept of social space for young Chinese. This wave of good work by the young was prompted by three events: a massive snowfall that paralysed transport links in much of the country around the Spring Festival holiday, a highly destructive earthquake in Sichuan in May, and the Olympic and Paralympic Games in Beijing in August and September. Volunteers were associated with each of these happenings, two unexpected and one long planned. On each of these occasions young people rallied in large numbers, recruited or brought together by the Internet, to assist victims of natural disaster or to enhance the national image, in the case of the sporting events. The latter attracted about a half million volunteers, not all of whom were young. The unpredicted disasters also brought out volunteer efforts from a range of citizens, though much of the impetus came from youths.

Volunteering was not unheard of before the momentous events of 2008. The Communist Youth League (CYL), a junior version and recruiting ground of the Communist Party, had traditionally been a means to do good work in society, on occasion organising neighbourhood cleanups or assisting victims of flooding or other disasters.[147] Reform and opening up after 1978 allowed for change in this limited pattern of social do-gooding. International NGOs, such as Save the Children, began working in China in the late 1980s while more home-grown organisations emerged, like the China Care Fund, founded in Hong Kong in the early 1990s to support poor rural schools on the mainland. The CYL was behind the establishment of the Chinese Young Volunteers Association, the only such national grouping, in December 1993. The United Nations Women's Conference in Huairou in suburban Beijing in 1995 involved a large number of volunteers to assist the thousands of international delegates to the gathering.[148] By 1996 students at high schools and universities were also involved with supporting backward rural areas. In 2002 a 'harmonious community service action plan' saw efforts to build 'harmonious neighbourhoods.'[149]

The youth volunteering in 2008 had a different caste. In the case of the natural disasters, it was more spontaneous, and with respect to the Olympics, attracted widespread public attention. It also raised the issue of the place of volunteerism in a nation ruled by a political party whose whole purpose was proclaimed to be a dedication to the advancement of society. Volunteering shifted social progress away from being the sole preserve of the ruling party. Optimists might argue that the rise of the volunteer heralded the emergence of a civil society in which the Party was but one player among many. Young people were at the heart of this shift. Their areas of work were identified in a survey of thirteen Zhejiang colleges. Neighbourhood or community service (*shequ fuwu*) appealed to twenty-six percent, the broader public welfare service (*shehui gongyi fuwu*) attracted 16.4 percent, environmental protection drew twelve percent, and helping poor and undeveloped regions also attracted twelve percent of volunteers. The top ranking declared motivations of these Zhejiang students in 2008 revealed an interesting mix of altruism and individual ambition. Raising grades and their assessment results was selected by thirty-eight percent of respondents, to better develop themselves was chosen by almost twenty-eight percent, while just under twenty-three percent selected 'wanting to do something for society and the masses.'[150]

The snowfalls that hit southern and central China in February 2008 disrupted millions of lives. Spring Festival, the celebration of the lunar New Year, always saw huge numbers of travellers, particularly on the railways and bus services. With the rise of migrant labourers in the booming factories and cities of the eastern and southern coastal provinces, the pressure on transport links at such holiday times had grown enormously. Millions of workers took advantage of the New Year celebration to return to their inland or rural homes to be with families and to bring back some of the fruits of their hard work in the export-oriented workshops of the globalised economy. Often this was the only holiday these workers were able to enjoy each year. Snow flung a huge spanner in the works in early 2008. Tens of thousands of migrant workers anxious to return home camped out, in freezing conditions, at railway stations across the country. Guangdong's railway stations were particularly hard hit. In addition to help provided by government organisations, volunteers also worked to provide food and temporary shelter to travellers disrupted by the unusually severe weather.

The 12 May earthquake that hit northwestern Sichuan and killed about seventy thousand people was a more shocking event. Television images from Wenquan at the epicentre of the quake had an immediate impact across the nation. Communist Party leaders, including premier Wen Jiabao and president Hu Jintao, rushed to show solidarity with the victims, and, through news cameras, their concern to the nation. Ordinary citizens, including young people, also hastened to assist. They were often brought together in this effort by the Internet, which provided detailed and frequently unofficial reports from the disaster zone. By mid-June the Chinese Red Cross had called up one hundred and eighty thousand volunteers, while Communist Youth League organisations at all levels in Sichuan had registered 1.185 million volunteers. All together, one count recorded over one and half million cases of volunteering a little over a month after the tremblor. Of those who immediately hired taxis or got on trains or planes to take themselves and supplies to Wenchuan, over ninety percent were young people.[151] Grassroots NGOs used the Internet to seek donations and people to help the relief effort. Groups of three to five friends spontaneously organised to offer support. Ten farmers from Shandong, for example, spent three days and nights driving their three-wheeled tractors to the quake area. Some residents of Tangshan, the scene of an even more destructive earthquake in July 1976, organised themselves as quake volunteers, pulling twenty-five victims from the rubble to safety in the critical first three days after the disaster. The Red Cross solicited blood donations on the street in major cities across China. The most-used Internet portal, QQ, set up a 'praying for blessings' (*qifu*) page immediately after news came of the 12 May earthquake. By the evening of 18 May, 5.7 million netizens had visited the site.[152] Youth in Chengdu established 'Our Sichuan' volunteer group, using QQ to agree on a set of principles, including not rushing to Wenchuan but instead doing fund-raising in Chengdu to support the rescue experts.[153] After the initial rescue efforts for the earthquake, as China prepared to host the Olympics, state propaganda outlets presented heroic stories of volunteers and other young people, including quake victims who had helped others. Somewhat in the manner of the *Supergirl* contest three years earlier, text messaging and the Internet gathered public support for those worthy of particular recognition. SMS and Internet votes from a pool of fifty young heroes helped select twenty named as 'heroic youths' in a televised Beijing ceremony in late June.[154]

Volunteering for the Beijing Olympics had sporting precedents in the 1990 Asian Games and the 2001 Universiade, the international university games, both hosted in Beijing. These sporting events, however, had been monopolised by volunteers from a strictly limited number of sources, including the Communist Youth League. Half the volunteers for the 2001 event were aged between fifty and seventy-five.[155] The 2008 Olympics cast the net for volunteers somewhat wider. Already just under two years out from the games almost a quarter million people, young and old, had registered for volunteer positions.[156] Olympic volunteers contributed to a wide variety of duties, including staffing mobile enquiry booths on Beijing's streets to answer tourists' questions. The half million volunteers who started work in July 2008 had been selected from 1.1 million aspirants from China and abroad.[157]

Motivations for young people to volunteer their time were identified in 2008 as a mixture of old and new. Traditional motivations included a sense of responsibility to others, which perhaps had roots in Confucian values. But more modern motives were linked with ideas of social development, and what one researcher identified as the postmodern motivation of pleasure.[158] As one volunteer told him: '[My volunteer work] represents a group who were born after the 1970s. When you see so many people like those of the 1950s, they always say: "Hit on the head, sprinkle hot blood" [a reference to Red Guard violence]. Nineteen-sixties people say, "I used my youth to gamble on tomorrow" [an oblique reference to the Tiananmen demonstrators in 1989]. Nineteen-seventies people say: "I want to use a relaxed life to approach every day." This is the shared view of me and the people around me.'[159] But this determination to eschew politics and enjoy prosperity did not obliterate a sense of commitment to others. The kind of psychological pleasure from helping others had, of course, been evident in the heyday of the Lei Feng cult and was rooted in the service of educated youth in assisting their rural hosts in the 1970s. But in the past, the official line about social service was embedded in Marxist notions of class solidarity and rejection of enemies. The new youth volunteers of the 2000s did not need these justifications to feel fulfilled in their service to others.[160] One university student, who had never served as a volunteer, reflected many of his peers' attitude when he mocked the annual, short-lived, virtually ritual push to learn from Lei Feng featured in the media and on the Internet each March on the anniversary of Mao's 1963 article commemorating the young soldier.[161] Half of almost 300 young Beijing volunteers surveyed in 2007 identified their motivation as 'a citizen's duty,' with only five respondents selecting 'doing something for the nation.' Seventeen percent thought volunteering would get them free access to Olympic events, twelve percent wanted to increase their experience of society, and almost five percent admitted that volunteering might help them find a job in the future, presumably by helping enhance their resumés. Almost one in five Beijing youth declared that they had experience of volunteering.[162]

### NEW SPACES, NEW DREAMS, AND NEW SOCIALISATION

Chinese youth subcultures were transformed by the Internet in the first decade of the new century. The 'Net gave young people the tools to take mainstream culture and shape its content and forms in ways that served youths' needs to create their own subcultures and assert their own identities. Sociologist Yang Cong noted in mid-2008 that the heroes of the Internet games that had such appeal to the young were characteristically 'high, wide, and handsome,' qualities found in the heroes of traditional fiction.[163] He could have extended these features to include Mao era heroes as well. Yang noted that the Internet allowed youth to shape subcultures in their 'original state' (yuansheng tai), without passing through some outside filter or necessarily being subject to adult or official censorship. The subcultures could use their own language (such as 'Martian'), post statements, hang together (*baotuan*), have fan contests (including PK, knockout contests), parodies and skits (*xixue ergao*), or search for pornography or cute friends. 'Youth subcultures are no longer merely confined to their own community. It's no longer a case of "my territory where I'm boss." They can have influence on mainstream culture and even mount a major attack on it.' The most obvious evidence of this impact was the change in written and spoken language usage throughout society. In the consumer economy, mainstream culture was constantly incorporating aspects of youth subcultures, seen in the triumphant rise of *Supergirl* and similar phenomena. Yang Cong ended his overview by suggesting that, compared to earlier generations, young people in the Internet age knew much more about society.[164]

A 2008 survey of 372 Hebei higher education students (from universities and specialist academies) showed the power of the Internet in shaping knowledge, particularly the speed with which catch phrases from television or the 'Net and the names and unofficial labels for recent public incidents took hold on young people's imaginations.[165] Three in four of the students rated the Internet as the top source of their knowledge and use of catch phrases. Films and television were also an influential source for the expressions and slang used on campus. They were identified by two in three students, including those who delighted in using the phrase 'There are serious consequences' (*Houguo hen yanzhong*), from Feng Xiaogang's film *A World without Thieves* (*Tianxia wu zei*, 2005).[166] The Hebei survey authors concluded on a distinctly positive note that the issues and expressions popular among university students reflected these young persons' civic consciousness and global citizenship. These qualities were enhanced by their exposure to the Internet. The students also showed their competitive spirit and commitment to their individualistic identity and values. Over half the students identified with the phrase 'no forsaking, no giving up' (*bu paoqi, bu fangqi*), much used by the determined young soldiers in the highly popular *Soldiers' Sortie* (*Shibing tuji*), a serial shown on CCTV in 2006. This belied, the researchers argued, the usual characterisation of this cohort of youth as 'a generation without ideals' (*meiyou lixiang de yidai*).[167]

The Internet could replace older media and express group identity. This was the intention of the four university students who in the early 2000s came up with the idea of '80s Internet broadcasting.' By this time the notion of a distinctive cohort of young people born in the 1980s and reaching university and maturity in the new century had taken hold in public discourse. These were the children of the era of 'reform and opening up.' Having no television in their dormitory apparently led to thoughts of a radio-style DJ (disk jockey) broadcast carried over the

Internet to appeal to members of their age cohort. Their programmes, including 'Men's Time' (*Nanshi shijian*), were carried on QQ.[168] The programmes, initially recorded in rather backward conditions, attracted an enthusiastic audience precisely because of the targeting that the broadcasts adopted. Snippets of dialogue from favourite movies of the 1980s generation, for example, took on an extended existence as catch phrases for these listeners.[169] As they noted in a 2004 interview:

> These days most people don't have a good feeling about those born in the 1980s. In their view this generation grew up eating 'Western food' (*yangfan*) and drinking 'Western milk' (*yangnai*). They are prone to be show-offs, unsociable and wild. We just wanted to provide this group of [young] people with a place (*di'er*) where they could pour out their feelings and respect to each other. To construct a cosy home (*jia*) for all brothers and sisters born in the 1980s, this was our original intention in setting up the broadcasts.[170]

As they explained:

> The '80s decade' doesn't just represent a symbol, it's more a kind of spirit. This is the element that we had to pour into the programmes we made. To say our generation is shut-off to ourselves (*zibi*), that is created by the environment. Most of those born in the 1980s were only children, and especially for those of us who grew up in the cities, you could say our whole childhoods were spent in the confines of our apartment blocks. Although we were only separated from the girl next door by a barred, anti-theft door, that distance seemed really remote. A generation growing up in that environment has thoughts and feelings it doesn't want to share with parents. Instead they want to find people of the same age to pour out their heart (*qingsu*). Only people the same age can understand and count it as a personal favor.[171]

The rise of 'cyber-hedonism' among young people around the world was noted by commentators by the end of the first decade of the new century. A relatively new phenomenon in the 2000s was using the Internet to find sexual partners with whom to share an apartment.[172] This was a major advance on the relatively simple personal advertisements in magazines in the late 1980s. The *Economist* weekly cited a Chinese survey in which two-thirds of respondents agreed with the statement 'It's possible to have real relationships purely online.' In contrast only one-fifth of Americans surveyed took the same view.[173] But, if the conclusions of Don Tapscott, the sociologist who coined the label 'the 'Net generation' in 1997, apply to China as much to the Western youth which are his focus of research, the rise of the Internet in the lives of China's young people was a positive development. Tapscott argued, in a 2008 follow-up study, that young netizens are articulate, well-informed, and enjoy social interaction with their peers. These conclusions counter a picture of isolated, obsessive, and alienated teens hunched over computer monitors and more at home in a virtual world.[174]

Figure 5.4. Youthful rebellion re-created from the Cultural Revolution in a publicity shot for *In the Heat of the Sun* (directed by Jiang Wen, 1995).
*Source:* Author's collection.

Young people in surveys claimed to watch over seven hours of television weekly. This was ahead of listening to music (over four hours) and reading nonschool books (3.6 hours), magazines, and newspapers (2.5 hours). Curiously, use of the 'Net did not figure in this early 2001 overview. The phrase 'I'm me' (*wo jiu shi wo*) encapsulated the new attitudes of China's youth, with its suggestion of difference from previous generations and its focus on the individual. University students were now much more attracted to entertainment programmes on television than to news or social issues. In this respect such students had gone from being 'the ideological vanguard' (*sixiang xianfeng*), an indirect reference perhaps to events in 1989, to being 'the fad vanguard' (*shishang xianfeng*).[175] The strong visuality of this new generation meant that they preferred watching films and television to reading. China's ancient classics, including works of philosophy and vernacular literature, were known to the young through picture book versions and television adaptations. Of more interest were American visual products, including the all-conquering *Titanic*, although around the year 2000 young Chinese television viewers also delighted in Hunan Television's historical romance serial *Princess Pearl* (*Huanzhu gege*), with its glossy fantasy of young love among the lower ranks in the Qing imperial palace.[176]

The mediascape in which those born in the 1980s had grown up was very different from that of previous generations. The virtual spaces and real connections made possible by the Internet meant that netizens were unlike consumers of other media: film, television, radio, and print media. Some commentators wondered if the moral standards of the new generation might be even worse than those of the Red Guards during the Cultural Revolution, widely seen as destructive and frequently cruel young people. Reassurance came from noting that for the Special Olympics held in Shanghai in September 2007, two-thirds of the forty thousand volunteers were university students, mostly born in the 1980s.[177] The following year, after the Sichuan earthquake and for the Beijing Olympics, the extent of youthful volunteerism was again seen as a sign of the maturity and service ethos of the new generation. Karsten Giese has shown how the mass media, including the Internet, have taken the place in China formerly occupied by the work unit (*danwei*) in providing the framework for personal reference and individual identity formation, particularly for young Chinese.[178] As the power of the state-owned work unit shrank from the 1980s onward, more young urban Chinese found themselves after their schooling ended beyond the reach of the unit or the state. The Internet became a major vehicle for the political socialisation of these young people. Microblogs had become an enhanced way for young and older citizens to connect by the second decade of the new century. Launched by Sina.com in August 2009 as an equivalent of Twitter, microblogs (*weibo*) had about a quarter billion users by mid-2011.[179]

The volunteering phenomenon of 2008, just like the rise of youth dependence on and creativity with the Internet, marked a profound shift in Chinese society and the position of young people in relation to power structures and social organisation. Imaginative worlds like those of the various reincarnations of Wang Shuo, volunteering, and the 'Net offered new spaces in which all citizens, including the young, could construct their own identities and versions of the real world. These spaces were symptomatic of the shift from a society organised around the work unit to one in which wider ranging and constantly changing connections were possible.[180] These new connections offered greater agency, even a degree of autonomy, to Chinese youth than any previous generations had dared to imagine. These new senses of independence might only exist in an imaginative or virtual, electronic space and were the equivalent five decades earlier of the realm of hand-copied novels or two decades previously defined in defiant rock songs. But these new spaces were more powerfully shaped by young people themselves, in a multilocal, multidirected dance of individual and social commitment.

The film *Red Sorghum* gave impetus in the late 1980s to the early flourishing of youth culture in China. At the end of the first decade of the new century, four films captured youthful imaginations, creating four different imaginative spaces. To mark the sixtieth anniversary of the founding of the People's Republic of China, *The Founding of a Republic* (*Jianguo daye*, directed by Huang Jianxin, maker of 1988's *Samsara*, and Han Sanping) was released amid fanfare and citizens were encouraged to attend screenings. The film told the official version of the events of the late 1940s. Young viewers found much to entertain them, as unlike the equivalent 1989 feature film, the 2009 version was teeming with a slew of celebrity actors.[181] As Internet reactions also showed, some of the dialogue (on corruption and the limits of relying on one-party rule in Republican China, for example) had application to circumstances in the People's Republic six decades on.[182]

Zhang Yimou in December 2009, amid huge media attention, released a new film which mixed the local and the global. *A Woman, A Gun and a Noodle Shop* (*San qiang pai'anjinqi*) was a remake of the Coen brothers' *Blood Simple* (1984), but set in a fantastical, northwest Chinese landscape. It was peopled by farcical characters and used the Northeast folk performance form of *errenzhuan* (song and dance duet, or 'two-person twist'), in which men dress as somewhat clumsy women. This hybrid combination of the native in a foreign-inspired story was in general not well-received, according to Internet discussion, though some commentators admired Zhang's effort at reinvention after the martial arts, costume extravaganzas of his recent films, and the Beijing Olympics opening ceremony.[183]

In early 2010 two films competed for young China's attention: *Confucius* and James Cameron's *Avatar*. The Chinese film was directed by Hu Mei, a member of Zhang Yimou's Beijing Film Academy class of '82. As a praise song to a Chinese icon, *Confucius* received priority on its release. Reportedly 2-D screenings of the American film were restricted in order to give the Chinese work space to find its audience. There were even reports of tickets for *Confucius* being bundled with those for *Avatar* to help fill seats.[184] Internet comment was not so easily directed. Some netizens made the point that the Chinese sage represented class oppression and obedience by the lower orders and that the Hollywood fantasy stood for resistance and action. Discussants on the 'Net revived the old Cultural Revolution mocking name for Confucius, 'Cuckold Kong' (*Kong lao'er*).[185] To me, watching Hong Kong actor Chow Yun-fat (Zhou Yunfa) playing the noble philosopher surrounded by admiring followers, the film took on the feel of one of the 1960s revolutionary war films that Zhang Yimou, Hu Mei, and her Red Guard contemporaries had grown up with almost five decades earlier.

# CHAPTER 6

# Conclusion

## *Consuming Identities*

Youth in China since the 1960s has been a site for complex interactions between and reworkings of local and international influences. Emerging in a period of relative national isolation and introspection, youth cultures established their power from an ability to serve a wide range of needs and expectations. In the space of four decades China's young people seemed to have gone through a process that had taken several generations in Western Europe and North America. The kinds of expressions of sometimes alienated youth identity that emerged in Western societies from at least the 1930s became common in China in half a generation. This study has tried to show that expressions of youth identity and their social impact took on distinctly China-based characteristics. Former Red Guards became the managers and promoters of rock bands in the 1980s, providing a new soundtrack to lives undergoing rapid change as the economy grew by ten percent each year in the subsequent decades. But these transformations in the lives of all Chinese, including youth, cannot be understood through mapping phenomena according to grid patterns of simple binaries: Chinese and Western, local and global, or traditional and modern. The developments were more complex and also spontaneous, ungoverned, uneven, and unpredictable. An assumed teleology from local to global is misleading, as Chinese elements coexisted and intermingled with the international and were transformed and reinvented. In short, Chinese youth cultures emerged, grew, and were elaborated by a myriad of influences large and small. This was their strength and attraction to participants.

### ECHOES ACROSS FIVE DECADES

Looking at this study's forty years, covering five decades, many continuities, links, and echoes are obvious. The importance of performance to Chinese young people, their creativity in even the most constrained circumstances, and their attachment to heroes or idols connect the three time nodes that we have used. Performing loyalty dances to Chairman Mao or their own reworkings of the official cultural canon gave Red Guards and sent-down youth a sense of solidarity and purpose. Dancing, body building, and enjoying the new-style music had performative aspects in the 1980s. By the twenty-first century, the Internet opened a stage for netizens to present themselves (or a version of themselves) to a wide (or narrow) audience.

Young people's creativity was evident in the handcopied novels circulating among sent-down youth, in the folk-inspired new rock music of the 1980s, in slogan T-shirts and the greater cynicism and delight in word play, parody, and satire enjoyed by netizens in the new century. The names of three writers are emblems of this creativity and of the changing circumstances in which their works were circulated and enjoyed: Zhang Yang (original author of the handcopied *The Second Handshake*), hoodlum novelist Wang Shuo, and race driver celebrity blogger Han Han. Creativity could be achieved in small ways, in making play with Maoist clichés in the 1970s and 1980s, or, later, in enjoying the codes of Martian language with friends. The Internet made accessible the efforts of bloggers, pranksters, and ordinary folk in making parodic jokes about almost anything. Innovation and experimentation reworked official culture, borrowed from outside China, and drew upon local roots.

Idols were important in young Chinese lives throughout the period of this study. Mao Zedong, father figure, or Li Tiemei, young heroine of the model opera *Red Lantern*, were presented as models for youthful behaviour and for connection with the national project before the 1980s. With 'opening up' young people identified their own heroes, such as rocker Cui Jian and Gong Li, the beautiful star of *Red Sorghum*, and, later, L'Oréal advertisements in which she assured viewers 'We're worth it.' *Supergirl* and other talent quests in the new century created instant idols for, often fleeting, youthful consumption. Grandparents might observe the replacement of the worship of Mao by the worship of money, but many youngsters seemed to take a more knowledgeable view of changing fads, judging by the popularity of parodic and copycat commentary on the Internet.

By the twenty-first century, Chinese youth cultures seemed all-consuming. The majority of urban youngsters were from one-child families, though the effectiveness of that policy was uneven and sometimes exaggerated in foreign perceptions. The Internet gave many of these youth a powerful means to connect with others, to perform, create, and show off. Ironically, just as youth cultures triumphed in Chinese informal public discourse, China's society entered a new era. The aging of society, seen in Japan and Western Europe, began to be noted in China too. The relative importance of young people aged between fourteen and twen-ty-five is set to decline markedly in the next few decades. Whether this demographic transformation serves to intensify or weaken youth cultures in China remains to be seen.

Youth rebellion was characteristic of Western European and North American societies, a condition made possible by the achievement of living standards that allowed for such expressions of difference. Urban Chinese families began to reach such levels of material security in the 1980s, but rebellion, resistance, or alienation took on different guises than in other countries. The sent-down youth of the 1970s were highly circumscribed in what they could openly express and even in more private contexts had to be cautious. In a political system in which the governing party aspired to control society, youthful rebellion took less obvious forms. But the old saying that 'the mountains are high and Beijing is far away' had perti-nence for some young people in the countryside and construction corps in the 1970s. The sense of liberation that had come from the end of regu-lar schooling in 1966, factional fighting, and 'establishing ties' could not be ignored in the subsequent decade. Urban salons and private groups in the countryside were spaces in which to circulate titillating handcopied fiction and thoughts on the need for political reform. The spontaneous revolt against the Gang of Four in late 1976 had deep roots.

The short-lived Democracy Wall movement of 1978–9 grew out of this Cultural Revolution ferment of underground ideas. Ten years on, China's youth appeared to have abandoned political engagement for a wholesale embracing of Westernisation in its most enticing forms: songs and popu-lar culture. Michael Jackson had replaced Mao as a youth icon by 1988, the cassette tape Mao's little red book of quotations. The undertow of politics, however, could not be ignored. We have seen how singer Cui Jian and his Chinese-style rock anthems could be heard as plaintive love songs and as laments over alienation and powerlessness. In a nation where the party-state still assumed it could direct citizens' lives, even playing a song from Hong Kong or the United States could be a political statement. Cui Jian, Canto-pop, and other music provided a soundtrack for the youth-ful demonstrators in Tiananmen Square in the spring of 1989, for whom official corruption was a more pressing issue than abstract notions of democracy.

Twenty years further on, the Chinese political landscape had ostensi-bly not changed. But in many ways the political engagement of China's youth had shifted dramatically. Most would have said they were not interested in politics, a wisely self-protective response. Consuming and

material concerns seemed to have taken over from the kind of eager participation in the fate of the nation that Red Guards or student protestors
had shown earlier. Quietly, however, in the glow of countless computer
and mobile phone screens, politics continued by other means. As in the
clandestine singing of a Western ballad in a barracks in a construction
corps on the northern wasteland in the mid-1970s or in the dancing to
a foreign beat in a campus hall in the 1980s, anonymously joining a discussion on the Internet about a newly released movie that was backed
by a huge official publicity effort could have political implications. With
the rise of the virtual domains of the Internet, the distinctions between
public and personal, official and unofficial, and youth and mainstream
became more blurred. This is not to deny the distinctive spaces inhabited
by youth cultures and subcultures on the Internet, but to acknowledge
that young Chinese throughout these forty years were able and happy to
roam widely across the cultural terrain.

This youth cultural terrain was a major element in the redelineation
of public space in contemporary China. Our analysis of youth activities
during the Cultural Revolution decade has suggested that even when the
Maoist state was at its most insistent on trying to control civil society,
young people found ways of self-expression and solidarity on the margins or beyond the recognised public domain. The lessons of that decade
for the Communist Party leadership led to a pulling back from ambitions
to direct all economic developments. Consequently spaces began to open
up for the expression of new ideas and new cultural practices. With rising prosperity in cities and the countryside, young Chinese in particular seized opportunities to try new things and to differentiate themselves
from parents, children, authority figures including teachers, as well as
from each other. These uncoordinated, uneven, and haphazard changes
did not create a commonly acknowledged youth or public domain. But
youth's enthusiasms were a major part of reintroducing and reinforcing
the notion of a commons in which such activities were tolerated and even
accepted as normal. Television, with its variety of programming and its
near saturation reach by the mid-1990s, played a vital role in expanding
on this acceptance of a commons.

Despite the student protests and the breathtaking boldness of these
youth in occupying Tiananmen Square in spring 1989, the mapping out
of boundaries in a new sense of publicness did not mean a Habermasian
progression to pressure for a democratic space. Most young Chinese in
the 1980s and subsequent decades were not politically engaged beyond
a vague sense of expectation that the state should continue to step back
from its earlier intervention in people's everyday lives. As economic
reform widened and deepened and as public material expectations rose,
so this acknowledgment grew of a public space in which politics played a

secondary or minor role.[1] The coming of the Internet and its conquest of youthful spare time and horizons reinforced this acknowledgment. Youth cultures were one important part of this space but did not monopolise it, as all generations found opportunities for less filtered expression. In the spring of 2011, softly whistling in public the tune of the much-loved folk-song 'Jasmine' (*Molihua*) could serve a rebellious purpose, referencing the 'Jasmine Revolution' in North Africa.[2] By then the microblog served as another means for mobilisation of young and old on public issues, including railway safety and polluting factories.

## YOUTH AND THE WORLD

As the youth cultures mapped here over five decades emerged and became more elaborate and differentiated, the world in which these changes occurred also underwent considerable transformation. In the late 1960s China's place in the world, in the eyes of ordinary citizens including edu-cated young people, was as the driving force of world revolution. While relations with Western countries were relatively restricted, China enjoyed apparently wide and close relationships with Third World nations, engaged, as China was, in expunging the colonial legacy. This self-image placed China in a central position globally and engendered a sense of national worthiness and pride. The formerly tight relationship with the Soviet Union had turned into bitter denunciation and rivalry, but Soviet influence persisted as the most recent wave of Western cultural exposure in China. Young China in the 1970s sang 'Moscow Nights' rather than Elvis Presley, but the effect was somewhat similar, an act of mild nos-talgia for the lost Western connection and for the exotic associations of that old link. Richard Nixon stepping foot on Chinese soil in February 1972 allowed at least the possibility of a restoration of wider relations with Western popular culture, though official caution and economic real-ity delayed this potential for China to rejoin the whole of the rest of the world.

Deng Xiaoping's reforms after 1978 and the 'opening up' of Chinese popular culture to a much less restricted and more widespread acquain-tance with Hong Kong, Taiwan, and Western equivalents broadened the possibilities to an unprecedented extent. Not only did official guardians of popular taste loosen their grip, but rising living standards provided ordinary young people with the means to access the new cultural influx. Television sets in private homes brought the world to China to a degree never seen before in its history. The at-home context allowed for an inti-mate engagement with the presentation of life and popular culture around the world, unlike the mostly collective consumption of usually didac-tic representations of life outside China in cinemas and workplaces in the past. Similarly, the cassette tape recorder and later the video cassette recorder and DVD further enhanced this engagement for youth, with the former portable outside the home and away from adult supervision. The growth in an older Chinese technology, printing, brought a new range of images and accounts of aspects of international youth culture in the pages of invigorated and only partially supervised magazines and other publications. A new, tabloid press sold knowledge of the world and of China to eager and often gullible readers. By 1988 the relative isolation of the Cultural Revolution years had become a distant memory for young people and their parents. China's place in the world had changed and a sense of the need to catch up with the developed world had taken hold. Catching up for China's young was a stronger imperative in the cultural domain.

By the turn of the century, a new technology was again changing China's place in the world and youth perceptions of that position. The personal computer opened up seemingly infinite acquaintance with connected humanity beyond China. This huge space, both real and virtual, was a domain dominated by the young, who were in part its very creators. An army of Internet censors aimed to provide guidance to the youthful navigators of this galaxy of entertainment, knowledge, and nonsense, but the scope of this space was so extensive that any kind of youth culture could find niches and means of self-expression. In this new, interconnected, but also splintered or fragmented world, China had both a place and no place. On the one hand, many young Chinese citizens on the Internet expressed a fervent and unrestrained nationalism that could become xenophobia. On the other, nations did not need to matter any more, as netizens roamed wide over a universe of possibilities. A sense of shared temporality, the circulation and remodelling of other, particularly East Asian modernities, and a new notion of publicness or commons, as Koichi Iwabuchi describes them, extended beyond national boundaries in a new, youth cultural landscape. The nation had become too large and too small to take care of the various issues of globalisation, so a reworking of the nation was required.[3]

This study has examined the range of global influences to which China's youth were exposed over forty years. Third World countries, socialist comrades in arms, and limited Western contacts gave way to an opening up in the 1980s that broadened the choices available. The importance of reworkings of these influences, through versions coined in marginal Chinese societies in Taiwan and Hong Kong, via South Korean elaborations of Los Angeles culture, and through Chinese youth's own selectivity and taste showed the irrelevance of any local versus global binary. Creative responses to these outside entanglements were characteristic of youthful incorporations of popular culture throughout these five decades.

Bodies were presented, rhythms heard, and spaces opened up that were distinctive to the places and young people who made them.

We do not need to subscribe to a Marxist view of history to acknowledge the material basis for the developments in youth cultures in China presented in this study. In 1968 and through the 1970s Chinese living standards were low, though most bellies were not empty and protein consumption relatively high. But aspiring Red Guards had to ask their mothers or sisters to resew old clothes to make a passable uniform and sent-down youth had to scavenge to make props and costumes for their performances as a culture of subsistence prevailed in most lives. By 1988, after ten years of 'reform and opening up' the range of choices available to Chinese youth had expanded enormously. This was particularly the case for urban youth with money. Spare time activities, including entertainment and sports, clothes, shopping, and even finding a job were open to individual selection from a spectrum of possibilities. The consumer revolution was taking root, even if the crudeness of some of the choices had roots in a command economy past. The trajectory of the career of the writer Wang Shuo, from hoodlum novelist in the 1980s to Internet entrepreneur in the new century, traces this growing commercialism and fragmentation in culture.

By the year of the Beijing Olympics a casual observer could conclude that consuming had become a consuming passion for China's youth and their parents. Idol shows on television tapped into this urge for entanglement in a world of shopping, possession, and celebrity. Unequal access to this spending boom engaged the attention of some young people, able to share their views and find confirmation of their opinions on the Internet. Incidents in which drivers of luxury vehicles knocked down humble cyclists and then showed no concern, for example, caused outrage on the 'Net. Urban demolition and rebuilding and encroachment on farm land likewise saw protests on the streets and in virtual space. The rise of the volunteer was not simply a case of young people seeking to enhance their CVs but a symptom also of a growing unease at social inequality. But rising living standards also gave more people a stake in maintaining social and political stability. Jon Savage's description of the idea of the teenager: 'living in the now, pleasure-seeking, product-hungry, embodying the new global society where social inclusion was to be granted through purchasing power,' could have been written in Beijing or Shanghai.[4]

If a virtual meeting could be arranged between an educated youth from 1972 and a netizen from forty years later, the encounter would reveal many differences. For one, a notebook is a small book of lined paper encased by a plastic cover; for the other, a notebook has a lit-up screen with a modem to connect to the world. The confines of a former Red Guard's view of the world and the limits in which they created a virtual space for themselves would seem claustrophobic to a young Chinese from the early twenty-first century. But the two youthful representatives would have little difficulty in recognising much of each other's aspirations. Finding and asserting a place in the world, distinctive and satisfying, was a shared ambition. Should they be joined by a counterpart from 1988, they would all see a lot of themselves in the others. Clandestine group songs, cheeky T-shirts, shouted folk-inspired anthems, and clever word play shared with thousands in a virtual space were all expressions of youthful world weariness that did not challenge the political status quo, merely underscored its potential irrelevance. Energetic youthful bodies found rhythms and spaces with which to share a sense of distance from adult or official orthodoxy. Youth cultures keep changing but the driving forces shaping the changes remain remarkably constant.

# Notes

## 1 INTRODUCTION: FINDING YOUTH IN CHINA

1 Jon Savage, *Teenage: The Creation of Youth Culture*, New York: Penguin, 2007, p. xviii.

2 One of the best overviews of subcultural studies is Ken Gelder, ed., *The Subcultures Reader (Second Edition)*, London and New York: Routledge, 2005. For a rethinking of subcultures and the work of the Birmingham Centre for Contemporary Cultural Studies, see Andy Bennett and Keith Kahn-Harris, eds., *After Subculture: Critical Studies in Contemporary Youth Culture*, Basingstoke and New York: Palgrave Macmillan, 2004.

3 Frank Dikötter, *Sex, Culture and Modernity in China: Medical Science and the Construction of Sexual Identities in the Early Republican Period*, Honolulu: University of Hawaii Press, 1995, pp. 146–50.

4 Mao Tse-tung, *Quotations from Chairman Mao Tse-tung*, Beijing: Foreign Languages Press, 1966, p. 288.

5 See, for example, Luo Xu, *Searching for Life's Meaning: Changes and Tensions in the World Views of Chinese in the 1980s*, Ann Arbor: University of Michigan Press, 2002, pp. 51–71.

6 For a collection in English of recollections by former Red Guards of their lives since the 1960s, see Yarong Jiang and David Ashley, eds, *Mao's Children in the New China: Voices from the Red Guard Generation*, London: Routledge, 2000.

7 See Jing Fang, *Wo shi 60 hou (1969–1979) (I am the Sixties generation, 1969–1978)*, Beijing: Xinxing chubanshe, 2010, in which the author presents vignettes of life in the 1970s, including watching movies outdoors, play-acting characters from the model operas, and everyday activities, illustrated by watercolour sketches. Another label, applied to the '90s cohort in particular, was 'the Bird's Nest generation' (*Niaowo yidai*), referring to the National Stadium built for the 2008 Beijing Olympics. On the 1980s cohort, see Yunxiang Yan, 'Little Emperors or Frail Pragmatists? China's '8oers Generation,' *Current History: A Journal of Contemporary World Affairs*, 105 (692) (2006), 255–62.

8 See, for example, Stanley Rosen, 'Contemporary Chinese Youth and the State,' *Journal of Asian Studies*, 68, 2 (2009), 359–69; Stanley Rosen, 'Chinese Youth and State-Society Relations' in Peter Hays Gries and Stanley Rosen,

eds, *Chinese Politics: State, Society and the Market*, London and New York: Routledge, 2010, pp. 160–78; Stanley Rosen, 'Youth and Social Change in the PRC,' in Ramon Myers, ed., *Two Societies in Opposition: The Republic of China and the People's Republic of China after Forty Years*, Stanford: Hoover Institution Press, 1991, pp. 288–315; Stanley Rosen, 'Value Change Among Post-Mao Youth,' in Perry Link, Richard Madsen, and Paul G. Pickowicz, eds, *Unofficial China: Popular Culture and Thought in the People's Republic*, Boulder: Westview Press, 1989, pp. 193–216. For a useful post-1949 overview, see Thomas B. Gold, 'Youth and the State,' *The China Quarterly*, 127 (September 1991), 594–612.

9  Lu Yulin, *Dangdai Zhongguo qingnian wenhua yanjiu*, Beijing: Renmin chubanshe, 2009.

## 2   MARKING OUT NEW SPACES: RED GUARDS, EDUCATED YOUTH, AND OPENING UP

1  Mark Kurlansky's *1968: The Year That Shook the World*, New York: Ballantine, 2004 includes a total of less than two pages on China in its 600-plus pages.

2  This kind of internal migration was not new in 1968. Beginning in the 1950s millions of urban residents had been sent to undeveloped rural areas to contribute to the modernisation of the economy: see Ding Yizhuang, *Zhongguo zhiqing shi: chulan (1953–1968) (History of China's educated youth: first wave 1953–1968)*, Beijing: Zhongguo shehui kexue chubanshe, 1998. The standard Chinese work on the Cultural Revolution movement is Liu Xiaomeng, *Zhongguo zhiqing shi: Dachao (1966–1980 nian) (History of China's educated youth: great tide, 1966–1980)*, Beijing: Zhongguo shehui kexue chubanshe, 1998 (reissued in 2009). In English, see the early study by Thomas P. Bernstein, *Up to the Mountains and Down to the Villages: The Transfer of Youth from Urban to Rural China*, New Haven: Yale University Press, 1977. For a typical literary recollection, see Deng Xian, *Zhongguo zhiqing zhongjie (The end of Chinese educated youth)*, Beijing: Renmin wenxue chubanshe, 2003.

3  Wang Dongcheng, '"Laosanjie" de wenhua lishi mingyun' ("The historical fate of *laosanjie* culture"), Zhongguo qingnian yanjiu (China youth research), 1994, 3 (May), pp. 22–4.

4  For a general outline, see Roderick MacFarquhar and Michael Schoenhals, *Mao's Last Revolution*, Cambridge: Harvard University Press, 2006, pp. 102–17. For a view from the countryside, see Anita Chan, Richard Madsen, and Jonathan Unger, *Chen Village under Mao and Deng*, Berkeley: University of California Press, 1992.

5  The changing social origins of successive waves of Red Guards is presented, for example, in Lei Yi and Shi Yun, 'Kuangre, huanmie, pipan: "Wen'ge" 10 nian qingnian sichao chutan' ("Fanatical, disillusioned, criticized: a first exploration of youth ideological trends in the Cultural Revolution ten years"), Qingnian yanjiu (Youth research), 1991, 2 (February), pp. 30–5, esp. pp. 30–2. For a pioneering exploration of Red Guard politics, written by four scholars perhaps in 1986 seeking safety in numbers, see Tang Can, Mi Hedou, Lu Jianhua, and Yin Hongbiao, 'Sikao yidai de ziwo fansi: yi xiang guanyu Hongweibing qi tongdairen de sixiang guiji de yanjiu' ("Reflections

on a generation's self rethinking: some research on the ideological orbit of Red Guards and their generation"), *Qingnian yanjiu*, 1986, 11 (November), pp. 21–5, 31 and 12 (December), pp. 12–17.

6 Yin Hongbiao quoted in Tang Can and others, *Qingnian yanjiu*, 1986, 11 (November), pp. 23–4. By the early 1960s, Mao had stepped back from his paramount position, humiliated by the failure of his most recent political campaign, the Great Leap Forward (1958).

7 For a comprehensive summary of such activities in colleges in Shanghai, see 'Zhuanji yi: "Wenhua da geming" zhong de Shanghai Hongweibing yundong' (Appendix 1: "The Shanghai Red Guard movement in the Great Cultural Revolution"), in Shanghai Youth Gazetteer editorial board, *Shanghai qingnian zhi* (*Shanghai Youth Gazetteer*), Shanghai: Shanghai shehui kexueyuan chubanshe, 2002, pp. 533–50, esp. p. 533.

8 *Shanghai Youth Gazetteer* editorial board, p. 534.

9 *Shanghai Youth Gazetteer* editorial board, p. 535.

10 *Shanghai Youth Gazetteer* editorial board, p. 542. Mao had also identified with Sun Wukong, praising the monkey hero in his writings.

11 On Red Guard uniforms, see Antonia Finnane, *Changing Clothes in China: Fashion, History, Nation*, New York: Columbia University Press, 2008, pp. 227–55 and Verity Wilson, 'Dress and the Cultural Revolution,' in Valerie Steele and John S. Major, eds., *China Chic: East Meets West*, New Haven: Yale University Press, 1999, pp. 167–86.

12 Red Guards at the Central Academy of Arts and Crafts in Beijing were typical in their determination to embrace the attractions of militancy in dress, lifestyle, and rhetoric. Zhang Dingzhi, a professor in the clothing design department, was cited for his alleged poisoning of young minds with revisionist ideas about fashion. He and his colleagues had promoted new dress designs for women in fashion magazine *May First* (*Wuyi*): 'Xiuzhengzhuyi wenyi heixian duhai qingnian de zuizheng' ("Proof of the crimes of the revisionist black line in literature and art poisoning the young"), Jinggangshan zhanbao (Jinggangshan battlefield report), 9 December 1967, p. 4 in *Xinbian Hongweibing ziliao* (*A New Collection of Red Guard Publications*), Oakton VA: Center for Chinese Research Materials, 1999, p. 4430.

13 See Melissa Schrift, *The Biography of a Chairman Mao Badge: The Creation and Mass Consumption of a Personality Cult*, New Brunswick: Rutgers University Press, 2001 and a 350-page illustrated catalogue of badges: Wang Anting, ed., *Mao Zedong xiangzhang tupu* (*Illustrated catalogue of Mao Zedong badges*), Beijing: Zhongguo shudian chubanshe, 1993.

14 For a full discussion of these model performances, see Clark, *The Chinese Cultural Revolution*, pp. 26–62 and pp. 158–68 (ballets). For an assessment of changing importance (or otherwise) of these performances, see Paul Clark, 'Model Theatrical Works and the Remodelling of the Cultural Revolution,' in Richard King, ed., *Art in Turmoil: The Chinese Cultural Revolution 1966–1976*, Vancouver: UBC Press, 2010, pp. 167–87.

15 See Mary Farquhar, *Children's Literature in China: From Lu Xun to Mao Zedong*, Armonk: M.E. Sharpe, 1999.

16 Yang Zirong, derring-do hero of *Taking Tiger Mountain by Strategy* (*Zhiqu Weihushan*), is hardly old and the fighters in their shorts and leggings in the ballet *The Red Detachment of Women* (*Hongse niangzijun*) are young women, as is the central character, Qinghua.

17  Writer Liu Jialing records his astonishment and excitement at seeing the Cultural Revolution ballet *The Red Detachment of Women* (*Hongse niangzijun*) for the first time as a young teenager sent to Beijing to avoid Red Guard armed conflict in his hometown of Shenyang: Liu Jialing, *Jiyi xianhong* (*Memories bright red*), Beijing: Zhongguo qingnian chubanshe, 2002, pp. 16–19.

18  For a typical, lengthy illustrated report, see 'Shengshi haoda de shoudu gongnongbing wenyi huiyan zuotian kaishi' ("The impressive worker-peasant-soldier artistic joint performances start yesterday in the capital"), *Tianjin ribao* (*Tianjin Daily*), 22 May 1967, pp. 2–3.

19  Cited in *Tianjin ribao*, 22 May 1967, p. 3.

20  Qu Zhe, 'Fendou, qiusuo, shizhong shi zhei yi dai ren de zhutiqu' ("Struggle and striving in the final analysis were the theme tune of this generation"), in Liu Xiaomeng, *Zhongguo zhiqing koushushi* (*An oral history of China's educated youth*), Beijing: Zhongguo shehui kexue chubanshe, 2004, p. 73.

21  Liu Jialing, p. 150.

22  Liu Jialing, pp. 152–5.

23  Liu Jialing, pp. 168–71.

24  Yang Jian, 'Wenhua da geming zhong de Hongweibing huaju' ("Red Guard plays in the Great Cultural Revolution"), *Zhongguo qingnian yanjiu*, 1995, 1 (January), p. 37.

25  Yang Jian, 'Wenhua … huaju,' p. 35.

26  Another version of this story is described in Clark, *The Chinese Cultural Revolution*, pp. 195–6. See also Yang Jian, 'Wenhua da geming zhong de Hongweibing huaju, xu' ("Red Guard plays in the Great Cultural Revolution, Part Two"), *Zhongguo qingnian yanjiu*, 1995, 2 (March), p. 26.

27  Ma Chengxiang, 'Hei xi "Xin shidai de kuangren" zai Ha shangyan shuoming le shenme?' ("What does the performance of 'Madman of the New Age' in Harbin tell us?"), *Heilongjiang ribao*, 26 March 1968, p. 2.

28  'Wei gongnongbing zhanling wenyi wutai relie huanhu' ("An ardent call for worker-peasant-soldiers to occupy the literary and art stage"), *Renmin ribao*, 21 May 1967, p. 4.

29  Yang Jian, 'Wenhua … huaju, xu,' p. 27.

30  Mingren County Shuren Commune High School Propaganda Team, 'Yizhi Hongweibing wenyi xuanchuandui' ("A Red Guard Literature and Art Propaganda Team"), *Heilongjiang ribao*, 15 March 1970, p. 3.

31  Yang Jian, 'Wenhua da geming shiqi de Hongweibing yinyue' ("Red Guard music in the Great Cultural Revolution"), *Zhongguo qingnian yanjiu*, 1997, 2 (March), pp. 24–8. For background, see Isabel K. F. Wong, '*Geming Gequ*: Songs for the Education of the Masses,' in Bonnie S. McDougall, ed., *Popular Chinese Literature and Performing Arts in the People's Republic of China, 1949–1979*, Berkeley: University of California Press, 1984, pp. 112–43. On mass singing's historical origins, see Hong-yu Gong, 'Missionaries, reformers, and the beginnings of Western music in late imperial China (1839–1911),' Ph.D. thesis in Asian Studies, The University of Auckland, 2006.

32  Yang Jian, 'Wenhua … yinyue', pp. 27–8.

33  See, for example, Wang Jiaping, 'Hongweibing "xiaobao" ji qi shige de jiben xingtai' ("Red Guard 'little papers' and the basic features of their poetry"), *Wenyi zhengming* (*Literature and art debates*), 2001, 5 (May), pp. 4–9.

34  An anonymous poem from June 1967, quoted by Wang Jiaping, p. 7 and p. 9n24.

35  The kind of discourse in Red Guard newspapers allowed for no acceptable alternative view. It was a totalising discourse that assumed complete dominance of logic and rhetorical devices. This point is made by Ma Yue, 'Hongweibing huayu de wenhua biaozheng: cong yi zhang fahuang de Hongweibing xiaobao shuo qi' ("The cultural features of Red Guard discourse: thoughts from a yellowing page of a Red Guard newspaper"), *Zhongguo qingnian yanjiu*, 1996, 6 (November), pp. 26–8.

36  *Geming zaofan wenyi*, 18 July 1967, pp. 3–8, reprinted in *Xinbian Hongweibing ziliao*, p. 1987–92.

37  For an account of this in a book of sent-down youth memoirs, see Zhu Zhenghui and Jin Guangyao, eds., *Zhiqing buluo: Huangshan jiaoxia de 10,000 ge Shanghai ren (Educated youth tribe: Ten thousand Shanghainese at the foot of Huangshan)*, Shanghai: Shanghai guji chubanshe, 2004, pp. 216–25. These kinds of memoirs need to be treated with caution. The writers have generally done well, at least in the years after the Cultural Revolution, and their recollections are not direct evidence of spontaneity or autonomy, being compiled years after the events described.

38  Liu Jialing includes a number of chapters on fond memories of film watching. Wang Shuo's career will be discussed in Chapter 5.

39  Interview with Huang Jianzhong, Beijing, 6 July 2002. For a Red Guard diary of a journey from Beijing to Shaoshan, Mao's birthplace, over four months beginning in November 1966, see Fang Guangsheng, *Hongweibing Changzheng riji (Red Guard Long March Diary)*, Hong Kong: Zhongguo xinwen chubanshe, 2004.

40  Interview with Tian Zhuangzhuang, Beijing, 8 June 1988. For an autobiographical account of the excitement of 'establishing ties,' see Mu Zhai, *Lishi de huashi: zhiqing shiwu nian (Fossils of history: fifteen years of educated youth)*, Beijing: Dongfang chubanshe, 2009, pp. 100–8.

41  Interview with Wu Ziniu, Fuzhou, 5 July 1988. For more on *chuanlian* by the future Fifth-Generation filmmakers, see Paul Clark, *Reinventing China: A Generation and Its Films*, Hong Kong: Chinese University Press, 2005, pp. 25–6.

42  Tian Jingqing, *Beijing dianying ye shiji, 1949–1990 (Achievements of the Beijing film industry)*, Beijing: Zhongguo dianying chubanshe, 1999, pp. 157–8.

43  Jin Dalu, 'Shanghai jiedai waishengshi Hongweibing de wu ge jieduan' ("Five periods in Shanghai's receiving of Red Guards from other provinces and cities"), *Qingnian yanjiu*, 2005, 9 (September), pp. 42–8 (figures are from p. 42). As the apparent precision of these statistics indicates, despite the upheaval, the Chinese bureaucratic traditions of paperwork and counting ploughed on.

44  Jin Dalu, 'Shanghai jiedai waishengshi Hongweibing de san ge tezheng' ("Three characteristics of Shanghai's receiving of Red Guards from other provinces and cities"), *Qingnian yanjiu*, 2005, 12 (December), p. 32.

45  These activities are described in Jin Dalu, Shanghai ... tezheng, pp. 32–5.

46  Jin Dalu, Shanghai ... tezheng, pp. 36–7. Jin emphasises the monumental effort by ordinary, mostly middle-aged Shanghainese to receive and serve the incomers. On official attitudes, see Jin Dalu, 'Chen Pixian, Cao Diqiu deng fandui Hongweibing da chuanlian de taidu he jucuo' ("The attitudes and actions of Chen Pixian and Cao Diqiu against the Red Guard great 'establishing ties' movement"), *Qingnian yanjiu*, 2010, 3 (June), 77–87.

47  Jin Dalu, 'Shanghai ... jieduan,' p. 46.

48  Jin Dalu, 'Shanghai ... jieduan,' p. 46.

49  Jin Dalu, 'Shanghai ... jieduan,' p. 48.

50  Jin Dalu, 'Shanghai Hongweibing waichu da chuanlian' ("Shanghai Red Guard going out to establish ties"), *Qingnian yanjiu*, 2008, 2 (February), pp. 40–9. and Part Two, 2008, 4 (April), pp. 26–35.

51  Jin Dalu, Part Two, pp. 26–9.

52  Jin Dalu, Part Two, pp. 30–1.

53  Liu Jialing, pp. 144–5.

54  Li Yuqi, '*1966–1967* 'da chuanlian' fengchao shimo' ("The ins and outs of the 'great establishing ties' tide, 1966–1967"), *Zhongguo qingnian yanjiu*, 1994, 3 (May), pp. 29–32.

55  Li Yuqi, '*1966–1967* "da chuanlian" qunsheng zhutai' ("Popular characteristics of the 'great establishing ties,' 1966–1967"), *Zhongguo qingnian yanjiu*, 1994, 4 (July), pp. 35–7, esp. p. 37. In her third article in this series, Li Yuqi describes much of the episode as 'absurd' (*huangtang*): '1966–1967 "da chuanlian" lishi fansi' ("Historical reflection on the 'great establishing ties,' 1966–1967"), *Zhongguo qingnian yanjiu*, 1994, 5/6 (October), pp. 54–7, esp. pp. 55–6.

56  Li Hua in 1993, quoted in Li Yuqi, p. 56. Li Yuqi describes much of the episode as 'absurd' (*huangtang*), pp. 55–6.

57  Zhao Jie, 'Lun Hongweibing wenhua' ("On Red Guard culture"), *Qingnian yanjiu*, 1991, 7 (July), pp. 1–6. Zhao's analysis is somewhat negative, suggesting that the five features of Red Guard culture were adoration (*chongbaixing*), destruction (*pohuaixing*), negation (*foudingxing*), fantasy/illusion (*huanxianging*), and savagery (*yemanxing*).

58  Future film director Chen Kaige spent almost two years on a rubber farm in Xishuangbanna starting in June 1968; see Clark, *Reinventing China*, p. 32.

59  Liu Xiaomeng, *Zhongguo zhiqing shi*, tables on pp. 179 and 183.

60  The fourteen million figure is calculated from a table in Liu Xiaomeng, Ding Yizhuang, Shi Weimin, and He Lan, *Zhongguo zhiqing shidian* (*Encyclopedia of China's educated youth*), Chengdu: Sichuan renmin chubanshe, 1995, p. 917. A December 1971 report on efforts in Shanghai to encourage enthusiasm for the 'up to the mountains, down to the villages' movement is an indication of resistance to the transfer of urban youth to the countryside. Some sent-down youth were brought back to the city to report on the splendid situation among their peers in the countryside: 'Jiaqiang dui zhishi qingnian shangshan xiaxiang gongzuo de lingdao' ("Strengthen management of the work of educated youth going up to the mountains and down to the villages"), *Heilongjiang ribao*, 24 December 1971, p. 2 See a similar, though front-page, report on strengthening political education on the movement: *Heilongjiang ribao*, 22 December 1971, p. 1.

61  Xinhua News Agency report, 'Quanguo guangda pinxiazhongnong he xiaxiangshangshan zhishiqingnian gongdu geminghua chunjie' ("Nationwide broad masses of poor and lower-middle peasants and educated youth going down the countryside and up to the mountains celebrate a revolutionary Spring Festival together"), *Heilongjiang ribao*, 20 February 1969, p. 2.

62  Yang Qizhang, in Shi Xiaoyan, ed., *Beidahuang fengyunlu* (*Trials and tribulations on the Great Northern Wasteland*), Beijing: Zhongguo qingnian chubanshe, 1990, pp. 299–300.

63 Xie Qianhong, 'Nongcun xuanchuandui shishi' ("Incidents from a country propaganda team"), in Yang Zhiyun and others, eds., *Zhiqing dang'an, 1962–1979: Zhishi qingnian shangshan xiaxiang jishi* (*Educated-youth archive, 1962–1979: Records of educated youth going up to the mountains and down to the villages*), Chengdu: Sichuan wenyi chubanshe, 1992, pp. 255–7.

64 This account is drawn from Mao Peiling, 'Balei zhi hua' ("Flowers of ballet"), in Shi Xiaoyan, pp. 21–3. See also a memoir by writer Liu Heng (b. 1954), 'Kanxi' ("Watching plays"), Xin juben ("New scripts"), 2000, 4 (August), pp. 94–5.

65 Hunan dianying faxing fangying gongsi (Hunan film distribution and projection company), *Yingpian (changpian jiemu) pianming paicibiao* (*Films [feature length] title list*), Changsha, 1978, p. 24. The same listing includes seventy-two film copies of the earlier videotaped version of the model opera in circulation from late July 1970. For an analysis of this listing, see Paul Clark, 'Closely watched viewers: a taxonomy of Chinese film audiences from 1949 to the Cultural Revolution seen from Hunan,' *Journal of Chinese Cinemas*, 5, 1 (2011), pp. 73–89. Reported popular enthusiasm for the latter version of *Tiger Mountain* and *The Red Lantern* can be found in *Heilongjiang ribao*, 23 September 1970, p. 1.

66 See, for example, a photo essay about the Harbin Railway Bureau's contributions to the campaign over a half page in *Heilongjiang ribao*, 29 October 1970, p. 2.

67 Zhang Ren, 'Wo zheige ren xihuan xinxian' ("I really like new things"), in Liu Xiaomeng, *Zhongguo zhiqing koushushi*, pp. 33–4.

68 'Sheng yijiuqiwu nian wenyi diaoyan dahui shengli jieshu' ("Provincial 1975 literature and art performance festival successfully concludes"), *Liaoning wenyi* (*Liaoning literature and art*), 1975, 12 (December), inside back cover. See also the first report of the festival in the same journal, 1975, 10 (October), p. 29.

69 For a fuller account, see Clark, *Reinventing China*, pp. 29–30, 39–41.

70 For a broad assessment of the event, see Cheng Dizhao, 'Laizi guangkuo tiandi de zhandou yishu: xikan wosheng nongken xitong zhishi qingnian yeyu wenyi chuangzuo jiemu diaoyan' ("Art from the vast, all-embracing struggle: joy at watching the amateur literature and art creative programme performances of the educated youth of our province's agricultural reclamation system"), *Yunnan wenyi* (*Yunnan literature and art*), 1975, 2 (February), pp. 69–71.

71 The following is based on Yang Jianhua, 'Shenshan li de balei' ("Ballet deep in the mountains"), in *Qingchun wuyi: Yunnan zhibian shenghuo jishi* (*Regrets for youth: Records of life at the margins*), Chengdu: Sichuan wenyi chubanshe, 1991, pp. 115–21.

72 Yang Jianhua, pp. 116–17. For a similar makeshift, amateur performance of a model ballet at a construction corps in the Northeast, see Shen Jianbing and Gang Dongliang, 'Jianding de zou zai Mao zhuxi geming wenyi luxian shang: ji Heilongjiang shengchan jianshe bingtuan moutuan 'Baimaonü' yeyu yanchudui dali puji geming yangbanxi de shiji' ("Staunchly following Chairman Mao's revolutionary literature and art line: on the achievements of a certain corps of the Heilongjiang production and construction corps *White-haired Girl* amateur performance troupe in vigorously popularising

the revolutionary model performances"), *Heilongjiang ribao*, 26 May 1971, p. 3.

73   Yang Yusheng, 'Ganga de "bianju"' ("Awkward 'playwrighting'"), in *Yang Zhiyun*, pp. 568–9.

74   Feng Zhicheng, 'Zhiqing geyao' ("Educated youth ballads"), in *Yang Zhiyun*, p. 360.

75   Feng Zhicheng, pp. 362–3.

76   Feng Zhicheng, pp. 363–5.

77   Wang Tianhui, 'Kexi le neiben "Waiguo minge 200 shou"' ("What a pity about that *Two Hundred Foreign Songs* book"), in *Yang Zhiyun*, pp. 212–13. For a discussion of vulgar songs in the PRC, see Anders Hansson, 'The Return of Yellow Music,' *CHIME Journal*, 16/17 (2005), 148–79.

78   Duan Detian, 'Anxian bu "an"' ("An county is not 'safe' as its name suggests"), in *Yang Zhiyun*, p. 273.

79   Duan Detian, pp. 373–4. Duan goes on to explain that accusations by a former classmate that these eight young men were involved in a bank robbery in Chengdu that day were dispelled by the audience attesting to them all being on stage presenting a model opera.

80   This discussion of sent-down youth songs is drawn from musicologist Dai Jiafang's 'Wutuobang li de aige: "Wen-ge" qijian zhiqing gequ de yanjiu' ("Mournful songs in Utopia: Research on educated youth songs in the Cultural Revolution"), *Zhongguo yinyuexue* (*Musicology in China*), 2002, 3 (September), pp. 5–25.

81   Quoted by Dai Jiafang, p. 7.

82   Dai Jiafang, pp. 8–9.

83   Dai Jiafang, pp. 10–12.

84   Dai Jiafang, pp. 11–12.

85   Yang Jian, *Wenhua dageming dixia wenxue* (*Underground literature in the Cultural Revolution*), Beijing: Chaohua chubanshe, 1993, p. 117. See also Dai Jiafang, p. 15.

86   Dai Jiafang, p. 13. See also Yang Jian, *Dixia wenxue*, p. 342. Ah Cheng's 1984 novella *King of Chess* (*Qiwang*) centres on such travelling expert. It is translated by Bonnie McDougall in Ah Cheng, *Three Kings: Three Stories from Today's China*, London: Collins Harvill, 1990.

87   Yang Jian, *Dixia wenxue*, pp. 130–1. See also Dai Jiafang, p. 17.

88   Quoted by Dai Jiafang, p. 18. As noted already regarding Red Guard plays, the notion of a madman having a clearer understanding of the state of the world than the so-called sane was used by Lu Xun in his 1918 seminal denunciation of Confucian morality.

89   Yan Xiaoli, 'Ganjiawan jishi' ("Records of Ganjiawan"), in *Yang Zhiyun*, pp. 387–8.

90   Dai Jiafang, pp. 25–6. As musicologist Dai Jiafang notes, the more popular (and to him more vulgar and lazy) qualities of post-1976 songs owed something to their sent-down youth predecessors. Ren Yi only left prison in 1979 when his case was overturned.

91   Yang Jian, 'Lishi goule: Neimeng yu Dongbei de zhiqing wenyi' ("Outline history: educated youth literature and art in Inner Mongolia and the Northeast"), *Zhongguo qingnian yanjiu*, 1998 5 (September), p. 33.

92   Yang Jian, 'Lishi goule …', p. 33. See Yang's brief account of the earliest salon, in Yang Jian, 'Hongweibing jituan xiang zhiqing jituan de lishixing

guodu (xu yi)' ("The historical transition from Red Guard to educated youth cliques, part two"), *Zhongguo qingnian yanjiu*, 1996, 3 (May), 4–8.

93 Yu Yinghua, '"Hong shaobing" de nahan' ("Cry of *Red Sentry*"), in Shi Xiaoyan, pp. 304–7. The broadsheets provided an outlet for youthful artists, whose drawing shifted from agit-prop portraits of Mao to more personal visual documentation of everyday life in the construction corps and on communes: see Wang Hongyi, 'Zhiqing meishu yuanliu shulüe' ("A brief account of the origin and development of educated youth fine art"), *Yishu tansuo* (*Arts Exploration: Journal of Guangxi Arts College*), 2008, 4 (August), pp. 5–13, 19.

94 See Liu Xiaomeng, *Zhongguo zhiqing shi*, p. 183.

95 Qu Zhe, p. 107.

96 Yang Jian, 'Lishi goule ... ,' p. 34. Many of these writings were modified and published after the end of the Cultural Revolution. For an overview, see Perry Link, 'Hand-Copied Entertainment Fiction from the Cultural Revolution,' in Perry Link, Richard Madsen, and Paul G. Pickowicz, pp. 17–36.

97 Yang Lian, 'Lishi goule ... ,' pp. 34–5.

98 Zheng Mengbiao, 'Bu zai chandou de linghun' ("A spirit that will not tremble again"), in Liu Xiaomeng, *Zhongguo zhiqing koushushi*, p. 363.

99 Zhuang Weiliang, 'Zhongguo de shi, "aibingbisheng"' ("China's affairs; victory comes when pushed to the wall") in Liu Xiaomeng, *Zhongguo zhiqing koushushi*, p. 535.

100 Cai Yongxian, p. 132. For other memories of the importance to sent-down youth of reading banned books, see Du Tianlin, 'Nanwang de qinghuai: xiaxiang biji' ("Unforgettable feelings: notes on going to the villages"), in Zhang Qi, ed., *Mo bu qu de jiyi: lao sanjie, xin san ji* (*Unerasable memories: old three classes, new three third class*), Beijing: Zhonggong dangshi chubanshe, 2009, pp. 82–4; Wang Zhenya, 'Hunfei xuezhua, suiyue liuhen' ("Frightening snow flies, the years leave marks") in Zhang Qi, pp. 465–8; Luo Dan, *Zhiqing biji* (*Notes of an educated youth*), Guangzhou: Huaheng chubanshe, 2010, pp. 120–5; Pan Yupeng, 'Yuanwang' ("Aspirations"), in Jin Dalu, ed., *Kunnan yu fengliu:'lao sanjie' ren de daolu (xiudingban)* (*Difficulties and distinction: the road of members of the 'old three classes': revised edition*), Shanghai: Shanghai shehui kexueyuan chubanshe, 2008, pp. 136–7; and Wang Tianyun, 'Liri rong canshuang' ("Bright sun melts the cruel frost"), in Jin Dalu, *Kunnan yu fengbo*, pp. 161–3.

101 Zhou Que, 'Wang bu liao, na shanwawa li de anfang' ("Unforgettable, that darkroom in the valley"), in Shi Xiaoyan, pp. 310–1. Zhou joined the regiment film projection team in 1973.

102 Han Xiuqing, 'Yinwei ni meiyou cuo!' ("Because you did not do wrong!"), in Shi Xiaoyan, pp. 451–2.

103 Zhong Ying, 'Jinyibu fazhan nongmin dianying fangying wang' ("Further develop the film projection network in the countryside"), *Hongqi*, 1975, 6 (June), pp. 50–3.

104 'Wosheng dianying faxing fangying gongzuo pengbo kaizhan' ("Province's film distribution and projection work vigorously develops"), *Heilongjiang ribao*, 14 February 1973, p. 1.

105 For a typical report see 'Shi fangying dui you shi xuanchuan dui' ("Both a projection team and a propaganda team"), *Heilongjiang ribao*, 20 February

1973, p. 4. Like most reports, this also emphasises the projection team's participation in agricultural work alongside the local peasants. On the same page as the above items is a report on how one Heilongjiang projection team saved state funds through an economy drive. Apparently some teams were wasteful of resources.

106  'Wosheng dianying faxing ... ,' p. 1.

107  Zhu Tianze, 'Ban hao nongcun dianying fangying dui' ("Run country film projection teams properly"), *Heilongjiang ribao*, 20 February 1973, p. 4. A Heilongjiang film projection team made sterling efforts after August 1970 to take the film of the videotaped version of *Taking Tiger Mountain by Strategy* to the peasants in Anda county, ensuring in fifty days that even the most remote of the 256 production brigades in the county had had an opportunity to see a screening: 'Puji geming yangbanxi de qingqibing: ji Anda xian nongcun dianying fangyingdui manqiang reqing wei pinxia zhongnong fuwu de xianjin shiji' ("Light cavalry in the popularization of the revolutionary model performances: on the advanced achievements of the Anda county country film projection team in whole-heartedly serving the poor and lower-middle peasants"), *Heilongjiang ribao*, 26 May 1971, p. 3.

108  For more on screenings of these banned films, see Clark, *Chinese Cultural Revolution*, p. 149.

109  In Inner Mongolia, 'barefoot doctor' An Haiyan recalled the appeal these films had to local children, who had not had much opportunity to see films before the influx of sent-down youth in the district. She also wondered why the explosive power on display in *Mine Warfare* could not be harnessed in creating irrigation canals in her district: An Haiyan, 'Wo yongyou zheme fengfu jingcai de jingli, zhen bu zhu lai renshi!' ("To have had such a rich and wonderful experience, what a world!"), in Liu Xiaomeng, *Zhongguo zhiqing koushushi*, pp. 318–19.

110  The 1994 film *In the Heat of the Sun* (*Yangguang canlan de rizi*) includes in its nostalgic portrayal of teenage life in Beijing in the early 1970s a sequence in which an outdoor screening of the model performance ballet film *The Red Detachment of Women* (*Hongse niangzijun*) suddenly stops due to a film break. The projectionist hastily puts on a reel from one of the Lenin films. As it starts several wags on stools in the front rows recite the dialogue just before it is heard on screen, to the general hilarity of their companions.

111  Zeng Zhicheng, pp. 26–7.

112  Sun Chunming, 'Yege' ("Night song"), in Shi Xiaoyan, pp. 133–4.

113  Tian Jingqing, pp. 184–5.

114  Dong Qiangsheng, 'Ai, "Mai hua guniang"!' ("Ah, *The Flower Seller*!"), in Shi Xiaoyan, pp. 449–50.

115  Nie Ming, 'Buyao yong puke gao mixin huodong' ("Don't use playing cards for superstitious activities"), *Liaoning qingnian* (*Liaoning Youth*), 1974, 2 (January), p. 45. See also Liu Xiaomeng, *Zhongguo zhiqing shidian*, p. 206.

116  Duan Zhishu, 'Yi ben "huang" shu' ("A 'yellow' book"), in Shi Xiaoyan, pp. 324–5. The owner of the book was identified as a class enemy and sentenced to fifteen years' imprisonment, in part because of his circulation of such books in his platoon.

117  See Clark, *Chinese Cultural Revolution*, pp. 228–9. For an outline, see Shuyu Kong, *Consuming Literature: Best Sellers and the Commercialization of*

*Literary Production in Contemporary China*, Stanford: Stanford University Press, 2005, pp. 120–4.

118 Shangganling Forest Bureau News Group and Yichun Region News Group, 'Fahui yeyu wenyi xuanchuandui de zhandou zuoyong' ("Develop the fighting role of amateur literature and art propaganda teams"), *Heilongjiang ribao*, 26 September 1972, p. 2.

119 Zeng Zhicheng, 'Zhibian shenghuo wu lezhang' ("Five happy chapters from life at the margins"), in *Qingchun wuyi*, p. 25.

120 This account is based on Wang Dawen, 'Shouchaoben' ("Hand-copied books"), in Shi Xiaoyan, pp. 28–30.

121 In spring 1976, at Peking University on a tiny and cheap ($5 U.S.) Sony transistor radio bought in Hong Kong I listened to interviews with U.S. presidential hopefuls, including Jimmy Carter, on VOA.

122 Zhu Shenzhi, 'Niu dawang' ("King of talk"), in Shi Xiaoyan, pp. 143–5.

123 This discussion is based on Gao Youpeng, 'Guanyu 'Wen'ge' shiqi de minjian wenxue wenti' ("On the question of Cultural Revolution period folk literature"), *Henan daxue xuebao (shehui kexue ban)* (*Henan University journal: social science edition*), 1999, 2 (March), pp. 27–30. These were collected after 1976 and some were published in magazines in the 1980s. But because this so-called literature created at the grassroots was created and circulated as an oral literature rather than being written down, it was difficult to collect. Parts of these folk stories found their way into features films, set during the Cultural Revolution, made in the late 1970s and early 1980s. They thus became even more widely circulated, though this time above ground: Gao Youpeng, p. 30.

124 Chen Qiguang, *Zhongguo dangdai wenxue shi* (*History of contemporary Chinese literature*), Guangzhou: Jinan daxue chubanshe, 1998, p. 327.

125 See Zhang Yang, *Wo yu 'Di'er ci woshou'* (*The Second Handshake and I*), Beijing: Zhongguo dangshi chubanshe, 2007, which reworks his earlier 'Di'er ci woshou' wenziyu (The Second Handshake literary inquisition), Beijing: Zhongguo shehui kexue chubanshe, 1999.

126 Yang Jian, *Zhongguo zhiqing wenxue shi* (*History of Chinese educated youth literature*), Beijing: Zhongguo gongren chubanshe, 2002, p. 175.

127 For an account of some of these literary groups, see Zhang Ming and Liao Yiwu, *Chenlun de shengdian: Zhongguo ershi shiji 70 niandai dixia shige yizhao* (*Sinking holy place: death pictures of underground poetry in China's 1970s*), Urumqi: Xinjiang qingshaonian chubanshe, 1994. See also Li Runxia, 'Lun "Baiyangdian shiqun" de wenhua tezheng' ("On the cultural characteristics of the 'Baiyangdian poetry group'"), reprinted in Jin Dalu and Jin Guangyao, eds., *Zhongguo zhishi qingnian shangshanxiaxiang yanjiu wenji* (*Collected research on China's educated youth going to the mountains and to the villages*), Shanghai: Shanghai shehui kexue chubanshe, 2009, pp. 388–98.

128 See Yang Jian, *Zhongguo zhiqing wenxue shi* and his earlier (now banned) *Wenhua dageming zhong de dixia wenxue* (1993). For a brief oral history account of informal circulation of ideas among sent-down youth and salons, see Yin Hongbiao, "'Wen'ge' shiqi de "Qingnian sixiang cunluo": jianzheng sixiang jiefang zhi lu' ("'Youth ideological villages' in the Cultural Revolution: witnessing the road of ideological liberation"), *Zhongguo qingnian yanjiu*, 2010, 3 (March), pp. 84–9, 104. For a succinct

review of poetry in these years, see Bonnie S. McDougall and Kam Louie, *The Literature of China in the Twentieth Century*, New York: Columbia University Press, 1997, pp. 421–7.

129  See *Shanghai wenhua shizhi tongxun (Bulletin of the Shanghai cultural history gazetteer)*, No. 22 (October 1992), p. 11.

130  Paul Clark, *Reinventing China*, pp. 35, 41–3.

131  For a Western journalist's account of the excitement of these years, see Roger Garside, *Coming Alive: China after Mao*, New York: McGraw-Hill, 1981. See Wei Jingsheng, *The Courage to Stand Alone: Letters from Prison and Other Writings*, New York: Viking, 1997. For ex-sent-down youth reminiscences of the period, see Dongfang chuban zhongxin, ed., *Wode qiqi, qiba (My '77 and '78)*, Shanghai: Dongfang chuban zhongxin, 2008; Weiming [Anonymous], ed., *Yongyuan de 1977 (Eternal 1977)*, Beijing: Beijing daxue chubanshe, 2007; and *Daxue meng yuan* Editorial Board, *Daxue meng yuan: wode 1977, 1978 (University dream fulfilled)*, Yinchuan: Ningxia renmin chubanshe, 2005. For an orthodox account of intellectual developments, see Luo Pinghan, *Chuntian: 1978 nian de Zhongguo zhishijie (Spring: Chinese intellectual circles in 1978)*, Beijing: Renmin chubanshe, 2008.

132  This outline is based on my observations during several visits to Beijing, Shanghai, and Xi'an during 1986–1987. For an outline of reform developments, see Harry Harding, *China's Second Revolution: Reform after Mao*, Washington, DC: The Brookings Institution, 1987.

133  "Han's 'Homecoming?'" (*Gui qu lai*, 1985), a story of a sent-down youth, created a primitive and grotesque rural world that seemed to mix the illustrations of Maurice Sendak with Latin American magical realism that was having an impact on Chinese writers at the time.

134  The novellas are titled 'King of the Children,' 'King of Chess,' and 'King of Trees': see Ah Cheng, *Three Kings*. All were made into art house films in the 1980s. For an excellent overview from 1987, see Bonnie McDougall, 'Breaking Through: Literature and the Arts in China 1976–1986,' in Bonnie S. McDougall, *Fictional Authors, Imaginary Audiences: Modern Chinese Literature in the Twentieth Century*, Hong Kong: Chinese University Press, 2003, pp. 171–204.

135  For one overview of these developments, see Wu Bin and Han Chunyan, *Zhongguo liuxing wenhua sanshinian (1978–2008) (Thirty years of Chinese popular culture)*, Beijing: Jiuzhou chubanshe, 2009. On publishing, see Shuyu Kong, pp. 124–30.


## 3  BODIES: UNDRESSED, FASHIONED, ADMIRED, AND MOVING

1  Ancient traditions, however, still have power. My Grandmother's arranged marriage to the leper, in exchange for a donkey and other financial inducements, is clearly an imposition from the patriarchal family system.

2  Li Shenzhi, 'Zhongguo: yijiubaba (xu)' ("China: 1988, part two"), *Dangdai qingnian yanjiu (Contemporary Youth Research)*, 1989, 3 (May), p. 47.

3  The win was reported in a small item at the bottom of the first page of *Renmin ribao*, 25 February 1988, p. 1. Zhang's return to Beijing warranted a photo and story: *Renmin ribao*, 26 February 1988, p. 3.

4   For an account of the Beijing Film Academy 1982 graduates, including Zhang
    Yimou, see Paul Clark, *Reinventing China*, esp. pp. 77–89 and 109–12.

5   I attended an afternoon of final auditions in Xi'an in late April 1986, where
    Wu explained that properly trained actors tended to be too citified and not
    look like peasants, and the untrained may have looked the part, but were
    often unable to grasp the subtleties of the roles.

6   Li Tong, 'Huode shuzhan xie, paide satuo xie: fang Zhang Yimou' ("Living
    more cheerfully, filming more freely: an interview with Zhang Yimou"),
    *Renmin ribao*, 16 January 1988, p. 8. Zhang expressed similar aims in his
    'Chang yi zhi shengming de zan'ge' ("Sing a song in praise of life"), *Dangdai
    dianying* (*Contemporary Film*), 1988, 2 (April), pp. 81–3. Zhang felt some
    confidence in setting out to make his first film as director, because the north-
    western peasant setting was similar to that of *The Yellow Earth*, for which
    he had won several international awards for his cinematography: interview
    with Zhang Yimou, Xi'an, 30 April 1986.

7   Chen Huai'ai (1920–1994) was the father of Chen Kaige, Zhang Yimou's
    Fifth Generation classmate and collaborator on *The Yellow Earth*: 'Zhumu
    "Hong gaoliang"' ("Looking at *Red Sorghum*"), *Dianying yishu* (*Film Art*),
    1988, 4 (August), pp. 3–10 (Chen's view is on p. 7).

8   Jin Zhongqiang, 'Cong kaobeishu kan dangqian dianying taishi' ("The pres-
    ent-day film situation from the point of view of the number of copies"),
    *Dazhong dianying* (*Popular Film*), 1989, 1 (January), pp. 2–3. Jin includes
    a list of the least copied films, starting with two titles for which no copies
    were struck, and showing *King of the Children* (*Haizi wang*), Chen Kaige's
    1987 feature, had a mere six copies in domestic distribution. For a claim that
    cinemas showing *Red Sorghum* were 95.1 percent full in Beijing in the first
    half of 1988, see Gao Jun, 'Lieqi: xiandai chengshi guanzhong xinli guankui'
    ("Chasing novelty: the narrow psychology of modern city audiences"),
    *Dazhong dianying*, 1988, 9 (September), pp. 12–13.

9   Director Zhang was himself associated with the birthplace of the ancient
    Chinese state, having been dubbed 'a son of Qin' (*Qinguo ren*) after the artistic
    success of *The Yellow Earth*. It did not hurt that he was from Xi'an, near where
    the first Chinese emperor had his capital and that his face and physique resem-
    bled those of the buried terracotta army beside that emperor's grave. Chen
    Kaige, director of *The Yellow Earth*, used the phrase *Qinguo ren* in a 1985
    article in praise of his cinematographer: Clark, *Reinventing China*, p. 180.

10  Wang Xiaobu, '"Hong gaoliang" de guanzhong' ("Red Sorghum's audi-
    ence"), *Zhongguo dianying bao* (*China Film Gazette*), 5 May 1988, p. 2.
    Wang tells the story of a Communist Party branch secretary in Beijing telling
    his driver not to let his two sons see such a pernicious film.

11  Cai Wanlin, 'Shen diandian de "Hong gaoliang"' ("Deep galloping *Red
    Sorghum*"), *Zhongguo dianying bao*, 5 May 1988, p. 2.

12  'D. W.,' '"Hong gaoliang" shi chouhua Zhongguoren de yingpian' ("*Red
    Sorghum* is a film which uglifies the Chinese"), *Zhongguo dianying bao*,
    5 May 1988, p. 2. The article is carefully dated April 1988. Note the shared
    initials with D. W. Griffith, the American film pioneer.

13  *Dazhong dianying*, 1988, 5 (May), pp. 4–5.

14  *Dazhong dianying*, 1988, 6 (June), pp. 2–4.

15  *Dazhong dianying*, 1988, 7 (July), pp. 8–11. Less than a year later, after
    events around June 4, an article in another popular magazine dismissed

foreign film prizes as worthless baubles rewarding directors who showed China as backward and weak: Zhang Yuezhong, 'Dui guoji dejiang dianying de yidian sikao' ("Thoughts on films that win international awards"), *Liaoning qingnian*, 1989, 14 (July), pp. 26–27.

16  Li Shui, 'Liu Zaifu tan dianying' ("Liu Zaifu on films"), *Dazhong dianying*, 1988, 10 (October), pp. 8–9.

17  Guo Yuhua, 'Guanyu qigong de youlü'("On worries about *qigong*"), *Daxuesheng (Campus Life)*, 1988, 10 (October), pp. 15–16.

18  'Shi ren gandai kunhuo: dianying "Hong gaoliang" guan hou' ("Causing puzzlement: after watching *Red Sorghum*"), *Huhehaote ribao (Huhehot Daily)*, 20 April 1988, p. 4.

19  Li Houji, 'Chou yu, mei yu?! "Hong gaoliang" guan hou' ("Ugly or beautiful?!: after watching *Red Sorghum*"), *Tianjin ribao*, 15 August 1988, p. 5.

20  Xu Hongli, '"Chou" ye shi yi zhong mei' ("'Ugly' is also a kind of beauty"), *Liaoning qingnian*, 1988, 18 (September), pp. 34–6.

21  Benbao pinglunyuan, 'Kexi de "Hong gaoliang" xianxiang' ("The gratifying '*Red Sorghum* phenomenon'"), *Renmin ribao*, 14 September 1988, p. 1. The story contrasted this treatment of a controversial film with the treatment meted out to *The Life of Wu Xun (Wu Xun zhuan)* in 1951, the first campaign against a work of art in the People's Republic of China and initiated by Mao Zedong himself: see Paul Clark, *Chinese Cinema: Culture and Politics since 1949*, Cambridge: Cambridge University Press, 1987, pp. 44–54.

22  Li Tong, '"Hong gaoliang" xixing' ("*Red Sorghum*'s westward travels"), *Renmin ribao*, 13 March 1988, p. 5.

23  The concert was organised by the Oriental Red Song and Dance Company (*Dongfang gewutuan*), a venerable outfit that had shown considerable entrepreneurial flair in the 1980s.

24  The preceding paragraph is based on my attending the two nights of the concert and spending time with Zhang Yimou in Beijing in the summers of 1988, 1989, and 1990.

25  Zhou Shirong, 'Hei tudi yunyu de yishu shengming: zan wuju "Gaoliang hun"' ("Artistic life bred in the black soil: in praise of 'Sorghum Soul'"), *Wenyi bao (Literature and Art Gazette)*, 15 October 1988, p. 5.

26  For more on the music, see Chapter 4.

27  Xiao Yu, 'Jingcheng "renti youhua dazhan" suo yinqi de …' ("Caused by the 'Nude Oil Painting Exhibition' in the capital …"), *Qingchun suiyue (Youth Era)*, 1989, 5 (May), pp. 33–5.

28  For a report of what the organisers of the exhibition thought, see Yi Xiaoxia, 'Renti yishu zai jinri zhi Zhongguo' ("Nude art in today's China"), *Qingchun suiyue*, 1989, 3 (March), pp. 45–6.

29  Jian Mei, 'Zhongguo potianhuang: Beijing mote'er fengbo suxie' ("Unprecedented in China: Notes on the model storm in Beijing"), *Daxuesheng*, 1989, 3 (March), pp. 18–24.

30  Yu Tian, 'Zouchu yunhuhu de meishuguan' ("On leaving the dizzying art gallery"), *Daxuesheng*, 1989, 3 (March), pp. 25–26. The inaugural issue of *Daxuesheng* in January 1988 had included the relatively rare reproduction of a nude oil painting.

31  *Renmin ribao*, 21 February 1989, p. 4 reported these Nanjing developments under a subheading: 'The sham is real; good and bad are mixed up' (*yumu-hunzhu, nishajuxia*).

32  Liu Xu, 'Zhongguo xiandai yishuzhan de fengbo' ("The storm over the China modern art exhibition"), *Daxuesheng*, 1989, 3 (March), inside front and back covers. For another report, with different dates for the exhibition, see Fang Wei, "'89' Zhongguo xiandai yishu dachao' ("The modern art wave in 1989"), *Qingchun suiyue*, 1989, 6 (June), pp. 30–2.

33  These two incidents are recorded in Jian Mei, pp. 19–20, and the former in *Renmin ribao*, 21 February 1989, p. 4. See also Maria Galikowski, *Art and Politics in China, 1949–1984*, Hong Kong: The Chinese University Press, 1998, p. 180 and Figure 42, and Julia F. Andrews, *Painters and Politics in the People's Republic of China, 1949–1979*, Berkeley: University of California Press, 1994, pp. 390–2.

34  I met with members of this class in a visit to the academy in October 1980. An illustrated academic book, Chen Zui, *Luoti yishu lun* (*On nude art*), Beijing: Zhongguo wenyi chubanshe, was first published in November 1987 and eight months later in a second printing reached a remarkable one hundred and twenty thousand copies in circulation. A Chinese translation of Kenneth Clark's *The Nude: A Study of Ideal Life* (1985) was published in December 1988 with a large print run of sixty thousand copies. Even with the rise of the Internet, readers' interest in artists' handbooks, featuring photographs of nudes, remained high in Beijing bookstores into the 2000s, judging from the state of most display copies.

35  Yu Tian, p. 25.

36  Li Hongbin, 'Zhongguo "renti chao"' (China's 'nude upsurge'), *Qingnian yu shehui* (*Youth and Society*), 1989, 7 (July), p. 47.

37  He Ren, 'Jinqiu shijie jiali huiqu Yangcheng, woguo jiang xuanchu shi daming mo' ("China's ten top models are chosen at a beautiful gathering in autumnal Guangzhou"), *Ba xiaoshi yiwai* (*Beyond eight hours*), 1988, 4 (July), p. 57.

38  Jian Mei, p, 20. For an overview of bodybuilding in the 1980s and after, see Susan Brownell, *Training the Body for China: Sports in the Moral Order of the People's Republic*, Chicago: University of Chicago Press, 1995, pp. 265–77.

39  Susan Brownell touches on this aspect of the sport: pp. 274–5.

40  *Qingchun suiyue*, 1989, 2 (February), p. 43. The August 1988 issue of *Qingnian shidai* (*Youth Era*) reprinted a short article from *Jiating kexue bao* (*Household Science News*) on appearance medicines, ending with a cautionary note that doctors were best relied upon in prescribing these drugs rather than using self-medication: *Qingnian shidai*, 1988, 8 (August), p. 49.

41  Chen Shaojian, 'Guoguanzhanjiang de "wu lianguan"' ("The 'five successive title' holder overcoming all obstacles"), *Qingchun yu shehui*, 1989, 10 (October), 10–11.

42  See the introduction, with colour stills, in *Dazhong dianshi* (*Popular Television*), 1988, 11 (November), last page of middle colour section, before p. 17.

43  Tao Ran, 'Deng Lijun jianmei youfang' ("Deng Lijun's exercising on the right track"), *Ba xiaoshi yiwai*, 1988, 4 (July), p. 57. Teresa Teng died suddenly from complications from asthma at the age of forty-two, much to the distress of her legions of Chinese fans.

44  *Dazhong dianshi*, 1989, 6 (June) centre page. The bottom corner of the fold-out page (at Ms Li's right hip) and the bottom of the page (across her right

leg and the sea) was an advertisement for traditional Chinese medicine from Huqingyutang.

45  Qin Zhen, 'Huang pifu shi xi bu bai de' ("Yellow skin can't be washed white"), *Qingnian yu shehui*, 1989, 2 (February), p. 1.

46  Chen Weiyun, 'Tiyu: tianshen de huanyue' ("Sport: a divine rejoicing"), *Daxuesheng*, 1988, 10 (October), pp. 36–8.

47  Wu Liping, 'Qingnian de shenmei tedian yu fuzhuang de liuxing quishi' ("Youth's aesthetic characteristics and popular fashion trends"), *Zhongguo qingnian yanjiu*, 1991, 3 (May), pp. 36–8, esp. p. 37. Taking Beijing's lead, khaki greatcoats were the rage in Shenyang in the winter and spring of 1988: Bai Qing, 'Qingnian zhong weishenme liuxing jundayi? ("Why are military coats fashionable among the young?"), *Liaoning qingnian*, 1988, 5 (March), pp. 28–9. For an overview of twenty-one clothing trends, from bell-bottomed trousers in the early 1980s to silk-brocade 'Shanghai Tang' jackets in the 2000s, see http://www.youthol.cn:3789/news/48/20943.html (accessed on 24 March 2010).

48  Zhao Zhiqin, 'Zai fushi wenhua xiandai bianqian zhong: Shencheng qingnian fushi xianxiang xilie sumiao' ("In the midst of modern changes in fashion culture: Set sketches of fashion phenomena among Shanghai youth"), *Qingnian xuebao* (*Youth Journal*), 1992, 1 (Spring), pp. 6–9.

49  Zhao Zhiqin, pp. 6–7.

50  These two examples are in Zhao Zhiqin, p. 7.

51  Wang Lin, '1991 nian Jingcheng "wenhua shan" xianxiang' ("The 1991 slogan T-shirt phenomenon in Beijing"), *Qingnian yanjiu*, 1992, 4 (April), p. 1. The best account of this T-shirt phenomenon is the chapter on 'Consuming T-shirts in Beijing' in Geremie Barmé, *In the Red: On Contemporary Chinese Culture*, New York: Columbia University Press, 1999, pp. 145–78.

52  Wang Lin, pp. 2–3. Grain ration tickets were used in Beijing until 1993.

53  Wang Lin, pp. 3–4. Wang traces the three or four key people, identified by surname only and by disguised work unit, responsible for the appearance of these shirts in March 1991 in Beijing. He also outlines the official response, including a 29 June notice from the Beijing City Commercial and Industrial Management Bureau that called for tight control on the sale of these T-shirts. *Qingnian yanjiu*, published by the Chinese Academy of Social Sciences, at the time was still a restricted circulation (*neibu*) publication. Barmé discusses Kong Yongqian's contributions to the T-shirt phenomenon at length.

54  Wang Lin, p. 5. The translations and origin of the phrase are from Barmé, pp. 162 and 430n83.

55  Wang Lin, p. 6. Eventually thirty-four slogan T-shirts were banned, though the onset of cooler autumn weather largely removed them from public awareness: Wang Lin, pp. 6 and 12.

56  Jiao Runming, 'Cong "wenhua shan" xianxiang tanjiu qingnian liuxing wenhua de fazhan' ("Exploration of the development of youth popular culture from the 'slogan T-shirt' phenomenon"), *Qingnian yanjiu*, 1992, 4 (April), pp. 7–12, esp. pp. 11–12.

57  Zhao Zhiqin, p. 9. Another such space for the expression of youthful views was the desk tops of China's universities. 'Desktop literature' (*kezhuo wenxue*) was the object of the earnest attention of several sociologists in the early 1990s. Like their counterparts in other countries, Chinese university students could express their boredom in lectures, their frustrations, and

their wit by writing or carving phrases in the desk tops in lecture halls and library reading rooms. Indeed the anonymity of such surreptitious graffiti was one of the attractions: Students could write what they really thought, however rude or spontaneous: See, for example, Liu Yiguo, 'Daxue "kezhuo wenxue" yanjiu' ("Research on university 'desktop literature'"), *Qingnian yanjiu*, 1991, 3 (March), pp. 15–19, 31.

58 *Elle* magazine appeared in a Chinese version (*Shijie shizhuan zhi yuan*, co-published by Hachette, France and the Shanghai Translation Publishing House) in 1994. *Cosmopolitan* (*Shishang*) appeared in 2004, and *Esquire* (*Shishang xiansheng*) in 2005. For a stylishly packaged account of the emergence of these magazines, see Wang Shouzhi, *Shishang shidai* (*Trends Era*), Beijing: Zhongguo lüyou chubanshe, 2008. On these kinds of magazines and their market, see Sun Yanjun, Kang Jianzhong, Mei Yuanmei, and Liu Zaixing, *Qikan Zhongguo* (*Periodical China*), Beijing: Zhongguo shehui kexue chubanshe, 2003, pp. 52–101. For an earlier view not focused on youth, see Julia F. Andrews and Kuiyi Shen, 'The New Chinese Woman and Lifestyle Magazines in the Late 1990s,' in Perry Link and others, pp. 137–62.

59 This is set out by Li Caijiao, 'Qingnian yu fushi xianxiang guanxi yanjiu' ("Research on the relations between youth and fashion phenomena"), *Zhongguo qingnian yanjiu*, 2007, 4 (April), pp. 21–6. She outlines the influence of Soviet Russian styles on Chinese fashion in the 1950s, the army look during the Cultural Revolution, and the rise of jeans, flares, and other youth fashions in the 1980s. Cosplay is discussed at the end of this chapter.

60 *Guqiguaishou* ['Strange Monster'], *Chuncui shaonian*, Beijing: Taihai chubanshe, 2001. For a typical item for young women, see the illustrated advice in a Fujian magazine on using hair extensions and false braids in *Qingchun chao* (*Youth Power*), 2000, 6 (June), pp. 54–5.

61 Nie Ping and Wei Ran, *Shishang youzui*, Beijing: Kexue jishu wenxian chubanshe, 2005. On the cover the character *zui* (guilt) has a line through it, as on a road sign, an indication of the playful approach of the book.

62 Shen Yibing, 'Wenshen yu fuhao: dushi qingnian wenshen xianxiang toushi' ("Tattoos and marks: A perspective on the tattoo phenomenon among urban youth"), *Zhongguo qingnian yanjiu*, 2006, 6 (June), pp. 69–73. See also Ren Peng, 'Tongku de fengliu: qingshaonian wenshen xianxiang toushi' ("A painful distinction: Perspectives on the young people's tattoo phenomenon"), *Qingnian tansuo* (*Youth Explorations*), 1994, 6 (November), pp. 20–3. The criminal association of tattoos caused problems for prospective army recruits who had the marks.

63 Jian Mei, p. 20.

64 See the page of stills and story outline in *Dazhong dianshi*, 1989, 11 (November), opposite p. 17.

65 'Guanyu "dianying zenyang biaoxian xing'ai? Nengfou zhanshi luoti?" de shi ge you zhengyi de wenti' ("Ten controversial questions on 'How should films present sexual love? and Should nudity be shown?'"), *Dazhong dianying*, 1989, 4 (April), pp. 2–3. Question 9 asked whether a ratings system (similar to 'general audiences' and R16) was needed, many years before this issue again became the object of agitation from frustrated filmmakers and distributors in China. In the May issue (1989, 5, pp. 2–5) one of six articles likened nude shots to Chinese film's 'Rubik's cube,' it was such a complicated

issue for audiences to contend with. The writer referred to New Zealand-born U.S. sexologist John Money on a visit to China in the mid-1970s viewing three contemporary Chinese films and discovering the absence of any reference to sex (p. 3).

66 Xing Kai, Wen Huai, and Jing Bin, 'Dui seqing duwu wenti de diaocha yu sikao' ("Investigation and thoughts on the issue of pornographic books"), *Qingchun suiyue*, 1988, 10 (October), p. 20. Private bookstores and bookstalls paid regular publishers a cut of the likely profits from a title to have a book printed with an official standardised book number. For a brief account of such unofficial publishing, see A Man, 'Yeshi "changxiaoshu" jingyi ji' ("A surprising record of nightime 'bestsellers'"), *Fujian qingnian*, 1988, 8 (August), pp. 16–17. See also Huang Ruixu, 'Seqing chongjibo: yinhui wupin yu qingshaonian zuicuo' ("A pornographic shockwave: Obscene goods and youngsters' criminal errors"), *Qingnian yanjiu*, 1989, 4 (April), pp. 33–8.

67 *Qingnian yu shehui*, 1988, 6 (June), p. 47. See also 1988, 5 (May), p. 47; 1988, 8 (August), p. 45. See also an identical section in *Qingchun suiyue*, 1988, 2 (February), p. 47; 1988, p. 3 (March), pp. 47–8; 1988, 4 (April), pp. 46–7; 1988, 5 (May), pp. 48 and 47; 1988, 6 (June), pp. 47–8; and 1989, 1 (January), p. 48.

68 See *Dazhong dianshi*, 1988, 6 (June), p. 29, and similar pages in the following months through to December 1989. The issue published June 1989 notably did not carry such a page. February 1989 (p. 31) oddly included two sixty-year-old actors' photos and bios, along with that of a thirty-four-year-old and five others ranging in age from sixteen to twenty-five. Other months with an actor in their thirties were August, October, and November 1989. Typical of the new commercialism of the 1980s, these pages included an advertisement for equipment or insurance, with a note at the top of how the featured enterprise (or even the named enterprise head) welcomed the blossoming of new talent on Chinese television, and with more advertising for that company across the bottom of the page. For new ways in the new century of finding marriage partners (and entertaining millions), see the discussion on the television show *If You Are the One* in Chapter 4. An analysis of the changing criteria men and women applied to such searches, as reflected in that 2010 programme, see Wang Fang and Rong Yan, 'Cong dianshi xiangqin jiemu kan nanxing ze'ou: yi Jiangsu Weishi "Feng cheng wu rao" 344 wei nan jiabing wei lie,' ("Men's mate searching seen in television dating shows: 344 male guests on Jiangsu Satellite TV's *If You Are the One* as illustration"), *Qingnian yanjiu*, 2011, 2 (April), pp. 31–40.

69 Detailed ballroom dancing instruction was provided for readers of *Qingchun suiyue*, 1988, 10 (October), p. 45. See an account of ballroom dancing in Inner Mongolia, which notes the youth of participants, in *Huhehaote wanbao* (*Huhehot Evening News*), 23 July 1988, p. 2.

70 A dance hall is the setting for a typical one-page photo drama, featured in many youth-oriented magazines in the late 1980s, designed to teach a lesson about behavior: 'Yongheng de tan'ge' ("Eternal tango"), *Fujian qingnian*, 1988, 8 (August), p. 46.

71 Zhang Yuan, 'Wuting: tamen lai le' ("Dance hall: the women have come"), *Qingnian yu shehui*, 1988, 7 (July), p. 33.

72 For a brief overview of these dances, including 'seniors' disco' (*laonian diske*), see Wu Zhenwen, 'Jiaoyiwu, diske, yunlücao' ("Ballroom dancing, disco, aerobic dance"), *Ba xiaoshi yiwai*, 1988, 6 (November), p. 56. A brief

defence of 'seniors disco' and 'Peking opera disco' can be found in Ruo Da, 'Cong laonian disike shuoqi' ("Starting with seniors' disco"), *Qingchun suiyue*, 1988, 4 (April), p. 19. The death of disco for the young once old folk took it up is noted in Lu De and Zhang Xiong, 'Qingchun de guiji: 90 niandai Zhongguo neidi qingshaonian shishang redian gaishu' ("The locus of youth: A summary of the fashion hot-spots of 1990s Chinese mainland youth"), *Zhongguo qingnian yanjiu*, 2000, 1 (January), p. 24.

73  Hu Ke and Hou Xiaofeng, 'He qingnian pengyou tan piliwu' ("Talking with young friends about breakdancing"), *Dazhong dianying*, 1988, 4 (April), p. 17.

74  This point is made in Bai Lingling, 'Piliwu qinggan shijie de jiaoluo' ("A corner of the world of breakdancing friendship"), *Wudao (Dance)*, 1988, 11 (November), pp. 34–5.

75  Wang Feng, 'Shenghuo de xuanlü: Zhongyang renmin guangbo diantai 9.20 ri "Wujian banxiaoshi"' ("The melody of life: Chinese People's Radio Station 'Noontime half-hour,' 20 September"), *Wudao (Dance)*, 1988, 11 (November), p. 32–3.

76  Wang Feng, p. 33. After Wang Feng's report, the radio host added earnest words about the need to ensure that breakdancing developed in a healthy direction, to avoid the negative elements in all this youthful enthusiasm. The song is discussed in Chapter 4.

77  Huang Xianguo, 'Zagan yu qingtian pili' ("Random thoughts on sunny day breakdancing"), *Wudao*, 1988, 11 (November), p. 36.

78  Note by Lei Ming [lit. thunder-peal] for a photo essay, 'Pili: zai Shancheng penfa' ("Breakdance: Gushes in Guiyang"), *Qingnian shidai*, 1988, 7 (July), inside front cover.

79  Lu Xianbiao, 'Wo yu piliwu' ("Break-dancing and I"), *Wudao*, 1988, 8 (August), p. 39 (reprinted from *Shanghai wudao yishu (Shanghai Dance Art)*, 1988, p. 1.

80  On-set conversation with Tian Zhuangzhuang, Beijing, 11 July 1988.

81  For background on the rise of the Fifth Generation filmmakers, mostly 1982 graduates of the Beijing Film Academy, see Paul Clark, *Reinventing China*.

82  See Paul Clark, p. 113. The 1940s novel adaptation was *The Drum Singers (Gushu yiren)*, which had a relatively low number of distribution copies struck (twenty-two) in 1988: *Dazhong dianying*, 1989, 1 (January), p. 3.

83  I learned this from chatting with several performers at a soundstage at the army's August First Film Studio, where I was smuggled into the military facility, which was then usually off limits to foreigners: 11 July 1988.

84  Tian Zhuangzhuang and others, '"Yaogun qingnian" dui guanzhong shuo' ("*Rock 'n Roll Kids* talks with its audience"), *Dazhong dianying*, 1989, 3 (March), pp. 18–19.

85  This nativist attraction of *qigong* was also part of its appeal to the mostly retired bulk of its actual practitioners, as well shown by David A. Palmer, in his *Qigong Fever: Body, Science, and Utopia in China*, New York: Columbia University Press, 2007. Palmer's focus is on the networks and organisational impact of the movement, particularly in the 1990s.

86  *Qigong yu kexue (Qigong and Science)*, 1988, 2 (February), inside front cover, and 1988, 3 (March), pp. 17–18. The urge to bring *qigong* into modern scientific discourse was apparent in the pages of a popular magazine, *Qigong yu kexue*. Founded in early 1983 by the Guangdong Province Qigong Scientific Research Association, the magazine set out to popularise

and give modern legitimacy to the various activities associated with deep breathing exercises and martial arts.

87  Wang Deming, 'Yishen zhenqi qianbanyong' ("A single individual's inborn vitality has a thousand uses"), *Huhehaote wanbao*, 3 September 1988, p. 2.

88  *Qigong yu kexue*, 1988, 9 (September), pp. 23–4. A popular study of *qigong* first published in 1987 reached over forty-three thousand copies in a second printing from the People's Health Press in July 1988: Zhao Baofeng, Tian Hongji, and Zhang Tiange, *Zhongguo qigong xue gailun* (*Introduction to Chinese qigong studies*), Beijing: Renmin weisheng chubanshe, 1987.

89  Ke Jun, 'Qigong re yu guominxing' ("*Qigong* fever and national characteristics"), *Huhehaote wanbao*, 17 April 1989, p. 3.

90  Bo Ya, '"Qigong re" xijuan Beida' ("*Qigong* fever sweeps through Peking University"), *Daxuesheng*, 1988, 6 (June), pp. 34–5.

91  Palmer, p. 137. Yan had been a sent-down youth in the Cultural Revolution before studying Chinese medicine in Chengdu from 1974 to 1977.

92  Ban Chengnong, 'Shenmi, shenqi, shenwang: qigong dashi Yan Xin fagong mujiji' ("Mysterious, magical, enrapturing: An eyewitness account of a demonstration by *qigong* master Yan Xin"), *Qingnian shidai*, 1988, 3 (March), pp. 24–25.

93  Mo Kai, 'Xianhua qigong' ("*Qigong* chat"), *Qingnian yu shehui*, 1988, 7 (July), p. 23.

94  See *Qigong yu kexue*, 1988, 12 (December), back cover; 1988, 4 (April), pp. 2–3, 19–20; 1988, 5 (May), pp. 2–4; 1988, 9 (September), pp. 32–3. See also Zong Yi and He Yanping, 'Cong shenmi zouxiang kexue: Zhongguo qigong re quxiang tanxi' ("Going from mystery to science: An analysis of the tendency of the *qigong* fever"), *Liaowang* (*Observation*), 1989, 14 (April), pp. 25–7. See also Mai Ning, 'Bi tiankong geng guangkuo de: qingnian qigongshi Li Chengzhi yinxiang' ("Vaster than the sky: Impressions of the young *qigong* master Li Chengzhi"), *Qingnian yu shehui*, 1989, 12 (December), pp. 14–15.

95  Zong Yi and He Yanping, pp. 25–6. See also Xiao Zhenhua, 'Wode yici qigong yan' ("My one *qigong* experience"), *Fujian qingnian*, 1988, 12 (December), p. 39.

96  Guo Yuhua, 'Guanyu qigong de youlü' ("Worry about *qigong*"), *Daxuesheng*, 1988, 10 (October), pp. 15–16 (the quotes are from p. 15).

97  Wang Hongguang, 'Qigong de zhendang' ("*Qigong* quake"), *Qingnian yidai*, 1988, 1 (January), pp. 22–3. See a story of a soldier using *qigong* to treat sick soldiers on the front line, though the whereabouts of the line is not explained: Jie Cheng, 'Laoshan "qigongshi"' ("'*Qigong* master' in the deep mountains"), *Qingchun suiyue*, 1988, 6 (June), pp. 16–17.

98  The billiards craze extended to other cities. In the summer of 1988 some streets in Shenyang in the northeast also saw tables set up and young people enthusiastically playing: Shi Tongxiang, 'Taiqiu re de zhenhan' ("Reverberations of the billiard fever"), *Liaoning qingnian*, 1988, 16 (August), pp. 16–17.

99  Su Ning, 'Jinghua chuxia "taiqiu re"' ("'Billiard fever' in early summer Beijing"), *Renmin ribao*, 2 June 1988, p. 4.

100  Dayu was the third of the legendary first emperors of China, credited with inventing irrigation.

101  Liu Hongsen, 'Qingnian qiumi xintai fenxi' ("Analysis of youth ball game fan mentality"), *Qingnian xuebao*, 1990, 3 (Fall), pp. 7–9.

102  Liu Hongsen, p. 9.

103 This account is based largely on Wang Nianning and Zhang Jingyan, 'Beijing gongren tiyuchang shijian jiqi sikao' ("The Beijing Workers' Stadium incident and reflections"), *Qingnian yanjiu*, 1985, 8 (August), pp. 18–21. As noted earlier, at the time *Qingnian yanjiu* was a restricted publication. The groundspeople collected 2,600 plastic bottles, over one hundred glass bottles, and more than two hundred buns and other bread (p. 20).

104 Wang Nianning and Zhang Jingyan, pp. 18–19. The Chinese failure in 1981 was the result of an unexpected win by the New Zealand team over Kuwait in a match in Singapore, a thwarting of Chinese ambitions that some middle-aged Chinese fans refer to even thirty years later.

105 Wang Nianning and Zhang Jingyan, pp. 20–1.

106 Yu Yuan, 'Fanzui "qiumi" de xinli pouxi: laizi Nanchong de baogao' ("Analysis of the psychology of criminal 'sports fans': a report from Nanchong"), *Tiyu bolan (Sports Panorama)*, 1988, 10 (October), pp. 4–8.

107 Yu Yuan, p. 4.

108 Yu Yuan, p. 7.

109 Yu Yuan, p. 8.

110 Lan Baogang and Gu Qing, '"Zhong-Yi zhi zhan," Shenyang qiupiao fengchao' ("The 'China–Iran battle,' Shenyang sports ticket unrest"), *Liaoning qingnian (Liaoning Youth)*, 1989, 18 (September), pp. 4–7. China established a national professional football (soccer) league in 1994. Basketball followed in 1995.

111 See the introduction and extract translation from *Sha'ou* by Zhou Xueliin in a Chinese Film special issue of *Renditions: A Chinese-English Translation Magazine*, No. 71 (Spring 2009), pp. 58–64.

112 Fan Lei, 'Beijing daxuesheng tan Aoyunhui shili' ("Beijing university students discuss the Olympic Games setbacks"), *Daxuesheng*, 1988, 11 (November), pp. 8–10.

113 Zhang Qing, 'Luojia shanxia, qizuibashe hua Aoyun: Wuhan daxue bufen tongxue zuotan Aoyunhui guangan jilu' ("Under Luojia Mountain, talking all at once about the Olympics: Record of observations by Wuhan University students discussing the Olympic Games"), *Daxuesheng*, 1988, 11 (November), pp. 11–13.

114 This paragraph draws on Bian Dengwei, Wo shi wang: Li Ning, cong ticao wangzi dao shangjie yingxiong ("I am a king: Li Ning, from prince of gymnastics to business hero"), Beijing: Guangming ribao chubanshe, 1999, esp. pp. 68–78, 90, 149. I watched Li Ning celebrate his graduation with his law school class from Peking University in June 2002. In August 2008 he lit the Olympic flame, suspended high above the National ('Bird's Nest') Stadium.

115 For a discussion of the rise of basketball in youth imaginations, see Andrew Morris, '"I Believe You Can Fly": Basketball Culture in Postsocialist China,' in Perry Link, Richard P. Madsen, and Paul G. Pickowicz, eds., *Popular China: Unofficial Culture in a Globalizing Society*, Lanham: Rowman & Littlefield, 2002, pp. 9–38. On another global sports phenomenon, see Tim Sedo, 'Dead-Stock Boards, Blown-Out Spots, and the Olympic Games: Global Twists and Local Turns in the Formation of China's Skateboarding Community,' in Petra Rethmann, Imre Szeman, and William D. Coleman, eds., *Cultural Autonomy: Frictions and Connections*, Vancouver: UBC Press, 2010, pp. 257–82.

116 Liu Xiang, *Wo shi Liu Xiang* (I am Liu Xiang), Shanghai Sanlian chubanshe, 2004, p. 133.

117 Liu's virtual sainthood was confirmed when he appeared in Shanghai primary school textbooks in the spring of 2005. This was the fastest textbook appearance by a contemporary figure: Gao Fusheng, 'Yeah! Liu Xiang "pao" jin xiaoxue keben' ("Yeah! Liu Xiang has 'run' into primary school textbooks"), *Liaoning qingnian*, 2005, 8 (April), p. 25. For another adulatory account, emphasising how handsome and talented the young hurdler is, see Lan Chunhui, 'Liu Xiang: yong zixin, pinbo, yongqi aozhan shijie tiantan' ("Liu Xiang: taking on world athletics with confidence, courage, and with all his might"), *Liaoning qingnian*, 2004, 19 (October), pp. 6–8.

118 A one-page account of where the payment for such advertising appearances goes appeared in *Liaoning Youth* magazine: Gao Zhiguo, 'Liu Xiang guanggao shouru fenpei mingdan lou le shui' ("Who is revealed by the list of names of the revenue from Liu Xiang's advertisements"), *Liaoning qingnian*, 2004, 24 (December), p. 22.

119 Liu's richly illustrated autobiography is emblazoned on the cover with the phrase 'I, Liu Xiang, ask you all to believe that in Beijing in 2008 I will fly through the air (*feixiang*, using his personal name).' This is a modified version of the last sentences in the book's postscript (p. 133).

120 As one fan noted sarcastically, 'With so much money riding on one leg, how *could* he run?': see on http://blog.stnn.cc/huangqiyi/Efp_b1_1002168441. aspx (accessed on 5 January 2010). Netizens noted that Liu covered up a Japanese logo on his running singlet at the Tenth National Games in nanjing in 2006, not from patriotism, but because of his obligations to his own sponsor's logo: http://tieba.baidu.com/f?z=132717581&ct+335544 320&lm+0&sc=0&rn=30&tn=baiduPostBrowser&word=%B3%AC%B C%B6%C5%AE%C9%F9&pn=0 (accessed on 2 January 2010). One of the relatively few female sports celebrities for China's youth was Olympic diver Guo Jingjing (born 1981). By 2009 she was followed as much for her engagement to the scion of one of Hong Kong's richest families as for her achievements on the diving board. On Chinese television in 2009 and 2010 she helped sell Yili brand milk products.

121 Manyou wenhua, *Manyou COSPLAY 100 xilie: pianyi huanxiang* (*Cartoon friend* [a magazine title] *Cosplay 100 series: on the wings of fantasy*), Harbin: Heilongjiang meishu chubanshe, 2006.

122 STOKIS, *Shaonian huawu STOKIS* (*Juvenile picture dance STOKIS*), Harbin: Heilongjiang shaonian ertong chubanshe, 2007.

## 4 RHYTHMS: THE SOUNDTRACKS OF CONNECTION AND ASSERTION

1 For a recent version of this story, see Ryan Moore, *Sells Like Teen Spirit: Music, Youth Culture, and Social Crisis*, New York: New York University Press, 2010.

2 For an overview of songs in the New China, see the serialised account by Chen Feng, 'Jiyi de suiyue zai gesheng zhong yongheng: xin Zhongguo gequ chuangzuo licheng huiwang' ("Times remembered in song are forever: A look back at the course of song creation in New China"), published monthly in the back two pages of the magazine *Gequ* (*Songs*) from April 2005 (issue 4) to January 2008 (issue 1) and covering the period from 1949 to 2000.

3   The theme song is the first on an album from 1980 published by the China
    Record Corporation and named after the other song in the film *Little Flower*,
    'Velvet Flowers' (*Ronghua*). The other nine songs on the disk were all from
    films or television serials: Record M-2511 (song slip sheet in the author's
    collection).

4   Li Luxin, *Liuxing gequ: dangdai qingnian de jiayuan* (*Popular songs: home-
    land of contemporary youth*), Beijing: Huaxia chubanshe, 1993, p. 2. Zhou
    Dianfu also notes the influence of television in awareness of the new songs:
    'Cong liuxing gequ kan qingnian wenhua jianshe ("Youth culture construc-
    tion from the point of view of popular songs"), *Qingnian yanjiu*, 1990,
    1 (January), p. 20.

5   Li Luxin comments on the absence of difficulty with songs in Cantonese on
    pp. 20–2.

6   By 1991, the state-owned record company reported that Hong Kong and
    Taiwan albums were expected to sell in the hundreds of thousands, whereas
    local artists could expect a tenth or less of such sales levels: Li Luxin, p. 5.

7   A young sales assistant surnamed Su, quoted by Li Luxin, p. 6.

8   Li Luxin cites the *Renmin yinyue* article, couched as a dialogue between an
    earnest teacher and a youth, on pp. 10–11. For a later defence of popular
    music, see Liao Ye, 'Zai kaifang de chaoliu zhongqiu fazhan: dui woguo
    tongsu yinyue chuangzuo wenti de sikao' ("Developing in the currents of
    opening up: Thoughts on the issue of popular music creation in China"),
    *Renmin ribao*, 5 January 1988, p. 5.

9   For a discussion of the emergence of new notions of popular music in the
    1980s, see the pioneering study by Andrew F. Jones, *Like a Knife: Ideology
    and Genre in Contemporary Chinese Popular Music*, Ithaca: Cornell East
    Asia Series, 1992, pp. 35–90. On the notion of 'happy, smiling natives,' more
    prone than Han Chinese to burst into song and dance, see Paul Clark, 'Ethnic
    minorities in Chinese films: Cinema and the exotic,' *East-West Film Journal*,
    1, 2 (1987), pp. 15–31.

10  Wang Yunlong, 'Tongsu gequ de kexi chaoyue' ("The gratifying excess of
    popular music"), *Qingnian yu shehui*, 1988, 9 (September), p. 45.

11  In 1979 one of the first Sanyo mono cassette player/recorders available in
    Shanghai cost 220 yuan at a time when the average monthly wage for a
    worker was about eighty yuan: mentioned in passing in Wang Weiming, '*Pop
    music: dangdai qingnian xinling licheng de xiezhao*' (*Pop music: Portrait
    of the spiritual course of contemporary youth*), *Qingnian xuebao*, 1992,
    1 (Spring), p. 20.

12  Cheng Yun, 'Zhongguo dangdai tongsu yinyue huanshilu' ("A comprehen-
    sive view of popular songs in contemporary China"), *Renmin yinyue*, 1988,
    2 (February), pp. 2–6. In the June issue of the magazine, an earnest discus-
    sion on the Chineseness of popular songs was another indication of their
    firm arrival on the Chinese musical scene: Song Yang, 'Tongsu gequ de min-
    zuxing' ("The national characteristics of popular songs"), *Renmin yinyue*,
    1988, 6 (June), pp. 26–8.

13  Li Tianyi, 'Tongsu gequ heyuan luoru digu' ("How did popular music fall
    to such a low ebb?"), *Renmin yinyue*, 1989, 11 (November), pp. 26–7) and
    Huang Rongzan, 'Liuxing gequ sikao: yinyue wenhua yao zhuyi "shengtai
    pingheng"' ("Reflections on in vogue music: Musical culture must pay atten-
    tion to 'ecological balance'"), *Renmin yinyue*, 1989, 10 (October), pp. 34–6.
    The magazine's editors provided the birthdates and biographical details of

these two writers: 1959 and 1920 respectively, suggesting that the former could not be considered an old fogey.

14  Li Luxin, pp. 17–18. For the song's patriotic lyrics, see Li Luxin, p. 23. See also Li Yueyun, 'Huaichuai yi ke "Zhongguo xin"' ("Carrying a 'Chinese heart'"), *Qingnian yu shehui*, 1989, 3 (March), pp. 10–11. For similar coverage of other singers, see (on Wang Hong) Chen Kangsheng, '"Qiu-liu wuyi" de "Zhongguo honghong": Nü gexing Wang Hong he jizhe yi xi tan' ("'China's Honghong' with 'no interest in coming or going': A snatch of conversation between the female singing star Wang Hong and a journalist"), *Qingchun suiyue*, 1988, 7 (July), pp. 26–7, and Huang Zhaocun, 'Nanguo getan shuangxing: Tang Biao yu An Li' ("Twin stars of the southern song stage: Tang Biao and An Li"), *Guangzhou wenyi* (*Guangzhou Literature and Art*), 1989, 4 (April), 46–9.

15  Xing Jian, '*Gang-Tai gequ bu zai duba Guangzhou getan*' (Hong Kong and Tawian songs will not monopolise the Guangzhou song scene again), *Huhehaote ribao*, 1 April 1989, p. 2.

16  Another Taiwan singer gaining attention in the late 1980s was Hou Dejian (born 1956). For a brief report on a concert by him, see Wu Zhe, 'Ting Hou Dejian chang ge' ("Listening to Hou Dejian singing"), *Renmin ribao*, 18 March 1989, p. 2. Hou crossed the Taiwan Straits and began living in China in his mid-twenties. On 3 June 1989 he was one of the last three prominent figures to leave Tiananmen Square and the following year was deported in a fishing boat back to Taiwan. An early 1988 article on his relations with his young mainland lover (when he had a wife in Taiwan) is typical of coverage of Hou, quoting from his love song lyrics: Hu Sisheng, 'Zhiyin zhi lian: ji Cheng Lin, Hou Dejian de xiangshi, xiangzhi he xianglian' ("Music lovers: The meeting, acquaintance, and love between Cheng Lin and Hou Dejian), *Ba xiaoshi yiwai*, 1988, 1 (January), pp. 36–9.

17  On this packaging of song stars, see Li Luxin, pp. 29–37, who notes the importance of television in creating stars. Hong Kong singer Leon Lai held a concert in Beijing in October 1992, the same month as Taiwan singer–actress Lin Ch'ing-hsia (Lin Qingxia) performed at the opening of a 'Taiwan City' in Shanghai: Tian Feng, 'Ai "xing" mei shangliang: dangdai qingshaonian "zhuixing xianxiang"' ("Never talked about loving 'stars': The 'star chasing phenomenon' among contemporary young people"), *Zhongguo qingnian yanjiu*, 1993, 3 (May), p. 26.

18  Li Luxin, p. 42.

19  Yang Zhonghue, 'Liu Huan de lu' ("Lu Huan's road"), *Ba ge xiaoshi yiwai*, 1988, 4 (July), pp. 45–6. By the next decade radio and television request shows were helping popularise the new music: Xiang Ronggao, 'Qingnian "diange re" tanxi' ("Analysis of the youth 'song request craze'"), *Qingnian yanjiu*, 1995, 8 (August), pp. 21–2, 30.

20  For coverage of a Hebei amateur singer in the third national youth TV singing contest, see Yang Mingyuan, 'Ha ha, bandao gong' ("Haha, making a job of it"), *Qingchun suiyue*, 1988, 4 (April), pp. 12–13. See also the interview with a judge clarifying the selection process for that same third National Youth Singing Television Prize (and explaining the failure of contestants from the northeast): Wang Wei and Jiang Qi, 'Qingnian geshou dianshi dajiangsai de huawai yin' (Off-screen at the Youth Singing Television Prize Contest), *Liaoning qingnian*, 1988, 18 (September), pp. 30–2. The same issue of the northeastern youth magazine included assurance that 'High schoolers

singing love songs is not worth fussing about' (*Zhongxuesheng chang qingge bubi dajingxiaoguai*) (pp. 24–5) on the same pages as advice to a reader from Henan that 'Curing masturbation is not hard' (*Zhiliao shouyin bing bu nan*).

21  Yi Da, 'Hong gexing "zouxue" yanchu de gao shouru ji tou loushui de qishi' ("Enlightening star singers 'moonlighting' performances' high incomes and tax evasion"), *Liaowang*, 1989, pp. 22–3 (5 June), pp. 38–9.

22  For a relatively early discussion of 'star chaser' (*zhuixingzu*) fans, see Tian Feng, pp. 26–8.

23  Noted by Scott Kara in a television review of a New Zealand music documentary series in the *New Zealand Herald*, 17 June 2008, A16. Another source dates rock in China from a 1981 visit to Tianjin by Japanese student pop group Godaigo (*Houtihu* in Chinese, literally post-clarified butter, named after an ancient Japanese emperor), which had roots in Tsukuba University near Tokyo: Guo Dong, 'Zhongguo yaogun gouchen' ("The sinking of Chinese rock"), *Qingnian xuebao*, 1995, 2 (Summer), p. 16. My thanks to Wayne Lawrence for the background on Godaigo. Shanghai's alleged first self-employed musician (*yinyue getihu*), He Zhendong, played the guitar and ran a coaching business. His 'Present situation of guitar music in China' had appeared in the Hong Kong magazine *Guitar* (*Jita*) in October 1983: Huo Tong, 'Jita guanjun getihu' ("Award-winning guitar entrepreneur"), *Qingchun suiyue*, 1988, 9 (September), pp. 7–8.

24  Jing Yufeng, 'Xiaoyuan liuxing ge ji qita' ("Popular songs and other matters on campus"), *Qingnian yu shehui*, 1988, 1 (January), p. 39. For a more critical assessment of pop music on campus, see Dong Weilong, 'Xiaoyuan liuxing qu xunli' ("A tour of campus popular music"), *Qingnian yanjiu*, 1989, 10 (October), pp. 38–9, 17.

25  Jin Zhaojun, 'Cui Jian yu Zhongguo yaogunyue' ("Cui Jian and China's rock music"), *Renmin yinyue*, 1989, 4 (April), pp. 32–3. Jin argues that the concert marked China's pop music's shift from modeling itself on Hong Kong and Taiwan examples. For an outline of Cui's career, see the comprehensive and opinionated history of Chinese rock music by Guo Facai, *Jiasuo yu benpao: 1980–2005 Zhongguo yaogun yue duli wenhua shengtai guancha* (*Chains and running: an independent survey of the cultural ecology of China's rock music, 1980–2005*), Wuhan: Hubei Changjiang chuban jituan, 2007, pp. 109–15.

26  Interest in foreign youth culture (especially music) was apparent among the third-year students of the Central Institute of Arts and Crafts with whom I spent time in October and November 1980 on a film research visit to Beijing. For a succinct outline of early rock groups from 1980, see Guo Facai, p. 5.

27  Special Report, 'Zhongguo yaogun dashiji' ("China rock chronology"), *Guoji yinyue jiaoliu* (*International Music Exchange*), 2002, 5 (May), p. 23.

28  Special Report, p. 23. At about the same time Hou Dejian and Cheng Lin released their 'New Shoes, Old Shoes' (*Xin xiezi jiu xiezi*).

29  Zhou Dianfu, '10 nian liuxing gequ suo zhaoshi de qingnian xinli' ("Youth mentality shown by ten years of popular songs"), *Zhongguo qingnian yanjiu*, 1990, 2 (March), p. 23. Cui's band used block capitals (ADO) for its name rather than having a name in Chinese characters. Such a foreign-sounding name emphasised the mixed origins of his musicians. ADO may have been a sly reference to the English expression 'much ado (about nothing).'

30  Gu Tu, 'Cong "Yiwusuoyou" shuodao yaogunyue: Cui Jian de zuopin weish-enme shou huanying' ("Speaking of rock music from 'Nothing to My Name': why are Cui Jian's works so popular?"), *Renmin ribao*, 16 July 1988, p. 7.

31  Jin Zhaojun, p. 32.

32  For another translation of the full lyrics, see Andrew F. Jones, *Like a Knife: Ideology and Genre in Contemporary Chinese Popular Music*, Ithaca: Cornell East Asia Series 57, 1992, pp. 138–40. *Renmin ribao*, 14 March 1989, p. 4 included a photo of Cui Jian at the 12 March Beijing Exhibition Hall theatre concert. The brief report makes no reference to 'A Piece of Red Cloth.'

33  Yibing Huang, in his discussion of Cui, agrees with this interpretation: *Contemporary Chinese Literature: From the Cultural Revolution to the Future*, New York: Palgrave Macmillan, 2007, pp. 11–16.

34  Jin Zhaojun, p. 33. See also Zhao Jinqing, 'Dalu yaogun geci poyi' ("Decoding mainland rock lyrics"), *Zhongguo qingnian yanjiu*, 1994, 1 (January), pp. 40–2.

35  Liu Qing, 'Cong 'Wo bu xiangxin' dao "Yiwusuoyou": xin shengdai wenhua de yanjiu beiwanglu' ("From 'I do not believe' to 'Nothing to My Name': Research memorandum on the culture of the Newborn Generation"), *Dangdai qingnian yanjiu*, 1988, 8 (August), p. 5. For a translation of the poem, see Bei Dao, *The August Sleepwalker*, translated by Bonnie S. McDougall), London: Anvil Press Poetry, 1988, p. 33. Despite Liu's dismissal here, Bei Dao's poetry inspired many young demonstrators in the spring of 1989.

36  Liu Qing, p. 6. Liu cites Engels and Margaret Mead on the way new genera-tions represented the spirit of their times.

37  Liu Qing, p. 6.

38  *Liaoning qingnian*, 1989, 19 (1 October), inside front cover.

39  Quoted in Yang Xiong, 'Yaogunyue yu qingnian wenhua' ("Rock music and youth culture"), *Qingnian yanjiu*, 1991, 12 (December), p. 19. Yang notes the excitement at Peking University in 1986 when Cui gave three concerts on campus (pp. 19–20). For the extended views of four Beijing youth about Cui Jian, see Yang Changzheng, 'Guanyu "Cui Jian, yaogun chao" de caifang' ("Interviews about 'Cui Jian, the rock wave'"), *Qingnian xuebao*, 1991, 1 (Spring), pp. 16–17.

40  Yang Xiong, p. 20, quoting Cui. See also the extended discussion in Yang Xiong and Lu Xinhe, 'Guanyu yaogunyue yu qingnian liuxing wenhua de duihua' ("A dialogue on rock music and youth popular culture"), *Qingnian yanjiu*, 1993, 8 (August), pp. 6–10.

41  Yibing Huang, p. 15 includes an English version of the title song. For an interview on Cui's insistence on live sound at his concerts, see Jiang Xiaoyu, 'Bu zhenshi cai tongku: Cui Jian tan zhenchang yundong' ("If it's not real it's a pain: Cui Jian on the 'live sound' movement"), *Beijing jishi* (*Beijing Events*), 2005, 9 (September), pp. 20–3; and for a report on Cui's 2006 Super Live concerts commemorating twenty years of Chinese popular music, see Yang Wenjie, 'Cui Jian: Zher de yaogunyue jiu shi yi ge xiaohua' ("Cui Jian: Rock music here is just a joke"), *Beijing qingnian bao* (*Beijing Youth News*), 8 July 2006, B7.

42  See Zhou You, ed., *Beijing yaogun buluo* (*Beijing rock tribes*), Tianjin: Tianjin shehui kexue chubanshe 1994, pp. 36–50, where the group is presented as 'China's Bon Jovi.' In an interview, band members make no mention of the African American connection to their name, citing instead the view that a

panther was rare (*xihan*), like their heavy metal music (Zhou Yu, p. 47). For more on the band, see Guo Facai, pp. 116–24.

43 Zhou Yu, pp. 37–8.

44 Guo Facai, p. 112.

45 For an indication of what young China was rebelling against, see the readers' poll on the best songs and singers of the ten years of the 'new era' (post-1978) conducted in the pages of *Renmin ribao* in late 1988. The list of nominees included Cui Jian (thirtieth in thirty-one names, according the number of strokes used in writing in his surname) and 'Nothing to My Name' (fifty-seventh in a list of one hundred songs): 10 November 1988, p. 8. The results (24 December 1988, p. 8) gave just the top ten singers. Liu Huan was number two, but most of the rest were more mainstream, easy-listening stars. 'Nothing to My Name' was listed as the fourteenth favourite song, ahead of the Wine Song from *Red Sorghum* in nineteenth place. Of foreign songs, the winner was the theme song from a Japanese television serial shown on CCTV at the beginning of the decade.

46 For an outline of their origins, style, and performances through 2005, see Guo Caifu, pp. 9–11. Pages 125–9 include a series of interviews with band members. For a 2002 lament on the decline of Tang Dynasty for failing to develop their sound, see Yan Jun, *Di dixia: xin yinyue qinaxing ji (Really underground: A secret record of the new music)*, Beijing: Wenhua yishu chubanshe, 2002, pp. 123–7. Another useful resource on Cui Jian and other rockers is Lu Lingtao and Li Yang, eds., *Nahan: weile Zhongguo cengjing de yaogun (Scream: For China's former rock)*, Guilin: Guangxi shifan daxue chubanshe, 2008. An early account is Huang Liaoyuan and others, eds., *Shi nian: 1986–1996 Zhongguo liuxing yinyue jishi (Ten years: Chronicle of Chinese popular music, 1986–1996)*, Beijing: Zhongguo dianying chubanshe, 1997.

47 Zhou Yu, pp. 51–63.

48 '1966' was composed for the documentary film *1966: My Time of* [sic] *the Red Guards (1966: wo de Hongweibing shidai)*, made in 1993 by independent documentarist Wu Wenguang: Guo Dong, p. 17.

49 I attended the two nights of this concert, organised by the Oriental Song and Dance Troupe and featuring songs from *Red Sorghum*. The programme listing for the concerts reverses the usual phrase in the title of Sun's song. It is usually *wanzhang gaolou pingdi qi* (literally, mighty towers grow out of the flat ground). On Sun Guoqing, see Li Yueyun, 'Yaogun gexing Sun Guoqing' ("Rock song star Sun Guoqing"), *Qingnian yu shehui*, 1989, 1 (January), pp. 16–17.

50 Fan Guo'an and Niu Xiufen, 'Gechang ba "Ge tihu"' ("Sing 'song Nirvana'"), *Ba xiaoshi yiwai*, 1988, 3 (May), pp. 15–16.

51 Jiao Yongfu, 'Liuxing gequ he wenhua shichang' ("Popular music and the culture marketplace"), *Renmin ribao*, 25 January 1989, p. 8. Li Luxin argues that the smaller capital spent on producing mainland albums meant they could not compete with songs from well-resourced music companies in Hong Kong and Taiwan: pp. 53–5.

52 Wang Siqi, *Zhongguo dangdai chengshi liuxing yinyue: yinyue yu shehui wenhua huanjing hudong yanjiu (Contemporary Chinese urban popular music: on the interaction between music and the cultural environment)*, Shanghai: Shanghai jiaoyu chubanshe, 2009, p. 78. See also Xiang Ronggao,

'"Kala OK re" yu dangdai qingnian shehuihua' ("The 'karaoke fever' and the socialization of contemporary youth"), *Zhongguo qingnian yanjiu*, 1992, 1 (January), pp. 25–8. Xiang reports that Shanghai's first karaoke bar was established in 1986. There were more than twenty in the city by 1988, and in the first four months of 1990 the numbers rose from 125 to 194 with another thirty-two waiting for approval. An incomplete count in Beijing was over 100 by 1991. Nationally there were eighty thousand karaoke outlets in about 300 cities (p. 25). In addition home karaoke sets enjoyed a brisk sale.

53 Wang Siqi, pp. 80–2.

54 Quoted in Xiang Ronggao, p. 25. Xiang reports forty-two percent of surveyed young workers in Shanghai often visited karaoke lounges, with nine percent spending more than one hundred yuan a month (fifty-six percent of their living expenditure) on their hobby (p. 25). National and local contests were organised and the Communist Party's Propaganda Department did a brisk trade in a compilation of songs (p. 26), bringing old revolutionary favorites from the Maoist era a new lease on life.

55 Xiang Ronggao, pp. 26–7. One investigation of 274 karaoke disks in Shanghai found 296 of the six thousand songs had 'reactionary and salacious content.' Another survey found Chinese mainland songs were only 0.6 percent of twelve thousand songs on more than six thousand laser disks in Shanghai (p. 27).

56 VCDs (video compact disks) were a predecessor to the DVD, used for movies and TV shows. They played on DVD machines. Guo Facai discusses the ways in which the Internet facilitated the distribution and fan discussion of *dakou* CDs: pp. 277–90. See also Jeroen de Kloet, 'Popular Music and Youth in Urban China: The *Dakou* Generation,' *The China Quarterly*, 183 (September 2005), pp. 609–26. Yan Jun notes that the first *dakou* CDs came from Japan: *Di dixia*, pp. 396–7; see also pp. 71–3.

57 Shu Zechi and Zeng Yi, 'Liuxing yinyue yu cidai shichang xianzhuang pingxi' ("An analysis of the present conditions in popular music and the tape market"), *Liaowang*, 1989, 10 (March), pp. 31–3.

58 Shu Zechi and Zeng Yi, pp. 32–3.

59 Guo Facai discusses the role of capital in promoting Chinese rock music in Hong Kong, Taiwan and beyond in the late 1980s and 1990s: pp. 296–321.

60 The three characters that made up *xintianyou* meant 'trust, sky, roving.'

61 On the origins of the Northwest Wind, see Wang Siqi, pp. 36–7. Su Hong was another emerging star in 1988. She was born in Wuhan in 1961, and had joined the city's song and dance troupe in the last year of the Cultural Revolution. She first achieved fame in nationally televised youth song contests in 1986 and 1987: Peng Tong, 'Gechang shi liti de yishu: ji 1988 nian jinxing Su Hong' ("Singing is a three-dimensional art: On Su Hong, the 1988 golden star"), *Renmin ribao*, 18 April 1989, p. 4.

62 Li Luxin, p. 44. For a similar, though far from enthusiastic, explanation of the appeal of the songs, see Zhang Lei, 'Yewei de "Xibeifeng" yinhe shou huanying?' ("Why has the wild 'Northwest Wind' been welcomed?"), *Liaoning qingnian*, 1989, 6 (March), pp. 32–3. Marc L. Moskowitz contrasts masculinist Beijing-based rock music with the more female tones of Mandopop (pop songs in Mandarin, unlike Canto-pop), with origins in Taiwan, which predominated in the south in his *Cries of Joy, Songs of Sorrow: Chinese Pop Music and Its Cultural Connotations*, Honolulu: University of Hawai'i Press, 2010.

63  Jinwan bao, 'Woguo getan "Xibeifeng" zheng jing: cong mofang zhengzha er chu, zhao zhenzheng Zhongguo qipai' ("The 'Northwest Wind' in China's song circles is really strong: From struggling to imitate to seeking a genuinely Chinese proud style), reprinted in *Huhehaote wanbao*, 28 July 1988, p. 3. See also Zhang Mingfu, 'Getan guaqi "Xibeifeng"' ("The 'Northwest Wind' blows in song circles"), *Huhehaote wanbao*, 9 July 1988, p. 2.

64  This is the argument of Guo Fengrun, who also suggests influence from American (country and) Western music: 'Getan jingchui "Xibeifeng"' ("The 'Northwest Wind' blows hard in song circles"), *Ba xiaoshi yiwai*, 1988, 6 (November), pp. 54–5.

65  Tu also argues that the syrupy songs of the immediate post-Gang of Four popular music suited its times, just as the forceful, dramatic Northwest Wind songs suited its era: Tu Keshan, 'Daxuesheng heyi tong "Xibeifeng" qihe' ("Why do university students feel a connection with the 'Northwest Wind'?"), *Renmin yinyue*, 1989, 1 (January), pp. 30–1. For a similar view, see Jin Zhaojun, 'Feng cong nali lai?: ping getan "Xibeifeng"' ("Where is the wind from?: On the 'Northwest Wind' in song circles"), *Renmin ribao*, 23 August 1988, p. 5.

66  This is the view of Zhou Guimian, '"Hong gaoliang" yu "Xibeifeng"' ("*Red Sorghum* and the 'Northeast Wind'"), *Renmin yinyue*, 1988, 12 (December), p. 20. Jin Zhaojun, cited previously, agrees, pointing out the delay between the Northwest Wind's first appearance in 1986 and young people's frenzy for it in 1988.

67  In the *People's Music* special section on the Northwest Wind in late 1988, Yang Ruiqing identified its 'manly style' (*yanggang fengge*) as the first of three attractions of the song style. The others were its Chineseness (*minzu fengge*) and its popular or ordinary style (*tongsu fengge*). Yang also noted recent songs that represented a Central Plains Wind (*Zhongyuan feng*): 'Miandui "Xibefeng' gechao de sikao' ("Thoughts confronting the Northwest Wind song wave"), *Renmin yinyue*, 1988, 12 (December), p. 21.

68  For two interviews with Zhao Jiping in which he explains the earthy, direct intentions behind the music of *Red Sorghum*, see Li Erwei, 'Zhao Jiping: huang tudi shang de fanggezhe' ("Zhao Jiping: loud singer on the yellow earth"), *Dianying yishu*, 1994, 1 (January), pp. 16–22, 53; and Dong Dayong, 'Cong gouhe zongheng de huang tudi shang qifei' ("Flying out of the yellow earth criss-crossed by ravines"), *Renmin yinyue*, 1989, 3 (March), pp. 18–19.

69  Han Yinghong, 'Xibeifeng daodi neng gua duojiu' ("How long can the Northwest Wind really keep blowing"), *Renmin yinyue*, 1988, 12 (December), pp. 20–1.

70  See, for example, Fu Yinchu, 'Tan "Huangtu re"' ("On the 'Yellow Earth craze'"), *Renmin yinyue*, 1989, 2 (February), p. 27.

71  *Jinwan bao*, p. 3.

72  Zhong Yuming, 'Man tai "Xibeifeng"guanzhong bu ai ting' ("Audience does not like to hear a whole concert of 'Northwest Wind'"), *Renmin ribao*, 14 April 1989, p. 4.

73  Jin Zhaojun, 'Feng xiang hefang qu?: ping "Xibeifeng" zhi houguo' ("Where has the wind gone?: A critique of the aftermath of the 'Northwest Wind'"), *Renmin ribao*, 24 May 1989, p. 8.

74  Duan Ruizhong, 'Gongji "Huangtu gaopo"' ("Attacking 'The Hills of Yellow Earth'"), *Renmin yinyue*, 1989, 3 (March), pp. 30–31. Duan noted a

contradiction between the praise for the television documentary series *River Elegy*, which argued for a rejection of the earth-bound tradition epitomised on the loess plain, and the ubiquity of Northwest Wind songs eulogising life in that region.

75    Qiong Xiaoming and Li Shiding, 'Weimiao de beilun: ping "Gongji Huangtu gaopo" de yiyuan siwei moshi ("A subtle paradox: A critique of the monistic pattern of thinking in 'Attacking 'The Hills of Yellow Earth''"), *Renmin yinyue*, 1989, 8 (August), pp. 24–5. The same pages included a second counterattacking piece. A more balanced assessment of the pluses (native traditions enhanced) and minuses (sameness and narrowness) of the Northwest Wind came in Wang Yongling, 'Xibu gequ re chuxian hou de li yu bi' ("The benefits and harm after the Western song craze appeared"), *Renmin yinyue*, 1989, 6 (June), p. 31.

76    In addition, in late 1988 and early 1989, a new music craze took hold of Chinese youth, the 'convict song,' similar in plaintive style to the better known song craze, drawn from the songs made by prisoners in labor camps and popularised by films like *Juvenile Delinquents* (*Shaonian fan*, directed by Zhang Liang, 1985). According to an executive of a Shenzhen recording company, legal and illegal tapes of these kinds of songs rivaled Northwest Wind compilations: Ling Xuan, '"Xibeifeng" yu "qiuge"' ("'Northwest Wind' and 'convict songs'"), *Renmin yinyue*, 1989, 5 (May), pp. 37–8.

77    Chun Xiao, 'Shei ba Abao tuixiang le wutai?' ("Who pushed Abao onto the stage?"), *Liaoning qingnian*, 2007, 7A (July), pp. 4–6. *Xingguang dadao* was a play on the phrase for 'golden highway,' the title of the Cultural Revolution Hao Ran novel *Jinguang dadao* (*The Golden Road*).

78    See, for example, the brief overview by Li Luxin, pp. 52–5.

79    Li Luxin, pp. 14–16.

80    Guo Dong, p. 16.

81    On the 2002 Midi festival, see Yan Jun, pp. 292–312. For a report on a more recent version, see Chen Nan, 'High-voltage action,' *China Daily*, 25 September 2008, p. 13.

82    As one critic noted in 2006, the just concluded twelfth CCTV youth singing star contest was an unfair mix of four kinds of singing styles (bel canto, national/folk, popular, and singing groups), in which the first style was most admired: Wu Yue, 'Qing ge sai de "bu gongping"' ("'Unfairness' at the Youth Song Contest"), *Beifang yinyue* (*Northern Music*), 2006, 6 (June). p. 27.

83    Ryan Moore, pp. 25–6.

84    Jeroen de Kloet, *China with a Cut: Globalisation, Urban Youth and Popular Music*, Amsterdam: Amsterdam University Press, 2010, esp. pp. 25–36. Curiously South Korea is hardly mentioned by de Kloet, despite his analysis extending into the first decade of the new century. Similarly, the Internet is largely absent from his discussion.

85    Li Xin (b. 1976), 'Xi'an diqu yaogunyue de chubu kaocha' ("A preliminary survey of rock music in the Xi'an region"), *Jiaoxiang: Xi'an yinyue xueyuan xuebao* (*Symphony: Journal of the Xi'an Conservatory of Music*), 19, 4 (December 2000), pp. 74–5. For an article on one member of the band Flying who went on to a solo career, see Chen Quanzhong, 'Xu Wei yanli de "wanmei shenghuo"' ("The 'beautiful life' in Xu Wei's eyes"), *Liaoning qingnian*, 2005, 23 (December), pp. 28–9.

86    Li Xin, pp. 75–6. Li goes on to record the establishment of the Xi'an New Music Alliance (*Xi'an xin yinyue lianmeng*) in mid-1997, which brought together various rock musicians and groups and published its own magazine,

and the more underground Xi'an Youth Music Federation (*Xi'an qingnian yinyue lianhehui*), which was more oriented to rock music. The latter's slogan was 'join us, pay attention to creativity.'

87 Li Xin. p. 77. For a case of a rock bar in Kunming in Yunnan in 1996, see Xiao Dao, 'Cong yaogun "fenqing" dao diannao laoban' ("From rock 'angry youth' to computer boss"), *Shidai fengcai (Elegant Times)*, 2003, 2 (February), pp. 4–6. Yan Jun reports on the underground music scene in Lanzhou in Yan Jun, pp. 151–67 and 207–19.

88 Xu Bing, 'Da huo'er de liuxingyue he wo de xianyansuiyu: Zhongguo liuxing gequ zouxiang' ("Our popular music and my idle comments: Chinese popular song trends"), *Qingnian xuebao*, 1990, 4 (Winter), pp. 21–2, 13.

89 Lu Xinhe and others, 'Xiandai yaogunyue de boxing he qingnian wenhua fazhan: yi ci yaogun taolunhui de bufen shilu' ("The rise of contemporary rock music and development of youth culture: extracts from a discussion on rock"), *Qingnian xuebao*, 1991, 1 (Spring), p. 12.

90 Lu Xinhe, p. 12–13. This quote is composed from three separate interventions by Zheng in the discussion. In the last sentence he uses the English word *rock*. The two-page transcript ends with an unusual plea to readers to contribute to the ongoing discussion about rock music and youth culture (p. 13).

91 Xu Fei, 'Gexing yu gemi yu san bai xuesheng tong "kan"' ("Singers and fans and three hundred students together 'with dignity'"), *Zhongguo qingnian yanjiu*, 1993, 3 (May), pp. 13–16. The writer was in the propaganda department of the Communist Party branch at Anhui Normal University.

92 Ou Ning, 'Nanfang de "Xin qunzhong" zhi sheng' ("Cry of the South's 'New Masses'"), *Zhongguo qingnian yanjiu*, 1995, 4 (July), inside front cover, including photos of excited fans.

93 See the section of five articles edited by Yang Changzheng, 'Liuxing yinyue yu qingshaonian chengzhang' ("Popular music and young people's growing up"), *Zhongguo qingnian yanjiu*, 2003, 1 (January), pp. 4–29. The nationwide research interviewed forty people aged between fourteen and twenty-five years old.

94 Quoted in Lü Jie, 'Qian zai qingchun de rizi li: daxuesheng yu liuxing yinyue' ("Embedded in days of adolescence: University students and popular music"), *Zhongguo qingnian yanjiu*, 2003, 1 (January), p. 9.

95 Quoted in Shi Xiaojie, 'Nongganfeixin fei zhenwei: shehui qingnian yu liuxing yinyue' ("Rich, sweet, fat, and pungent, but without real flavor: Working youth and popular music"), *Zhongguo qingnian yanjiu*, 2003, 1 (January), p. 14. Wu noted that his parents were big pop music fans, which meant they were open to new ideas and experiences (p. 15).

96 Wang Shaopo, '"Zhongxuesheng yu liuxing yinyue" fangtan shilu' ("'High schoolers and popular music' interview record"), *Zhongguo qingnian yanjiu*, 2003, 1 (January), pp. 16–19.

97 Liu Yang, 'Suiyue ru ge: "qingshaonian yu liuxing yinyue" fangtan bijiao' ("Time like a song: Comparison of interviews on 'young people and popular music'"), *Zhongguo qingnian yanjiu*, 2003, 1 (January), pp. 20–2, 24, 25, 26.

98 See, for example, comment on the Baidu Cui Jian site: http://tieba.baidu. com/f?kz=651506230 (accessed on 21 December 2009). Teenagers expressed their fandom for Cui on a long thread started in October 2005 that had more than 300 postings four years later: http://tieba.baidu.com/f?z=53885 282&ct=335544320&lm=0&sc=0&rn=30&tn=baiduPostBrowser&word= %B4%DE%BD%A1&pn=0 (accessed 21 December 2009).

99 For a comprehensive journalistic overview of the Korean Wave in Asia and around the world, see the essays in *The Korean Herald*, ed., *Korean Wave*, Seoul: Jimoondang, 2008. China and South Korea had begun trading directly on a large scale in the 1980s, but only in 1992 did the two countries establish full diplomatic relations. The South Korean government in 1999 adopted a soft diplomacy policy to promote its culture, including modern manifestations and youth culture. For an analysis of the emotional appeal of such dramas, see Ding Li, 'Cong "Dongji linage" kan wenhua "Hanliu"' ("Looking at the cultural 'Korean Wave' from *Winter Sonata*"), *Dangdai dianshi (Contemporary TV)*, 2005, 8 (August), pp. 64–5. For a brief description of Korean TV dramas appearing on Chinese television in the mid-1980s and discussion of their appeal, see Gui Qingshan, '"Hanliu" xianxiang de wenhua shenshi' ("A cultural examination of the 'Korean Wave' phenomenon"), *Dianying yishu*, 2002, 6 (November), pp. 52–4, 45. Jian Cai, 'China's first taste of the Korean Wave,' in *Korean Herald*, ed., p. 101. Cai makes the point that the success of *Daejanggeum* (in Chinese *Dachangling*, in English *Jewel in the Palace*) in 2005 drove the price of Korean TV dramas out of the reach of most provincial stations in China (p. 107–8). For a skeptical view of the alleged popularity of Korean TV dramas, see Ma Fan, 'Hanju zhen you neme "hong"? ("Are Korean dramas really that 'popular'?"), *Dazhong dianying*, 2006, 4 (February), pp. 12–15. Ma cites statistics showing that in twelve major cities *Daejanggeum* commanded the attention of an average 10.86 percent of actual viewers (p. 13).

100 One Chinese scholar suggests the Korean Wave was the successor to the Western influences dominant in China in the 1980s and the Japanese influence of the 1990s: Yang Ying, '"Hanliu" xianxiang tanxi' ("Analysis of the 'Korean Wave' phenomenon"), *Qingnian tansuo*, 2002, 6 (November), p. 40. On the cultural conservative values promulgated by Korean TV serials, see Cheng Qijin, 'Hanliu qinxi: guochanju lianhong' ("The Korean Wave sneak attack: Local dramas embarrassed"), *Xinwen zhoukan (News Weekly)*, 24 June 2002, p. 76.

101 Noted by scholars at a 2005 discussion of the phenomenon: Sun Xiaozhong, 'Quyuxing zai xiangxiang: 2005 nian "'Hanliu' zai Zhongguo" guoji yantaohui shuping' ("Visualizing regionally again: Review of the 2005 'Korean Wave in China' international symposium"), *Shanghai daxue xuebao (shehui kexue ban) (Journal of Shanghai University [Social Sciences])*, 2006, 1 (January), pp. 159–60. For examples of popular Chinese magazines providing information on websites devoted to Korean music, food, study, and stars, see, *for example, Ma Ning, 'Wangshang Hanliu' ("Korean Wave on the 'Net")*, Wangluo yu xinxi ("Internet and information"), 2001, 8 (August), pp. 30–1; Ma Ning, 'Hanliu laixi' ("The Korean Wave attacks"), *Wangluo yu xinxi*, 2002, 10 (November), pp. 32–3. On translated Korean romantic fiction, see Ma Ning, 'Wangshang Hanliu "hua"' ("'Flowers' of the Korean Wave on the 'Net"), *Wangluo yu xinxi*, 2003, 4 (April), p. 23.

102 Sung Sang-yeon, 'Why are Asians attracted to Korean pop culture?' in *Korean Herald*, p. 15.

103 Yang Ying, '"Hanliu": you yi zhong zhuixing de xin fanshi?' ("'Korean Wave': yet another new kind of fandom?"), *Zhongguo qingnian yanjiu*, 2004, 1 (January), p. 9.

104 Quoted in Xu Jin, '"Hanliu" denglu Zhongguo 6 nian' ("Six years of the Korean Wave landing in China"), *Zhongwai wenhua jiaoliu* (*China–Foreign Cultural Relations*), 2003, 10 (November), p. 22.

105 Bai Yuandan (South Korea), 'Chuixi Dongya de "Hanliu"' ("Pushing East Asia's Korean Wave"), *Wenyi lilun yu piping* (*Literature and Art Theory and Criticism*), 2002, 1 (January), 86.

106 Chinese fans of Rain adopted a way of rendering their names to express their shared adoration of the handsome young star, adding the word *qin* (close relative) to their given names. Thus Zhang Ke became to her fellow fans, including on the Internet, Kekeqin: cited in Luo Xuehui, *Shifei Hanliu* (*All about the Korean Wave*), *Zhongguo xinwen zhoukan* (*China News Weekly*), 2005, 46 (December), p. 57.

107 Piao Guanghai, '"Hanliu" zai Zhongguo de boji yu yingxiang' ("The spread and impact of the 'Korean Wave' on China"), *Dangdai Hanguo*, 2003, 1 (June), pp. 71–72, 74. On the Korean five-person girl band, Baby Vox, see Anon, 'Qingjing Hanliu xiji neilu' ("Powerful Korean Wave makes a surprise attack on the mainland"), *Yinyue shijie* (*Music World*), 1999, 12 (December), p. 21. This page on Baby Vox, providing birthdates, height, and hobbies of the five members, is followed by a quarter-page story on another Korean-American girl group, S.E.S, and a three-quarter-page report on Britney Spears (p. 22).

108 Rowan Pease, 'Internet, Fandom, and K-Wave in China,' in Keith Howard, ed., *Korean Pop Music: Riding the Wave*, Folkstone: Global Oriental, 2006, pp. 179–80.

109 Quoted in Yang Dian, '"Hanliu" weihe zheme re' ("Why is the 'Korean Wave' so hot?"), *Baike zhishi* (*Encyclopedia Knowledge*), 2002, 4 (April), p. 49. For a typical example of a 'moral panic' about the impact of the Korean Wave on youth, see Wang Hui, '"Hanliu" yu Zhongguo qingnian wenhua jianshe' ("The 'Korean Wave' and the cultural construction of Chinese youth"), *Shaanxi qingnian guanli ganbu xueyuan xuebao* (*Journal of the Shaanxi Youth Management/Officials Academy*), 2006, 2 (June), pp. 16–19. Wang argues that stories set in contemporary Seoul were readily transferable to the lives of young people in Beijing or Shanghai (p. 16).

110 Rowan Pease, p. 181.

111 Pease, p. 177. Pease argued at a November 2007 conference on contemporary Korea and East Asia at the University of Auckland that the music presented by groups like H.O.T. was 'culturally odorless' (to use Koichi Iwabuchi's phrase), having an appeal despite its Korean origins.

112 A survey of university students in Beijing in 2003 concluded that female students were more interested in Korean films and TV dramas, attracted by love stories: Chu Weihua, Liu Chaoxia, and Wang Yilin, 'Zhongguo daxuesheng yu "Hanliu": guanyu "Hanliu" de diaocha fenxi baogao' ("Chinese college students and the 'Korean Wave': An analytical report on a survey of the 'Korean Wave'"), *Zhongguo qingnian zhengzhi xueyuan xuebao* (*Journal of the China Youth University for Political Sciences*), 2003, 7 (July), pp. 11–17. For a similar view of the wider, female population, see Han Weijuan, '"Hanliu" heyi xijuan nianqing nüxing ("How has the 'Korean Wave' engulfed young women?"), *Zhongguo dianshi* (*Chinese Television*), 2008, 6 (June), pp. 33–6.

113 Liu Weiheng, *Xin shiji Hanliu dianfeng dang'an* (*New Century Edition Korean Wave Summit Archive*), Haikou: Nanfang chubanshe, 2003. The

influence of Korean pop models can be seen in the two-boy group from the Northeast, *Liang tuanhuo* (Two Gangsters), who triumphed at a 1994 Chinese MTV national song contest. Both around twenty years old and dressed in a South Korean, campus-look style (decidedly not gangster-like), one of the singers' surnames, Jin (and their performance to commemorate the first anniversary of China–South Korean diplomatic relations) suggests he may be Korean–Chinese, though the story does not mention this: Zhang Biao, 'Dongbei getan "Liang tuanhuo"' ("'Two Gangsters' of Northeast song circles"), *Beijing qingnian*, 1995, 3 (March), pp. 16–17.

114 Chen Jiuguo and Luo Aiai, 'Hanliu: qingnian de jingshen houhuayuan' ("The Korean Wave: The back garden of youth's spirit"), *Dangdai qingnian yanjiu*, 2006, 1 (January), p. 12.

115 Yang Xin, 'Dangdai qingnian wenhua radian xianxiang shuping' ("Review of hot spot phenomena in contemporary youth culture"), *Guangdong qingnian ganbu xueyuan xuebao* (*Journal of the Guangdong Youth Leaders College*), 2007, 3 (March), pp. 39–40.

116 Yang Xin, p. 28.

117 Wu Yadan, 'Cong "Ha Hanju" kan "Ha Han" qingnian' ("From 'mad about Korean dramas' see 'mad about Korea' youth"), *Zhongguo qingnian yanjiu*, 2004, 1 (January), p. 32.

118 Luo Xuehui, p. 57.

119 Yang Dian, p. 48.

120 Yang Xin, p. 28 For brief coverage of Korean pop cultural influence in Shaanxi and Shanxi, see Fan Chao, 'Hanliu chongdong yu Xibu "hua" wen' ("The Korean Wave excitement and Western Region 'culture'"), *Xin Xibu* (*New West*), 2005, 12 (December), p. 51.

121 Chen Jiuguo and Luo Aiai, pp. 12–13.

122 Li Yiming, '"Hanliu" zou zai dalu shang' ("The 'Korean Wave' moves on the mainland"), *Dazhong dianying*, 2003, 4 (February), p. 17.

123 A 2002 student-led survey of 434 students at six high schools in Chengdu and its suburbs showed the extent of interest in animation, comic books, clothing, music, and food from Korea and Japan was high, with almost half expressing interest in these items: Chengdu Shude High School, Class 8 of Class of 2004 Survey Group, 'Guanyu Ri-Han wenhua dui Chengdu zhongxuesheng yingxiang de diaocha' ("Survey of the influence of Japanese and Korean culture on Chengdu high schoolers"), *Qingnian yanjiu*, 2002, 10 (October), pp. 33–9.

124 See http://www.haibao.cn/artile/55621.htm (accessed on 22 December 2009).

125 Yang Ying (2002) suggests that the Korean Wave offered a way for Chinese to 'show off ourselves' (liangchu women ziji), p. 42. Rowan Pease quotes one of her young Chinese informants: *Hahan* ('crazed for Korea') isn't just about liking something or other. I think that there are lots of areas that every Chinese should study. Isn't patriotism important? I think Korean people do that really well. I really respect them!' (p. 179).

126 Such had been the fan interest that supporters of the three finalists had been given names that played on their idols' names. Liu's fans were *Yumi* (literally corn, using a homophone for Liu's first given name Yu, and using a homophone for *mi*, meaning fan). Zhou's followers were *Bimi* (using her first given name, *bi* (writing brush or pen) and *mi* (fan, or to become enchanted with). Zhang's fans were *Liangfen* (literally bean jelly, using a homophone for an alternate reading of her first given name and playing on

*fenzi*, meaning a member or participant). These clever linguistic coinages were an indication of the extent to which Chinese television viewers had become engaged in the contest.

127 The theme song is reproduced in Lü Hui, '"Chaonü"! "Chaonü"!' ("'Supergirl'! 'Supergirl'!"), *Baogao wenxue (Reportage)*, 2005, 10 (October), p. 36.

128 On the rise of the Chinese New Year programme, see Ni Zi, Shan Liang, Ou Ran, *21 nian chunjie lianhuan wanhui neibu xiaoxi (The inner story of the twenty-one years of the Spring Festival Variety Show)*, Beijing: Xinhua chubanshe, 2004.

129 These instances are cited by Tang Delong, 'Chaoji nüsheng: yi ge yule shenhua de fayi' ("*Supergirl*: Fame and fortune in an entertainment fairy tale"), *Zhongguo shehui daokan* (China Society Periodical), 2005, 9 (September), p. 9.

130 Lü Hui, p. 39.

131 Lü Hui, pp. 41, 39–40. In the first *Supergirl* contest in 2004, sixty thousand women had registered to participate; in 2005 that number rose to one hundred and fifty thousand, covering ages eighty-nine to six. The final was watched by about five hundred million viewers on TV and computer screens: Xiang Ronggao, 'Chaoji nüsheng xianxiang toushi,' ("Perspective on the '*Supergirl* phenomenon"), *Qingnian yanjiu*, 2005, 10 (November), p. 45.

132 Xiang Ronggao, pp. 45–6.

133 Lü Hui provides a long list of judges' comments, pp. 41–2, including the immortal 'Don't frighten the remaining contestants' and 'Come back in ten years and sing that song.'

134 Lü Hui, p. 43.

135 Lü Hui, p. 44.

136 Reportedly, a beggar on the street turned down a donation from a young man, urging him instead to use the money to vote for a particular contestant: Xiang Ronggao, p. 47.

137 Quoted in Lü Hui, p. 45. The text voting was overwhelmingly an activity of teenagers and fans in their twenties: Zan Yulin, 'Qingnian wenhua radian de shidai toushi: "Chaoji nüsheng" re de leng sikao' ("A current perspective on hotspots of youth culture: A cold look at the '*Supergirl*' fever"), *Qingnian tansuo*, 2006, 1 (January), p. 23.

138 Lu Jun, '*Dazhong gouzao de « Chaonü » shenhua*' (The '*Supergirl*' fairy tale constructed by the masses), *Zhongguo shehui daokan*, 2005, 9 (September), 11. A similar view is expressed in Lian Weiqing, '*Chaoji nüsheng : Qingnian wenhua xin tezheng fenxi*' (Supergirl: analysis of the new features of youth culture), *Dangdai qingnian yanjiu*, 2006, 3 (March), 13–15. See also Luo Yunbin and Zhang Yi, '*Liuxing yinyue de qumei he fumei: jianping « Chaonü » xianxiang*' (The enchantments and disenchantments of popular music: a double analysis of the '*Supergirl*' phenomenon), *Nanchang daxue xuebao (renwen shehui kexue ban)* (Journal of Nanchang University (humanities and social sciences)), 2007, 1 (January), 134–137. Another scholar to emphasise the democratic qualities of the *Supergirl* contest (its low threshold for entry, the equal weight of each text vote, and the combination of judges, audience voting and text voting) was Lian Qingwei, '*Chaoji nüsheng : qongnian wenhua xin tezheng fenxi*' (Supergirl: analysis of the new features of youth culture), *Dangdai qingnian yanjiu*, 2006, 3 (March), 12–15.

139  Lü Hui, p. 46. A *Chinese Youth News* (*Zhongguo qingnian bao*) survey reportedly showed 60.8 percent of respondents agreeing that this asexuality was a normal expression of social diversity, while about ten percent felt alarmed by it: Xiang Ronggao, inside back cover.

140  Lu Jun, p. 11. One young husband was reported to have said his view of family planning had changed. Before, he had thought a son was best. Now, as a result of seeing the accomplished and confident young women on *Supergirl*, he realised having a daughter was just as good (p. 11). In mid-2009 Li Yuchun's lawyers took action against the unauthorised use of her image on a Chongqing family planning billboard sporting the slogan: 'Boys and girls are equally good. Girls can pass down the family line too.': *China Daily*, 25 June 2009, p. 8. Attacks on Chris Lee's sexuality were likened in blog postings to Cultural Revolution criticism campaigns.

141  The word *fensi* became much more widely used as a result of the popular impact of the 2005 song contest. See also Cai Qi and Liao Jie, 'Qingshaonian "fensi" xingwei tezheng ji xinli xuqiu kaocha fenxi' ("Investigation into the features of the actions of youthful 'fans' and their psychological needs"), *Zhongguo guangbo dianshi xuekan* (*China Radio and TV Journal*), 2009, 3 (March), pp. 35–6.

142  Lü Hui, pp. 46–7.

143  Lü Hui, p. 48.

144  Tang Delong, p. 10.

145  Some of these activities are described briefly in Zan Yulin, pp. 22–3.

146  Quoted by Lü Hui, p. 48.

147  Lü Hui, pp. 48–9.

148  Lü Hui, pp. 51–3.

149  Tang Delong, p. 10.

150  Paraphrased from Lü Hui, p. 54.

151  Li's English name is noted in a newspaper story on her ghostwritten commentary (along with that of third place winner Zhang Liangying (Jane) on the 2006 Football World Cup being published in twenty-six newspapers in China, illustrated with her meeting London mayor Ken Livingstone on the roof of the trendy Bund 18 building in Shanghai: *China Daily*, 8–9 July 2006, p. 3.

152  Lü Hui, pp. 54–5.

153  Lü Hui, p. 56. A survey of 726 students at four Nanjing high schools in 2005, around the time of that year's *Supergirl* contest, showed that the idols (*ouxiang*) of teenagers were overwhelmingly singing stars, though older boys also took a strong interest in sports stars. Three-quarters of teens' idols were either music or sporting figures. Both girls and boys directed their adulation mostly at male stars: Shi Xiaohui, 'Zhongxuesheng ouxiang chongbai xianzhuang diaocha' ("Survey of the present condition of high school student adoration of idols"), *Qingnian tansuo*, 2005, 6 (November), pp. 3–8.

154  Lü Hui makes these points on p. 59.

155  Lu Jun, p. 11.

156  Lü Hui, pp. 56–7.

157  Xiao Hui, 'Gexing shidai zai jueqi?' ("Is this the rise of an individualistic era?"), *Zhongguo shehui daokan*, 2005, 9 (September), pp. 17–18. Xiao Hui has a doctorate from the University of Illinois.

158 This salutary tale is told in Sha Zi, 'Qin'ai de "Yumi" bie yong zheizhong fangshi ai Chunchun' ("Dear 'Li Yuchun fans', don't use this way of loving Li Yuchun"), *Liaoning qingnian*, 2006, 5 (March), pp. 92–4.

159 Wang Ligang, 'Xuanxiu jiemu you duo re' ("How popular are talent shows"), *Qingnian jizhe* (*Youth Reporter*), 2006, 17 (September), pp. 15–16. Wang uses the conventional categories of performance skills from Peking opera in his listing.

160 Liu Hong, 'Cong dianshi xuanxiu xiang kaiqu' ("Wanting to go beyond television talent shows"), *Qingnian jizhe*, 2006, 17 (September), pp. 17–18.

161 Han Haoyue, in a column in *Xinjing bao* (*New Peking Times*), reprinted in *Qingnian jizhe*, 2006, 17 (September), p. 26.

162 'Guanyu xuanxiu jiemu de suiji diaocha' ("Random survey regarding talent shows"), *Qingnian jizhe*, 2006, 17 (September), pp. 26–7. In 2008 Li Yuchun was criticised on the Internet for faking a blood donation for the victims of the May Sichuan earthquake until detective work by supporters showed how photos had been flipped to make her appear to give blood from one arm and leave the clinic holding the other arm: see http://bbs. auto.china.com/viewthread.php?tid=12439951&extra=&page=1 (accessed on 11 January 2010).

163 Zhen Xiaofei, 'Touhao "Kuai nan" Chen Chusheng' ("First 'Happy Boy', Chen Chusheng"), *Nanfang zhoumou* (*Southern Weekend*), 26 July 2007, pp. 28, 27. Three years later on Chongqing TV another *Super Boy* (*Kuaile nansheng*) contest featured a competitor dressed, speaking, and singing like a young woman. Liu Zhu was a student at the Sichuan Conservatory, the same school as Li Yuchun, and had long identified as a woman. His/her position was similar to that of Korea's Harisu and Taiwan's Regine Wu, also transgender performers: see *Shanghaiist*, 5 May 2010 (shanghaiist. com/2010/05/02-week).

164 For a report on the final, see Raymond Zhou, 'A less than happy feeling,' *China Daily*, 11 September 2009, p. 18. A contestant on the 2009 *Happy Girl* contest had the temerity to sing 'Nothing to My Name.' Huang Ying was born in 1989 and older bloggers wondered if she understood the meaning and significance of the song: See, for example, the discussion threads on http://www.tianya.cn/publicforum/content/funstribe/1/167199. shtml (accessed on 21 December 2009) and the same site, page 167832. shtml (accessed on 21 December 2009).

165 'Shanghai wenguang xinwen chuanbo jituan fazhan yanjiubu,' ed., *Nianqing de zhanchang: SMG 'Hao nan'er' shi zenyang liancheng de* (*Young battlefield: how SMG My Hero was tempered*), Shanghai: Shanghai shiji chuban gufen youxian gongsi, 2007. The book's title plays on the title of the Soviet novel popular in the 1950s and 1960s, *How the Steel Was Tempered*.

166 For a brief analysis, see Gong Xingqiong, 'Zai "Mengxiang" de beihou: dui xuanxiulei dianshi yule jiemu de pipanxing jiedu' ("Behind the 'Dream': A critical deciphering of talent contest television entertainment programmes"), *Hubei jiaoyu xueyuan xuebao* (*Journal of Hubei Institute of Education*), 2007, 1 (January), pp. 41–3.

167 For typical discussion of the banning of the show, with skepticism about the alleged strong support for the move, see, for example, http://www.tianya. cn/publicforum/content/funinfo/1/1004522.shtml (accessed on 15 January 2010). A former contestant on *First Heartbeat*, Guo Xuanyu, blogged with

the real story of the show, including allegations that the text voting figures that featured so prominently in the competitions were faked. See the reposting in http://www.tianya.cn/publicforum/content/funstribe/1/115003.shtml (accessed on 15 January 2010).

168 Peng Guifang and chen Jiuguo, '*Cong fengkuang dao lixing zhi lu hai you duo yuan?: dui qingshaonian ouxiang chongbai de sikao*' (How far is there yet from madness to reason?: reflections on young people's idol worship), *Qingnian tansuo*, 2007, 4 (August), 91–94 is a typical earnest discussion of how to turn idol worship to positive purposes. See also Wang Li, '*Dazhong wenhua beihou de liliang: guanyu dianshi xuanxiu jiemu de ji dian sikao*' (The strength behind popular culture: some thoughts on television talent shows), *Hebei jiaoyu xueyuan xuebao*, 2007, 1 (January), 38–40.

169 See Lin Qi, 'Show takes turn for the worse,' *China Daily*, 5 July 2010, p. 2. On 23 July 2010 at a Politburo study session, Hu Jintao spoke of the need to 'oppose the three vulgarities' (*fan sansu*), namely things that were vulgar (*yongsu*), cheap (*disu*), and tasteless (*meisu*). See also the five sociological articles edited by Wang Linglong, 'Cong "Fei cheng wu rao" toushi dangdai qingnina de jiazhiguan' ("From *If You Are the One* examining contemporary youth values"), *Zhongguo qongnian yanjiu*, 2011, 4 (April), pp. 4–23.

170 Cao Hongbei, 'Xie Tianxiao: linjie' ("Xie Tianxiao: critical"), *Zhongguo xinwen zhoukan* (*China News Weekly*), 2005, 46 (December), pp. 62–3.

171 Ding Nan, 'Beijing you ge yaogun qingnian wutuobang' ("There's a rock youth Utopia in Beijing"), *Baixing* (*Common People*), 2001, 5 (May), pp. 26–7. This magazine was published for two years (2000–1) by the Ministry of Agriculture.

172 Chen Jie, 'All dolled up,' *China Daily*, 4 September 2007, p. 18. Cui Jian performed his first English-language song (called 'Outside Girl') at the event: *China Daily*, 12 September 2007, p. 21. The contrast is striking between this matter-of-fact reportage in 2007 and the breathless story in *Beijing Youth* on a sold-out February 1995 Beijing concert by U.S. pop group Roxette in the Capital Gymnasium (with ticket prices ranging from fifty to 600 yuan). The story includes a fan photo of audience members standing and waving their arms in delight behind a poker-faced, young policeman: Lei Fan, '"Luokesaite" menghuan Beijing' ("Roxette dream in Beijing"), *Beijing qingnian*, 1995, 4 (April), pp. 20–3.

173 For a sense of the diversity and commercialism of rock music in China by 2006, see the 430-page directory, including details on 180 bands, Li Hongjie, ed., *Zhongguo yaogun shouce* (*Encyclopedia of China Rock & Roll*), Chongqing: Chongqing chubanshe, 2006.

174 Yi Ran, 'Yaogun 20 nian, yong yinyue chang rensheng' (Twenty years of rock, using music to sing about life), *Liaoning qingnian*, 2006, 16 (August), p. 83.

175 Da Peng, 'Zouhao, Zhongguo yaogun' ("Good bye, Chinese rock"), *Guoji yinyue jiaoliu* (International Music Exchange), 2001, 1 (January), p. 133. For the continuing popularity of the heavy metal Tang Dynasty (most members of which were now in their late forties) in the new century, see Chen Nan, 'Rock for the ages,' *China Daily*, 9 July 2008, p. 18.

176 See, for example, Beijing Zhongshi Shengqi Cultural Media Company, ed., *Yu ni zai yiqi: Ma Tianyu tuwen xiezhen ji* (*Together with you: A pictorial portrait of Ma Tianyu*), Shanghai: Shanghai huabao chubanshe, 2006. The title played on the second given name of the Shandong-born singer, using it

as a homophone for *yu* (meaning with). Among other setups, Mr Ma is pictured sprawled on a bed, dressed in singlet and jeans. He is also portrayed in the Shandong countryside with his Muslim paternal grandfather in a wheelchair, suggesting filial virtue. Like most books in this genre, a DVD of the making of the book and with an interview with the singer is included. *Supergirl* 2005 spawned a large number of such fan books on the three finalists.

177 For an early discussion of hip-hop, with limited reference to Chinese youth, see Zhao Fang, 'Cong Hip-Hop yundong kan qingnian wenhua' ("Youth culture through the hip-hop movement"), *Qingnian yanjiu*, 2002, 12 (December), pp. 15–20. Zhao focuses on street dancing and skateboard cultures, noting their rebel stance and the importance of the Internet in their spread.

178 The words in italics are in English in the original. Quoted in Li Fanzhuo, 'Hip-hop wenhua zai qingshaonian zhong de liuxingxing fenxi' ("Analysis of the popularity of hip-hop culture among the young"), *Qingnian yanjiu*, 2004, 6 (June), p. 31.

179 See, for another example, the lyrics of the song *Xishuashua* by spiky-haired boy group Folk Band (*Hua'er yuedui*), which include the English 'kiss' and '1234Go': *Liaoning qingnian*, 2006, 3 (February), inside front cover. On breakdancing South Korean B-Boys, see Park Ju-yeon, 'Korea's B-Boys Capture the International Spotlight,' *Koreana*, 20, 4 (2006), pp. 80–4.

180 Li Fanzhuo, p. 32. The word 'free' is in English in Li's article. Andl is a U.S. brand favored by street players. De Kloet, *China with a Cut*, notes the strong identification of hip-hop with modernity and consumer culture in China (pp. 68–73). Cui Jian himself expressed strong endorsement of the expressive qualities of hip-hop: see the collected interview transcripts in Cui Jian and Zhou Guoping, *Ziyou fengge* (Freestyle), Guilin: Guangxi shifan daxue chubanshe, 2001, pp. 65–9.

## 5  SPACES: REAL, IMAGINED, AND VIRTUAL ARENAS

1 See Paul Clark, *Chinese Cultural Revolution*, pp. 3–4, 258, 261.

2 I was struck in 1988 and 1989 at the absence of customers in the China Film Import and Export Corporation's Beijing video store, despite its unique and relatively comprehensive inventory of Chinese feature films from 1949 onward.

3 Ke Xiaowei, *Dangdai Beijing can-yin shihua* (*Contemporary Beijing food and drink history*), Beijing: Dangdai Zhongguo chubanshe, 2009, pp. 158–60.

4 Ke Xiaowei, p. 159.

5 For a discussion of this literature and its readers, see Perry Link, *The Uses of Literature: Life in the Socialist Literary System*, Princeton: Princeton University Press, 2000.

6 Some of this biographical information is from Yu Wong, 'Wang's World,' *Far Eastern Economic Review* (Hong Kong), 8 August 1996, pp. 46–8. For a discussion of Wang and 'hoodlum literature,' see Geremie Barmé, pp. 62–98.

7 See Chen Shan, '"Tongsu wenxue re": yizhong chengshi wenhua xianxiang' ("The 'popular literature fever:' an urban culture phenomenon"), *Renmin ribao*, 22 September 1988, p. 5. A more sympathetic view of popular

literature came from established writer Feng Qiuchang a few weeks later. Feng argued that the defining characteristic of this kind of writing and the reason for its appeal to ordinary readers was that its creators not only expressed themselves directly but also spoke for ordinary people (*pingmin baixing*: another coinage that avoided any political connotations that words like the *masses* or the *people* carried in 1980s China). Such writing took empathy (*tong*: together) as its watchword, whereas more high-brow literature focused on difference (*yi*: other). One kind could not exist without the other. See Feng Qiuchang, 'Tongsu wenxue de shenmei tezheng' ("The aesthetic features of popular literature"), *Renmin ribao*, 11 October 1988, p. 5. The work of Wang Shuo is not mentioned.

8   Ru Shi, 'Waiguo wenxue chuban ying re zhong qiujing' ("The boom in foreign literature publishing"), *Renmin ribao*, 29 May 1989, p. 4.

9   For a discussion of Chinese cinema's efforts to create popular entertainment films in the 1980s, see Clark, *Reinventing China*, pp. 137–45.

10  This account is drawn from Shan Ren, '"Lunhui" paishe sanji' ("Notes on the filming of *Samsara*"), *Dazhong dianying*, 1988, 10 (October), p. 16 and from an all-night visit to the film shoot in Beijing's Jianguo Hotel in June 1988. For a comparison of Fifth Generation filmmakers' interests in questions of the nation and Wang Shuo's rather different take, see Jin Jianguo, '"Wanzhong' xianxiang," "Wang Shuo dianying" jiyu wenti' ("The issue of favorable circumstances in the '*Evening Bell* phenomenon' and 'Wang Shuo films'"), *Qingnian yu shehui*, 1989, 6 (June), pp. 15–16.

11  Conversations with Zhang Yimou, Beijing, June 1988.

12  Li Li, 'Yi pi zhongqingnian zuojia jinjun yingshi jie, Haima yingshe chuangzuo zhongxin zai Jing chengli' ("A group of middle-aged and young writers advance on film and TV circles, the Seahorse Film and Television Creative Centre is established in Beijing"), *Renmin ribao*, 12 January 1989, p. 3. See also Lu Yunyun, 'Wang Shuo he tade xiaoshuo' ("Wang Shuo and his novels"), *Renmin ribao*, 28 January 1989, p. 8.

13  These observations are from a visit to Beijing from 25 May to 8 June 1989.

14  Wang Yu, 'Wang Shuo de xin Jingwei xiaoshuo: ping "Wanr de jiu xintiao" ji qita' ("Wang Shuo's new Beijing-flavor novel: A review of *Playing for Thrills* and other matters"), *Renmin ribao*, 30 May 1989, p. 6.

15  Zuo Shula, 'Wang Shuo: yi ge ganyu miaoshi changgui de "suren,"' *Dazhong dianying*, 1989, 6 (June), pp. 14–15 and 7 (July), pp. 10–13.

16  Zuo Shula's admiring and picaresque two-part account of Wang Shuo's life is curiously punctuated by quotations from famous authors (Chinese and foreign) on the qualities of a successful writer. See the conservative views of youthful tastes in Yang Xiong, '1978–1989: Zhongguo qingnian shenmei gunanian de tuibian' ("The transformation of Chinese youth's aesthetic tastes"), *Dangdai qingnian yanjiu*, 1990, 4 (August), p. 12.

17  What amounted to a celebration of his quirky and clever writing and of his scorn for the public expectations of a proper writer appeared in the youth magazine *Seeking* (*Zhuiqiu*) in mid-1992. Wang Zhaoqian, '"Kanye" Wang Shuo' ("'Windbag' Wang Shuo"), *Zhuiqiu* (Seeking), 1992, 4 (April), pp. 2–4.

18  See, for example, Wang Dongcheng, 'Wang Shuo de "meisu" yu "fanzhi"' ("Wang Shuo's 'appealing to vulgar tastes' and 'anti-intellectualism'"), *Zhongguo qingnian yanjiu*, 1993, 3 (May), pp. 16–18 and Wang Xiaozhang, 'Jiazhi zhenkong shidai de "wenhua gu'er": xi Cui Jian, Wang Guozhen,

Wang Shuo xianxiang' ("'Cultural orphans' in an age of value vacuum: Explaining the Cui Jian, Wang Guozhen, and Wang Shuo phenomena"), *Qingnian yanjiu*, 1994, 11 (November), pp. 25–8.

19 Gao Bo, *Wang Shuo: Dashi haishi pizi*, Beijing: Beijing Yanshan chubanshe, 1993; Wang Shuo, *Wo shi Wang Shuo*, Beijing: Guoji wenhua chubanshe, 1992; Zhang Dexiang and Jin Huimin, eds., *Wang Shuo pipan*, Beijing: Zhongguo shehui kexue chubanshe, 1993.

20 The interview transcripts covered 101 pages of the 290-page book. The rest were extracts from Wang's key works of fiction to date: *Wo shi Wang Shuo* (1992).

21 Zhang Dexiang, front cover and pp. 1–2.

22 Gao Bo, pp. 1–3.

23 The bibliography of writings about Wang Shuo, arranged in chronological order of publication, in Ge Hongbing and Zhu Lidong, eds., *Wang Shuo yanjiu ziliao*, Tianjin: Tianjin renmin chubanshe, 2005, pp. 541–71, shows the extent of attention Wang attracted from literary critics, social commentators, and other writers from 1987 to 2003.

24 Chen Zufen, 'Wang Shuo he wenhua jingji: fang Wan Shuo tan zuojia xiahai' ("Wang Shuo and the cultural economy: Wang Shuo talks about writers entering the market economy"), *Beijing qingnian*, 1993, 11 (November), p. 41.

25 Chen Zufen, p. 41. But in the same interview Wang also admitted to literary ambitions such as recapturing the power of language. For a useful overview of Wang Shuo as an entrepreneur in the early 1990s, see Shuyu Kong, pp. 22–8.

26 *Beijing Youth* reported on the setting up of the company in early 1995 with a series of brief comments wishing the enterprise well from nine young writers, as well as from Wang himself: Weng Zhe, '"Langjian wenren" tanyan zhaoshang' ("Top writers frankly seek outside investment"), *Beijing qingnian*, 1995, 1 (January), pp. 54–5. Most of the writers confessed to hoping to participate in the new company's planned large-scale television serial production.

27 Liu Hong, 'Buganjimo de "wenhua shangren" Wang Shuo' ("Wang Shuo: a 'cultural businessman' unwilling to stay out of the limelight"), *Beijing qingnian*, 1995, 1 (January), pp. 8–11. A photo of Wang in full conversational flight illustrated each of the pages of the interview.

28 Liu Hong, *Buganjimo*, p. 11.

29 Liu Hong, *Buganjimo*, p. 11.

30 Weng Zhe, 'Wang Shuo pengchu haoshu yi luokuang: jieshao Shishi gongsi tuichu de congshu' ("Wang Shuo holds up a basket of good books: introducing the book series from the Current Affairs company"), *Beijing qingnian*, 1995, 4 (April), pp. 24–5.

31 Weng Zhe, p. 25.

32 Liu Hong, '"Shangdi" de hao-wu' ("The likes and dislikes of 'emperors'"), *Beijing qingnian*, 1995, 3 (March), pp. 24–5. The 'emperors' in the title is a way of referring to customers. The survey was not confined to youth respondents, but the commentary assumes that they predominated among the twenty thousand expressing their preferences.

33 Gong Li's worst actress award from Shanghai voters was probably related to their selection of *Soul of the Painter* (*Huahun*), in which Gong played a Republican-era artist, as their least favorite film. The film's female director,

Huang Shuqin, was chosen in Shanghai as the most unpopular director for 1994.

34  Liu Hong, 'Pai bu dianying ye tinghao' ("Making a film is also great"), *Beijing qingnian*, 1995, 11 (November), pp. 38–9.

35  See Shuyu Kong, '*Big Shot from Beijing*: Feng Xiaogang's *He Sui Pian* and Contemporary Chinese Commercial Film,' *Asian Cinema*, 14, 1 (Spring/Summer 2003), pp. 175–87.

36  Liu Hong, *Pai bu dianying*, p. 39.

37  Wu Hongfei, 'Wang Shuo xiongmeng' ("Wang Shuo ferocious"), *Nanfang renwu zhoukan* (*Southern People Weekly*), 21 March 2007, pp. 16–27.

38  Wu Hongfei, p. 17.

39  In an extended interview as part of this feature story, Wang labeled Li Ao, the Taiwan-based Phoenix Television commentator, a megalomaniac (*zidakuang*). This was perhaps an indication that Wang felt challenged by television celebrities like Li, who is as opinionated as him, and attracted a sizeable following to his weekly television programs: Wu Hongfei, p. 23.

40  Jiang Ni, *Wang Shuo mima: jiekai Wang Shuo 'chenggong' zhi mi* (*The Wang Shuo Code: Solving the Riddle of the Wang Shuo 'Success'*), Beijing: Zhongguo Sanxia chubanshe, 2007.

41  Sun Hong, 'Wang Shuo: "Wo de moshi nimen bu dong"' ("Wang Shuo: 'You don't understand my model'"), *Beifang yinyue* (*Northern Music*), 2007, 3 (March), pp. 32–3. The website name may have been a reference to his novella *Kanshangqu hen mei* (*Could be Beautiful*), a story about a kindergarten adapted by Sixth Generation director Zhang Yuan as *Little Red Flowers* (its English title) in 2004.

42  Sun Hong, p. 32.

43  Sun Hong, p. 33.

44  Sun Hong, p. 32.

45  Yunxiang Yan makes this point in 'Introduction: Conflicting Images of the Individual and Contested Process of Individualization,' in Mette Halskov Hansen and Rune Svarverud, eds., *iChina: The Rise of the Individual in Modern Chinese Society*, Copenhagen: NIAS Press, 2010, p. 18.

46  Han Renjun, *Erzi Han Han* (*My son Han Han*), Shanghai: Shanghai renmin chubanshe, 2000.

47  See, for example, Han Han, *Han Han zuopinji* (*Han Han: Collected works*), Beijing: Shijie zhishi chubanshe, 2006. For a survey showing the high level of high school student interest in his writings soon after his first novel, a high school story called *Three Doors* (*San zhong men*), was published, see Yu Danping, Yang Weiwei, He Jiayu and Zhang Yi, 'Ganshou "Han-liu" de weili: women yan zhong de "Han Han xianxiang"' ("Feeling the 'Han Wave': The 'Han Han phenomenon' in our eyes"), *Wangluo keji shidai* (*Nettime*), 2003, 11 (November), pp. 27–9. The title of the report played on Han's surname being the same as the word for South Korea used in the expression Korean Wave (*Hanliu*).

48  For an historical overview of youthful idol worship, see Yue Xiaodong and Liang Xiao, 'Qingshaonian ouxiang chongbai xilie zongshu zhi wu: lun bainian lai Zhongguo dalu qingshaonian ouxiang chongbai de bianqian' ("A fifth summary of a series of youthful idol worship: On one hundred years of changes in Chinese mainland youthful idol worship"), *Qingnian yanjiu*, 2010, 4 (August), pp. 70–9.

49  The 1999 figure is from Yang Xiong, 'Wangluo dui woguo qingnian de yingxiang pingjia' ("An evaluation of the impact of the Internet on China's youth"), *Qingnian yanjiu*, April 2000, p. 8. For an historical and political examination of the Internet, though without a focus on youth, see Zhou Yongming, *Historicizing Online Politics: Telegraphy, The Internet, and Political Participation in China*, Stanford: Stanford University Press, 2006.

50  Zhang Bingfu, Tu Minxia, and Liu Yuling, 'Guangzhou qingshaonian wangluo shenghuo diaocha baogao' ("Report on an investigation of Guangzhou young people's Internet life"), *Zhongguo qingnian yanjiu*, February 2006, p. 15. See also an earlier analysis of usage: Lan Jun and Lu Huiju, 'You wangluo sousuo redian yinfa de sikao: laizi san ge zhuming wangzhan sousuo paihangbang de diaocha baogao' ("Thoughts arising from the hottest Internet searches: A report on an investigation of the frequency order of searches on three prominent websites), *Zhongguo qingnian yanjiu*, December 2003, pp. 19–22.

51  Yang Xiong, 'Wangluo dui woguo ... ,' pp. 9–10.

52  Ji Qiufa, 'Qingshaonian xuesheng shiyong wangluo de shizheng yanjiu' ("Research on the concrete evidence of young people's use of the Internet"), *Beijing qingnian zhengzhi xueyuan xuebao (Journal of Beijing Youth Politics College)*, 2003, 2 (June), p. 17.

53  Ji Qiufa, p. 22 (Table 5).

54  Liu Lanping and Hua Tongxu, 'Lülun wangluo qingshaonian wenhua de jiankang fazhan: chengshi wenhua jianshi zhong de yige zhongyao fangmian' ("A brief discussion of the healthy development of young people's Internet culture: An important aspect of urban cultural construction"), *Guangdong shehui kexue (Guangdong Social Science)*, 2002, 4 (August), pp. 147–52.

55  Wang Haiming, Ren Juanjuan, and Huang Shaohua, 'Qingshaonian wangluo xingwei tezheng jiqi yu wangluo renzhi de xiangguanxing yanjiu' ("Comparative research on the features of young people's Internet behaviour and their Internet cognition), *Lanzhou daxue xuebao (shehui kexue ban) (Journal of Lanzhou University [Social Sciences])*, 2005, 33, 4 (July), pp. 102–11. This survey involved 1,691 respondents. See also Huang Shaohua, 'Qingshaonian wangmin de wangluo jiaowang jiegou' ("Young netizens' Internet communication structures"), *Lanzhou daxue xuebao (shehui kexue ban)*, 2009, 1 (January), pp. 70–8; Zhou Jinzhang, 'Wangluo wenti yu "qingshaonian kongjian" de yongzao' ("The Internet issue and building a young people's space'"), *Hongqi wengao (Red Flag Manuscripts)*, 2010, 5 (March), pp. 28–9 and Zhao Qingsi, 'Qingnian wangluo yawenhua de wenhua luoji' ("The cultural logic of youth Internet subcultures"), *Dangdai qingnian yanjiu*, 2010, 1 (January), pp. 28–33.

56  Wang Haiming and others, p. 111. The researchers explained the higher level of interest in sexual content on the Internet among university students (especially males) with the distance from parental supervision enjoyed by such students. See also Han Xianzhou, 'Cong Internet de fazhan kan qingnian wenti' ("Looking at youth issues from the development of the Internet"), *Zhongguo qingnian zhengzhi xueyuan xuebao*, 1999, 4 (August), p. 35; and Li Tao, 'Dui goujian qingshaonian wangluo lunli jingshen de sikao' ("Reflection on the cultivation of young people's ethical spirit on the Internet"), *Zhongguo qingnian zhengzhi xueyuan xuebao*, 2002, 2 (February), pp. 22–5. The Leshan survey is cited on p. 24.

57  Lin Yafei, Qi Aihua, and Ouyang Qinghua, Ningbo qingshaonian wangluo xingwei diaocha' ("An investigation into online behaviour among young people in Ningbo"), *Nongbo guangbo dianshi daxue xuebao (Journal of Ningbo Radio and Television University)*, 2006, 4 (September), p. 17 (survey questions), p. 19 (data). This article is rare in providing the text of the survey instrument and a chart of the percentage of responses to all forty-four questions. The conclusion about the honesty of the high school respondents is my own, not that of the article's three authors.

58  Wei Hongxin, 'Wangluo yu qingshaonian shehuihua' ("The Internet and young people's socialization"), *Gong'an daxue xuebao (Journal of Chinese People's Public Security University)*, 2001, 3 (June), pp. 94–7. The Dongguan example is on p. 96. The female researcher seems to pay particular attention to the negative impacts of the Internet on the young.

59  Ouyang Yanwen, 'Wangluo dui qingshaonian shehuihua de li yu bi' ("Pros and cons of the Internet for young people's socialization"), *Beijing qingnian zhengzhi xueyuan xuebao (Journal of Beijing Youth Politics College)*, pp. 15–18.

60  Chen Zhi, 'Lüelun wangluohua dui qingshaonian shehuihua de yingxiang' ("A brief discussion of the influence of Internet-ization on young people's socialization"), *Fujian shifan daxue xuebao (zhexue sheui kexue ban) (Journal of Fujian Normal University [Philosophy and Social Sciences Edition])*, 2003, 3 (June), pp. 141–6 (quote is from p. 143).

61  *Internet bar* is a translation of the Chinese *wangba*, the second syllable being a transliteration of 'bar.' There was no alcohol served in such places. Any beverages, including coffee, were in cans dispensed by a coin-operated machine.

62  Liu Shengzhi, 'Qingshaonian yu xiaofei wenhua: guanyu wangba de guannian chongtu yu liyi boyi' ("Young people and consumer culture: On conflicting ideas and the chess game about the benefits regarding Internet bars"), *Zhongguo qingnian yanjiu*, 2007, 10 (October), p. 56.

63  Liu Shengzhi, p. 56–57.

64  Liu Shengzhi, p. 57.

65  Discussed in Liu Shengzhi, p. 59.

66  Wang Sihai, Zhang Jianxin, and Dong Xueqing, 'Wangba heidong reng zai "bushi" qingshaonian' ("Black hole Internet bars still preying on young people"), *Liaowang xinwen zhoukan (Outlook News Weekly)*, 22 May 2006, pp. 17–18.

67  Wang Sihai, Zhang Jianxin, and Dong Xueqing, 'Qingshaonian weihe chenni "wangyou"' ("Why do young people wallow in 'Internet games'?"), *Liaowang xinwen zhoukan*, 22 May 2006, pp. 18–20 (p. 18).

68  Wang Sihai, Zhang Jianxin, and Dong Xueqing, 'Shei lai jianguan wangyou shichang' ("Who supervises the market for the Internet?"), *Liaowang xinwen zhoukan*, 22 May 2006, p. 20.

69  Wang Sihai, Zhang Jianxin, and Dong Xueqing, 'Youxiao jianghua wangluo huanjing' ("Effectively purify the Internet environment"), *Liaowang xinwen zhoukan*, 22 May 2006, pp. 22–3.

70  Su Wenliang, Liu Qinxue, Fang Xiaoyi, Fang Zhao, and Wan Jingjing, 'Dui daxuesheng wangluo chengyin de xingzhi yanjiu' ("Research on the features of university student Internet addiction"), *Qingnian yanjiu*, 2007, 10 (October), p. 11.

71  Su Wenliang and others, p. 12.

72  Su Wenliang, pp. 12–13.

73  Su Wenliang, p. 14. See also Feng Xiaotian, 'Chengshi zaizhi qingnian de wangluo jiechu: quanguo 12 chengshi 1786 ming zaizhi qingnian de diaocha fenxi' ("Urban employed youth's contact with the Internet: Analysis of a nationwide 12 city 1786 person survey of employed youth"), *Zhongguo qingnian yanjiu*, 2007, 12 (December), pp. 47–51.

74  Zhao Xue, 'Zai Flash li "shan" bian rensheng' ("A life changed in a flash"), *Liaoning qingnian*, 2005, 6 (March), pp. 52–3.

75  Zhang Yu, 'BBS wangluo kongjian de shehui jiaowang lingyu: yi Shuimu shequ de shizheng fenxi wei lie' ("The associative social domain of BBS Internet space: Concrete analysis of the Shuimu community as an example"), *Qingnian yanjiu*, 2007, 8 (August), pp. 22–9.

76  Zhang Yu, pp. 22–3.

77  Zhang Yu, pp. 24–5, Tables 3, 4, and 5.

78  Zhang Yu, p. 25. These were the English names used for pages that also had Chinese names.

79  Zhang Yu, pp. 25–6.

80  Pan Congyi, 'Daxuesheng feizhengshi qunti chizheng yanjiu' ("Impartial research on informal groups among university students"), *Dangdai qingnian yanjiu*, 2007, 6 (June), p. 41. Wenzhou University, in one of the most entrepreneurial boom towns in reform China, was formally established in 2006.

81  Pan Congyi, pp. 41–2. *Sanrenxing* was from an ancient phrase that 'if three men are walking, at least one is good enough to be my teacher' (*san ren xing, bi you wo shi*).

82  Pan Congyi, pp. 42–3.

83  Pan Congyi, pp. 43–4.

84  Pan Congyi, p. 44.

85  Pan Congyi, pp. 44–5.

86  These 2003 episodes are listed at the start of Luo Di and Mao Yuxi, 'Zhenglun zhong de "wangluo minzuzhuyi"' ("'Internet nationalism' in dispute"), *Zhongguo qingnian yanjiu*, 2006, 5 (May), p. 47.

87  Luo Di and Mao Yuxi, pp. 47–8. The headline used a mathematical equal sign with a line crossed through it. Other upsurges in popular nationalism among Chinese youth in the 1990s, including the disappointment in 1993 at not being awarded the 2000 Olympics hosting rights, the Milky Way (ship) incident, the U.S. accidental bombing of the Chinese embassy in Belgrade in May 1999, and the sentiments encapsulated in the publication in 1996 of *China Can Say 'No'* (*Zhongguo keyi shuo bu*) came before the popularisation of the Web in China.

88  Luo Di and Mao Yuxi, p. 48.

89  Luo Di and Mao Yuxi, pp. 48–9, 50–1.

90  Kevin Latham, 'SMS, communication, and citizenship in China's information society,' *Critical Asian Studies*, 39, 2 (2007), pp. 295–314.

91  Latham, pp. 301–2.

92  Latham, pp. 302–3.

93  Latham, p. 305.

94  Quoted by Latham, p. 308.

95  Jiang Yun, 'Wode dipan wo zuo zhu: shixi shouji dui qingshaonian siyu jinagou de yingxiang' ("I'm master of my territory: A preliminary analysis of

the influence of cell phones on the construction of young people's personal space"), *Qingnian yanjiu*, 2006, 1 (January), pp. 16–23. The title of the article incorporated the name of a current hit song ('My territory') by Taiwan singer Jay Chou (Zhou Jielun).

96 Jiang Yun, p. 18. In a revealing comment on the effectiveness of the one-child policy, 35.1 percent of the 360 high school students surveyed by Jiang had a brother or sister (p. 17).

97 Jiang Yun, p. 21.

98 Wu Zhengguo, 'Daxue xiaoyuan de "duanxin wenhua": qingnian xuesheng de xinli fuhao' ("University campus 'text message culture': A mark of youthful student psychology"), *Qingnian yanjiu*, 2003, 5 (May), p. 21.

99 Wu Zhengguo, pp. 22–3.

100 Jing Yongli, 'Mo rang xuesheng shouji biancheng shoulei' ("Don't let students' hand phones become hand grenades"), *Liaoning qingnian*, 2005, 23 (November), p. 26. See also Liu Haiyan, 'Qingshaonian shouji duanxin chuanbo de houxiandai wenti' ("The postmodern issue of young people's text messaging communication"), *Dangdai qingnian yanjiu*, 2008, 2 (February), pp. 43–7. Privacy did not require virtual space: Quiet chats with dormmates provided an opportunity for intimate sharing of thoughts: see Lin Yingying, 'Daxuesheng wotan xianxiang toushi' ("Perspective on the phenomenon of university student bed chatting"), *Qingnian tansuo*, 2008, 3 (May), pp. 87–90.

101 Wang Daoyong, 'Yiming de kuanghuan yu renxing de xianxian: dui 2006 nian ruogan wangluo jiqun shijian zhong wangmin xingwei de fenxi' ("Anonymous revelry and the revealing of humanity: An analysis of netizen behaviour from certain Internet mass incidents in 2006"), *Qingnian yanjiu*, 2007, 3 (March), pp. 21–7.

102 Wang Daoyong, pp. 21–2.

103 This is the argument of Xu Chuanxin and Zhang Le, '"Baobaotuan" xianxiang de shehuixue jiedu' ("Sociological deciphering of the 'hugging group' phenomenon"), *Zhongguo qingnian yanjiu*, 2007, 10 (October), pp. 8–10.

104 Wang Daoyong, p. 22–4.

105 Wang Daoyong, p. 23.

106 See, for example, Wan Meirong and Ye Lei, '21 shijichu qingshaonian liuxing wenhua de liubian' ("Later developments in early twenty-first-century young people's popular culture"), *Zhongguo qingnian yanjiu*, 2009, 4 (April), p. 27; Mao Yanling, 'Dui "shanzhai wenhua" de jiedu' ("Explaining 'copycat culture'"), *Zhongguo qingnian yanjiu*, 2009, 3 (March), pp. 84–6, 91; Su Zhicui, 'Jiexi hulian wangshi jiaoxia de qingshaonian shanzhai wenhua' ("Analysis of young people's copycat culture from the angle of mutual media"), *Qingnian tansuo*, 2009, 4 (July), pp. 66–9; and Lü Peng, 'Shanzhai wenhua de duoshijiao jiedu' ("A multi-perspective explanation of copycat culture"), *Zhongguo qingnian yanjiu*, 2009, 8 (August), pp. 84–6, 70. One example of the spread of *shanzhai* into mainstream discourse was the presentation of a so-called *shanzhai* Spring Festival Gala in early 2010 to compete with CCTV's venerable annual blockbuster.

107 Zhang Ting, 'Daxuesheng qunti yu "shanzhai" wenhua xianzhuang diaocha' ("Investigation of the current state of university student groups and 'copycat' culture"), *Dangdai qingnian yanjiu*, 2010, 1 (January), p. 35.

108 Ma Zhonghong, 'Wangluo qingnian yawenhua leixing tedian yu chuanbo lujing diaocha baogao: jiyu Jiangsu 21 suo gaoxiao de diaocha' ("Survey

report on the features of the kinds of youth Internet subcultures and dissemination access: Based on a survey of twenty-one tertiary institutes in Jiangsu"), *Zhongguo guangbo (China Advertising)*, 2009, 7 (July), p. 45. Amateur or grassroots activity (*zipa*) was another quality in youth Internet culture identified in this 2009 survey (p. 45). The survey showed that two-thirds of students accessed the 'Net in their dorm rooms and that one-half of students spent between 400 and 800 yuan on monthly living costs (p. 44). See also Pu Yingjuan, Su Yan, and Zheng Peng, 'Daxuesheng yu wangluo qingnian yawenhua guanxi yanjiu' ("Research on the connections between university students and youth Internet subcultures"), *Dangdai qingnian yanjiu*, 2009, 4 (April), pp. 44–5.

109 Li Ronghua, 'Qingnian "boke wenhua" de jiegou yu jiangou' ("The deconstruction and construction of youth 'blog culture'"), *Dangdai qingnian yanjiu*, 2007, 1 (January), pp. 13–16. A 2006 examination of blogs written by three university student bloggers showed that this writing was a way to try to control the presentation of the self: Sun Ran, 'Cong blog yu chuantong riji de qubie kan daxuesheng boke de xiezuo xinli' ("Examining the writing psychology of university student blogs from the difference between blogs and traditional diaries"), *Zhongguo qingnian yanjiu*, 2006, 1 (January), pp. 69–72.

110 Du Jinyan, 'Q-ban: jiti moqi de yawenhua' ("Q: A collective secret pact subculture"), *Qingnian yanjiu*, 2006, 9 (September), pp. 10–11.

111 Du Jinyan, pp. 10–11.

112 The following is based on Yang Chunrong and Yin Fangmin, 'Daxuesheng wangluo luoliao xingwei de duowei fenxi' (« A multidimensional analysis of university student 'naked chatting' behaviour »), *Dangdai qingnian yanjiu*, 2006, 12 (December), pp. 18–23.

113 Yang Chunrong and Yin Fangmin, p. 19. Commercial 'naked chatting' also occurred, taking advantage of the 'Net insatiable demand for pornography. Some university students spent over 100 yuan a day visiting such sites.

114 A respondent quoted in Yang Chunrong and Yin Fangmin, p. 20.

115 The following is based on Jing Yuan, 'Cong wangluo zhengyou kan dangdai qingnian de zeou biaozhun: dui "Wo ai Nankai BBS" queqiaoban neirong fenxi' ("How Internet personal adverts reveal contemporary youth's mate selection criteria: Examining the contents of the matchmaking site on the 'I love Nankai' BBS"), *Qingnian yanjiu*, 2007, 2 (February), pp. 9–16.

116 See the tables of fifteen aspects in the advertisements, Jing Yuan, pp. 11–12. Table 2 (page 12) shows relatively minor differences between male and female advertisers' criteria. As for requirements sought in a partner, 9.79 percent of men specified place of residence (meaning an urban resident), while 15.26 percent of women advertisers did this, suggesting a higher number of women seeing marriage as a means to gain urban residency.

117 See Wang Debao, 'Social networking gaining ground,' *China Daily*, 11 September 2009, S9. QQ had 350 million users (essentially all Chinese netizens), while kaixin001.com had forty million registered users. See also Gan Tian, 'Caught in the net,' *China Daily*, 25 June 2009, p. 18. Xiaonei became Renren (literally person person), China's answer to Facebook.

118 Yang Jing, 'Zhuguan qingshaonian wangluo fensi julebu qunti' ("Pay attention to young people's Internet fan club groups"), *Qingnian gongzuo luntan (Youth Work Forum* [Shandong]), 2008, 2 (March), pp. 23–6.

119 Yang Jing, p. 24.

120 Yang Jing, p. 25.

121	Yang Jing, p. 25. For a similar discussion of Internet fandom, see Huang Hailiang and Luo Anyuan, 'Wangluo "fensi" wenhua shequ chuanbo jizhi chutan' ("A first exploration of broadcast mechanisms of internet fan cultural communities"), *Chongqing jiaoyu xueyuan xuebao* (*Journal of the Chongqing Education Academy*), 2007, 1 (January), pp. 80–2.

122	Pease, p. 185. Street management committees are a part of the neighbourhood governance apparatus in Chinese cities.

123	Pease, p. 186.

124	Wang Ping and Liu Dianzhi, '"Tongren nü" xianxiang de fenxi yu sikao' ("Analysis and reflections on the 'gay-groupie girl' phenomenon"), *Qingnian yanjiu*, 2008, 10 (October), pp. 37–42.

125	These young women also formed the main Chinese audience for the U.S. television adaptation of *Angels in America*: Wang Ping and Liu Dianzhi, p. 38.

126	Both these quotes are from Wang Ping and Liu Dianzhi, pp. 38–9.

127	Wang Ping and Liu Dianzhi, p. 41.

128	Xue Yali, 'e-shidai de "wangluo wenxue"' ("E-times, internet literature'"), *Qingnian tansuo*, 2001, 5 (September), p. 34.

129	For a masterful discussion of Wang's fiction, see Bonnie S. McDougall, 'Self-narrative as group discourse: female subjectivity in Wang Anyi's fiction,' in McDougall, *Fictional Authors, Imaginary Audiences*, pp. 95–113.

130	Xue Yali, pp. 35–6. Xue ends with a customary warning about the negative effects of such Internet writing, though that does not negate the enthusiasm of the rest of the analysis.

131	Chen Si, '2002 nian Beijing gaoxiao liuxingyu zhangkuang diaocha' ("Survey of the situation of Beijing tertiary popular language in 2002"), *Zhongguo qingnian yanjiu*, 2002, 5 (May), p. 14. The most popular expression, chosen by over half those surveyed, was *yumen* (depressed or suppressed). Number two was *kao* (literally lean against), a substitute for the swear word *cao*, in the manner of English speakers who might say 'puck' instead of a common swear word.

132	Chen Si, p. 16.

133	Chen Si, pp. 16–17 (incl. Table 4).

134	Chen Si, pp. 17–18.

135	Chen Si, p. 18. For one kind of Internet novel, see Yang Linxiang, 'Qingnian qinglai wangluo: "chuan yue" xiaoshuo de shenceng yuanyin fenxi' ("Youth-favored Internet: An analysis of the deep reasons for novels that leap across time and place"), *Zhongguo qingnian yanjiu*, 2009, 6 (June), pp. 94–6.

136	Chen Yuanyuan and others, 'Man yi qingnian liuxing yuyan' ("Youth popular language rich in meaning"), *Zhongguo qingnian zhengzhi xueyuan xuebao*, 2003, 3 (June), pp. 26–7.

137	Chen Yuanyuan, p. 28–9. Speaker was Jin Yanna. This development could cause concern among those charged with guiding the young. As a Shanghai youth work cadre noted about this new language trend: 'The birth of each new thing [the speaker uses the Cultural Revolution expression *xinsheng shiwu*] must contain with it the danger of probing.' (p. 27)

138	See Xiao Weisheng and Wang Shulin, 'Lun wangluo yuyan de qingnian yawenhua texing' ("On the characteristics of the youth subculture of Internet language"), *Qingnian yanjiu*, 2008, 6 (June), pp. 21–6.

139	Xiao Weisheng and Wang Shulin, pp. 23–4.

140 See Dong Changdi, 'Jiedu "90 hou" wangmin "huoxing wen" xianxiang' ("Deciphering the phenomenon of 'Martian language' used by '90s generation' netizens"), *Shanxi qingnian guanli ganbu xueyuan xuebao (Journal of the Shanxi Youth Management Cadre Institute)*, 2008, 1 (January), pp. 24–7. Dong used the Baidu search engine to find 'Martian language' and received 11.5 million references (p. 27). See also Xu Liyan, 'Huoxing wen: "N dai" ren de wenhua fuhao' ("Martian language: Cultural signs used by the 'N[ineties] generation'"), *Shanxi qingnian guanli ganbu xueyuan xuebao (Journal of the Shanxi Youth Management Cadre Academy)*, 2008, 3 (September), pp. 18–20, reprinted in *Qingshaonian daokan*, 2009, 1 (January), pp. 54–7; Yang Liming, '"Fei zhuliu" yu "Huoxingwen" de yidai: "90 hou" wangluo meiti xingxiang chutan' ("The generation of 'non-mainstream' and 'Martian language': A first exploration of the form of Internet and media use by the 'nineties generation'"), *Zhongguo qingnian yanjiu*, 2009, 8 (August), pp. 74–80; and Chen Jingying and Ma Jianqing, 'Houxiandai jingyu zhong "Huoxingwen" de xinlixue jiedu' ("A psychological explanation of 'Martian language' in a postmodern milieu"), *Dangdai qingnian yanjiu*, 2010, 4 (April), pp. 42–6.

141 Dong Changdi, pp. 24–5. Dong cites an Internet survey of young people that he conducted showing that four in ten of the over five thousand respondents agreed that 'Martian' could have a bad influence on ordinary written language use and should be discouraged (pp. 25–6).

142 Anonymous, 'Jiedu xiaoyuan liuxing wangyu' (Deciphering internet language popular on campus), *Liaoning qingnian*, 2005, 22 (November), 118–119. FT was an abbreviation of the English 'to faint.' Some young people took the Shanghainese expression for fainting (*huntuo*) and pronounced the two characters like '*fen te*' to approximate the sound of the English word 'faint.' FT took on almost the frequency of *ku* ('cool') in BBS exchanges in particular, to express excitement or emotion at good or bad news: a classmate dumped by his girlfriend or a special purchase finally achieved, for example. A similar expression was *wo hun* (literally 'I faint'), meaning 'Amazing!' or such like.

143 See http://bbs.24xuexi.com/thread-134821-1-1.html (a compilation from March 2007), accessed on 18 November 2008 by Wu Xiaojing, to whom I am most grateful for providing this source.

144 The above source gives two separate definitions of *Zhengtai*, the second being a more innocent reference to boys under twelve without any sexual connotations. The *manga* first appeared in 1956 and told the story of a late World War II Japanese project to create giant robots. Shotaro, a twelve-year-old, was the son of the developer of the twenty-eighth version of the huge creatures. In Japan *Lolikon* (in Chinese *Luoli-kong*) and *Shotakon* (Chinese *Zhengtai-kong*) were the labels of the two sexual attractions to youngsters. Chinese Internet users seem to have adopted them directly from Japan. My thanks to Wayne P. Lawrence for this Japanese information.

145 Michael Wines, 'A Dirty Pun Tweaks China's Online Censors,' *The New York Times*, 12 March 2009, A1 (Internet version accessed on the *NYT* website on 16 March 2009).

146 Wines, *New York Times*.

147 In 2008 there were about seventy-five million CYL members aged between fourteen and twenty-eight, half of them students and organised into about

three million units: Tan Yingzi, 'Filling the need to help others,' *China Daily*, 5 December 2009, p. 7. For the origins of volunteering, see Chen Jinghuan, 'Zhongguo qingnian zhiyuan fuwu de fazhan yu tese' ("The development and characteristics of China's youth volunteerism"), *Qingnian tansuo*, 2011, 1 (January), pp. 41–6.

148 Cited in Yu Yiqun, Ji Qiufa, and Mu Qing, 'Xin shiji de Beijing qingnian, ("Beijing youth in the new century"), *Qingnian yanjiu*, 2003, 1 (January), 2. This article cites a modest local effort by young workers in a Beijing construction company to help the widows and children of deceased coworkers (p. 20).

149 Tan Yingzi, p. 7. For a useful overview, see Unn Målfrid H. Rolandsen, 'A Collective of Their Own: Young Volunteers at the Fringes of the Party Realm,' in Mette Halskov Hansen and Rune Svarverud, eds, pp. 132–163.

150 Zeng Li, 'Daxuesheng zhiyuan fuwu yu hexie shehui goujian' ("University student volunteer service and the construction of a harmonious society"), *Dangdai qingnian yanjiu*, 2008, 8 (August), p. 61.

151 The term used for cases of volunteering is *renci*. The ninety percent figure of youth volunteers may reflect a loose definition that extends into the thirties. See Liang Zhiquan, 'Qingnian zhiyuanzhe: kangzhen jiuzai zhong de zuzhi leixing yu gongneng fenxi' ("Youth volunteers: Analysis of organisational types and functions in the post-earthquake relief effort"), *Zhongguo qingnian yanjiu*, 2008, 10 (October), p. 9.

152 Liang Zhiquan, pp. 10–11. The Internet also helped people find relatives and friends feared harmed.

153 Nan Shan, '"5.12" da dizhen zhong qingnian qunti xingwei fenxi' ("Analysis of youth group actions in the May 12 earthquake"), *Dangdai qingnian yanjiu*, 2008, 8 (August), p. 42.

154 Hu Yinan, 'Heroic youths honored for rescue, relief work,' *China Daily*, 28–9 June 2008, p. 2. For an official book commemorating volunteers, see Communist Youth League Shanghai Committee, Shanghai Youth Literature and Art Association and Youth Work Committee of the Shanghai Propaganda System, *Xin xiang Wenchuan: Shanghai qingnian kangdi jiuzai jishi* (*Hearts towards Wenchuan: record of Shanghai youths' earthquake disaster relief efforts*), Shanghai: Shanghai shudian chubanshe, 2008.

155 Tang Jun, 'Zhiyuanzhe zhuangkuang yanjiu: di 21 jie Shijie daxuesheng yundonghui zhiyuanzhe zhuangkuang diaocha' ("Research on the condition of volunteers: A survey of the condition of volunteers for the Twenty-first World University Student Games"), *Qingnian yanjiu*, 2001, 11 (November), pp. 27–34. Of forty thousand volunteers at the games, fifteen thousand were from directly subordinate organisations (*zhishu*, including sports federations) and twenty-five thousand were 'mobile' (*jidong*) volunteers, who seem closer to Western notions of volunteerism (p. 29).

156 Zhang Zhufu, Bai Zhenyao and Teng Fei, 'Cong tuandui jianshe kan Beijing Aoyun zhiyuanzhe de youxiao guanli' ("Effective management of Beijing Olympic volunteers from the point of view of team building"), *Qingnian tansuo*, 2007, 3 (March), p. 70. Teng Fei was head of the Beijing Normal University Youth Volunteers Association (*qingnian zhiyuanzhe xiehui*).

157 Cui Xiaohuo, 'Help is at hand, as volunteers hit streets,' *China Daily*, 1 July 2008, p. 6.

158 Wu Luping, 'Zhiyuanzhe canyu dongji de jiegou zhuanxing he duoyuan gongsheng xianxiang yanjiu: dui 24 ming qingnian zhiyuanzhe de shendu

fangtan fenxi' ("Research on structural transformation of volunteer participation and motivation and multifarious phenomenon: an analysis of in-depth interviews with twenty-four youth volunteers"), *Zhongguo qingnian yanjiu*, 2008, 2 (February), pp. 5–10.

159 Wu Luping, p. 7.

160 On the pleasure of service, though expressed differently from here, see Wu Luping and Niu Xi, 'Zhiyuanzhe de shouhuo yu kuaile gongxiao yanjiu' ("Research on volunteers' rewards and pleasure effect"), *Zhongguo qingnian yanjiu*, 2008, 2 (February), pp. 11–15. On youth volunteer efforts closer to home, see Shi Xinming, 'Cesuo bu sao, heyi sao tianxia?: cong "Beike daxuesheng qingsao cesuo xiehui" tanqi' ("If the toilet isn't cleaned, how will the world be clean?: Speaking of the 'Beijing University of Science and Technology Students Toilet Cleaning Association'"), *Qingnian yanjiu*, 2001, 4 (April), pp. 38–9.

161 Quoted in Lu Ping and Tan Jie, 'Fei zhiyuanzhe bu canyu zhiyuan huodong de helihua jizhi yanjiu' ("Research on nonvolunteers' rationalization for not participating in volunteer activities"), *Zhongguo qingnian yanjiu*, 2008, 2 (February), p. 26.

162 Shen Jie, 'Beijing qingnian de zhiyuan xingdong canyu yiyuan: yi xiang dui butong qunti zhi jian de bijiao fenxi' ("The volunteer activity participatory aspirations of Beijing youth: A comparative analysis of different groups"), *Beijing qingnian zhengzhi xueyuan xuebao*, 2008, 1 (January), p. 55 (on motivations) and p. 56 (on participation rate).

163 Yang Cong, 'Qianxi wangluo shidai de qingnian yawenhua' ("A preliminary analysis of youth subcultures in the Internet age"), *Zhongguo qingnian zhengzhi xueyuan xuebao*, 2008, 5 (October), p. 55.

164 Yang Cong, p. 56.

165 Wei Tongru and Guo Limin, '2007 nian yilai daxuesheng qunti liuxingyu diaoyan baogao: yi Hebeisheng gaoxiao wei lie' ("Report of an investigation into university student group catchwords since 2007: The example of Hebei tertiary institutions"), *Zhongguo qingnian yanjiu*, 2008, 7 (July), pp. 83–6.

166 Wei Tongru and Guo Limin, pp. 84–5. This was the catch phrase of the thieves' leader, played by comic actor Ge You.

167 Wei Tongru and Guo Limin, pp. 85–6.

168 Cheng Haitao, '"Baling niandai": rang shengming high qilai' ('The '80s decade': Making life 'high'"), *Liaoning qingnian*, 2004, 23 (November), pp. 6–8.

169 Cheng Haitao, p. 7.

170 Cheng Haitao, p. 8.

171 Cheng Haitao, p. 8.

172 Zhong Yibiao, 'Qingshaonian wangluo tongju yawenhua de shehuixue fenxi' ("A sociological analysis of the subculture of young people living together through the Internet"), *Dangdai qingnian yanjiu*, 2006, 3 (March), pp. 8–11.

173 'Virtual pleasures: Cyber-hedonism,' *The Economist*, 7 February 2009, p. 54.

174 See Don Tapscott, *Grown Up Digital: How the Net Generation is Changing Your World*, New York: McGraw-Hill, 2008. Tapscott makes no mention of China in this book.

175 Wang Bin, 'Dazhong wenhua dui qingshaonian yidai de yingxiang' ("The influence of popular culture on a generation of young people"), *Qingnian yanjiu*, 2001, 1 (January), 11, pp. 14–16.

176  Wang Bin, pp. 16–17.

177  Huang Hongji, 'Zai gaige zhong chusheng, zai kaifang zhong chengzhang, zai fazhan zhong chengshu: wei "80 hou" zaoxiang' ("Born in the midst of reform, growing up in opening up, reaching maturity in the midst of development: For a portrait of the 'post-80' generation"), *Shanghai qingnian guanli ganbu xueyuan xuebao (Journal of the Shanghai Youth Management Cadre Academy)*, 2008, 1 (January), p. 8.

178  Karsten Giese, 'Speaker's Corner or Virtual Panopticon: Discursive Construction of Chinese Identities Online,' in Françoise Mengin, ed., *Cyber China: Reshaping National Identities in the Age of Information*, London: Palgrave Macmillan, 2004, pp. 19–36.

179  Chen Longxiang, 'China's *weibo* fever needs to be checked,' *China Daily*, 25 June 2011, p. 6. Microblogs mobilised public opinion forcefully against central and local government regarding a polluting factory in Dalian and a high-speed train crash near Wenzhou in mid-2011, for example.

180  Yu Yiqun and his cowriters note a shift from dependence on the *danwei* to wider concepts of *shequ* (usually translated as neighbourhood or community) in their 2003 article on Beijing youth in the new century: p. 2.

181  Supergirl Li Yuchun (Chris Lee) made her feature film debut in a similar historical epic in 2009, *Bodyguards and Assassins (Shiyue weicheng*, directed by Teddy Chan), a Hong Kong-made commemoration of Sun Yat-sen on a visit to Hong Kong in 1905 which also teems with celebrity actors.

182  The 1989 film was *The Birth of New China (Kaiguo dadian*, directed by Li Qiankuan and Xiao Guiyun). See http://blog.sina.com.cn/s/blog_49c2c43f0100fd20.html (accessed on 25 January 2010) and http://www.tianya.cn/publicforum/content.n004/9e5342599a92300b7ee09ff05831005a/1/0/1.shtml (accessed on 25 January 2010). Other bloggers noted the foreign passports or residences of a long list of the featured actors in the film. See, for example, http://www.tianya.cn/publicforum/content/n004/51120d49cb935f84a834516dcbf9655b/1/0/1.shtml (accessed on 25 January 2010).

183  See, for example, http://www.tianya.cn/publicforum/content/filmtv/1/278726 (accessed on 23 January 2010), http://hi.baidu.com/ghghok/blog/item/395c1c0a82a12e1494ca6b07.html (accessed on 25 January 2010), and, for a fifty-two-year-old's praise of the film's 'national characteristics' (*minzu tese*), which brought a flurry of condemnation from younger posters, see http://tianya.cn/publicforum/content/filmTV/1/279153.shtml (accessed on 23 January 2010).

184  See http://www.tianya.cn/publicforum/content/funinfo/1/1788628.shtml (accessed on 27 January 2010).

185  See for example, http://www.tianya.cn/publicofrum/content/filmtv/1/280488.shtml (accessed by 27 January 2010).

## 6  CONCLUSION: CONSUMING IDENTITIES

1  This new notion of the public perhaps lay behind singer Cui Jian's declaration in a 2001 interview that 'China needs a revolution in self-expression' and should abandon lies and gossip in favor of truth telling: Cui Jian and Zhou Guoping, pp. 150–1.

2  Puccini used the tune for the princess's theme in his *Turandot*, which Zhang Yimou directed in a New York Metropolitan Opera production at the Forbidden City in Beijing in 1998.

3  For a discussion of these themes, though not with a specific focus on youth, see Koichi Iwabuchi, 'Globalization, East Asian Media Cultures and Their Publics,' *Asian Journal of Communication*, 20, 2 (June 2010), 197–212.

4  Jon Savage, p. 465. For a discussion of the tensions between individualist desires and collectivist pressures, see Ian Weber, '*Shanghai Baby*: Negotiating Youth Self-Identity in Urban China,' *Social Identities*, 8, 2 (2002), 347–68.

# Bibliography

A Man, 'Yeshi "changxiaoshu" jingyi ji' (A surprising record of nightime 'bestsellers'), *Fujian qingnian*, 1988, 8 (August), pp. 16–17

Ah Cheng, *Three Kings: Three Stories from Today's China*, translated by Bonnie S. McDougall, London: Collins Harvill, 1990

An Haiyan, 'Wo yongyou zheme fengfu jingcai de jingli, zhen bu zhu lai renshi!' (To have had such a rich and wonderful experience, what a world!), in Liu Xiaomeng, *Zhongguo zhiqing koushushi*, pp. 268–347

Andrews, Julia F., *Painters and Politics in the People's Republic of China, 1949–1979*, Berkeley: University of California Press, 1994

Andrews, Julia F. and Kuiyi Shen, 'The New Chinese Woman and Lifestyle Magazines in the Late 1990s,' in Perry Link, Richard P. Madsen, and Paul G. Pickowicz, eds, *Popular China: Unofficial Culture in a Globalizing Society*, Lanham: Rowman & Littlefield, 2002, pp. 137–62

Anonymous, 'Jiedu xiaoyuan liuxing wangyu' (Deciphering Internet language popular on campus), *Liaoning qingnian*, 2005, 22 (November), pp. 118–19

'Qingjing Hanliu xiji neilu' (Powerful Korean Wave makes a surprise attack on the mainland), *Yinyue shijie (Music World)*, 1999, 12 (December), p. 21

Bai Lingling, 'Piliwu qinggan shijie de jiaoluo' (A corner of the world of break-dancing friendship), *Wudao (Dance)*, 1988, 11 (November), pp. 34–5

Bai Qing, 'Qingnian zhong weishenme liuxing jundaiyi? (Why are military coats fashionable among the young?), *Liaoning qingnian*, 1988, 5 (March), pp. 28–9

Bai Yuandan (South Korea), 'Chuixi Dongya de "Hanliu"' (Pushing East Asia's Korean Wave), *Wenyi lilun yu piping (Literature and Art Theory and Criticism)*, 2002, 1 (January), pp. 85–8

Bakken, Børge, *The Exemplary Society: Human Improvement, Social Control, and the Dangers of Modernity in China*, Oxford: Oxford University Press, 2000

Ban Chengnong, 'Shenmi, shenqi, shenwang: qigong dashi Yan Xin fagong mujiji' (Mysterious, magical, enrapturing: an eyewitness account of a demonstration by *qigong* master Yan Xin), *Qingnian shidai*, 1988, 3 (March), pp. 24–5

Baranovitch, Nimrod, *China's New Voices: Popular Music, Ethnicity, Gender, and Politics, 1978–1997*, Berkeley: University of California Press, 2003.

Barmé, Geremie, *In the Red: On Contemporary Chinese Culture*, New York: Columbia University Press, 1999

Bei Dao, *The August Sleepwalker*, translated by Bonnie S. McDougall, London: Anvil Press Poetry, 1988

Beijing Zhongshi Shengqi Cultural Media Company, ed., *Yu ni zai yiqi: Ma Tianyu tuwen xiezhen ji (Together with You: A Pictorial Portrait of Ma Tianyu)*, Shanghai: Shanghai huabao chubanshe, 2006

Benbao pinglunyuan, 'Kexi de '"Hong gaoliang" xianxiang' (The gratifying '*Red Sorghum* phenomenon'), *Renmin ribao*, 14 September 1988, p. 1

Bennett, Andy and Keith Kahn-Harris, eds, *After Subculture: Critical Studies in Contemporary Youth Culture*, Basingstoke and New York: Palgrave Macmillan, 2004

Bernstein, Thomas P., *Up to the Mountains and Down to the Villages: The Transfer of Youth from Urban to Rural China*, New Haven: Yale University Press, 1977

Bian Dengwei, Wo *shi wang: Li Ning, cong ticao wangzi dao shangjie yingxiong* (I am a King: Li Ning, From Prince of Gymnastics to Business Hero), Beijing: Guangming ribao chubanshe, 1999

Bo Ya, '"Qigong re" xijuan Beida' (*Qigong* fever sweeps through Peking University), *Daxuesheng*, 1988, 6 (June), pp. 34–5

Brownell, Susan, *Training the Body for China: Sports in the Moral Order of the People's Republic*, Chicago: University of Chicago Press, 1995

Cai, Jian 'China's first taste of the Korean Wave,' in *Korean Herald*, ed., pp. 100–8

Cai Qi and Liao Jie, 'Qingshaonian "fensi" xingwei tezheng ji xinli xuqiu kao-cha fenxi' (Investigation into the features of the actions of youthful 'fans' and their psychological needs), *Zhongguo guangbo dianshi xuekan (China Radio and TV Journal)*, 2009, 3 (March), pp. 35–6

Cai Wanlin, 'Shen diandian de "Hong gaoliang"' (Deep galloping *Red Sorghum*), *Zhongguo dianying bao*, 5 May 1988, p. 2

Cao Hongbei, 'Xie Tianxiao: linjie' (Xie Tianxiao: Critical), *Zhongguo xinwen zhoukan (China News Weekly)*, 2005, 46 (December), pp. 62–3

Chan, Anita, Richard P. Madsen, and Jonathan Unger, *Chen Village under Mao and Deng*, Berkeley: University of California Press, 1992

Chen Feng, 'Jiyi de suiyue zai gesheng zhong yongheng: xin Zhongguo gequ chuangzuo licheng huiwang' (Times remembered in song are forever: A look back at the course of song creation in New China), *Gequ (Songs)*, 2005, 4 (April) to 2008, 1 (January)

Chen Jie, 'All dolled up,' *China Daily*, 4 September 2007, p. 18

Chen Jinghuan, 'Zhongguo qingnian zhiyuan fuwu de fazhan yu tese' (The development and characteristics of China's youth volunteerism), *Qingnian tansuo*, 2011, 1 (January), pp. 41–6

Chen Jiuguo and Luo Aiai, 'Hanliu: qingnian de jingshen houhuayuan' (The Korean Wave: The back garden of youth's spirit), *Dangdai qingnian yanjiu*, 2006, 1 (January), pp. 12–14

Chen Kangsheng, '"Qiu-liu wuyi" de "Zhongguo honghong": Nü gexing Wang Hong he jizhe yi xi tan' ('China's Honghong' with 'no interest in coming or going': A snatch of conversation between the female singing star Wang Hong and a journalist), *Qingchun suiyue*, 1988, 7 (July), pp. 26–7

Chen Longxiang, 'China's *weibo* fever needs to be checked,' *China Daily*, 25 June 2011, p. 6

Chen Nan, 'High-voltage action,' *China Daily*, 25 September 2008, p. 13

'Rock for the ages,' *China Daily*, 9 July 2008, p. 18

Chen Qiguang, *Zhongguo dangdai wenxue shi* (History of Contemporary Chinese Literature), Guangzhou: Jinan daxue chubanshe, 1998

Chen Quanzhong, 'Xu Wei yanli de "wanmei shenghuo"' (The 'beautiful life' in Xu Wei's eyes), *Liaoning qingnian*, 2005, 23 (December), pp. 28–29

Chen Shan, '"Tongsu wenxue re": yizhong chengshi wenhua xianxiang' (The 'popular literature fever:' an urban culture phenomenon), *Renmin ribao*, 22 September 1988, p. 5

Chen Shaojian, 'Guoguanzhanjiang de "wu lianguan"' (The 'five successive title' holder overcoming all obstacles), *Qingchun yu shehui*, 1989, 10 (October), pp. 10–11

Chen Si, '2002 nian Beijing gaoxiao liuxingyu zhangkuang diaocha' (Survey of the situation of Beijing tertiary popular language in 2002), *Zhongguo qingnian yanjiu*, 2002, 5 (May), pp. 14–18

Chen Weiyun, 'Tiyu: tianshen de huanyue' (Sport: A divine rejoicing), *Daxuesheng*, 1988, 10 (October), pp. 36–8

Chen Yuanyuan and others, 'Man yi qingnian liuxing yuyan' (Youth popular language rich in meaning), *Zhongguo qingnian zhengzhi xueyuan xuebao* (*Journal of the China Youth University for Political Sciences*), 2003, 3 (June), pp. 26–31

Chen Zhi, 'Lüelun wangluohua dui qingshaonian shehuihua de yingxiang' (A brief discussion of the influence of Internet-ization on young people's social-ization), *Fujian shifan daxue xuebao (zhexue sheui kexue ban)* (*Journal of Fujian Normal University, Philosophy and Social Sciences Edition*), 2003, 3 (June), pp. 141–6

Chen Zufen, 'Wang Shuo he wenhua jingji: fang Wan Shuo tan zuojia xiahai' (Wang Shuo and the cultural economy: Wang Shuo talks about writers enter-ing the market economy), *Beijing qingnian*, 1993, 11 (November), p. 41

Chen Zui, *Luoti yishu lun* (*On Nude Art*), Beijing: Zhongguo wenyi chubanshe, 1987

Cheng Dizhao, 'Laizi guangkuo tiandi de zhandou yishu: xikan wosheng nong-ken xitong zhishi qingnian yeyu wenyi chuangzuo jiemu diaoyan' (Art from the vast, all-embracing struggle: Joy at watching the amateur literature and art creative programme performances of the educated youth of our prov-ince's agricultural reclamation system), *Yunnan wenyi* (*Yunnan Literature and Art*), 1975, 2 (February), pp. 69–71

Chengdu Shude High School, Class 8 of Class of 2004 Survey Group, 'Guanyu Ri-Han wenhua dui Chengdu zhongxuesheng yingxiang de diaocha' (Survey of the influence of Japanese and Korean culture of Chengdu high schoolers), *Qingnian yanjiu*, 2002, 10 (October), pp. 33–9

Cheng Haitao, '"Baling niandai": rang shengming high qilai' ('The '80s decade': Making life 'high'), *Liaoning qingnian*, 2004, 23 (November), pp. 6–8

Cheng Qijin, 'Hanliu qinxi: guochanju lianhong' (The Korean Wave sneak attack: Local dramas embarrassed), *Xinwen zhoukan* (*News Weekly*), 24 June 2002, p. 76

Cheng Yun, 'Zhongguo dangdai tongsu yinyue huanshilu' (A comprehensive view of popular songs in contemporary China), *Renmin yinyue*, 1988, 2 (February), pp. 2–6

China Filmmakers Association, ed., 'Zhumu "Hong gaoliang"' (Looking at Red Sorghum), Dianying yishu (Film Art), 1988, 4 (August), pp. 3–10

Chu Weihua, Liu Chaoxia, and Wang Yilin, 'Zhongguo daxuesheng yu "Hanliu": guanyu "Hanliu" de diaocha fenxi baogao' (Chinese college students and the Korean Wave: An analytical report on a survey of the Korean Wave), Zhongguo qingnian zhengzhi xueyuan xuebao, 2003, 7 (July), pp. 11–17

Chun Xiao, 'Shei ba Abao tuixiang le wutai?' (Who pushed Abao onto the stage?), Liaoning qingnian, 2007, 7A (July), pp. 4–6

Clark, Paul, Chinese Cinema: Culture and Politics since 1949, New York: Cambridge University Press, 1987

The Chinese Cultural Revolution: A History, New York: Cambridge University Press, 2008

'Closely watched viewers: A taxonomy of Chinese film audiences from 1949 to the Cultural Revolution seen from Hunan,' Journal of Chinese Cinemas, 5, 1 (2011), pp. 73–89

'Ethnic minorities in Chinese films: Cinema and the exotic,' East-West Film Journal, 1, 2 (1987), pp. 15–31

'Model Theatrical Works and the Remodelling of the Cultural Revolution,' in Richard King, ed., Art in Turmoil: The Chinese Cultural Revolution 1966–1976, Vancouver: UBC Press, 2010, pp. 167–87

Reinventing China: A Generation and Its Films, Hong Kong: Chinese University Press, 2005

Communist Youth League Shanghai Committee, Shanghai Youth Literature and Art Association and Youth Work Committee of the Shanghai Propaganda System, Xin xiang Wenchuan: Shanghai qingnian kangdi jiuzai jishi (Hearts towards Wenchuan: record of Shanghai youths' earthquake disaster relief efforts), Shanghai: Shanghai shudian chubanshe, 2008

Cui Jian and Zhou Guoping, Ziyou fengge (Freestyle), Guilin: Guangxi shifan daxue chubanshe, 2001

Cui Xiaohuo, 'Help is at hand, as volunteers hit streets,' China Daily, 1 July 2008, p. 6

D. W., '"Hong gaoliang" shi chouhua Zhongguoren de yingpian' (Red Sorghum is a film which uglifies the Chinese), Zhongguo dianying bao, 5 May 1988, p. 2

Da Peng, 'Zouhao, Zhongguo yaogun' (Good bye, Chinese rock), Guoji yinyue jiaoliu (International Music Exchange), 2001, 1 (January), p. 133

Daxue meng yuan Editorial Board, Daxue meng yuan: wode 1977, 1978 (University Dream Fulfilled), Yinchuan: Ningxia renmin chubanshe, 2005

Dai Jiafang, 'Wutuobang li de aige: "Wen-ge" qijian zhiqing gequ de yanjiu' (Mournful songs in Utopia: Research on educated youth songs in the Cultural Revolution), Zhongguo yinyuexue (Musicology in China), 2002, 3 (September), pp. 5–25

de Kloet, Jeroen, China with a Cut: Globalisation, Urban Youth and Popular Music, Amsterdam: Amsterdam University Press, 2010

'Popular Music and Youth in Urban China: The Dakou Generation,' The China Quarterly, 183 (September 2005), pp. 609–26

Deng Xian, Zhongguo zhiqing zhongjie (The End of Chinese Educated Youth), Beijing: Renmin wenxue chubanshe, 2003

Dikötter, Frank, Sex, Culture and Modernity in China: Medical Science and the Construction of Sexual Identities in the Early Republican Period, Honolulu: University of Hawaii Press, 1995

Ding Li, '*Cong "Dongji linage" kan wenhua "Hanliu"*' (Looking at the cultural Korean Wave from *Winter Sonata*), *Dangdai dianshi (Contemporary TV)*, 2005, 8 (August), pp. 64–5

Ding Nan, '*Beijing you ge yaogun qingnian wutuobang*' (There's a rock youth Utopia in Beijing), *Baixing (Common People)*, 2001, 5 (May), pp. 26–7

Ding Yizhuang, *Zhongguo zhiqing shi: chulan (1953–1968) (History of China's Educated Youth: First Wave 1953–1968)*, Beijing: Zhongguo shehui kexue chubanshe, 1998

Dong Changdi,'*Jiedu "90 hou" wangmin "huoxing wen" xianxiang*' (Deciphering the phenomenon of 'Martian language' used by ''90s generation' netizens), *Shanxi qingnian guanli ganbu xueyuan xuebao (Journal of the Shanxi Youth Management Cadre Institute)*, 2008, 1 (January), pp. 24–7

Dong Dayong, '*Cong gouhe zongheng de huang tudi shang qifei*' (Flying out of the yellow earth criss-crossed by ravines), *Renmin yinyue*, 1989, 3 (March), pp. 18–19

Dongfang chuban zhongxin, ed., *Wode qiqi, qiba (My '77 and '78)*, Shanghai: Dongfang chuban zhongxin, 2008

Dong Qiangsheng, '*Ai, "Mai hua guniang"!*' (Ah, *The Flower Seller*!), in Shi Xiaoyan, ed., *Beidahuang fengyunlu (Trials and Tribulations on the Great Northern Wasteland)*, Beijing: Zhongguo qingnian chubanshe, 1990, pp. 449–50

Dong Weilong, 'Xiaoyuan liuxing qu xunli' (A tour of campus popular music), *Qingnian yanjiu*, 1989, 10 (October), pp. 38–9, 17

Du Jinyan, 'Q-ban: jiti moqi de yawenhua' (Q: A collective secret pact subculture), *Qingnian yanjiu*, 2006, 9 (September), pp. 10–15

Du Tianlin, 'Nanwang de qinghuai: xiaxiang biji' (Unforgettable feelings: Notes on going to the villages), in Zhang Qi, ed., *Mo bu qu de jiyi: lao sanjie, xin san ji (Unerasable Memories: Old Three Classes, New Three Third Class)*, Beijing: Zhonggong dangshi chubanshe, 2009, pp. 81–91

Duan Detian, '*Anxian bu "an"*' (An county is not "safe" as its name suggests), in Yang Zhiyun and others, eds, *Zhiqing dang'an, 1962–1979: Zhishi qingnian shangshan xiaxiang jishi (Educated Youth Archive, 1962–1979: Records of Educated Youth Going up to the Mountains and Down to the Villages)*, Chengdu: Sichuan wenyi chubanshe, 1992, pp. 370–5

Duan Ruizhong, 'Gongji "Huangtu gaopo"' (Attacking 'The Hills of Yellow Earth'), *Renmin yinyue*, 1989, 3 (March) pp. 30–1

Duan Zhishu, '*Yi ben "huang" shu*' (A "yellow" book), in Shi Xiaoyan, *Trials and Tribulations on the Great Northern Wasteland*, pp. 324–5

Fan Chao, 'Hanliu chongdong yu Xibu "hua" wen' (The Korean Wave excitement and Western Region 'culture'), *Xin Xibu (New West)*, 2005, 12 (December), p. 51

Fan Guo'an and Niu Xiufen, 'Gechang ba "Ge tihu"' (Sing 'Song Nirvana'), *Ba xiaoshi yiwai*, 1988, 3 (May), pp. 15–16

Fan Lei, 'Beijing daxuesheng tan Aoyunhui shili' (Beijing university students discuss the Olympic Games setbacks), *Daxuesheng*, 1988, 11 (November), pp. 8–10

Fang Guangsheng, *Hongweibing Changzheng riji (Red Guard Long March Diary)*, Hong Kong: Zhongguo xinwen chubanshe, 2004

Fang Wei, '89' Zhongguo xiandai yishu dachao' (The modern art wave in 1989), *Qingchun suiyue*, 1989, 6 (June), pp. 30–2

Farquhar, Mary, *Children's Literature in China: From Lu Xun to Mao Zedong*, Armonk: M.E. Sharpe, 1999

Farrer, James C., *Opening Up: Youth Sex Culture and Market Reform in Shanghai*, Chicago: University of Chicago Press, 2002

Feng Qiuchang, 'Tongsu wenxue de shenmei tezheng' (The aesthetic features of popular literature), *Renmin ribao*, 11 October 1988, p. 5

Feng Xiaotian, 'Chengshi zaizhi qingnian de wangluo jiechu: quanguo 12 chengshi 1786 ming zaizhi qingnian de diaocha fenxi' (Urban employed youth's contact with the Internet: Analysis of a nationwide 12-city, 1,786-person survey of employed youth), *Zhongguo qingnian yanjiu*, 2007, 12 (December), pp. 47–51

Feng Zhicheng, 'Zhiqing geyao' (Educated youth ballads), in Yang Zhiyun, *Educated Youth Archive*, pp. 360–7

Finnane, Antonia, *Changing Clothes in China: Fashion, History, Nation*, New York: Columbia University Press, 2008

Fu Yinchu, 'Tan "Huangtu re"' (On the Yellow Earth craze), *Renmin yinyue*, 1989, 2 (February), p. 27

Galikowski, Maria, *Art and Politics in China, 1949–1984*, Hong Kong: The Chinese University Press, 1998

Gamble, Jos, *Shanghai in Transition: Changing Perspectives and Social Contours of a Chinese Metropolis*, Richmond: Curzon, 2003

Gan Tian, 'Caught in the net,' *China Daily*, 25 June 2009, p. 18

Gao Bo, *Wang Shuo: Dashi haishi pizi (Wang Shuo: Great Master or Rogue?)*, Beijing: Beijing Yanshan chubanshe, 1993

Gao Fusheng, 'Yeah! Liu Xiang "pao" jin xiaoxue keben' (Yeah! Liu Xiang has 'run' into primary school textbooks), *Liaoning qingnian*, 2005, 8 (April), p. 25

Gao Jun, 'Lieqi: xiandai chengshi guanzhong xinli guankui' (Chasing novelty: The narrow psychology of modern city audiences), *Dazhong dianying*, 1988, 9 (September), pp. 12–13

Gao Youpeng, 'Guanyu "Wen'ge" shiqi de minjian wenxue wenti' (On the question of Cultural Revolution period folk literature), *Henan daxue xuebao (shehui kexue ban) (Henan University Journal: Social Science Edition)*, 1999, 2 (March), 27–30

Gao Zhiguo, 'Liu Xiang guanggao shouru fenpei mingdan lou le shui' (Who is revealed by the list of names of the revenue from Liu Xiang's advertisements), *Liaoning qingnian*, 2004, 24 (December), p. 22

Garside, Roger, *Coming Alive: China after Mao*, New York: McGraw-Hill, 1981

Ge Hongbing and Zhu Lidong, eds, *Wang Shuo yanjiu ziliao*, Tianjin: Tianjin renmin chubanshe, 2005

Gelder, Ken, ed., *The Subcultures Reader (Second Edition)*, London and New York: Routledge, 2005

Giese, Karsten, 'Speaker's Corner or Virtual Panopticon: Discursive Construction of Chinese Identities Online,' in Françoise Mengin, ed., *Cyber China: Reshaping National Identities in the Age of Information*, London: Palgrave Macmillan, 2004, pp. 19–36

Gold, Thomas B., 'Youth and the State,' *The China Quarterly*, 127 (September 1991), 594–612

Gong, Hong-yu, 'Missionaries, reformers, and the beginnings of Western music in late imperial China (1839–1911),' Ph.D. thesis in Asian Studies, The University of Auckland, 2006

Gong Xingqiong, 'Zai "Mengxiang" de beihou: dui xuanxiulei dianshi yule jiemu de pipanxing jiedu' (Behind the 'Dream': A critical deciphering of talent contest television entertainment programs), *Hubei jiaoyu xueyuan xuebao* (*Journal of Hubei Institute of Education*), 2007, 1 (January), pp. 41–3

Guqiguaishou ['Strange Monster'], *Chuncui shaonian* (*Pure Teenager*), Beijing: Taihai chubanshe, 2001

Gu Tu, 'Cong "Yiwusuoyou" shuodao yaogunyue: Cui Jian de zuopin weishenme shou huanying' (Speaking of rock music from 'Nothing to My Name': Why are Cui Jian's works so popular?), *Renmin ribao*, 16 July 1988, p. 7

'Guanyu xuanxiu jiemu de suiji diaocha' (Random survey regarding talent shows), *Qingnian jizhe* (*Youth Reporter*), 2006, 17 (September), pp. 26–7

Gui Qingshan, '"Hanliu" xianxiang de wenhua shenshi' (A cultural examination of the Korean Wave phenomenon), *Dianying yishu*, 2002, 6 (November), pp. 52–4, 45

Guo Dong, 'Zhongguo yaogun gouchen' (The sinking of Chinese rock), *Qingnian xuebao*, 1995, 2 (Summer), pp. 16–19

Guo Facai, *Jiasuo yu benpao: 1980–2005 Zhongguo yaogun yue duli wenhua shengtai guancha* (Chains and running: An independent survey of the cultural ecology of China's rock music, 1980–2005), Wuhan: Hubei Changjiang chuban jituan, 2007

Guo Fengrun, 'Getan jingchui "Xibeifeng"' (The Northwest Wind blows hard in song circles), *Ba xiaoshi yiwai*, 1988, 6 (November), pp. 54–5

Guo Yuhua, 'Guanyu qigong de youlü' (On worries about *qigong*), *Daxuesheng* (*Campus Life*), 1988, 10 (October), pp. 15–16

Han Han, *Han Han zuopinji* (*Han Han: Collected Works*), Beijing: Shijie zhishi chubanshe, 2006

Han Renjun, *Erzi Han Han* (*My Son Han Han*), Shanghai: Shanghai renmin chubanshe, 2000

Han Weijuan, '"Hanliu" heyi xijuan nianqing nüxing (How has the Korean Wave engulfed young women?), *Zhongguo dianshi*, 2008, 6 (June), pp. 33–6

Han Xianzhou, 'Cong Internet de fazhan kan qingnian wenti' (Looking at youth issues from the development of the Internet), *Zhongguo qingnian zhengzhi xueyuan xuebao*, 1999, 4 (August), pp. 33–6

Han Xiuqing, '*Yinwei ni meiyou cuo!*' (Because you did not do wrong!), in Shi Xiaoyan, *Trials and Tribulations on the Great Northern Wasteland*, pp. 451–2

Han Yinghong, '"Xibeifeng daodi neng gua duojiu' (How long can the Northwest Wind really keep blowing), *Renmin yinyue*, 1988, 12 (December), pp. 20–1

Hansson, Anders, 'The Return of Yellow Music,' *CHIME Journal*, 16/17 (2005), pp. 148–79

Harding, Harry, *China's Second Revolution: Reform after Mao*, Washington, D.C.: The Brookings Institution, 1987

He Ren, 'Jinqiu shijie jiali huiqu Yangcheng, woguo jiang xuanchu shi daming mo' (China's ten top models are chosen at a beautiful gathering in autumnal Guangzhou), *Ba xiaoshi yiwai* (*Beyond Eight Hours*), 1988, 4 (July), p. 57

*Heilongjiang ribao* (*Heilongjiang Daily*), Harbin, 1968–1976

Howard, Keith, ed., *Korean Pop Music: Riding the Wave*, Folkstone: Global Oriental, 2006

Hu Ke and Hou Xiaofeng, 'He qingnian pengyou tan piliwu' (Talking with young friends about breakdancing), *Dazhong dianying*, 1988, 4 (April), p. 17

Hunan dianying faxing fangying gongsi (Hunan film distribution and projection company), *Yingpian [changpian jiemu] pianming paicibiao* (Films [feature length] title list), Changsha, 1978

Hu Sisheng, 'Zhiyin zhi lian: ji Cheng Lin, Hou Dejian de xiangshi, xiangzhi he xianglian' (Music lovers: The meeting, acquaintance and love between Cheng Lin and Hou Dejian), *Ba xiaoshi yiwai*, 1988, 1 (January), pp. 36–9

Hu Yinan, 'Heroic youths honored for rescue, relief work,' *China Daily*, 28–29 June 2008, p. 2

Hua'er yuedui, 'Xishuashua' (song), *Liaoning qingnian*, 2006, 3 (February), inside front cover

Huang Hailiang and Luo Anyuan, 'Wangluo "fensi" wenhua shequ chuanbo jizhi chutan' (A first exploration of broadcast mechanisms of Internet fan cultural communities), *Chongqing jiaoyu xueyuan xuebao* (*Journal of the Chongqing Education Academy*), 2007, 1 (January), pp. 80–2

Huang Hongji, 'Zai gaige zhong chusheng, zai kaifang zhong chengzhang, zai fazhan zhong chengshu: wei "80 hou" zaoxiang' (Born in the midst of reform, growing up in opening up, reaching maturity in the midst of development: For a portrait of the 'post-'80' generation), *Shanghai qingnian guanli ganbu xueyuan xuebao* (*Journal of the Shanghai Youth Management Cadre Academy*), 2008, 1 (January), pp. 6–8

Huang Liaoyuan and others, eds, *Shi nian: 1986–1996 Zhongguo liuxing yinyue jishi* (Ten years: Chronicle of Chinese popular music, 1986–1996), Beijing: Zhongguo dianying chubanshe, 1997

Huang Rongzan, 'Liuxing gequ sikao: yinyue wenhua yao zhuyi "shengtai pingheng"' (Reflections on in vogue music: Musical culture must pay attention to 'ecological balance'), *Renmin yinyue*, 1989, 10 (October), pp. 34–6

Huang Ruixu, 'Seqing chongjibo: yinhui wupin yu qingshaonian zuicuo' (A pornographic shockwave: Obscene goods and youngsters' criminal errors), *Qingnian yanjiu*, 1989, 4 (April), pp. 33–8

Huang Shaohua, 'Qingshaonian wangmin de wangluo jiaowang jiegou' (Young netizens' Internet communication structures), *Lanzhou daxue xuebao (shehui kexue ban)*, 2009, 1 (January), pp. 70–8

Huang Xianguo, 'Zagan yu qingtian pili' (Random thoughts on sunny day break-dancing), *Wudao*, 1988, 11 (November), p. 36

Huang, Yibing, *Contemporary Chinese Literature: From the Cultural Revolution to the Future*, New York: Palgrave Macmillan, 2007

Huang Zhaocun, 'Nanguo getan shuangxing: Tang Biao yu An Li' (Twin stars of the southern song stage: Tang Biao and An Li), *Guangzhou wenyi* (*Guangzhou Literature and Art*), 1989, 4 (April), pp. 46–9

Huo Tong, 'Jita guanjun getihu' (Award-winning guitar entrepreneur), *Qingchun suiyue*, 1988, 9 (September), pp. 7–8

Iwabuchi, Koichi, 'Globalization, East Asian Media Cultures and Their Publics,' *Asian Journal of Communication*, 20, 2 (June 2010), pp. 197–212

Ji Qiufa, 'Qingshaonian xuesheng shiyong wangluo de shizheng yanjiu' (Research on the concrete evidence of young people's use of the Internet), *Beijing qingnian zhengzhi xueyuan xuebao*, 2003, 2 (June), pp. 17–27

Jian Mei, 'Zhongguo potianhuang: Beijing mote'er fengbo suxie' (Unprecedented in China: Notes on the model storm in Beijing), *Daxuesheng*, 1989, 3 (March), pp. 18–24

Jiang Ni, *Wang Shuo mima: jiekai Wang Shuo 'chenggong' zhi mi* (*The Wang Shuo Code: Solving the Riddle of the Wang Shuo 'Success'*), Beijing: Zhongguo Sanxia chubanshe, 2007

Jiang Xiaoyu, 'Bu zhenshi cai tongku: Cui Jian tan zhenchang yundong (If it's not real it's a pain: Cui Jian on the 'live sound' movement), *Beijing jishi* (*Beijing Events*), 2005, 9 (September), pp. 20–3

Jiang, Yarong and David Ashley, eds, *Mao's Children in the New China: Voices from the Red Guard Generation*, London: Routledge, 2000

Jiang Yun, 'Wode dipan wo zuo zhu: shixi shouji dui qingshaonian siyu jinagou de yingxiang' (I'm master of my territory: A preliminary analysis of the influence of cellphones on the construction of young people's personal space), *Qingnian yanjiu*, 2006, 1 (January), pp. 16–23

Jiao Runming, 'Cong "wenhua shan" xianxiang tanjiu qingnina liuxing wenhua de fazhan' (Exploration of the development of youth popular culture from the 'slogan T-shirt' phenomenon), *Qingnian yanjiu*, 1992, 4 (April), pp. 7–12

Jiao Yongfu, 'Liuxing gequ he wenhua shichang' (Popular music and the culture marketplace), *Renmin ribao*, 25 January 1989, p. 8

Jie Cheng, 'Laoshan "qigongshi"' ('*Qigong* master' in the deep mountains), *Qingchun suiyue*, 1988, 6 (June), pp. 16–17

Jin Dalu, 'Chen Pixian, Cao Diqiu deng fandui Hongweibing da chuanlian de taidu he jucuo' (The attitudes and actions of Chen Pixian and Cao Diqiu against the Red Guard great 'establishing ties' movement), *Qingnian yanjiu*, 2010, 3 (June), pp. 77–87

    ed., *Kunnan yu fengliu: 'lao sanjie' ren de daolu (xiudingban)* (Difficulties and distinction: The road of members of the 'old three classes': revised edition), Shanghai: Shanghai shehui kexueyuan chubanshe, 2008

    'Shanghai Hongweibing waichu da chuanlian' (Shanghai Red Guard going out to establish ties), *Qingnian yanjiu*, 2008, 2 (February), pp. 40–9; Part Two, 2008, 4 (April), pp. 26–35

    'Shanghai jiedai waishengshi Hongweibing de san ge tezheng' (Three characteristics of Shanghai's receiving of Red Guards from other provinces and cities), *Qingnian yanjiu*, 2005, 12 (December), pp. 32–8

    'Shanghai jiedai waishengshi Hongweibing de wu ge jieduan' (Five periods in Shanghai's receiving of Red Guards from other provinces and cities), *Qingnian yanjiu*, 2005, 9 (September), pp. 42–8

Jin Dalu and Jin Guangyao, eds, *Zhongguo zhishi qingnian shangshanxiaxiang yanjiu wenji* (*Collected Research on China's Educated Youth Going to the Mountains and to the Villages*), Shanghai: Shanghai shehui kexue chubanshe, 2009, three volumes

Jin Jianguo, '"'Wanzhong' xianxiang", "Wang Shuo dianying" jiyu wenti' (The issue of favorable circumstances in the '*Evening Bell* phenomenon' and 'Wang Shuo films'), *Qingnian yu shehui*, 1989, 6 (June), pp. 15–16

*Jinwan bao*, 'Woguo getan "Xibeifeng" zheng jing: cong mofang zhengzha er chu, zhao zhenzheng Zhongguo qipai' (The Northwest Wing in China's song circles is really strong: From struggling to imitate to seeking a genuinely Chinese proud style), reprinted in *Huhehaote wanbao*, 28 July 1988, p. 3

Jin Zhaojun, 'Cui Jian yu Zhongguo yaogunyue' (Cui Jian and China's rock music), *Renmin yinyue*, 1989, 4 (April), pp. 32–3

    'Feng cong nali lai?: ping getan "Xibeifeng"' (Where is the wind from?: On the Northwest Wing in song circles), *Renmin ribao*, 23 August 1988, p. 5

'Feng xiang hefang qu?: ping "Xibeifeng" zhi houguo' (Where has the wind gone?: A critique of the aftermath of the Northwest Wind), *Renmin ribao*, 24 May 1989, p. 8

Jin Zhongqiang, 'Cong kaobeishu kan dangqian dianying taishi' (The present-day film situation from the point of view of the number of copies), *Dazhong dianying (Popular Film)*, 1989, 1 (January), pp. 2–3

Jing Fang, *Wo shi 60 hou (1969–1979)* (I am the Sixties generation, 1969–1978), Beijing: Xinxing chubanshe, 2010

Jing Yongli, 'Mo rang xuesheng shouji biancheng shoulei' (Don't let students' hand phones become hand grenades), *Liaoning qingnian*, 2005, 23 (November), p. 26

Jing Yuan, 'Cong wangluo zhengyou kan dangdai qingnian de zeou biaozhun: dui "Wo ai Nankai" BBS queqiaoban neirong fenxi' (How Internet personal adverts reveal contemporary youth's mate selection criteria: Examining the contents of the matchmaking site on the 'I love Nankai' BBS), *Qingnian yanjiu*, 2007, 2 (February), pp. 9–16

Jing Yufeng, 'Xiaoyuan liuxing ge ji qita' (Popular songs and other matters on campus), *Qingnian yu shehui*, 1988, 1 (January), p. 39

Jones, Andrew F., *Like a Knife: Ideology and Genre in Contemporary Chinese Popular Music*, Ithaca: Cornell East Asia Series, 1992

Ke Jun, 'Qigong re yu guominxing' (*Qigong* fever and national characteristics), *Huhehaote wanbao*, 17 April 1989, p. 3

Ke Xiaowei, *Dangdai Beijing can-yin shihua* (*Contemporary Beijing Food and Drink History*), Beijing: Dangdai Zhongguo chubanshe, 2009

Kong, Shuyu, '*Big Shot from Beijing*: Feng Xiaogang's *He Sui Pian* and Contemporary Chinese Commercial Film,' *Asian Cinema*, 14, 1 (Spring/Summer 2003), pp. 175–87

  *Consuming Literature: Best Sellers and the Commercialization of Literary Production in Contemporary China*, Stanford: Stanford University Press, 2005

Korean Herald, ed., *Korean Wave*, Seoul: Jimoondang, 2008

Kurlansky, Mark, *1968: The Year That Shook the World*, New York: Ballantine, 2004

Lan Baogang and Gu Qing, '"Zhong-Yi zhi zhan," Shenyang qiupiao fengchao' (The 'China-Iran battle,' Shenyang sports ticket unrest), *Liaoning qingnian (Liaoning Youth)*, 1989, 18 (September), pp. 4–7

Lan Chunhui, 'Liu Xiang: yong zixin, pinbo, yongqi aozhan shijie tiantan' (Liu Xiang: Taking on world athletics with confidence, courage and with all his might), *Liaoning qingnian*, 2004, 19 (October), pp. 6–8

Lan Jun and Lu Huiju, 'You wangluo sousuo redian yinfa de sikao: laizi san ge zhuming wangzhan sousuo paihangbang de diaocha baogao' (Thoughts arising from the hottest Internet searches: A report on an investigation of the frequency order of searches on three prominent websites), *Zhongguo qingnian yanjiu*, December 2003, pp. 19–22

Latham, Kevin, 'SMS, communication, and citizenship in China's information society,' *Critical Asian Studies*, 39, 2 (2007), pp. 295–314

Lei Fan, '"Luokesaite" menghuan Beijing' (Roxette dream in Beijing), *Beijing qingnian*, 1995, 4 (April), pp. 20–3

Lei Ming, 'Pili: zai Shancheng penfa' (Breakdance: Gushes in Guiyang), *Qingnian shidai*, 1988, 7 (July), inside front cover

Lei Yi and Shi Yun, 'Kuangre, huanmie, pipan: "Wen'ge" 10 nian qingnian sichao chutan' (Fanatical, disillusioned, criticized: A first exploration of youth ideological trends in the Cultural Revolution ten years), *Qingnian yanjiu* (*Youth Research*), 1991, 2 (February), 30–5

Li Caijiao, 'Qingnian yu fushi xianxiang guanxi yanjiu' (Research on the relations between youth and fashion phenomena), *Zhongguo qingnian yanjiu*, 2007, 4 (April), pp. 21–6

Li Erwei, 'Zhao Jiping: huang tudi shang de fanggezhe' (Zhao Jiping: Loud singer on the yellow earth), *Dianying yishu*, 1994, 1 (January), pp. 16–22, 53

Li Fanzhuo, 'Hip-hop wenhua zai qingshaonian zhong de liuxingxing fenxi' (Analysis of the popularity of hip-hop culture among the young), *Qingnian yanjiu*, 2004, 6 (June), pp. 29–33

Li Hongbin, 'Zhongguo "renti chao"' (China's 'nude upsurge'), *Qingnian yu shehui* (*Youth and Society*), 1989, 7 (July), p. 47

Li Hongjie, ed., *Zhongguo yaogun shouce* (*Encyclopedia of China Rock & Roll*), Chongqing: Chongqing chubanshe, 2006

Li Houji, 'Chou yu, mei yu?! "Hong gaoliang" guan hou' (Ugly or beautiful?!: After watching *Red Sorghum*), *Tianjin ribao*, 15 August 1988, p. 5

Li Li, 'Yi pi zhongqingnian zuojia jinjun yingshi jie, Haima yingshe chuangzuo zhongxin zai Jing chengli' (A group of middle-aged and young writers advance on film and TV circles, the Seahorse Film and Television Creative Centre is established in Beijing), *Renmin ribao*, 12 January 1989, p. 3

Li Luxin, *Liuxing gequ: dangdai qingnian de jiayuan* (*Popular Songs: Homeland of Contemporary Youth*), Beijing: Huaxia chubanshe, 1993

Li Ronghua, 'Qingnian "boke wenhua" de jiegou yu jiangou' (The deconstruction and construction of youth 'blog culture'), *Dangdai qingnian yanjiu*, 2007, 1 (January), pp. 13–16

Li Runxia, '*Lun "Baiyangdian shiqun" de wenhua tezheng*' (On the cultural characteristics of the 'Baiyangdian poetry group') in Jin Dalu and Jin Guangyao, *Collected Research on China's Educated Youth*, pp. 388–98

Li Shenzhi, 'Zhongguo: yijiubaba' (China: 1988), *Dangdai qingnian yanjiu* (*Contemporary Youth Research*), 1989, 2 (March), pp. 41–3
'Zhongguo: yijiubaba (*xu*)' (China: 1988, part two), *Dangdai qingnian yanjiu* (*Contemporary Youth Research*), 1989, 3 (May), pp. 46–8

Li Shui, 'Liu Zaifu tan dianying' (Liu Zaifu on films), *Dazhong dianying*, 1988, 10 (October), pp. 8–9

Li Tao, 'Dui goujian qingshaonian wangluo lunli jingshen de sikao' (Reflection on the cultivation of young people's ethical spirit on the Internet), *Zhongguo qingnian zhengzhi xueyuan xuebao*, 2002, 2 (February), pp. 22–5

Li Tianyi, 'Tongsu gequ heyuan luoru digu' (How did popular music fall to such a low ebb?), *Renmin yinyue*, 1989, 11 (November), pp. 26–7

Li Tong, '"Hong gaoliang" xixing' (*Red Sorghum*'s westward travels), *Renmin ribao*, 13 March 1988, p. 5
'Huode shuzhan xie, paide satuo xie: fang Zhang Yimou' (Living more cheerfully, filming more freely: An interview with Zhang Yimou), *Renmin ribao*, 16 January 1988, p. 8

Li Xin, 'Xi'an diqu yaogunyue de chubu kaocha' (A preliminary survey of rock music in the Xi'an region), *Jiaoxiang: Xi'an yinyue xueyuan xuebao* (*Symphony: Journal of the Xi'an Conservatory of Music*), 19, 4 (December 2000), pp. 74–7

Li Yiming, '"Hanliu" zou zai dalu shang' (The Korean Wave moves on the mainland), *Dazhong dianying*, 2003, 4 (February), p. 17

Li Yuqi, '1966–1967 "da chuanlian" fengchao shimo' (The ins and outs of the 'great establishing ties' tide, 1966–1967), *Zhongguo qingnian yanjiu*, 1994, 3 (May), pp. 29–32

'1966–1967 "da chuanlian" lishi fansi' (Historical reflection on the 'great establishing ties,' 1966–1967), *Zhongguo qingnian yanjiu*, 1994, 5/6 (October), pp. 54–7

'1966–1967 "da chuanlian" qunsheng zhutai' (Popular characteristics of the 'great establishing ties,' 1966–1967), *Zhongguo qingnian yanjiu*, 1994, 4 (July), pp. 35–7

Li Yueyun, 'Huaichuai yi ke "Zhongguo xin"' (Carrying a 'Chinese heart'), *Qingnian yu shehui*, 1989, 3 (March), pp. 10–11

'Yaogun gexing Sun Guoqing' (Rock song star Sun Guoqing), *Qingnian yu shehui*, 1989, 1 (January), pp. 16–17

Lian Weiqing, 'Chaoji nüsheng : Qingnian wenhua xin tezheng fenxi' (*Supergirl*: Analysis of the new features of youth culture), *Dangdai qingnian yanjiu*, 2006, 3 (March), pp. 13–15

Liao Ye, 'Zai kaifang de chaoliu zhongqiu fazhan: dui woguo tongsu yinyue chuangzuo wenti de sikao' (Developing in the currents of opening up: Thoughts on the issue of popular music creation in China), *Renmin ribao*, 5 January 1988, p. 5

Lin Qi, 'Show takes turn for the worse,' *China Daily*, 5 July 2010, p. 2

Lin Yafei, Qi Aihua and Ouyang Qinghua, 'Ningbo qingshaonian wangluo xingwei diaocha' (An investigation into online behaviour among young people in Ningbo), *Nongbo guangbo dianshi daxue xuebao* (*Journal of Ningbo Radio and Television University*), 2006, 4 (September), pp. 13–20

Lin Yingying, 'Daxuesheng wotan xianxiang toushi' (Perspective on the phenomenon of university student bed chatting), *Qingnian tansuo*, 2008, 3 (May), pp. 87–90

Ling Xuan, '"Xibeifeng" yu "qiuge"' (Northwest Wind and 'convict songs'), *Renmin yinyue*, 1989, 5 (May), pp. 37–8

Link, Perry, 'Hand-Copied Entertainment Fiction from the Cultural Revolution,' in Perry Link, Richard P. Madsen, and Paul G. Pickowicz, eds, *Unofficial China: Popular Culture and Thought in the People's Republic*, Boulder: Westview, 1989, pp. 17–36

*The Uses of Literature: Life in the Socialist Literary System*, Princeton: Princeton University Press, 2000

Link, Perry, Richard P. Madsen, and Paul G. Pickowicz, eds, *Popular China: Unofficial Culture in a Globalizing Society*, Lanham: Rowman & Littlefield, 2002

Liu Haiyan, 'Qingshaonian shouji duanxin chuanbo de houxiandai wenti' (The postmodern issue of young people's text messaging communication), *Dangdai qingnian yanjiu*, 2008, 2 (February), pp. 43–7

Liu Heng, 'Kanxi' (Watching plays), *Xin juben* (*New Scripts*), 2000, 4 (August), pp. 94–5

Liu Hong, 'Buganjimo de "wenhua shangren" Wang Shuo' (Wang Shuo: A 'cultural businessman' unwilling to stay out of the limelight), *Beijing qingnian*, 1995, 1 (January), pp. 8–11

'Pai bu dianying ye tinghao' (Making a film is also great), *Beijing qingnian*, 1995, 11 (November), pp. 38–9

'"Shangdi" de hao-wu' (The likes and dislikes of 'emperors'), *Beijing qingnian*, 1995, 3 (March), pp. 24–5

Liu Hong, 'Cong dianshi xuanxiu xiang kaiqu' (Wanting to go beyond television talent shows), *Qingnian jizhe*, 2006, 17 (September), pp. 17–18

Liu Hongsen, 'Qingnian qiumi xintai fenxi' (Analysis of youth ball game fan mentality), *Qingnian xuebao*, 1990, 3 (Fall), pp. 7–9

Liu Jialing, *Jiyi xianhong* (*Memories Bright Red*), Beijing: Zhongguo qingnian chubanshe, 2002

Liu Qing, 'Cong "Wo bu xiangxin" dao "Yiwusuoyou": xin shengdai wenhua de yanjiu beiwanglu' (From 'I do not believe' to 'Nothing to My Name': Research memorandum on the culture of the Newborn Generation), *Dangdai qingnian yanjiu*, 1988, 8 (August), pp. 5–6

Liu Shengzhi, 'Qingshaonian yu xiaofei wenhua: guanyu wangba de guannian chongtu yu liyi boyi' (Young people and consumer culture: On conflicting ideas and the chess game about the benefits regarding Internet bars), *Zhongguo qingnian yanjiu*, 2007, 10 (October), pp. 56–60

Liu Weiheng, *Xin shiji Hanliu dianfeng dang'an* (*New Century Edition Korean Wave Summit Archive*), Haikou: Nanfang chubanshe, 2003

Liu Xiang, *Wo shi Liu Xiang* (*I am Liu Xiang*), Shanghai Sanlian chubanshe, 2004

Liu Xiaomeng, *Zhongguo zhiqing koushushi* (*An Oral History of China's Educated Youth*), Beijing: Zhongguo shehui kexue chubanshe, 2004

*Zhongguo zhiqing shi: Dachao (1966–1980 nian)* (*History of China's Educated Youth: Great Tide, 1966–1980*), Beijing: Zhongguo shehui kexue chubanshe, 1998

Liu Xiaomeng, Ding Yizhuang, Shi Weimin, and He Lan, *Zhongguo zhiqing shidian* (*Encyclopedia of China's Educated Youth*), Chengdu: Sichuan renmin chubanshe, 1995

Liu Xu, 'Zhongguo xiandai yishuzhan de fengbo' (The storm over the China modern art exhibition), *Daxuesheng*, 1989, 3 (March), inside front and back covers

Liu Yang, 'Suiyue ru ge: "qingshaonian yu liuxing yinyue" fangtan bijiao' (Time like a song: Comparison of interviews on 'young people and popular music'), *Zhongguo qingnian yanjiu*, 2003, 1 (January), pp. 19–26

Liu Yiguo, 'Daxue "kezhuo wenxue" yanjiu' (Research on university 'desktop literature'), *Qingnian yanjiu*, 1991, 3 (March), pp. 15–19, 31

Lu De and Zhang Xiong, 'Qingchun de guiji: 90 niandai Zhongguo neidi qingshaonian shishang redian gaishu' (The locus of youth: A summary of the fashion hot spots of 1990s Chinese mainland youth), *Zhongguo qingnian yanjiu*, 2000, 1 (January), pp. 22–5

Lü Hui, '"Chaonü"! "Chaonü"!' (*Supergirl! Supergirl!*), *Baogao wenxue* (*Reportage*), 2005, 10 (October), pp. 36–59

Lü Jie, 'Qian zai qingchun de rizi li: daxuesheng yu liuxing yinyue' (Embedded in days of adolescence: University students and popular music), *Zhongguo qingnian yanjiu*, 2003, 1 (January), pp. 6–11

Lu Jun, 'Dazhong gouzao de "Chaonü" shenhua' (The *Supergirl* fairy tale constructed by the masses), *Zhongguo shehui daokan*, 2005, 9 (September), pp. 11–13

Lu Lingtao and Li Yang, eds, *Nahan: weile Zhongguo cengjing de yaogun* (*Scream: For China's Former Rock*), Guilin: Guangxi shifan daxue chubanshe, 2008

Lü Peng, 'Shanzhai wenhua de duoshijiao jiedu' (A multiperspective explanation of copycat culture), *Zhongguo qingnian yanjiu*, 2009, 8 (August), pp. 84–6, 70

Lu Ping and Tan Jie, 'Fei zhiyuanzhe bu canyu zhiyuan huodong de helihua jizhi yanjiu' (Research on nonvolunteers' rationalization for not participating in volunteer activities), *Zhongguo qingnian yanjiu*, 2008, 2 (February), pp. 25–8

Lu Xianbiao, 'Wo yu piliwu' (Breakdancing and I), *Wudao*, 1988, 8 (August), p. 39

Lu Xinhe and others, 'Xiandai yaogunyue de boxing he qingnian wenhua fazhan: yi ci yaogun taolunhui de bufen shilu' (The rise of contemporary rock music and development of youth culture: Extracts from a discussion on rock), *Qingnian xuebao*, 1991, 1 (Spring), pp. 12–13

Lu Yulin, *Dangdai Zhongguo qingnian wenhua yanjiu* (*Research on Contemporary Chinese Youth Culture*), Beijing: Renmin chubanshe, 2009

Lu Yunyun, 'Wang Shuo he tade xiaoshuo' (Wang Shuo and his novels), *Renmin ribao*, 28 January 1989, p. 8

Luo Dan, *Zhiqing biji* (*Notes of an Educated Youth*), Guangzhou: Huacheng chubanshe, 2010

Luo Di and Mao Yuxi, 'Zhenglun zhong de "wangluo minzuzhuyi"' ('Internet nationalism' in dispute), *Zhongguo qingnian yanjiu*, 2006, 5 (May), pp. 47–51

Luo Pinghan, *Chuntian: 1978 nian de Zhongguo zhishijie* (*Spring: Chinese Intellectual Circles in 1978*), Beijing: Renmin chubanshe, 2008

Luo Xuehui, *Shifei Hanliu* (All about the Korean Wave), *Zhongguo xinwen zhoukan* (*China News Weekly*), 2005, 46 (December), pp. 56–61

Luo Yunbin and Zhang Yi, 'Liuxing yinyue de qumei he fumei: jianping "Chaonü" xianxiang' (The enchantments and disenchantments of popular music: A double analysis of the 'Supergirl' phenomenon), *Nanchang daxue xuebao (renwen shehui kexue ban)* (*Journal of Nanchang University [Humanities and Social Sciences]*), 2007, 1 (January), pp. 134–7

Ma Chengxiang, 'Hei xi "Xin shidai de kuangren" zai Ha shangyan shuoming le shenme?' (What does the performance of 'Madman of the New Age' in Harbin tell us?), *Heilongjiang ribao*, 26 March 1968, p. 2

Ma Fan, 'Hanju zhen you neme "hong"?' (Are Korean dramas really that popular?), *Dazhong dianying*, 2006, 4 (February), pp. 12–15

Ma Ning, 'Hanliu laixi' (The Korean Wave attacks), *Wangluo yu xinxi*, 2002, 10 (November), pp. 32–3

'Wangshang Hanliu' (Korean Wave on the 'Net), *Wangluo yu xinxi* (*Internet and Information*), 2001, 8 (August), pp. 30–1

'Wangshang Hanliu "hua"' ('Flowers' of the Korean Wave on the 'Net), *Wangluo yu xinxi*, 2003, 4 (April), p. 23

Ma Yue, 'Hongweibing huayu de wenhua biaozheng: cong yi zhang fahuang de Hongweibing xiaobao shuo qi' (The cultural features of Red Guard discourse: Thoughts from a yellowing page of a Red Guard newspaper), *Zhongguo qingnian yanjiu*, 1996, 6 (November), pp. 26–8

Ma Zhonghong, 'Wangluo qingnian yawenhua leixing tedian yu chuanbo lujing diaocha baogao: jiyu Jiangsu 21 suo gaoxiao de diaocha' (Survey report on the features of the kinds of youth Internet subcultures and dissemination access: Based on a survey of twenty-one tertiary institutes in Jiangsu), *Zhongguo guangbo* (*China Advertising*), 2009, 7 (July), pp. 42–50

MacFarquhar, Roderick and Michael Schoenhals, *Mao's Last Revolution*, Cambridge: Harvard University Press, 2006

Mai Ning, 'Bi tiankong geng guangkuo de: qingnian qigongshi Li Chengzhi yinxiang' (Vaster than the sky: Impressions of the young *qigong* master Li Chengzhi), *Qingnian yu shehui*, 1989, 12 (December), pp. 14–15

Manyou wenhua, *Manyou COSPLAY 100 xilie: pianyi huanxiang (Cartoon Friend Cosplay 100 series: On the Wings of Fantasy)*, Harbin: Heilongjiang meishu chubanshe, 2006

Mao Peiling, '*Balei zhi hua*' (Flowers of Ballet), in Shi Xiaoyan, *Trials and Tribulations on the Great Northern Wasteland*, pp. 21–23

Mao Tse-tung, *Quotations from Chairman Mao Tse-tung*, Beijing: Foreign Languages Press, 1966

Mao Yanling, 'Dui "shanzhai wenhua" de jiedu' (Explaining 'copycat culture'), *Zhongguo qingnian yanjiu*, 2009, 3 (March), pp. 84–6, 91

McDougall, Bonnie S., *Fictional Authors, Imaginary Audiences: Modern Chinese Literature in the Twentieth Century*, Hong Kong: Chinese University Press, 2003

ed., *Popular Chinese Literature and Performing Arts in the People's Republic of China, 1949–1979*, Berkeley: University of California Press, 1984

McDougall, Bonnie S. and Kam Louie, *The Literature of China in the Twentieth Century*, New York: Columbia University Press, 1997

McMillin, Divya C., *Mediated Identities: Youth, Ageny, and Globalization*, New York, Peter Lang, 2009

Mo Kai, 'Xianhua qigong' (*Qigong* chat), *Qingnian yu shehui*, 1988, 7 (July), p. 23

Moore, Ryan, *Sells Like Teen Spirit: Music, Youth Culture, and Social Crisis*, New York: New York University Press, 2010

Morris, Andrew, '"I Believe You Can Fly": Basketball Culture in Postsocialist China,' in Perry Link, Richard P. Madsen, and Paul G. Pickowicz, eds, *Popular China: Unofficial Culture in a Globalizing Society*, Lanham: Rowman & Littlefield, 2002, pp. 9–38

Moskowitz, Marc L., *Cries of Joy, Songs of Sorrow: Chinese Pop Music and Its Cultural Connotations*, Honolulu: University of Hawai'i Press, 2010

Mu Zhai, *Lishi de huashi: zhiqing shiwu nian (Fossils of History: Fifteen Years of Educated Youth)*, Beijing: Dongfang chubanshe, 2009

Nan Shan, '"5.12" da dizhen zhong qingnian qunti xingwei fenxi' (Analysis of youth group actions in the May 12 earthquake), *Dangdai qingnian yanjiu*, 2008, 8 (August), pp. 39–43

Ni Zi, Shan Liang, Ou Ran, *21 nian chunjie lianhuan wanhui neibu xiaoxi (The Inner Story of the Twenty-one Years of the Spring Festival Variety Show)*, Beijing: Xinhua chubanshe, 2004

Nie Ming, 'Buyao yong puke gao mixin huodong' (Don't use playing cards for superstitious activities), *Liaoning qingnian (Liaoning Youth)*, 1974, 2 (January), p. 45

Nie Ping and Wei Ran, *Shishang youzui (Fashion Guilty)*, Beijing: Kexue jishu wenxian chubanshe, 2005

Ou Ning, 'Nanfang de "Xin qunzhong" zhi sheng' (Cry of the South's 'New Masses'), *Zhongguo qingnian yanjiu*, 1995, 4 (July), inside front cover

Ouyang Yanwen, 'Wangluo dui qingshaonian shehuihua de li yu bi' (Pros and cons of the Internet for young people's socialization), *Beijing qingnian zhengzhi xueyuan xuebao (Journal of Beijing Youth Politics College)*, pp. 15–18

Palmer, David A., *Qigong Fever: Body, Science, and Utopia in China*, New York: Columbia University Press, 2007

Pan Congyi, 'Daxuesheng feizhengshi qunti chizheng yanjiu' (Impartial research on informal groups among university students), *Dangdai qingnian yanjiu*, 2007, 6 (June), pp. 41–5

Park Ju-yeon, 'Korea's B-Boys Capture the International Spotlight,' *Koreana*, 20, 4 (2006), pp. 80–4

Pease, Rowan, 'Internet, Fandom, and K-Wave in China,' in Keith Howard, *Korean Pop Music*, pp. 176–89

Peng Guifang and Chen Jiuguo, 'Cong fengkuang dao lixing zhi lu hai you duo yuan?: dui qingshaonian ouxiang chongbai de sikao' (How far is there yet from madness to reason?: Reflections on young people's idol worship), *Qingnian tansuo*, 2007, 4 (August), pp. 91–4

Peng Tong, 'Gechang shi liti de yishu: ji 1988 nian jinxing Su Hong' (Singing is a three-dimensional art: On Su Hong, the 1988 golden star), *Renmin ribao*, 18 April 1989, p. 4

Piao Guanghai, '"Hanliu" zai Zhongguo de boji yu yingxiang' (The spread and impact of the Korean Wave on China), *Dangdai Hanguo*, 2003, 1 (June), pp. 71–5

Popular Film editors, 'Guanyu "dianying zenyang biaoxian xing'ai? Nengfou zhanshi luoti?" de shi ge you zhengyi de wenti' (Ten controversial questions on 'How should films present sexual love? and Should nudity be shown?'), *Dazhong dianying*, 1989, 4 (April), pp. 2–3

'Puji geming yangbanxi de qingqibing: ji Anda xian nongcun dianying fangyingdui manqiang reqing wei pinxia zhongnong fuwu de xianjin shiji' (Light cavalry in the popularization of the revolutionary model performances: On the advanced achievements of the Anda county country film projection team in wholeheartedly serving the poor and lower-middle peasants), *Heilongjiang ribao*, 26 May 1971, p. 3

Pu Yingjuan, Su Yan, and Zheng Peng, 'Daxuesheng yu wangluo qingnian yawenhua guanxi yanjiu' (Research on the connections between university students and youth Internet subcultures), *Dangdai qingnian yanjiu*, 2009, 4 (April), pp. 43–8

Qiong Xiaoming and Li Shiding, 'Weimiao de beilun: ping "Gongji Huangtu gaopo" de yiyuan siwei moshi (A subtle paradox: A critique of the monistic pattern of thinking in "Attacking 'The Hills of Yellow Earth'"), *Renmin yinyue*, 1989, 8 (August), pp. 24–5

Qin Zhen, 'Huang pifu shi xi bu bai de' (Yellow skin can't be washed white), *Qingnian yu shehui*, 1989, 2 (February), p. 1

*Qingchun wuyi: Yunnan zhibian shenghuo jishi* (Regrets for Youth: Records of Life at the Margins), Chengdu: Sichuan wenyi chubanshe, 1991

Qu Zhe, 'Fendou, qiusuo, shizhong shi zhei yi dai ren de zhutiqu' (Struggle and striving in the final analysis were the theme tune of this generation), in Liu Xiaomeng, *Zhongguo zhiqing koushushi*, pp. 56–124

Ren Peng, 'Tongku de fengliu: qingshaonian wenshen xianxiang toushi' (A painful distinction: Perspectives on the young people's tattoo phenomenon), *Qingnian tansuo (Youth Explorations)*, 1994, 6 (November), pp. 20–3

Rolandsen, Unn Målfrid H., 'A Collective of Their Own: Young Volunteers at the Fringes of the Party Realm,' in Mette Halskov Hansen and Rune Svarverud, eds, *iChina: The Rise of the Individual in Modern Chinese Society*, Copenhagen: NIAS Press, 2010, pp. 132–63

Rosen, Stanley, 'Chinese Youth and State-Society Relations' in Peter Hays Gries and Stanley Rosen, eds, *Chinese Politics: State, Society and the Market*, London and New York: Routledge, 2010, pp. 160–78

'Contemporary Chinese Youth and the State,' *Journal of Asian Studies*, 68, 2 (2009), pp. 359–69

'Value Change Among Post-Mao Youth,' in Perry Link, Richard P. Madsen, and Paul G. Pickowicz, eds, *Unofficial China: Popular Culture and Thought in the People's Republic*, Boulder: Westview Press, 1989, pp. 193–216

'Youth and Social Change in the PRC,' in Ramon Myers, ed, *Two Societies in Opposition: The Republic of China and the People's Republic of China after Forty Years*, Stanford: Hoover Institution Press, 1991, pp. 288–315

Ru Shi, '*Waiguo wenxue chuban ying re zhong qiujing*' (The boom in foreign literature publishing), *Renmin ribao*, 29 May 1989, p. 4

Ruo Da, 'Cong laonian disike shuoqi' (Starting with seniors' disco), *Qingchun suiyue*, 1988, 4 (April), p. 19

Savage, Jon, *Teenage: The Creation of Youth Culture*, New York: Penguin, 2007

Schrift, Melissa, *The Biography of a Chairman Mao Badge: The Creation and Mass Consumption of a Personality Cult*, New Brunswick: Rutgers University Press, 2001

Sedo, Tim, 'Dead-Stock Boards, Blown-Out Spots, and the Olympic Games: Global Twists and Local Turns in the Formation of China's Skateboarding Community,' in Petra Rethmann, Imre Szeman, and William D. Coleman, eds, *Cultural Autonomy: Frictions and Connections*, Vancouver: UBC Press, 2010, pp. 257–82.

Sha Zi, 'Qin'ai de "Yumi" bie yong zheizhong fangshi ai Chunchun' (Dear Li Yuchun fans, don't use this way of loving Li Yuchun), *Liaoning qingnian*, 2006, 5 (March), pp. 92–4

Shan Ren, '"Lunhui" paishe sanji' (Notes on the filming of *Samsara*), *Dazhong dianying*, 1988, 10 (October), p. 16

Shanghai wenguang xinwen chuanbo jituan fazhan yanjiubu, ed., *Nianqing de zhanchang: SMG 'Hao nan'er' shi zenyang liancheng de* (*Young battle-field: How SMG Go Boys! was Tempered*), Shanghai: Shanghai shiji chuban gufen youxian gongsi, 2007

*Shanghai wenhua shizhi tongxun* (Bulletin of the *Shanghai Cultural History Gazetteer*), No. 22 (October 1992), p. 11

Shanghai Youth Gazetteer editorial board, *Shanghai qingnian zhi* (*Shanghai Youth Gazetteer*), Shanghai: Shanghai shehui kexueyuan chubanshe, 2002

Shen Jianbing and Gang Dongliang, 'Jianding de zou zai Mao zhuxi geming wenyi luxian shang: ji Heilongjiang shengchan jianshe bingtuan moutuan "Baimaonü" yeyu yanchudui dali puji geming yangbanxi de shiji' (Staunchly following Chairman Mao's revolutionary literature and art line: On the achievements of a certain corps of the Heilongjiang production and con-struction corps White-haired Girl amateur performance troupe in vigorously popularising the revolutionary model performances), *Heilongjiang ribao*, 26 May 1971, p. 3

Shen Jie, 'Beijing qingnian de zhiyuan xingdong canyu yiyuan: yi xiang dui butong qunti zhi jian de bijiao fenxi' (The volunteer activity participatory aspira-tions of Beijing youth: A comparative analysis of different groups), *Beijing qingnian zhengzhi xueyuan xuebao*, 2008, 1 (January), pp. 47–58

Shen Yibing, 'Wenshen yu fuhao: dushi qingnian wenshen xianxiang toushi' (Tattoos and marks: A perspective on the tattoo phenomenon among urban youth), *Zhongguo qingnian yanjiu*, 2006, 6 (June), pp. 69–73

'Sheng yijiuqiwu nian wenyi diaoyan dahui shengli jieshu' (Provincial 1975 literature and art performance festival successfully concludes), *Liaoning wenyi* (*Liaoning Literature and Art*), 1975, 12 (December), inside back cover.

'Shengshi haoda de shoudu gongnongbing wenyi huiyan zuotian kaishi' (The impressive worker-peasant-soldier artistic joint performances start yesterday in the capital), *Tianjin ribao* (*Tianjin Daily*), 22 May 1967, pp. 2–3

'Shi fangying dui you shi xuanchuan dui' (Both a projection team and a propaganda team), *Heilongjiang ribao*, 20 February 1973, p. 4

'Shi ren gandai kunhuo: dianying "Hong gaoliang" guan hou' (Causing puzzlement: After watching *Red Sorghum*), *Huhehaote ribao* (*Huhehot Daily*), 20 April 1988, p. 4

Shi Tongxiang, 'Taiqiu re de zhenhan' (Reverberations of the billiard fever), *Liaoning qingnian*, 1988, 16 (August), pp. 16–17

Shi Xiaohui, 'Zhongxuesheng ouxiang chongbai xianzhuang diaocha' (Survey of the present condition of high school student adoration of idols), *Qingnian tansuo*, 2005, 6 (November), pp. 3–8

Shi Xiaojie, 'Nongganfeixin fei zhenwei: shehui qingnian yu liuxing yinyue' (Rich, sweet, fat and pungent, but without real flavor: Working youth and popular music), *Zhongguo qingnian yanjiu*, 2003, 1 (January), pp. 11–15

Shi Xiaoyan, ed., *Beidahuang fengyunlu* (*Trials and Tribulations on the Great Northern Wasteland*), Beijing: Zhongguo qingnian chubanshe, 1990

Shi Xinming, 'Cesuo bu sao, heyi sao tianxia?: cong "Beike daxuesheng qingsao cesuo xiehui" tanqi' (If the toilet isn't cleaned, how will the world be clean?: Speaking of the 'Beijing University of Science and Technology Students Toilet Cleaning Association'), *Qingnian yanjiu*, 2001, 4 (April), pp. 38–9

Shu Zechi and Zeng Yi, 'Liuxing yinyue yu cidai shichang xianzhuang pingxi' (An analysis of the present conditions in popular music and the tape market), *Liaowang*, 1989, 10 (March), pp. 31–3

Song Yang, '*Tongsu gequ de minzuxing*' (The national characteristics of popular songs), *Renmin yinyue*, 1988, 6 (June), pp. 26–8

Special Report, 'Zhongguo yaogun dashiji' (China rock chronology), *Guoji yinyue jiaoliu* (*International Music Exchange*), 2002, 5 (May), p. 23

STOKIS, *Shaonian huawu STOKIS* (*Juvenile Picture Dance STOKIS*), Harbin: Heilongjiang shaonian ertong chubanshe, 2007

Su Ning, '*Jinghua chuxia "taiqiu re"*' ('Billiard fever' in early summer Beijing), *Renmin ribao*, 2 June 1988, p. 4

Su Wenliang, Liu Qinxue, Fang Xiaoyi, Fang Zhao, and Wan Jingjing, 'Dui daxuesheng wangluo chengyin de xingzhi yanjiu' (Research on the features of university student Internet addiction), *Qingnian yanjiu*, 2007, 10 (October), pp. 10–16

Su Zhicui, 'Jiexi hulian wangshi jiaoxia de qingshaonian shanzhai wenhua' (Analysis of young people's copycat culture from the angle of mutual media), *Qingnian tansuo*, 2009, 4 (July), pp. 66–9

Sun Chunming, '*Yege*' (Night song), in Shi Xiaoyan, *Trials and Tribulations on the Great Northern Wasteland*, pp. 133–4

Sun Hong, '*Wang Shuo: "Wo de moshi nimen bu dong"*' (Wang Shuo: 'You don't understand my model'), *Beifang yinyue* (*Northern Music*), 2007, 3 (March), pp. 32–3

Sun Ran, 'Cong blog yu chuantong riji de qubie kan daxuesheng boke de xiezuo xinli' (Examining the writing psychology of university student blogs from the difference between blogs and traditional diaries), *Zhongguo qingnian yanjiu*, 2006, 1 (January), pp. 69–72

Sun Xiaozhong, '*Quyuxing zai xiangxiang: 2005 nian* "'*Hanliu*' *zai Zhongguo*" *guoji yantaohui shuping*' (Visualizing regionally again: Review of the 2005 'Korean Wave in China' international symposium), *Shanghai daxue xuebao (shehui kexue ban) (Journal of Shanghai University [Social Sciences])*, 2006, 1 (January), pp. 159–60

Sun Yanjun, Kang Jianzhong, Mei Yuanmei, and Liu Zaixing, *Qikan Zhongguo (Periodical China)*, Beijing: Zhongguo shehui kexue chubanshe, 2003

Sung, Sang-yeon, 'The *Hanliu* Phenomenon in Taiwan: TV dramas and Teenage Pop,' in Keith Howard, *Korean Pop Music*, 168–75

'Why are Asians attracted to Korean pop culture?', in *Korean Herald*, pp. 11–21

Tan Yingzi, 'Filling the need to help others,' *China Daily*, 5 December 2009, p. 7

Tang Can, Mi Hedou, Lu Jianhua, and Yin Hongbiao, '*Sikao yidai de ziwo fansi: yi xiang guanyu Hongweibing qi tongdairen de sixiang guiji de yanjiu*' (Reflections on a generation's self-rethinking: Some research on the ideological orbit of Red Guards and their generation), *Qingnian yanjiu*, 1986, 11 (November), pp. 21–5, 31 and 12 (December), pp. 12–17

Tang Delong, '*Chaoji nüsheng: yi ge yule shenhua de fayi*' (*Supergirl*: Fame and fortune in an entertainment fairy tale), *Zhongguo shehui daokan (China Society Periodical)*, 2005, 9 (September), pp. 9–10

Tang Jun, '*Zhiyuanzhe zhuangkuang yanjiu: di 21 jie Shijie daxuesheng yundonghui zhiyuanzhe zhuangkuang diaocha*' (Research on the condition of volunteers: A survey of the condition of volunteers for the Twenty-first World University Student Games), *Qingnian yanjiu*, 2001, 11 (November), pp. 27–34

Tao Ran, '*Deng Lijun jianmei youfang*' (Deng Lijun's exercising on the right track), *Ba xiaoshi yiwai*, 1988, 4 (July), p. 57

Tapscott, Don, *Grown Up Digital: How the Net Generation is Changing Your World*, New York: McGraw-Hill, 2008

Tian Feng, '*Ai "xing" mei shangliang: dangdai qingshaonian "zhuixing xianxiang"*' (Never talked about loving 'stars': The 'star chasing phenomenon' among contemporary young people), *Zhongguo qingnian yanjiu*, 1993, 3 (May), pp. 26–8

Tian Jingqing, *Beijing dianying ye shiji, 1949–1990 (Achievements of the Beijing Film Industry)*, Beijing: Zhongguo dianying chubanshe, 1999

Tian Zhuangzhuang and others, '"*Yaogun qingnian*" *dui guanzhong shuo*' (*Rock 'n Roll Kids* talks with its audience), *Dazhong dianying*, 1989, 3 (March), pp. 18–19

Tu Keshan, '*Daxuesheng heyi tong "Xibeifeng" qihe*' (Why do university students feel a connection with the Northwest Wind?), *Renmin yinyue*, 1989, 1 (January), pp. 30–1

'Virtual pleasures: Cyber-hedonism,' *The Economist*, 7 February 2009, p. 54

Wan Meirong and Ye Lei, '*21 shijichu qingshaonian liuxing wenhua de liubian*' (Later developments in early twenty-first-century young people's popular culture), *Zhongguo qingnian yanjiu*, 2009, 4 (April), pp. 24–7, 37

Wang Anting, ed., *Mao Zedong xiangzhang tupu* (Illustrated catalogue of Mao Zedong badges), Beijing: Zhongguo shudian chubanshe, 1993

Wang Bin, '*Dazhong wenhua dui qingshaonian yidai de yingxiang*' (The influence of popular culture on a generation of young people), *Qingnian yanjiu*, 2001, 1 (January), pp. 11–17

Wang Daoyong, '*Yiming de kuanghuan yu renxing de xianxian: dui 2006 nian ruogan wangluo jiqun shijian zhong wangmin xingwei de fenxi*' (Anonymous revelry and the revealing of humanity: An analysis of netizen behavior from certain Internet mass incidents in 2006), *Qingnian yanjiu*, 2007, 3 (March), pp. 21–7

Wang Dawen, '*Shouchaoben*' (Handcopied books), in Shi Xiaoyan, *Trials and Tribulations on the Great Northern Wasteland*, pp. 28–30

Wang Debao, 'Social networking gaining ground,' *China Daily*, 11 September 2009, p. 9

Wang Deming, '*Yishen zhenqi qianbanyong*' (A single individual's inborn vitality has a thousand uses), *Huhehaote wanbao*, 3 September 1988, p. 2

Wang Dongcheng, '"*Laosanjie*" de wenhua lishi mingyun' (The historical fate of *laosanjie* culture), *Zhongguo qingnian yanjiu* (*China Youth Research*), 1994, 3 (May), pp. 22–4

'*Wang Shuo de "meisu" yu "fanzhi"*' (Wang Shuo's 'appealing to vulgar tastes' and 'anti-intellectualism'), *Zhongguo qingnian yanjiu*, 1993, 3 (May), pp. 16–18

Wang Fang and Rong Yan, '*Cong dianshi xiangqin jiemu kan nanxing ze'ou: yi Jiangsu Weishi "Feng cheng wu rao" 344 wei nan jiabing wei lie*,' (Men's mate searching seen in television dating shows: 344 male guests on Jiangsu Satellite TV's *If You Are the One* as illustration), *Qingnian yanjiu*, 2011, 2 (April), pp. 31–40

Wang Feng, '*Shenghuo de xuanlü: Zhongyang renmin guangbo diantai 9.20 ri "Wujian banxiaoshi"*' (The melody of life: Chinese People's Radio Station 'Noontime half-hour,' 20 September), *Wudao*, 1988, 11 (November), pp. 32–3

Wang Haiming, Ren Juanjuan, and Huang Shaohua, '*Qingshaonian wangluo xingwei tezheng jiqi yu wangluo renzhi de xiangguanxing yanjiu*' (Comparative research on the features of young people's Internet behaviour and their Internet cognition), *Lanzhou daxue xuebao (shehui kexue ban)* (*Journal of Lanzhou University [Social Sciences]*), 2005, 33, 4 (July), pp. 102–11

Wang Hongguang, '*Qigong de zhendang*' (*Qigong* quake), *Qingnian yidai*, 1988, 1 (January), pp. 22–3

Wang Hongyi, '*Zhiqing meishu yuanliu shulüe*' (A brief account of the origin and development of educated youth fine art), *Yishu tansuo (Arts Exploration: Journal of Guangxi Arts College)*, 2008, 4 (August), pp. 5–13, 19

Wang Hui, '"*Hanliu*" yu Zhongguo qingnian wenhua jianshe' (The Korean Wave and the cultural construction of Chinese youth), *Shaanxi qingnian guanli ganbu xueyuan xuebao (Journal of the Shaanxi Youth Management/ Officials Academy)*, 2006, 2 (June), pp. 16–19

Wang Jiaping, '*Hongweibing "xiaobao" ji qi shige de jiben xingtai*' (Red Guard 'little papers' and the basic features of their poetry), *Wenyi zhengming (Literature and Art Debates)*, 2001, 5 (May), pp. 4–9

Wang Li, '*Dazhong wenhua beihou de liliang: guanyu dianshi xuanxiu jiemu de ji dian sikao*' (The strength behind popular culture: Some thoughts on television talent shows), *Hebei jiaoyu xueyuan xuebao*, 2007, 1 (January), pp. 38–40

Wang Ligang, '*Xuanxiu jiemu you duo re*' (How popular are talent shows), *Qingnian jizhe*, 2006, 17 (September), pp. 15–16

Wang Lin, '*1991 nian Jingcheng "wenhua shan" xianxiang*' (The 1991 slogan T-shirt phenomenon in Beijing), *Qingnian yanjiu*, 1992, 4 (April), pp. 1–6, 12

Wang Linglong, section editor, '*Cong "Fei cheng wu rao" toushi dangdai qingnian de jiazhiguan*' (From *If You Are the One* examining contemporary youth values), *Zhongguo qongnian yanjiu*, 2011, 4 (April), pp. 4–23

Wang Nianning and Zhang Jingyan, '*Beijing gongren tiyuchang shijian jiqi sikao*' (The Beijing Workers' Stadium incident and reflections), *Qingnian yanjiu*, 1985, 8 (August), pp. 18–21

Wang Ping and Liu Dianzhi, '"*Tongren nü" xianxiang de fenxi yu sikao*' (Analysis and reflections on the 'gay-groupie girl' phenomenon), *Qingnian yanjiu*, 2008, 10 (October), pp. 37–42

Wang Shaopo, '"*Zhongxuesheng yu liuxing yinyue" fangtan shilu*' ('High schoolers and popular music' interview record), *Zhongguo qingnian yanjiu*, 2003, 1 (January), pp. 16–19

Wang Shouzhi, *Shishang shidai* (*Trends Era*), Beijing: Zhongguo lüyou chubanshe, 2008

Wang Shuo, *Wo shi Wang Shuo* (*I am Wang Shuo*), Beijing: Guoji wenhua chubanshe, 1992

Wang Sihai, Zhang Jianxin, and Dong Xueqing, '*Qingshaonian weihe chenni "wangyou"*' (Why do young people wallow in 'Internet games'), *Liaowang xinwen zhoukan*, 22 May 2006, pp. 18–20

'*Shei lai jianguan wangyou shichang*' (Who supervises the market for the Internet?), *Liaowang xinwen zhoukan*, 22 May 2006, pp. 20–1

'*Wangba heidong reng zai "bushi" qingshaonian*' (Black hole Internet bars still preying on young people), *Liaowang xinwen zhoukan* (*Outlook News Weekly*), 22 May 2006, pp. 17–18

'*Youxiao jianghua wangluo huanjing*' (Effectively purify the Internet environment), *Liaowang xinwen zhoukan*, 22 May 2006, pp. 22–3

Wang Siqi, *Zhongguo dangdai chengshi liuxing yinyue: yinyue yu shehui wenhua huanjing hudong yanjiu* (*Contemporary Chinese Urban Popular Music: On the Interaction between Music and the Cultural Environment*), Shanghai: Shanghai jiaoyu chubanshe, 2009

Wang Tianhui, '*Kexi le neiben "Waiguo minge 200 shou"*' (What a pity about that *Two Hundred Foreign Songs* book), in Yang Zhiyun, *Educated Youth Archive*, pp. 212–13

Wang Tianyun, '*Liri rong canshuang*' (Bright sun melts the cruel frost), in Jin Dalu, *Kunnan yu fengbo*, pp. 161–3

Wang Wei and Jiang Qi, '*Qingnian geshou dianshi dajiangsai de huawai yin*' (Off-screen at the Youth Singing Television Prize Contest), *Liaoning qingnian*, 1988, 18 (September), pp. 30–2

Wang Weiming, '*Pop music: dangdai qingnian xinling licheng de xiezhao*' (Pop music: Portrait of the spiritual course of contemporary youth), *Qingnian xuebao*, 1992, 1 (Spring), pp. 20–3

Wang Xiaobu, '"*Hong gaoliang" de guanzhong*' (*Red Sorghum*'s audience), *Zhongguo dianying bao* (*China Film Gazette*), 5 May 1988, p. 2

Wang Xiaozhang, '*Jiazhi zhenkong shidai de "wenhua gu'er": xi Cui Jian, Wang Guozhen, Wang Shuo xianxiang*' ('Cultural orphans' in an age of value vacuum: Explaining the Cui Jian, Wang Guozhen, and Wang Shuo phenomena), *Qingnian yanjiu*, 1994, 11 (November), pp. 25–8

Wang Yongling, '*Xibu gequ re chuxian hou de li yu bi*' (The benefits and harm after the Western song craze appeared), *Renmin yinyue*, 1989, 6 (June), p. 31

Wang Yu, '*Wang Shuo de xin Jingwei xiaoshuo: ping "Wanr de jiu xintiao" ji qita*' (Wang Shuo's new Beijing-flavor novel: A review of *Playing for Thrills* and other matters), *Renmin ribao*, 30 May 1989, p. 6

Wang Yunlong, '*Tongsu gequ de kexi chaoyue*' (The gratifying excess of popular music), *Qingnian yu shehui*, 1988, 9 (September), p. 45

Wang Zhaoqian, ,"*Kanye*" *Wang Shuo*' ('Windbag' Wang Shuo), *Zhuiqiu* (*Seeking*), 1992, 4 (April), pp. 2–4

Wang Zhenya, '*Hunfei xuezhua, suiyue liuhen*' (Frightening snow flies, the years leave marks) in Zhang Qi, *Mo bu qu de jiyi: lao sanjie, xin san ji*, pp. 463–72

Weber, Ian, '*Shanghai Baby*: Negotiating Youth Self-Identity in Urban China,' *Social Identities*, 8, 2 (2002), pp. 347–68.

'*Wei gongnongbing zhanling wenyi wutai relie huanhu*' (An ardent call for worker-peasant-soldiers to occupy the literary and art stage), *Renmin ribao*, 21 May 1967, p. 4

Wei Hongxin, '*Wangluo yu qingshaonian shehuihua*' (The Internet and young people's socialization), *Gong'an daxue xuebao* (*Journal of Chinese People's Public Security University*), 2001, 3 (June), pp. 94–7

Wei Jingsheng, *The Courage to Stand Alone: Letters from Prison and Other Writings*, New York: Viking, 1997

Wei Tongru and Guo Limin, '2007 nian yilai daxuesheng qunti liuxingyu diaoyan baogao: yi Hebeisheng gaoxiao wei lie' (Report of an investigation into university student group catchwords since 2007: The example of Hebei tertiary institutions), *Zhongguo qingnian yanjiu*, 2008, 7 (July), pp. 83–6

Weiming [Anonymous ], ed., *Yongyuan de 1977* (Eternal 1977), Beijing: Beijing daxue chubanshe, 2007

Weng Zhe, '"*Langjian wenren*" *tanyan zhaoshang*' (Top writers frankly seek outside investment), *Beijing qingnian*, 1995, 1 (January), pp. 54–5

'*Wang Shuo pengchu haoshu yi luokuang: jieshao Shishi gongsi tuichu de congshu*' (Wang Shuo holds up a basket of good books: Introducing the book series from the Current Affairs company), *Beijing qingnian*, 1995, 4 (April), pp. 24–5

Wilson, Verity, 'Dress and the Cultural Revolution,' in Valerie Steele and John S. Major, eds, *China Chic: East Meets West*, New Haven: Yale University Press, 1999

Wines, Michael, 'A Dirty Pun Tweaks China's Online Censors,' *The New York Times*, 12 March 2009, p. A1

'*Wosheng dianying faxing fangying gongzuo pengbo kaizhan*' (Province's film distribution and projection work vigorously develops), *Heilongjiang ribao*, 14 February 1973, p. 1

Wong, Isabel K. F., '*Geming Gequ*: Songs for the Education of the Masses,' in Bonnie S. McDougall, ed., *Popular Chinese Literature and Performing Arts in the People's Republic of China, 1949–1979*, Berkeley: University of California Press, 1984, pp. 112–43.

Wu Bin and Han Chunyan, *Zhongguo liuxing wenhua sanshinian (1978–2008)* (Thirty years of Chinese popular culture), Beijing: Jiuzhou chubanshe, 2009

Wu Hongfei, 'Wang Shuo xiongmeng' (Wang Shuo ferocious), *Nanfang renwu zhoukan* (*Southern People Weekly*), 21 March 2007, pp. 16–27

Wu Liping, '*Qingnian de shenmei tedian yu fuzhuang de liuxing quishi*' (Youth's aesthetic characteristics and popular fashion trends), *Zhongguo qingnian yanjiu*, 1991, 3 (May), pp. 36–8

Wu Luping, '*Zhiyuanzhe canyu dongji de jiegou zhuanxing he duoyuan gongsheng xianxiang yanjiu: dui 24 ming qingnian zhiyuanzhe de shendu fangtan fenxi*' (Research on structural transformation of volunteer participation and motivation and multifarious phenomenon: An analysis of in-depth interviews with twenty-four youth volunteers), *Zhongguo qingnian yanjiu*, 2008, 2 (February), pp. 5–10

Wu Yadan, '*Cong "Ha Hanju" kan "Ha Han" qingnian*' (From 'mad about Korean dramas' see 'mad about Korea' youth), *Zhongguo qingnian yanjiu*, 2004, 1 (January), pp. 31–8

Wu Yue, '*Qing ge sai de "bu gongping"*' ('Unfairness' at the Youth Song Contest), *Beifang yinyue (Northern Music)*, 2006, 6 (June). p. 27

Wu Zhe, '*Ting Hou Dejian chang ge*' (Listening to Hou Dejian singing), *Renmin ribao*, 18 March 1989, p. 2

Wu Zhengguo, '*Daxue xiaoyuan de "duanxin wenhua"*: qingnian xuesheng de xinli fuhao*' (University campus 'text message culture': A mark of youthful student psychology), *Qingnian yanjiu*, 2003, 5 (May), pp. 21–6

Wu Zhenwen, '*Jiaoyiwu, disike, yunlücao*' (Ballroom dancing, disco, aerobic dance), *Ba xiaoshi yiwai*, 1988, 6 (November), p. 56

Xiang Ronggao, '"*Chaoji nüsheng xianxiang*" toushi*' (Perspective on the 'Supergirl' phenomenon'), *Qingnian yanjiu*, 2005, 10 (November), p. 45, inside back cover

'"Kala OK re" yu dangdai qingnian shehuihua' (The 'karaoke fever' and the socialization of contemporary youth), *Zhongguo qingnian yanjiu*, 1992, 1 (January), pp. 25–8

'Qingnian "diange re" tanxi' (Analysis of the youth 'song request craze'), *Qingnian yanjiu*, 1995, 8 (August), pp. 21–3, 30

Xiao Hui, 'Gexing shidai zai jueqi?' (Is this the rise of an individualistic era?), *Zhongguo shehui daokan*, 2005, 9 (September), pp. 17–18

Xiao Weisheng and Wang Shulin, 'Lun wangluo yuyan de qingnian yawenhua texing' (On the characteristics of the youth subculture of Internet language), *Qingnian yanjiu*, 2008, 6 (June), pp. 21–6

Xiao Yu, 'Jingcheng "renti youhua dazhan" suo yinqi de…' (Caused by the 'Nude Oil Painting Exhibition' in the capital …), *Qingchun suiyue (Youth Era)*, 1989, 5 (May), pp. 33–5

Xiao Zhenhua, 'Wode yici qigong yan' (My one *qigong* experience), *Fujian qingnian*, 1988, 12 (December), p. 39

Xie Qianhong, '*Nongcun xuanchuandui shishi*' (Incidents from a country propaganda team), in Yang Zhiyun, *Educated Youth Archive*, pp. 255–9

*Xinbian Hongweibing ziliao (A New Collection of Red Guard Publications)*, Oakton VA: Center for Chinese Research Materials, 1999

Xing Jian, 'Gang-Tai gequ bu zai duba Guangzhou getan' (Hong Kong and Tawian songs will not monopolise the Guangzhou song scene again), *Huhehaote ribao*, 1 April 1989, p. 2

Xing Kai, Wen Huai, and Jing Bin, 'Dui seqing duwu wenti de diaocha yu sikao' (Investigation and thoughts on the issue of pornographic books), *Qingchun suiyue*, 1988, 10 (October), pp. 20–2

Xinhua News Agency report, 'Quanguo guangda pinxiazhongnong he xiaxiangshangshan zhishiqingnian gongdu geminghua chunjie' (Nationwide broad masses of poor and lower-middle peasants and educated youth going down the countryside and up to the mountains celebrate a revolutionary Spring Festival together), *Heilongjiang ribao*, 20 February 1969, p. 2

Xu Bing, 'Da huo'er de liuxingyue he wo de xianyansuiyu: Zhongguo liuxing gequ zouxiang' (Our popular music and my idle comments: Chinese popular song trends), *Qingnian xuebao*, 1990, 4 (Winter), pp. 21–2, 13

Xu Chuanxin and Zhang Le, '"Baobaotuan" xianxiang de shehuixue jiedu' (Sociological deciphering of the 'hugging group' phenomenon), *Zhongguo qingnian yanjiu*, 2007, 10 (October), pp. 8–10

Xu Fei, 'Gexing yu gemi yu san bai xuesheng tong "kan"' (Singers and fans and
three hundred students together 'with dignity'), *Zhongguo qingnian yanjiu*,
1993, 3 (May), pp. 13–16

Xu Hongli, '"Chou" ye shi yi zhong mei' ('Ugly' is also a kind of beauty), *Liaoning
qingnian*, 1988, 18 (September), pp. 34–6

Xu Jin, '"Hanliu" denglu Zhongguo 6 nian' (Six years of the Korean Wave landing
in China), *Zhongwai wenhua jiaoliu (China-Foreign Cultural Relations)*,
2003, 10 (November), pp. 22–4

Xu Liyan, 'Huoxing wen: "N dai" ren de wenhua fuhao' (Martian language:
Cultural signs used by the 'N[ineties] generation'), *Shanxi qingnian guanli
ganbu xueyuan xuebao (Journal of the Shanxi Youth Management Cadre
Academy)*, 2008, 3 (September), pp. 18–20, reprinted in *Qingshaonian daokan*, 2009, 1 (January), pp. 54–7

Xu, Luo , *Searching for Life's Meaning: Changes and Tensions in the World
Views of Chinese in the 1980s*, Ann Arbor: University of Michigan Press,
2002

Xue Yali, 'e-shidai de "wangluo wenxue"' (E-times, 'Internet literature'), *Qingnian
tansuo*, 2001, 5 (September), pp. 34–6

Yan Jun, *Di dixia: xin yinyue qinaxing ji* (Really underground: A secret record
of the new music), Beijing: Wenhua yishu chubanshe, 2002

Yan Xiaoli, '*Ganjiawan jishi*' (Records of Ganjiawan), in Yang Zhiyun, *Educated
Youth Archive*, 385–8

Yan, Yunxiang, 'Introduction: Conflicting Images of the Individual and Contested
Process of Individualization,' in Mette Halskov Hansen and Rune Svarverud,
eds, *iChina: The Rise of the Individual in Modern Chinese Society*,
Copenhagen: NIAS Press, 2010, pp. 1–38.

'Little Emperors or Frail Pragmatists? China's '8oers Generation,' *Current
History: A Journal of Contemporary World Affairs*, 105 (692) (2006),
pp. 255–62

Yang Changzheng, 'Guanyu "Cui Jian, yaogun chao" de caifang' (Interviews about
'Cui Jian, the rock wave'), *Qingnian xuebao*, 1991, 1 (Spring), pp. 14–17

ed., 'Liuxing yinyue yu qingshaonian chengzhang' (Popular music and young
people's growing up), *Zhongguo qingnian yanjiu*, 2003, 1 (January),
pp. 4–29

Yang Chunrong and Yin Fangmin, 'Daxuesheng wangluo luoliao xingwei de
duowei fenxi' (A multidimensional analysis of university student 'naked
chatting' behavior), *Dangdai qingnian yanjiu*, 2006, 12 (December),
pp. 18–23

Yang Cong, 'Qianxi wangluo shidai de qingnian yawenhua' (A preliminary analysis of youth subcultures in the Internet age), *Zhongguo qingnian zhengzhi
xueyuan xuebao*, 2008, 5 (October), pp. 53–6

Yang Dian, '"Hanliu" weihe zheme re' (Why is the 'Korean Wave' so hot?), *Baike
zhishi (Encyclopedia Knowledge)*, 2002, 4 (April), pp. 48–9

Yang Jian, 'Hongweibing jituan xiang zhiqing jituan de lishixing guodu (xu yi)'
(The historical transition from Red Guard to educated youth cliques, part
two), *Zhongguo qingnian yanjiu*, 1996, 3 (May), pp. 4–8

'Lishi goule: Neimeng yu Dongbei de zhiqing wenyi' (Outline history: Educated
youth literature and art in Inner Mongolia and the Northeast), *Zhongguo
qingnian yanjiu*, 1998, 5 (September), pp. 33–5

*Wenhua dageming dixia wenxue (Underground Literature in the Cultural
Revolution)*, Beijing: Chaohua chubanshe, 1993

'Wenhua da geming zhong de Hongweibing huaju' (Red Guard plays in the Great Cultural Revolution), *Zhongguo qingnian yanjiu*, 1995, 1 (January), pp. 34–7

'*Wenhua da geming zhong de Hongweibing huaju, xu*' (Red Guard plays in the Great Cultural Revolution, Part Two), *Zhongguo qingnian yanjiu*, 1995, 2 (March), pp. 25–8

'*Wenhua da geming shiqi de Hongweibing yinyue*' (Red Guard music in the Great Cultural Revolution), *Zhongguo qingnian yanjiu*, 1997, 2 (March), pp. 24–8

*Zhongguo zhiqing wenxue shi* (*History of Chinese Educated Youth Literature*), Beijing: Zhongguo gongren chubanshe, 2002

Yang Jianhua, '*Shenshan li de balei*' (Ballet deep in the mountains), in *Qingchun wuyi*, pp. 115–21

Yang Jing, '*Zhuguan qingshaonian wangluo fensi julebu qunti*' (Pay attention to young people's Internet fan club groups), *Qingnian gongzuo luntan* (*Youth Work Forum* [*Shandong*]), 2008, 2 (March), pp. 23–6

Yang Liming, '"*Fei zhuliu*" yu "*Huoxingwen*" de yidai: "90 hou" wangluo meiti xingxiang chutan' (The generation of 'non-mainstream' and 'Martian language': A first exploration of the form of Internet and media use by the 'nineties generation'), *Zhongguo qingnian yanjiu*, 2009, 8 (August), pp. 74–80

Yang Linxiang, '*Qingnian qinglai wangluo : "chuan yue" xiaoshuo de shenceng yuanyin fenxi*' (Youth-favored Internet : An analysis of the deep reasons for novels that leap across time and place), *Zhongguo qingnian yanjiu*, 2009, 6 (June), pp. 94–6

Yang Mingyuan, '*Ha ha, bandao gong*' (Haha, making a job of it), *Qingchun suiyue*, 1988, 4 (April), pp. 12–13

Yang Ruiqing, 'Miandui "Xibefeng" gechao de sikao' (Thoughts confronting the Northwest Wind song wave), *Renmin yinyue*, 1988, 12 (December), p. 21

Yang Wenjie, 'Cui Jian: Zher de yaogunyue jiu shi yi ge xiaohua' (Cui Jian: Rock music here is just a joke), *Beijing qingnian bao* (*Beijing Youth News*), 8 July 2006, p. B7

Yang Xin, 'Dangdai qingnian wenhua radian xianxiang shuping' (Review of hot spot phenomena in contemporary youth culture), *Guangdong qingnian ganbu xueyuan xuebao* (*Journal of the Guangdong Youth Leaders College*), 2007, 3 (March), pp. 38–41

Yang Xiong, '*1978–1989: Zhongguo qingnian shenmei gunanian de tuibian*' (The transformation of Chinese youth's aesthetic tastes), *Dangdai qingnian yanjiu*, 1990, 4 (August), pp. 8–14

'Wangluo dui woguo qingnian de yingxiang pingjia' (An evaluation of the impact of the Internet on China's youth), *Qingnian yanjiu*, April 2000, pp. 7–14

'Yaogunyue yu qingnian wenhua' (Rock music and youth culture), *Qingnian yanjiu*, 1991, 12 (December), pp. 19–23

Yang Xiong and Lu Xinhe, 'Guanyu yaogunyue yu qingnian liuxing wenhua de duihua' (A dialogue on rock music and youth popular culture), *Qingnian yanjiu*, 1993, 8 (August), pp. 6–10

Yang Ying, '"Hanliu" xianxiang tanxi' (Analysis of the Korean Wave phenomenon), *Qingnian tansuo*, 2002, 6 (November), pp. 40–2

'"Hanliu": you yi zhong zhuixing de xin fanshi?' (Korean Wave: Yet another new kind of fandom?), *Zhongguo qingnian yanjiu*, 2004, 1 (January), pp. 9–15

Yang Yusheng, 'Ganga de "bianju"' (Awkward 'playwrighting'), in Yang Zhiyun, Educated Youth Archive, pp. 568–71

Yang Zhiyun and others, eds, Zhiqing dang'an, 1962–1979: Zhishi qingnian shangshan xiaxiang jishi (Educated Youth Archive, 1962–1979: Records of Educated Youth Going Up to the Mountains and Down to the Villages), Chengdu: Sichuan wenyi chubanshe, 1992

Yang Zhonghua, 'Liu Huan de lu' (Lu Huan's road), Ba ge xiaoshi yiwai, 1988, 4 (July), pp. 45–6

Yi Da, 'Hong gexing "zouxue" yanchu de gao shouru ji tou loushui de qishi' (Enlightening star singers 'moonlighting' performances' high incomes and tax evasion), Liaowang, 1989, pp. 22–3 (5 June), pp. 38–9

Yi Ran, 'Yaogun 20 nian, yong yinyue chang rensheng' (Twenty years of rock, using music to sing about life), Liaoning qingnian, 2006, 16 (August), p. 83

Yi Xiaoxia, 'Renti yishu zai jinri zhi Zhongguo' (Nude art in today's China), Qingchun suiyue, 1989, 3 (March), pp. 45–6

Yin Hongbiao, '"Wen'ge" shiqi de "Qingnian sixiang cunluo": jianzheng sixiang jiefang zhi lu' ('Youth ideological villages' in the Cultural Revolution: Witnessing the road of ideological liberation), Zhongguo qingnian yanjiu, 2010, 3 (March), pp. 84–9, 104

'Yongheng de tan'ge' (Eternal tango), Fujian qingnian, 1988, 8 (August), p. 46 (picture story)

Yu Danping, Yang Weiwei, He Jiayu, and Zhang Yi, 'Ganshou "Han-liu" de weili: Women yan zhong de "Han Han xianxiang"' (Feeling the 'Han Wave': The 'Han Han phenomenon' in our eyes), Wangluo keji shidai (Nettime), 2003, 11 (November), pp. 27–9

Yu Tian, 'Zouchu yunhuhu de meishuguan' (On leaving the dizzying art gallery), Daxuesheng, 1989, 3 (March), pp. 25–6

Yu Wong, "Wang's World," Far Eastern Economic Review (Hong Kong), 8 August 1996, pp. 46–8.

Yu Yiqun, Ji Qiufa, and Mu Qing, 'Xin shiji de Beijing qingnian, (Beijing youth in the new century), Qingnian yanjiu, 2003, 1 (January), pp. 1–12

Yu Yinghua, '"Hong shaobing" de nahan' (Cry of Red Sentry), in Shi Xiaoyan, Trials and Tribulations on the Great Northern Wasteland, pp. 304–7

Yu Yuan, 'Fanzui "qiumi" de xinli pouxi: laizi Nanchong de baogao' (Analysis of the psychology of criminal 'sports fans': A report from Nanchong), Tiyu bolan (Sports Panorama), 1988, 10 (October), pp. 4–8

Zan Yulin, 'Qingnian wenhua radian de shidai toushi: "Chaoji nüsheng" re de leng sikao' (A current perspective on hotspots of youth culture: A cold look at the Supergirl fever), Qingnian tansuo, 2006, 1 (January), pp. 22–4

Zeng Li, 'Daxuesheng zhiyuan fuwu yu hexie shehui goujian' (University student volunteer service and the construction of an harmonious society), Dangdai qingnian yanjiu, 2008, 8 (August), pp. 59–64

Zeng Zhicheng, 'Zhibian shenghuo wu lezhang' (Five happy chapters from life at the margins), in Qingchun wuyi, pp. 10–27

Zhang Biao, 'Dongbei getan "Liang tuanhuo"' ('Two Gangsters' of Northeast song circles), Beijing qingnian, 1995, 3 (March), pp. 16–17

Zhang Bingfu, Tu Minxia, and Liu Yuling, 'Guangzhou qingshaonian wangluo shenghuo diaocha baogao' (Report on an investigation of Guangzhou young people's Internet life), Zhongguo qingnian yanjiu, February 2006, pp. 10–16

Zhang Dexiang and Jin Huimin, eds, Wang Shuo pipan (Critique of Wang Shuo), Beijing: Zhongguo shehui kexue chubanshe, 1993

Zhang Lei, 'Yewei de "Xibeifeng" yinhe shou huanying?' (Why has the wild Northwest Wind been welcomed?), *Liaoning qingnian*, 1989, 6 (March), pp. 32–3

Zhang Ming and Liao Yiwu, *Chenlun de shengdian: Zhongguo ershi shiji 70 niandai dixia shige yizhao (Sinking holy place: Death pictures of underground poetry in China's 1970s)*, Urumqi: Xinjiang qingshaonian chubanshe, 1994

Zhang Mingfu, 'Getan guaqi "Xibeifeng"' (The Northwest Wind blows in song circles), *Huhehaote wanbao*, 9 July 1988, p. 2

Zhang Qi, ed, *Mo bu qu de jiyi: lao sanjie, xin san ji (Unerasable Memories: Old Three Classes, New Three Third Class)*, Beijing: Zhonggong dangshi chubanshe, 2009

Zhang Qing, 'Luojiashan xia, qizuibashe hua Aoyun: Wuhan daxue bufen tongxue zuotan Aoyunhui guangan jilu' (Under Luojia Mountain, talking all at once about the Olympics: record of observations by Wuhan University students discussing the Olympic Games), *Daxuesheng*, 1988, 11 (November), pp. 11–13

Zhang Ren, 'Wo zheige ren xihuan xinxian' (I really like new things), in Liu Xiaomeng, *Zhongguo zhiqing koushushi*, pp. 22–55

Zhang Ting, 'Daxuesheng qunti yu "shanzhai" wenhua xianzhuang diaocha' (Investigation of the current state of university student groups and 'copycat' culture), *Dangdai qingnian yanjiu*, 2010, 1 (January), pp. 34–7

Zhang Yang, *'Di'er ci woshou' wenziyu (The Second Handshake Literary Inquisition)*, Beijing: Zhongguo shehui kexue chubanshe, 1999
Wo yu *'Di'er ci woshou' (The Second Handshake and I)*, Beijing: Zhongguo dangshi chubanshe, 2007

Zhang Yimou, 'Chang yi zhi shengming de zan'ge' (Sing a song in praise of life), *Dangdai dianying (Contemporary Film)*, 1988, 2 (April), pp. 81–3

Zhang Yu, 'BBS wangluo kongjian de shehui jiaowang lingyu: yi Shuimu shequ de shizheng fenxi wei lie' (The associative social domain of BBS Internet space: Concrete analysis of the Shuimu community as an example), *Qingnian yanjiu*, 2007, 8 (August), pp. 22–9

Zhang Yuan, 'Wuting: tamen lai le' (Dance hall: The women have come), *Qingnian yu shehui*, 1988, 7 (July), p. 33

Zhang Yuezhong, 'Dui guoji dejiang dianying de yidian sikao' (Thoughts on films that win international awards), *Liaoning qingnian*, 1989, 14 (July), pp. 26–7

Zhang Zhufu, Bai Zhenyao, and Teng Fei, 'Cong tuandui jianshe kan Beijing Aoyun zhiyuanzhe de youxiao guanli' (Effective management of Beijing Olympic volunteers from the point of view of team building), *Qingnian tansuo*, 2007, 3 (March), pp. 70–2

Zhao Baofeng, Tian Hongji, and Zhang Tiange, *Zhongguo qigong xue gailun (Introduction to Chinese Qigong Studies)*, Beijing: Renmin weisheng chubanshe, 1987

Zhao Fang, 'Cong Hip-Hop yundong kan qingnian wenhua' (Youth culture through the hip-hop movement), *Qingnian yanjiu*, 2002, 12 (December), pp. 15–20

Zhao Jie, 'Lun Hongweibing wenhua' (On Red Guard culture), *Qingnian yanjiu*, 1991, 7 (July), pp. 1–6

Zhao Jinqing, 'Dalu yaogun geci poyi' (Decoding mainland rock lyrics), *Zhongguo qingnian yanjiu*, 1994, 1 (January), pp. 40–2

Zhao Qingsi, 'Qingnian wangluo yawenhua de wenhua luoji' (The cultural logic of youth Internet subcultures), *Dangdai qingnian yanjiu*, 2010, 1 (January), pp. 28–33.

Zhao Xue, 'Zai Flash li "shan" bian rensheng' (A life changed in a flash), *Liaoning qingnian*, 2005, 6 (March), pp. 52–3

Zhao Zhiqin, 'Zai fushi wenhua xiandai bianqian zhong: Shencheng qingnian fushi xianxiang xilie sumiao' (In the midst of modern changes in fashion culture: Set sketches of fashion phenomena among Shanghai youth), *Qingnian xuebao* (*Youth Journal*), 1992, 1 (Spring), pp. 6–9

Zhen Xiaofei, 'Touhao "Kuai nan" Chen Chusheng' (First Happy Boy, Chen Chusheng), *Nanfang zhoumou* (*Southern Weekend*), 26 July 2007, pp. 28–7 [*sic*]

Zheng Mengbiao, 'Bu zai chandou de linghun' (A spirit that will not tremble again), in Liu Xiaomeng, *Zhongguo zhiqing koushushi*, pp. 348–89

Zhong Yibiao, 'Qingshaonian wangluo tongju yawenhua de shehuixue fenxi' (A sociological analysis of the subculture of young people living together through the Internet), *Dangdai qingnian yanjiu*, 2006, 3 (March), pp. 8–11

Zhong Ying, 'Jinyibu fazhan nongmin dianying fangying wang' (Further develop the film projection network in the countryside), *Hongqi* (*Red Flag*), 1975, 6 (June), pp. 50–3

Zhong Yuming, 'Man tai "Xibeifeng"guanzhong bu ai ting' (Audience does not like to hear a whole concert of Northwest Wind), *Renmin ribao*, 14 April 1989, p. 4

Zhou Dianfu, 'Cong liuxing gequ kan qingnian wenhua jianshe (Youth culture construction from the point of view of popular songs), *Qingnian yanjiu*, 1990, 1 (January), pp. 19–22, 10

'10 nian liuxing gequ suo zhaoshi de qingnian xinli' (Youth mentality shown by ten years of popular songs), *Zhongguo qingnian yanjiu*, 1990, 2 (March), pp. 23–5

Zhou Guimian, '"Hong gaoliang" yu "Xibeifeng"' (*Red Sorghum* and the Northeast Wind), *Renmin yinyue*, 1988, 12 (December), p. 20

Zhou Jinzhang, 'Wangluo wenti yu "qingshaonian kongjian"de yongzao' (The Internet issue and building a young people's space'), *Hongqi wengao* (*Red Flag Manuscripts*), 2010, 5 (March), pp. 28–9

Zhou Que, '*Wang bu liao, na shanwawa li de anfang*' (Unforgettable, that darkroom in the valley), in Shi Xiaoyan, *Trials and Tribulations on the Great Northern Wasteland*, pp. 310–11

Zhou Shirong, 'Hei tudi yunyu de yishu shengming: zan wuju "Gaoliang hun"' (Artistic life bred in the black soil: In praise of 'Sorghum Soul'), *Wenyi bao* (*Literature and Art Gazette*), 15 October 1988, p. 5

Zhou Xueliin (introduction and translation), '*Sha Ou*: excerpt,' *Renditions: A Chinese-English Translation Magazine*, No. 71 (Spring 2009), pp. 58–64

*Young Rebels in Contemporary Chinese Cinema*, Hong Kong: Hong Kong University Press, 2007

Zhou Yan, 'Cong yingshi "Hanliu" zhong kan Zhongguo chuantong wenhua de huigui' (Finding the return of Chinese traditional culture in films and television of the Korean Wave), *Mei yu shidai* (*Beauty & Times*), 2006, 6 (June), pp. 20–1

Zhou Yongming, *Historicizing Online Politics: Telegraphy, The Internet, and Political Participation in China*, Stanford: Stanford University Press, 2006

Zhou You, ed, *Beijing yaogun buluo* (*Beijing Rock Tribes*), Tianjin: Tianjin shehui kexue chubanshe 1994

Zhu Shenzhi, '*Niu dawang*' (King of talk), in Shi Xiaoyan, *Trials and Tribulations on the Great Northern Wasteland*, pp. 143–5

Zhu Tianze, 'Ban hao nongcun dianying fangying dui' (Run country film projection teams properly), *Heilongjiang ribao*, 20 February 1973, p. 4

Zhu Zhenghui and Jin Guangyao, eds, *Zhiqing buluo: Huangshan jiaoxia de 10,000 ge Shanghai ren* (*Educated Youth Tribe: Ten Thousand Shanghainese at the Foot of Huangshan*), Shanghai: Shanghai guji chubanshe, 2004

Zhuang Weiliang, 'Zhongguo de shi, "aibingbisheng"' (China's affairs; victory comes when pushed to the wall) in Liu Xiaomeng, *Zhongguo zhiqing koushushi*, pp. 530–92

Zong Yi and He Yanping, 'Cong shenmi zouxiang kexue: Zhongguo qigong re quxiang tanxi' (Going from mystery to science: An analysis of the tendency of the *qigong* fever), *Liaowang* (*Observation*), 1989, 14 (April), pp. 25–7

Zuo Shula, 'Wang Shuo: yi ge ganyu miaoshi changgui de "suren,"' *Dazhong dianying*, 1989, 6 (June), pp. 14–15 and 7 (July), pp. 10–13

# Index